EXPANDING THE BOUNDARIES
OF WOMEN'S HISTORY

EXPANDING THE BOUNDARIES OF WOMEN'S HISTORY

Essays on Women in the Third World

EDITED BY

CHERYL JOHNSON-ODIM

AND

MARGARET STROBEL

Published for the *Journal of Women's History* by
INDIANA UNIVERSITY PRESS
Bloomington and Indianapolis

"Industrialization and Employment: Changes in the Patterns of Women's Work in Puerto Rico," by Luz del Alba Acevedo, was first published in *World Development*, Vol. 18, No. 2, 1990. *World Development* is published by Pergamon Journals, Ltd., Oxford, United Kingdom.

"The Voices of Doria Shafik: Feminist Consciousness in Egypt 1940-1960," by Cynthia Nelson, is published by permission of Transaction Publishers, from *Feminist Issues*, Vol. 6, No. 2. Copyright © 1986 by *Feminist Issues*.

© 1992 by Indiana University Press

All rights reserved

No part of this book may be reproduced or utilized in any form or by any means, electronic or mechanical, including photocopying and recording, or by any information storage and retrieval system, without permission in writing from the publisher. The Association of American University Presses' Resolution on Permissions constitutes the only exception to this prohibition.

The paper used in this publication meets the minimum requirements of American National Standard for Information Sciences—Permanence of Paper for Printed Library Materials, ANSI Z39.48-1984.

Manufactured in the United States of America

Library of Congress Cataloging-in-Publication Data

Expanding the boundaries of women's history: essays on women in the Third World / edited by Cheryl Johnson-Odim and Margaret Strobel.

    p.   cm.
   ISBN 0-253-33097-1 (cloth). —- ISBN 0-253-20734-7 (paper)
   1. Women—Developing countries—History—19th century.
2. Women—Developing countries—History—20th century. I. Johnson-Odim, Cheryl, date. II. Strobel, Margaret, date.
  HQ1870.9.E97 1992
  305.4'09172'4—dc20   91-42654
 1 2 3 4 5 96 95 94 93 92

This book is dedicated to Jessica and Maya
with love and bright hopes for the future.

CONTENTS

III. Women as Workers

IV. Issues in Methodology and Analysis

INTRODUCTION

CHERYL JOHNSON-ODIM AND MARGARET STROBEL

This book is a collection of essays focusing on women's history in the nineteenth and twentieth centuries in countries in Africa, Asia, Latin America and the Caribbean, and the Middle East. The readings provide a multicultural introduction to the history of women, examine the discourse between Third World and Western cultures, and raise theoretical and methodological questions about comparative women's history.

The book emerges out of a collaboration now almost a decade old. This collaboration began with a grant proposal to prepare packets on women's history in the above-named regions of the world. These packets, edited by us and written by eight others, were produced by the Organization of American Historians with a planning grant from the National Endowment for the Humanities and a multiple-year grant from the Fund for the Improvement of Post-Secondary Education.[1] Subsequently we were asked to co-edit two special internationally focused issues of the *Journal of Women's History* (vol. 1, no. 2, and vol. 2, no. 1). The success of these publications and the encouragement of those who used them inspired the creation of this book.

Given our past experience, we were well aware of the advantages and disadvantages of producing such a collection. How can a single volume of essays cover such vast and diverse regions and populations? It can't, other than arbitrarily. We plead guilty to that. Although we have tried to choose carefully, we do not pretend to be representative in other than a random way. Yet we feel there is merit in providing in one volume exposure to women's lives in a number of settings outside Europe and the United States. We hope the variety that the book offers will discourage tunnel vision and challenge gender-focused analyses and theories to broaden their scope.

Questions of terminology and intellectual cohesion pose similar problems. Although still the most frequent term of choice, "Third World" is sometimes controversial and misunderstood.[2] How is the Third World defined? Is it merely an ahistorical, descriptive term for underdeveloped areas of the world? Or does it more accurately designate places whose main commonality is the exploitative and often racist nature of their domination by the major Western powers, for varying lengths of time, over the last five hundred years? The term "Third World" delineates diverse regions which, through ever-changing historical processes, have found themselves simultaneously struggling with Western colonialism and/or imperialism and with internal dynamics sometimes connected to and sometimes independent of Westernization. Although we believe the term "Third World" can be useful, we caution that the histories of its people, even in the nineteenth and twentieth centuries when the major Western powers were so much in evidence in many places, cannot be subsumed or even understood by relegating them to having been merely a reaction to Western domination.

The term "non-Western" is also complex. South and Central America and parts of the Caribbean, areas where the cultures of many countries are an amalgam of Amerindian, African, and European influences, cannot be considered entirely non-Western. Additionally, many of the descendants of African, Asian, and other "non-Western" cultures who reside in Europe and the United States consider themselves to be Third World people because of their origins and the material conditions of their communities. They, too, cannot be considered entirely non-Western. Moreover, as we have stated elsewhere, it seems less affirming to refer to people by a negative term denoting something they are not. Still, the terms "non-Western" and "Third World" can be useful for particular purposes if we remain aware of their limitations.

The term "feminism" can also be problematic. Generally understood as a belief in the equality of women and men, it is often identified in the Third World as a struggle which defines sexism as the only oppressive force in women's lives. Since such things as class relations, structural poverty, illiteracy, hunger, and imperialism also figure prominently in the oppression of most Third World women, many of them do not choose to refer to themselves as feminists. This does not mean that they have not been active proponents of gender equality; certainly this collection shows that they have. Rather, many of them wish to define feminism broadly enough to be able to address the multiple oppressions against which they struggle. As the international feminist movement moves to identify issues such as apartheid, imperialism, poverty, and racism as feminist issues, the term "feminism" grows in acceptance.

The question of the intellectual cohesion of this collection is related to but not entirely covered by the discussion of terminology. Just as Third World women are united by that designation, they are sometimes separated by class, culture, ethnicity, ideology, national origin, religion, and "race" or color. They often labor under indigenous patriarchal forces exacerbated by the patriarchal doctrines and systems imposed by the West. Yet, the conditions of women in the Third World are tied as much to the position of their countries in the international economy as to patriarchy.

Especially for women, Western and indigenous influences have interacted in an uneven, often unintended, and sometimes ambiguous fashion. Although the racism and xenophobia attendant to Western colonial and imperial expansion militated against it, anti-imperialist and antisexist forces in the Third World and in the West have sometimes fought together to end such oppression and in that process have defined common terrain. Knowing that this cooperative activity did sometimes exist lends better potential definition and direction to an international women's movement. Of course, unfortunately, the opposite is also shown to be true. The common bond of gender, for instance, did not always preclude the participation of European women in the oppression of Third World women. These cases must be analyzed as well.

These essays employ several methodologies, including the use of statistical analysis, archival and documentary sources, newspapers and personal diaries, interviews, biography and life history, and comparative philosophy. All are based on extensive fieldwork in the regions discussed. The authors of the theoretical pieces have also worked and lived in the Third World.

The collection is divided into four sections. The first, "Cross-Cultural Contact and Issues of Discourse," contains essays that address discourse between Western and non-Western/Third World cultures. In discussing the southern African nation of Zambia, Karen Hansen brings cultural and ideological factors to bear on an explanation of why the domestic service corps was primarily male during the colonial period, a practice continuing into the present. She delineates historically how and why African women's gender in Zambia became constructed in sexual terms that made colonial white women reluctant to employ them as household servants. Janaki Nair examines the constructions of Indian womanhood in the thought of Englishwomen who accompanied officials of the Raj (British rule) or who were missionaries, employees, or travelers in their own right. In asserting that these women (directly or indirectly) enjoyed privilege and power vis-à-vis Indian women, she seeks to locate their visions of Indian womanhood at the intersection of two sets of discourses: the growing resistance in India to British imperialism and the changing configuration of forces in the feminist movement in the late nineteenth and early twentieth centuries. E. Frances White analyzes the ways African-Americans use the African past to construct a counterdiscourse against racist ideology and oppression. While the political memory of the African past is used to foster pride, she argues that it is also used to shape and judge gender relations among black people in ways that can be confining and conservative even as a radical stance toward racist oppression is maintained. In India, Anand Yang attempts to identify the many faces of *sati* in the early nineteenth century. In investigating the social and economic circumstances underlying this practice of widow self-immolation, he aims to understand *sati* as part of the fabric of the local societies in which widows lived. For many widows *sati* was a form of ritual suicide, and the statistics for the early nineteenth century reveal that most of these women were elderly, a substantial number of them poor. Yang's focus on the victims themselves conveys a more intimate picture and seeks to answer a different set of questions from those pursued hitherto in the literature, which has focused on British attempts to abolish the practice.

The second section, "Women as Activists," contains five essays that chronicle women in various socio-political struggles and movements. To different degrees all of these essays explore the interaction between feminist and nationalist aspirations and agitation, which at times have been in tension with one another. Janet Afary examines women's political participation and early feminist activism during the 1906-1911 Constitutional Revolution in Iran in *anjumans*, semisecret women's councils that established schools, hospitals, and theaters for women, without support from the major political institutions such as parliament. The experience of Iranian women in the last century, she argues, demonstrates that women's liberation cannot be reduced to greater educational and professional opportunities and that feminism must have a broader vision. In her biography of Deng Yuzhi (Cora Deng), Emily Honig focuses on the relationship between Christianity, feminism, and communism in Deng's life. These ideologies were sometimes in competition for primacy, and Deng herself was torn between her identities. This essay reminds us that activists are also individuals making personal as well as political choices, that in fact, as the adage goes, the personal is political. Cheryl Johnson-Odim's biography of Funmilayo Ransome-Kuti chronicles and analyzes the life of a Nigerian feminist who was as committed to the struggles for national independence and social democracy as to the enfranchisement and empowerment of women. Ransome-Kuti was active in the local, national, and international arenas, and her struggle for support required her to walk a tightrope between her roles as mother, wife, and activist, between adherents to various ideological poles, and between feminist and nationalist movements. Cynthia Nelson's study of Doria Shafik examines Shafik's role as a feminist activist in mid-twentieth-century Egypt. Shafik's life is a crystal which refracts the dominant historical trends of the time in which she lived. Barbara Ramusack explores historically a question of immense and contemporary interest to women: birth control. In looking at the debate over birth control in India between 1920 and 1940, she finds key differences between the arguments put forward by men and women, as well as critical cooperation between indigenous proponents and foreign supporters.

Section three, "Women as Workers," does not preclude discussion of the activist struggles of women workers but focuses on the national and international ideologies of women's work and women as workers. Iris Berger examines the historical literature on women, industrial labor, and trade unions as a guide to formulating the questions and theoretical issues most relevant to understanding South African labor history. While acknowledging that the literature's lack of attention to racial issues and state power is a serious limitation, she shows that it yields important insights into the culture and significance of women's work, the main issues involved in organizing women workers, and the relationships between gender, class, and community. Luz del Alba Acevedo discusses her study of the changes in the sectoral and occupational distribution of female employment in Puerto Rico from 1947 to 1982. Using the results of her study, she analyzes the current debate on the impact of industrialization and the employment of women in developing countries—are women integrated into or marginalized from the labor market by industrialization? She finds that while women's participation in the labor force grew with industrialization, the types of occupations they filled remained sex-segregated with few exceptions, and that integration into the labor force does not necessarily mean an improvement in women's employment. Asunción Lavrin looks at the interrelation of gender and political ideology in the attitudes of anarchists and socialists in Argentina and Chile toward the entry of women into the wage-labor force from 1890 to 1925. She finds differences between the two political groupings but ultimately argues that the Left did not significantly change gender relations in these countries in the early decades of the twentieth century. Mary Kay Vaughan utilizes the life histories of three women school teachers to focus on the interaction between their work as teachers and socio-political movements and state formation during the Mexican Revolution.

Section four, "Issues in Methodology and Analysis," contains two essays that address some methodological and philosophical questions of doing feminist history. Susan Geiger discusses the relationship between doing women's oral history and a feminist understanding and approach. She argues that many issues must be addressed in order for oral history research with women to be considered a feminist methodology. Embedded in her approach to the development of a feminist methodology is a critique of several common concepts of social science research that have tended to undercut serious consideration of oral accounts and, more particularly, women's oral accounts. Sharon Sievers discusses the writing of feminist history and of histories of feminism. She urges historians not to eliminate non-Western societies and political movements from discussions of feminism, but in including them to be wary of cultural imperialism.

We hope that this collection of essays will make a contribution toward internationalizing our curricula and our consciousnesses, toward recognizing gender as the central historical theme that it is, and toward replacing simplistic polarizations with more considered analyses.

NOTES

1. The authors of the packets are Iris Berger and E. Frances White for Africa; Barbara Ramusack and Sharon Sievers for Asia; Virginia Sanchez Korrol and Marysa Navarro for Latin America and the Caribbean; Guity Nashat and Judith

Tucker for the Middle East. The packets are available for purchase as a whole set or as individual region sets from the Organization of American Historians, 112 North Bryan Street, Bloomington, Indiana, 47408-4199.

2. For early usage of the term "Third World," see Sue Ellen Charlton, *Women in the Third World*, p. 13, and Wayne Clegern, "What Is the Third World," in *Technos* 8 (January-December 1980). Early on the designation "Third World" was applied to those countries which were not aligned with Western or socialist bloc nations, though in time the term took on an economic meaning as well. Most agree, however, that it is fundamentally a political concept.

I

Cross-Cultural Contact and
Issues of Discourse

BODY POLITICS

SEXUALITY, GENDER, AND
DOMESTIC SERVICE IN ZAMBIA

Karen Tranberg Hansen

Many maids come in the house as innocent as a new born babe. But the attitudes of some women to treat their maids almost like slaves or rivals certainly changes their outlook and behavior towards house work. Do you blame the maids if they look at the husband as a prize catch?[1]

During the colonial period in Northern Rhodesia and today in independent Zambia, employers of domestic servants prefer to hire men. Rather than reducing domestic service in that country to an archaic remnant of a once widespread form of wage labor relationship in the west, I view it as a comparative and historical problem whose similarities to, and differences from, domestic service in other times and places must be explained. Such an approach yields insights into those aspects of servant/employer relationships that inhere in their structure and those that are mediated by historical and cultural factors. My special concern in this paper is with the historical and cultural factors in that I seek to explore a culturally constructed gender convention invested with ambiguous sexual meanings that have not been seriously examined in the Africanist research context. For this reason, I barely treat the comparative and structural questions that I have dealt with at length elsewhere.[2] The paper, thus, is an attempt at approaching an analysis of some effects on gender relations across race and class of culturally constructed notions of gender and sexuality.[3] Last but not least, because of the near total silence in the conventional source materials about sexual interaction across race and class lines, the paper is also a demonstration of the challenge and difficulty of attempting to think through and write about engendered cultural constructions whose meanings today's readers may find troublesome.

By bringing cultural and ideological factors to bear on my analysis of the gender question in domestic service in Zambia, I argue that structural and ideological factors operate in complex and at times contradictory interaction to shape social action and practice. I mobilize these culturally constructed notions in the context of a historical case study in which I seek to illustrate the effects of such ideas on actual social interaction across race, gender, and class. The case under scrutiny is the failed attempt by colonial officials in Northern Rhodesia during the post-World War II years to recruit African women into domestic service. The ensuing discussion, labelled the African womanpower debate in the colonial correspondence, provides dramatic evidence of the workings of colonial gender ideology and of the social impacts of its sexual assumptions. In the paper's first section, I present the empirical and theoretical backdrop for my subsequent analysis. I next identify the strands of the womanpower debate and then briefly delineate the historical background against which cultural notions of gender and sexuality emerged. I go on to explore how the race, gender, and class dynamics in white colonial households were affected by these notions. I finally discuss and explain why such ideas persist in changed form, but for different reasons, in domestic service in postcolonial Zambia and bring out a peculiar body politic between the madam, as female employers of servants invariably are called in southern Africa, her female servant, and the madam's husband.

Background and Problem

The existing studies of domestic service in Africa pertain almost exclusively to the southern region.[4] The South African studies offer a kaleidoscopic story of women of all races and men passing through domestic service. After the abolition of slavery in 1834, poor Afrikaner women and British women brought over from Europe worked as domestics in white households. As members of household staffs consisting mainly of African men, the presence of these white women proved problematic, and they were replaced by African men soon after the turn of the century. African men persisted in domestic service on the Witwatersrand till the late 1930s but were replaced by "coloured" and African women in the Cape much earlier.[5] With growing demand for African men's labor on the mines, women gradually became more numerous in domestic service also on the Witwatersrand. Today in South Africa, domestic service is considered an African woman's job, and it remains a life-long occupation through which married and unmarried women as well as single mothers pursue a series of dead-end jobs.[6]

In Southern Rhodesia, domestic service remained a male occupational preserve longer than in South Africa.[7] Recent research by Janet Bujra is likely to unravel the gender dynamics in domestic service in Tanzania.[8] But for much of the rest of Africa, our knowledge about gender and domestic service remains anecdotal. There is a widespread assumption that African men, rather than women, everywhere were the first to be recruited into domestic service during the colonial period and that women have been replacing them to different degrees after independence. The challenge to scholarship is not to take these assumptions for granted but to examine the changing interaction of structural, historical, and cultural factors involved in producing particular gender conventions in employment. Although the ways in which such factors have combined across space and time may result in similar employment conventions, the individual factors may carry varying weight because they are invested with different cultural meanings and thus, as in the case I am about to explore, produce conclusions that may be at variance with those of scholars who have explored the gender dynamics in domestic service elsewhere.

Colonial officials in Northern Rhodesia often referred to experiences in South Africa and Southern Rhodesia when arguing about the direction of change in the colony. By the post-World War II years, African women had established a strong presence in domestic service in South Africa and were beginning to take on this job in larger numbers also in Southern Rhodesia. These experiences influenced the thinking of colonial officials in Northern Rhodesia when, during the post-World War II years, they became increasingly preoccupied with labor shortages. The copper mining industry was booming in the wake of the Korean war, secondary industry was developing, and labor was scarce across town and country. In their concern to alleviate the labor shortage, they suggested a solution: the recruitment of African women into domestic service in order to release men for more productive work elsewhere. The African womanpower campaign they set into motion for that purpose between the late 1940s and 1956 was a failure.

If colonial officials were to succeed in staging a gender transition from male to female in domestic service in Northern Rhodesia, they would have needed ingenuity, for domestic service in that country was defined in gender terms as an African man's job. During the early decades of white settlement, some white women had been employed as governesses and ladies' companions in colonial households. As more whites settled, a small number of African women, many of whom were "coloureds" from South Africa, were hired as "nurses" or nannies, but even in this field, juveniles (meaning "nurse boys") were taken on more frequently than African women. Although more women have entered the occupation after independence in 1964, they are greatly outnumbered by men who continue to be preferred as domestic workers.

The question of gender in domestic service has to a large extent been considered self-evident in the existing scholarship on the transformations of this occupation in the west and its ongoing changes in the Third World.[9] The historical experience of the west, of women replacing men servants towards the end of the seventeenth century, their employment peaking in the early decades of the twentieth century, and the occupation's decline as a major source of urban wage income for women as new job opportunities opened up elsewhere, has been linked in the main to economic and demographic changes.[10] Extrapolating from the twentieth-century employment pattern of women domestics in the west when making predictions about the place of gender in the process of socio-economic change in Third World countries, much existing scholarship has underestimated the singularity of this pattern.[11]

The issue of domestic service, as Belinda Bozzoli has observed, "can better be understood as the outcome of a complex series of domestic struggles, rather than an institution designed to serve the interests of capital in an uncomplicated fashion."[12] The unsuccessful outcome of the African womanpower campaign was not the result only of labor market factors. Nor is today's predominance of men as paid domestic workers in Zambia to be solely attributed to the lack of postcolonial labor market developments. Scholarship on gender construction promises to flesh out the question of gender in domestic service in more detail, qualifying overly economistic accounts by actively implicating cultural and ideological factors in analysis.

Gender roles, as Michelle Rosaldo has pointed out, are not the product of the tasks women undertake or of their biology. Rather, their construction is a result of the meanings women's activities acquire through actual social interaction.[13] Cautioning against conflating gender and sexuality, Patricia Caplan has encouraged us to raise questions about whether, and if so, how, when, and why they become linked.[14] Notions of gender and sexuality were not given at the onset of the colonial encounter in Northern Rhodesia but created through it and the processes it set into motion. Although the lives of both colonizer and colonized were influenced by sexual attitudes and practices, sexuality has been placed on the scholarly agenda of colonial history only recently, and the exploration of African women's and men's experience of sexuality has barely begun.[15] Sexuality, considered as symbols pertaining to gender and to eroticism, is invested with culturally variable meanings.[16] In Northern Rhodesia, its meanings were manipulated and used by women and men of both races in ways that reflected the impact of race, class, and gender and other factors on the structure of their society. I suggest in this paper that African women's gender role hinged on constructed notions of sexuality that were the products of interactions across race and sex from the onset of colonial rule and onwards. These ideas came to the fore in the case under scrutiny, which enables me to tease out the convergence of gender and sexuality that invested the gender construction of the African female servant with ambiguous sexual meanings.

The African Womanpower Campaign

Gender and Wage Labor in Northern Rhodesia

As in much of the rest of the southern part of the African continent, the development of the migrant labor system in Northern Rhodesia from the last decades of the nineteenth century through the time of the Great Depression resulted in a geographical division of labor in which African men were recruited into wage labor on farms and in mines, while African women remained in the rural areas working the fields and taking care of children and the old. The viability of village life depended overwhelmingly on women's work, which also subsidized migrant workers' substandard wages without cost to the administration.[17] Deteriorating rural conditions and lack of agricultural extension services had by the 1930s adversely affected rural livelihoods, prompting more and more women and children to migrate to towns.[18] African women were largely excluded from urban wage labor, and many secured a living by joining men as wives or consorts and/or by trading or marketing.[19] Despite the dubious nature of colonial statistics and lack of gender categorized employment data till 1951, the available statistics show that very few African women were employed in domestic service. A total of 250 African women compared to 30,000 men domestic servants were enumerated in 1951 when the occupation formed the third largest male employment category after mining and agriculture.[20] During World War II, when Northern Rhodesia experienced extreme food scarcities, the colonial government tried to stem the urban influx of women and children, devising a variety of measures to get them back to the villages as food producers.[21] These attempts were largely ineffectual. Due to growing white immigration and continued migration of rural Africans, the urban populations increased rapidly during the decade 1946-56, and the previous era's skewed adult sex ratios of both Africans and whites became more balanced.[22] To increase productivity, the colonial administration copied the practice followed since the 1930s by some of the mining companies, allowing African male workers to live with wives and dependents.[23] During the early 1940s, primary education was for the first time made compulsory for urban African children between 12 and 16 years of age. Newly established welfare departments involved themselves in shaping African urban patterns of leisure and in the teaching of western notions of domesticity to urban African women.[24] These, and other developments, contributed to the creation of a more stabilized urban African community.

The scope the colonial administration grudgingly had granted African urbanites to organize their households was not left undisturbed. When labor shortages grew during the post-World War II period, the colonial administration sought to intrude in order to tap the available labor supply.

Assuming that units of labor were mutually interchangeable, they argued that African women should replace men in domestic service to release the latter for work elsewhere.[25] The ambiguous and at times contradictory attitudes of whites and Africans, males and females, to the question of employing women in domestic service was laid open in the debate that followed.

The Debate about African Womanpower

Being female or male was far from an irrelevant factor in the Northern Rhodesian labor market, and, for historical reasons, domestic service had become construed in gender terms as male. In the view of male administrators and white women, there were three chief "problems" that made the prospective employment of African female domestic servants difficult. There was no housing for them, they were not trained, and their men would object. They claimed that African women could not work as servants in white households until hostels were built for them outside of the white residential areas. Living there under the supervision of a white woman, they would be less likely to become involved with men. The reverse had never been argued, namely the need to house African men servants away from their employers' residences in order to reduce their possible sexual involvement with white madams. It seems that white women in Northern Rhodesia had been accustomed to African men servants living in their backyards for decades. Why now this fuss about African women?

It was argued over and over again that African women needed education before they would be able to go into service. African women, it seems, were not considered domestic "by nature." And white women appear to have been unwilling to socialize them into domestic labor on the job as they had done with previous generations of African men servants. In the past, men's work as servants had not been deemed problematic because they had little education. On the contrary, in the early days of settlement, and according to my informants, up through the 1940s if not later, many employers avoided "mission boys" (Africans who had received some education) who were considered rogues of the first order, and several white madams had, indeed, preferred "raw natives," that is, young men fresh from the villages, whom they trained themselves. Holding African women's lack of education against them, white women chose to disregard that the curriculum in girls' schools, such as they were at this point in time, was heavy on domestic science subjects with the intention of making African women into good mothers and proud housewives. Yet these mutually contradictory attitudes did not cancel each other out. In the view of white madams, African women servants were less controllable than men; they were less tractable and caused more problems in the running of the white colonial household. Training of African women, wrote four white women in a 1950 letter to a newspaper's editor, should be undertaken by "honest-to-goodness women with a sound knowledge of Rhodesian homes . . .

[because] only women who have lived among Africans have a glimmering idea of the primitive condition of the African female."[26]

These, and other comments made during the debate, indicate white women's doubt that African women would be able to take over from men in domestic service, and they themselves made little effort to see to it that they were. Nor did white male officials of the labor department who, at a 1950 conference, declared African women as "absolutely raw material." In spite of advocating the employment of African women servants, the colonial administration did little to facilitate it, resisting suggestions from churches and philanthropic groups to finance both training and hostels for women servants.[27]

As for African men, colonial authorities described them as "loth, not without some reason, to allow their wives to work away from home." The colonial assumption was that African wives would involve themselves sexually with other men. I suggest that several additional factors may have influenced African men's attitudes toward women's work as domestics. Their reluctance to send wives, sisters, and daughters into service in colonial white households may reflect their unwillingness to expose women to a demeaning work relationship for which very low wages were paid. The matter of wages was never addressed in the debate. The few African women who did participate in a short-lived African Charwoman Scheme at the copperbelt town of Ndola in 1954 preferred to change from an hourly basis to "whole time employment as being more secure." Their statement implies that part-time domestic service hardly was worthwhile economically.

Last but not least, paid household service conflicted with the demands placed on African women's own domestic labor as broadly defined in cultural terms among the region's different ethnic groups. Across much of Africa, women and men regard the home as women's place and childcare and household tasks as their most important endeavors. Married women's ability to prioritize this work was, and continues to be, influenced by cultural practices that shape gender relations within households and by the viability of their household economy. This viability is affected by the region's productive potential, by the economic needs and political capacity of the state to incorporate women as wage laborers, and by women's personal initiatives. Single women, and women who entered short-term relations with men, may have preferred their own work or self-employment to ill-paid wage labor in domestic service. African women in Northern Rhodesia were thus better able to resist the colonial government's sudden attempt to incorporate them into domestic service than their sisters in different parts of South Africa where the proletarianization process had eroded household viability much earlier.[28]

In Northern Rhodesia's urban African communities in the postwar years, the demands on women's domestic work from within their own households did not differ much by class. This is reflected in the reactions of three African men of elite status in the colonial structure who took part in a radio debate in 1952 about women servants.[29] They objected to the idea of women going into service in white households because they had enough to attend to in their own households. When colonial authorities complained that urban African women were idle and lazy, they failed to recognize the time-consuming tasks of food processing and preparation and the constant demands that children and their care placed on women. Despite mentioning the need for childcare facilities for urban African women, authorities never attended to it. Thus, beyond African men's sexual needs for women, authorities drew no conclusions about contending claims on women's labor from within their own households.

Perhaps most importantly, the African women themselves, crucial actors to the outcome of the campaign to hire them as domestic servants, were not called upon to express their opinion. But although the debate gave them no voice, they spoke by their action, preferring to do their own work at home or in trade. The African women of the early 1950s are likely to have shared the view on domestic service held by the women I interviewed in Lusaka in the 1980s as part of my follow-up research of low-income household developments since the early 1970s: a woman with small children just doesn't leave her own household to attend to someone else's.[30] And if she does, it is as a last resort, for who wants to be ordered around by another woman all the time on a slave wage?

The debate about hiring African women for domestic service dragged on through the first half of the 1950s. The number of women domestics had increased to 855 in 1956 when a total of 33,000 men were employed in the occupation.[31] The labor commissioner was clearly fed up. His longhand remarks at the end of the official correspondence in 1956 indicate his frustrations: "It is a pity but I do not think we can force the issue any more." There was no need to do so. The postwar boom had been succeeded by an economic downturn, beginning in 1954, when for the first time in many years labor was plentiful. The unemployment figures for all races grew when copper prices dropped sharply in 1957. The ensuing recession lasted through the first years after independence in 1964. The argument that African women should replace men in domestic service so as to release them for more productive work elsewhere was no longer heard.

Sexual Imagery and Ideology of Gender

Although economic factors had pushed toward the employment of African women in domestic service during the post-World War II economic boom, the effort between the late 1940s and 1956 to recruit them was a dismal failure. This was not only due, as the participants in the debate claimed, to lack of suitable housing for women servants, their lack of education, or the opposition of African men. Although these factors certainly influenced the outcome, they masked the more important issue of sexuality. African women's gender, I suggest, had become constructed in the white mind in a highly selective and idiosyncratic manner that accentuated their sexuality. This notion of sexuality was a by-product of pre-World War I interaction between white men and African women in the days when the white sex ratio was skewed and white settlement yet too scattered and small for social pressures for European notions of "civilized standards" to become effective. These relationships set the scene for later developments of sexual and gender relations across race. Although the way in which late-Victorian, early Edwardian society defined the sexuality of white men and women played a likely role in the shaping of their reactions to sexual relationships in what they considered as "darkest Africa," an analysis of its role lies beyond the scope of this paper.

When white women came to the colony in larger numbers from the post-World War II years and on, they used the distorted image of African women's sexuality strategically to refrain from employing them in their own households. The image of overexaggerated sexuality colonial white women ascribed to African women was informed by normative notions of moral laxity and looseness which this generation of whites attributed to African social organization in general and to such marriage and descent practices as polyandry and matriliny in particular. Turn-of-the-century white perceptions of matriliny (the practice of tracing descent in the female line that was prevalent among many local African groups) and of polyandry (the practice of women having more than one "husband" at the same time widely reported in the literature on the region)[32] had come to constitute an ambiguous image of African women as the embodiment of sexuality associated with a "savage" eroticism in need of control. The Baila, noted a native commissioner in 1923 about one of the matrilineal, polyandrous groups in the district he administered, are "chiefly noted for their low state of morality." "These remarks," he continued, were "not much out of place if applied to the Balenje or Balovale. . . . Morally the sub-district . . . might now be called the brothel of Northern Rhodesia."[33]

Although the pronounced invidious stance in colonial whites' interpretation of African social organization lessened as the years went on, the sedimented cultural weight of this image helped to construe the gender division of labor in domestic service in terms that made African men better suited for it than women. So much taken for granted was this division of labor in the outlook of white women from the employing class that in my interviews and correspondence with postwar residents of Northern Rhodesia, who now have retired to England, I appeared to be questioning what to them were common-sense statements. Women's standard answer to my question of why so few African women worked as servants then was that it simply did not come into question or that it just was not done. Men's standard answer was that it was not looked well upon having an African woman servant for, given the legacy of pioneer days, the suspicion lingered that she was sexually available to the master of the house. Whether such statements are true or false, the ideology they express had significance by affecting social practice, in this case the convention of not employing African women as servants.

Sexual and Gender Dynamics

The impact that deep-seated European cultural assumptions about African women's sexuality had on the outcome of the campaign to hire them for domestic service must be viewed in the light of the power dynamics between colonial white women and men within the private household and in society beyond it. The campaign to hire African women workers for domestic service had been the product of male officials who, vaguely doubting it would work, could easily argue in the abstract the pros and cons of male versus female labor for domestic service. They left to their wives the practical matters involving servants and their management. I suggest that the difficulties to which white officials had alluded when anticipating the failure of the campaign concerned the sexual ramifications of the scheme. Their gender became African women's liability and not an asset that "naturally" predisposed them for domestic work. Young African girls were considered dangerous in colonial households, for they were assumed to be sexually precocious, and married African women were suspected of adulterous sexual assignations. Then there was the unspoken question of how an African woman servant and the white madam's husband would confront one another.

It is not surprising that colonial white women defended their place as mistresses of their own households when encouraged by male officials to hire African women. White women in Northern Rhodesia had little scope for autonomous activity and power acquisition in their own right in this class and race conscious society. To understand this, we must reckon with their status as incorporated wives whose ascribed social character was a function of their husbands' occupation and culture.[34] Their private lives easily merged into officialdom and made their role into that of "silent partner." Emily Bradley, the wife of a long-time colonial officer in Northern Rhodesia from 1929-42 used that term. In a mores and customs handbook Bradley wrote for a fictitous bride-to-be of a young colonial officer, she told her that it was "the rule rather than the exception out there . . . that the men can get along without us."[35]

White colonial women were well aware of their limited powers. What these women said about interracial sexuality remains unarticulated in the public discourse of the late colonial period's strained racial atmosphere, no doubt silenced by the need to keep up propriety in white "civilized society." These were events of which it was not polite to talk in public, although there was substantial intimate knowledge about them.[36] But writers in the literary vein captured popularly shared sentiments. Women's knowledge about inter-racial sex and their reactions are illustrated dramatically in the only novel by best-selling Southern Rhodesian writer, Gertrude Page, whose plot features sex between a white male administrator and an African woman and is set in Northern Rhodesia.[37] On her outward journey to marry a white administrator, the British bride-to-be in the novel is informed about his African "harem" by a woman fellow-passenger. The bringer of unspeakable news explained to her friend that many white women overlooked their husbands' sexual habits; they had no choice, she said. Colonial white women's chief choice was to identify with their husbands, regardless of the latters' extramarital involvements.[38]

But there were other choices: departure for one thing. Employing language and sentiments that we today find objectionable, a contemporary white woman observer recalled this choice when she "thought of the game rangers and planters and men of the administration, too, who had gone to England and brought back pretty young English brides who, when they . discovered that their husbands owned large families of coloured piccanins [children of mixed racial parentage] had fled as fast as their sturdy legs could carry them, back to their homes across the sea."[39] Her comments on colonial life in the 1940s at the small town of Fort Jameson (now Chipata) in the eastern part of the country showed empathy neither for such white men nor these African women: "the native women themselves [are] a travesty of womanhood as we [women] of the West understand it."[40]

Because of their position, white men were in contact with a broader range of people and more on the move than white women. Yet white women did have other choices than condoning their men's extramarital affairs or quitting the scene. These were but two of several possible ones, involving both sexes and the two races. Liaisons between white women and African men were another choice, though one Europeans considered even more despicably than relations between white men and African women. They did occur but were not widespread.[41] Judging from contemporary writers such as those quoted above and the women I interviewed, white women were very conscious of themselves as the embodiment of white womanhood and of the propriety expected of them in their roles as wives to powerful men.

The decision to play the role of incorporated wife to the hilt may have been these women's best choice. Given the dominant ideology of exclusivity in race and sex that developed over the preceding decades in response to what whites saw as "uncivilized" surroundings, it is perhaps not surprising that colonial white women drew clear distinctions by sex in their household employment practices. Since white women considered them to be potential if not actual prostitutes in any case, African women would cause too many problems for the proper running of a white "civilized" household. White women were unwilling to dispense with their men servants. They used the unexpected political platform created by the campaign for African womanpower to their own advantage: keeping the men servants they had been used to for so long rather than upsetting the already delicate race, sex, and class hierarchy within the colonial household. Being aware of white men's sexual involvement with African women, white women may have seen any possibility for such liaisons as placing themselves in jeopardy. A very similar ideology affects interaction across gender and class in Zambian servant-employing households today. Although its terms rarely are charged with the colonial era's racial notions, they produce the same effects on interaction within domestic service as did the distinctions called on in the colonial discourse: they mark a class divide.

The Postcolonial Sexuality Argument

Postcolonial Changes

The recession Zambia experienced in the immediate postindependence years gave way to an economic expansion lasting into the first half of the 1970s. New economic reforms stimulated the indigenization of the economy, and changed demographics brought about changes within the servant employing class after independence. The expatriate population declined and, unlike in the past, the majority of today's employers of servants are black Zambians. Servants earn low wages, which makes them affordable by a broad cross-section of society, including some segments of low-income earners. In addition to paid servants or instead of them, many Zambian householders make use of the unpaid labor of young relatives in return for upkeep. Yet in postcolonial Zambia, men still dominate in domestic service in terms of numbers of people employed. This statement is based on my own conservative estimate, for domestic service has not been enumerated as a separate category of the labor force since 1968. That year, some 36,491 men and 1,758 women were employed as paid servants in private households.[42] The Zambia National Provident Fund has of late begun to provide statistics on servant employment for pension purposes. The 1983 count showed 45,760 registered servants of both sexes across the country's towns.[43] The ZNPF figures give a poor indication of the extent and nature of domestic employment. Far from all employers register their servants, and the ZNPF figures are not categorized by sex or task specialization.[44] My own sample survey of workers and employers in 187 servant-keeping households in mid- to upper-income areas in the capital city, Lusaka, showed that women comprised between one-third and one-fourth of the domestic workers, and that the majority of these women had been hired for one particular task: childcare. My findings suggest that domestic service in Zambia in the mid-1980s forms the single largest sector of the paid wage labor force, outnumbering employment in mining, which has dropped steadily. Domestic service kept on growing when overall employment shrank in the economic decline that set in during the first half of the 1970s and has persisted to this day.

Women, Men, and Domestic Service

In the mid-1980s Zambia, domestic service continues to be an important entry-level occupation for people with few marketable skills and for migrants newly arrived from the countryside. Although more women work in domestic service than during the colonial period, the occupation is not in my view at the present time undergoing a gender transition in which women are replacing men. Most of the women who enter service are not taking over men's jobs but doing something different. They are, in the main, hired as nannies and to perform tasks associated with childcare. They may do other things within the house, but these are secondary to their main duty: childcare. Men, thus, remain employed as the chief domestic workers, and the expanded number of women who today work as nannies is contributing to the extension of an occupational domain without transforming its long established gender division of labor.

Because of the difference in childbearing and childrearing patterns between Zambian women today and the white women of the colonial era, a special niche has opened up within domestic service for women to work as paid nannies for other wealthier Zambian women. This is not to say that African women never worked as nannies during the colonial period. Some certainly did, as I noted at the outset, and persons who employed African women went to great length to relate the troublesome nature of their employment to me. The point is, rather, that the African female nanny then was a "rare bird," as one of their contemporary employers expressed it. She was the exception, not the rule. Many colonial white women used paid childcare facilities for their children during the daytime. To push the pram and to wash the nappies at home, they more often employed "nurse boys" than African women. Few colonial white women worked away from home until the post-World War II years. These white women had fewer children than today's Zambian women householders. Because children usually were sent away to schools in what then was Southern Rhodesia, to South Africa or Great Britain, their mothers had fewer worries about their day-to-day supervision than have postcolonial Zambian women who bear children much more frequently and with shorter intervals.

Zambian women, thus, need nannies to attend to their children while they themselves go out to work. And many Zambian women who do not work away from home want relief from childcare if they can afford it. Childcare facilities and nursery schools do not have sufficient places for the growing number of preschool children. Even if places were available, they would be too expensive for most Zambian mothers.

My study shows that women who work in domestic service fall into two broad categories of marital status: 35 percent of women servants (compared to 67 percent men) were married and lived with their spouses; 13 percent of women servants had not married (compared to 20 percent men); and 52 percent of women supported their own households after separation, divorce, or widowhood (compared to 13 percent men). The married women were, in the main, nannies in Zambian and expatriate households; they earned median range wages; and they all lived-out, often walking long distances to and from work. The unmarried women were young school drop-outs from rural areas who had come to town, sometimes leaving a child behind with relatives. They worked in the very low paid jobs, primarily as nannies in Zambian households, and they sometimes lived-in there. The single heads of households tended to be middle aged, close to or beyond the end of their child-bearing years, often long-term urban residents who worked in better paid jobs especially in expatriate households with larger servant staffs, and they lived-out.

In my interviews with them, Zambian madams described their "nanny problems" as beginning at the birth of their first child. At this point in their household's development cycle, they typically fetch, or are brought, a female relative from the countryside, often a teenage girl who has dropped out of school or whose parents are unable to pay her education. She is fed and clothed and shares sleeping space with members of the household, yet is at their beck and call. She rarely lasts from the birth of one baby to the next, which is to say that she is employed for at most two to three years before being dismissed. Problems of discipline readily arise, for young girls develop a dislike for being ordered around, and they want to do things their own way. They want freedom to explore the city as well. If they stay for three years, they are generally returned by their urban relations or collected by their parents or guardians in order not to "detain" them for too long since this may reduce their marriage chances. The longer they stay in town, the more likely they are to become "spoiled," that is, made pregnant, which reduces the size of bridewealth their fathers or guardians may claim. After their trials with young country relatives, Zambian women turn to paid women servants and their problems with nannies grow rather than diminish. Many of the Zambian women I interviewed preferred to hire rural women new to town, for they assume them to be less venturesome in matters of sex. They deliberately do not keep them too long, for with length of stay develops familiarity and a fear of likely intimate encounters with the male household head. These problems last for as long as they have preschool children, and they typically "go through" more nannies than they care to remember. Once their last-born child has entered school or the older children are considered responsible enough to watch their younger siblings, Zambian women employ men servants.

Evaluated poorly, paid miserably, and spoken of in invidious terms, paid domestic work does not in the Zambian view constitute proper women's work, for it is not considered "natural" for a woman with small children to leave her own household to attend to someone else's. In my interviews, Zambian madams recounted their experiences of employing women servants in a troubled voice: women servants are insolent and cheeky; they do only the work they feel like doing; in addition, they steal; they go through your panties and toiletries. But worst of all, before you know it they move into the bedroom and take over the house.[45] The sexuality issue, thus, continues to shape the gender construction of women servants in postcolonial Zambia, although those who frame it have changed in terms of race. But this shift is largely irrelevant for women whom circumstances leave no other option than paid domestic work. Their gender role continues to be constructed in sexual terms.

Body Politics

The persistence, if not growth, of domestic service in postcolonial Zambia masks changes at several levels of society alluded to in the foregoing discussion at the same time as the apparent continuity of gender construction reveals a sexually charged contest that is fueled by growing economic disparity between servants and employers. Zambian women householders attribute their problems in domestic service to the loose morals of their female domestics whom they claim to be always on the lookout for a man either to marry or to "keep them nicely." Being kept nicely in Zambia means receiving shelter, food, and occasional clothing. Poor women's attempts to secure their own and their dependents' livelihood through support from a spouse or consort clash with middle-to-upper income Zambian women's needs for childcare: the woman who takes a job as a nanny seeks to quit as soon as she has some economic means in her own household.

To account for this, we must grapple with the power dynamics within the household between the sexes and the way these dynamics enter into, and affect, women's and men's places in the wider social context. Most urban studies in Zambia have shown that male/female relations are difficult and very unstable.[46] Regardless of the ethnic background of the towns' heterogeneous populations, the gender dynamics within private households turn on an age- and male-based hierarchy of authority. Across class, male/female relations are largely authoritarian and asymmetric, and, although there are exceptions, husbands generally assume domestic authority. Many marital relations are fraught with tensions, in part due to the persistence of customary marriage practices that permit polygyny and, perhaps influenced by this, to the existence of a double standard that condones extramarital sex for men. Zambian madams anticipate and fear their husbands' extramarital affairs, not only with women domestics but with the wife's young relatives, women at the workplace, or women they meet at bars or on the streets. To attract their man's love and assure his financial support, Zambian women will go to great expense to buy love medicines.[47] Yet they also know that they cannot rely on men. Unlike in many West African countries, cultural norms in Zambia do not oblige men to distribute part of their resources to wives for household purposes. Even if Zambian men have ample economic means, only a portion of their income reaches their own households.

While women seek to get and maintain support from men, they are also concerned to ensure the day-to-day survival of their children and to make some economic gains in their own right. As they grow older, and their children are leaving the household, Zambian women become less concerned with the pursuit of men's attentions and concentrate more of their efforts on making an income they control themselves. This shift helps account for the dual participation pattern in domestic service identified earlier: the young women who come and go in the low paid jobs are struggling to establish their own households, whereas the middle-aged and older women in longer-term employment and at better wages often are single heads of households after the death or divorce of a husband. Men may come and go in their lives for they do not mind being kept nicely, yet they do not want them around on a permanent basis.

These tensions characterize gender relations in Zambian households across class. Because of the sexual double standard, men may feel freer than women to pursue sex and change partners. Zambian women householders seek to identify themselves sexually as their husbands' women at the same time as they are aware that husbands have other choices. They will make statements to that effect, if not about their own husbands then about a neighbor's. A sexualized gender role is attributed not only to female domestics but to any category of women a wife perceives as a threat to her marriage. To prevent compromising sexual affairs from happening within their own households, Zambian women prefer to employ men servants. Their distrust of their women domestics expresses itself in an idiom of sexuality that accentuates and dramatizes their women servants' struggle for a livelihood. It also distances them from their less fortunate sisters who may have neither husbands nor homes of their own. Underneath these expressions lies a difference of lifestyle, a class gap, which they make sure not to bridge. Yet they do have much in common: the servant wants a person to support her and her children so that she no longer needs to do someone else's domestic work, and her female employer wants a husband, certainly to support her children and to legitimate her economic and social pursuits as a mature social person, properly married.

The gender role Zambian women householders attribute to their women servants is a product of the way they interpret sexual activities and interaction in general, and it produces a special body politic within their own households. Since they believe that their women servants may indulge in sexual affairs with their husbands, they restrict them by rules that reduce their opportunity for contact with the male head of household. The chief rules revealed in my study concerned bedrooms and the preparation of food. In colonial white households, male servants commonly entered bedrooms, bringing in the early morning tea; they made the beds and washed the underwear of white male and female employers alike; cooks were almost without exception men, for white householders claimed that Zambian women "cannot cook." In postcolonial Zambian households, these activities and domains have become reorganized spatially in sexually charged terms: the bedroom is the private space from which even children, aside from infants, are excluded; madams and their daughters wash their own underwear; and food preparation is a domain of activity in which the wife exerts individual care to please her husband.[48] In most of the Zambian households I studied, neither men nor women servants were allowed to enter bedrooms, and in several of them, the women servants were asked not to cook for the madam's husband. In these cases, the Zambian women householders feared that the female servant would mix love potions into the husband's food in order to attract his sexual attentions. Those servants who did cook were mostly men, and even in some of these cases, the wife took personal charge of preparing her husband's main meals. Only because of their need for child care do they tolerate the presence of their Zambian nannies. As these nannies come and go, their madams' problems with them are reenacted, and the structured inequality between the two main protagonists is recreated anew. While couched in sexual idioms, the contest between women servants and employers is a battle over the status quo. Their shared interest in men creates a sexual antagonism that further distances these two categories of women who have such different marketable skills and are involved in fundamentally different relationships to the economy.

The Gender Question in Domestic Service:
The Zambian Case

Few scholars today speak unequivocally about how economic change is affecting the gender division of labor; rather, they are turning toward much finer grained analyses. My account shares this concern in its attempt to free this field of study from constraining assumptions, to anchor it in time, and to leave analytical space for the human social actor. I have suggested that interaction between whites and Africans during the early colonial period was instrumental in constructing a female gender role that in a selective and idiosyncratic manner accentuated African women's sexuality. Thus, a culturally constructed notion of gender must be reckoned with when we seek to explain the division of labor that evolved in private household employment in Northern Rhodesia's towns from the close of the depression years and onwards. Over time, the ideology embodied in the female gender construct was articulated by the white dominant class and absorbed into social practice to the point of "naturalizing" a convention of not employing African women in wage labor and particularly not in domestic service. In the late 1940s and early 1950s, when by all accounts African women were readily available in towns, authorities argued in vain for their recruitment into domestic service. Believing that they knew what was good for them, white male colonial officials, white madams, and African men did not solicit African women's opinion when discussing the possibility of them working as servants in colonial white households. The chief performers absented themselves: white women did not want African women in their homes for fear of their sexuality, and African women, having different priorities, resisted this sudden claim on their labor power. The coming of independence has not broken this employment practice, although differences having to do with class rather than race help to account for its persistence and to explain why, in the view of some social segments in Zambia today, women's easy virtue remains a notion that exercises constraints on their employability.

My conclusions may be at variance with those of scholars who have explored the gender dynamics in domestic service in other African countries and elsewhere.[49] If so, our differences may have to do in part with the variable meanings with which notions of gender and sexuality are invested and with the ways in which they are transformed or persist as societies undergo change. While recognizing the constraining effects of economic and demographic processes on domestic service in Zambia, I have in this paper been chiefly concerned with the cultural and idiosyncratic dimension of gender construction and the resulting body politics that both influenced and were the products of domestic struggles across race and class. In my attempt to account for the influence of culturally constructed notions of gender on private household employment practices, I have purposefully sought to problematize commonsense knowledge about sexuality by asking questions about, rather than contributing to, the folklore of domestic service. Gender ideology, in short, has a legitimate place on the research agenda as part of the study of socio-economic change and its effects on women and men.

NOTES

This paper draws on extensive archival research begun in 1982, and field research in Zambia, 1983-85, including the collection of life history data from retired employers of colonial servants in Great Britain (5 interviews; 19 written communications) and Zambia (a minority of the white employers of servants interviewed as part of the sample survey), elderly servants (16 men; 12 women), and a sample survey in 187 servant employing households in Lusaka involving separate interviews with the chief domestic servant and the employer. Parts of the research were funded in 1982 by the McMillan Fund and the Office of International Programs at the University of Minnesota, from 1983-85 by the U.S. National Science Foundation grant no. BNS 8303507, and by faculty grants from Northwestern University in 1985 and 1986. Versions of this paper have been presented on several occasions, among them the seminar series on Women, Colonialism and Commonwealth at the Institute of Commonwealth Studies, University of London, June 25, 1987. Among the many who have offered critical comments and suggestions, I am grateful to Carol B. Eastman for constructive advice and to Margaret Strobel for continous prodding and for always being a stimulating critic.

1. Geoff Zulu, "Maids Wreaking Havoc in Homes," *Zambia Daily Mail*, Weekend Entertainment Section, May 27, 1989, 4.

2. Karen Tranberg Hansen, *Distant Companions: Servants and Employers in Zambia, 1900-1985* (Ithaca, N.Y.: Cornell University Press, 1989).

3. Because of the nature of my sources, most of my discussion of European or white attitudes refers to the British. The fact that African, Asian ("Indians"), and Afrikaans-speaking households also employed servants does not mean that the master-servant relationship in British households was atypical or out of the ordinary. On the contrary, since the British were the dominant group in political terms, they set the norms and standards against which social interaction and practices were evaluated.

4. Among the chief studies are Michael G. Whisson and William Weil, *Domestic Servants: A Micrososm of "The Race Problem"* (Johannesburg: Institute of Race Relations, 1971); Eleanor Preston-Whyte, "Race Attitudes and Behavior: The Case of Domestic Employment in White South African Homes," *African Studies* 35 (1976): 71-89; special issue on domestic labor of the *South African Labour Bulletin* 6 (1980); Jacklyn Cock, *Maids and Madams: A Study in the Politics of Exploitation* (Johannesburg: Ravan Press, 1980); and Suzanne Gordon, *A Talent for Tomorrow: Life Stories of South African Servants* (Johannesburg: Ravan Press, 1985).

5. Charles van Onselen, "The Witches of Suburbia: Domestic Service on the Witwatersrand, 1890-1914," in van Onselen, ed., *Studies in the Social and Economic History of the Witwatersrand 1886-1914* (London: Longman, 1982), 2 vols., *New Nineveh*, 2: 1-73; Deborah Gaitskell, Judy Kimble, Moira Maconachie, and Elaine Unterhalter, "Race, Class and Gender: Domestic Workers in South Africa," *Review of African Political Economy* 27/28 (1984): 86-108.

6. Eleanor Preston-Whyte develops this point in "Families without Marriage: A Zulu Case Study, " in *Social System and Transition in South Africa: Essays in Honour of Eileen Krige,* ed. John Argyle and Eleanor Preston-Whyte (Cape Town: Oxford University Press, 1978), 55-85.

7. Duncan G. Clarke, *Domestic Workers in Rhodesia: The Economics of Masters and Servants* (Gwelo: Mambo Press, 1974), and chapters on servants and employers in A. K. Weinrich, *Mucheke: Race, Status, and Politics in a Rhodesian Community* (New York: Holmes and Meier, 1976).

8. Janet Bujra, "Men at Work in the Tanzanian Home: How Did They Ever Learn?" in *African Encounters with Domesticity*, ed. Karen Tranberg Hansen (New Brunswick: Rutgers University Press, 1992).

9. Recent Third World studies include Elsa M. Chaney and Mary Garcia Castro, eds., *Muchachas No More: Household Workers in Latin America and the Caribbean* (Philadelphia: Temple University Press, 1989); Jacklyn Cock, *Maids & Madams: A Study of the Politics of Exploitation* (Johannesburg: Ravan Press, 1980); and Shellee Coleen and Roger Sanjek, eds., *At Work in Homes: Household Workers in Third World Countries* (Washington, DC: American Ethnological Society, forthcoming).

10. On these changes in the west, see for example, Faye E. Dudden, *Serving Women: Household Service in Nineteenth-Century America* (Middletown, Conn: Wesleyan University Press, 1983); David Katzman, *Seven Days a Week: Women and Domestic Service in Industrializing America* (New York: Oxford University Press, 1978); Sarah Maza, *The Uses of Loyalty: Domestic Service in Eighteenth Century France* (Princeton, N.J.: Princeton University Press, 1983); Pamela Horn, *The Rise and Fall of the Victorian Servant* (New York: St. Martin's Press, 1975). On race and domestic service in America, see Evelyn Nakano Glenn, *Issei, Nisei, War Bride: Three Generations of Japanese American Women in Domestic Service* (Philadelphia: Temple University Press, 1986); Judith Rollins, *Between Women: Domestics and Their Employers* (Philadelphia: Temple University Press, 1985).

11. See for example, Ester Boserup, *Woman's Role in Economic Development* (New York: St. Martin's Press, 1970), and David Chaplin, "Domestic Service and Industrialization," *Comparative Studies in Sociology* 1 (1978): 97-127.

12. Belinda Bozzoli, "Marxism, Feminism and South African Studies," *Journal of Southern African Studies* 9(1983): 159.

13. Michelle Z. Rosaldo, "The Use and Abuse of Anthropology: Reflections on Feminism and Cross-cultural Understanding," *Signs* 5 (1980): 399-400.

14. Pat Caplan, ed., *The Cultural Construction of Sexuality* (London: Tavistock, 1987).

15. Ronald Hyam, "Empire and Sexual Opportunity," *Journal of Imperial and Commonwealth History* 14 (1986): 34-90. For studies concerning the former British colonies, see Kenneth Ballhatchet, *Race, Sex and Class under the Raj* (London: Weidenfeld and Nicolson, 1980), and Amirah Inglis, *The White Women's Protection Ordinance: Sexual Anxiety and Politics in Papua* (London: Sussex University Press, 1974). For American discussions of sexuality, see Ann Snitow, Christine Stansell, and Sharon Thompson, eds., *Powers of Desire: The Politics of Sexuality* (New York: Monthly Review Press, 1983).

16. Sherry B. Ortner and Harriet Whitehead, "Introduction: Accounting for Sexual Meanings," in *Sexual Meanings: The Cultural Construction of Gender and Sexuality*, ed. Sherry B. Ortner and Harriet Whitehead (New York: Cambridge University Press, 1981), ix.

17. Lionel Cliffe, "Labour Migration and Peasant Differentiation: Zambian Experiences," *Journal of Peasant Studies* 5 (1978): 326-46.

18. Andrew Roberts, *A History of Zambia* (London: Heinemann, 1976), 190-94.

19. George Chauncey, Jr., "The Locus of Reproduction: Women's Labour in the Zambian Copperbelt, 1927-1953," *Journal of Southern African Studies* 7 (1981): 135-64.

20. Hansen, *Distant Companions*, 130.

21. Helmuth Heisler, *Urbanization and the Government of Migration* (New York: St. Martin's Press, 1974), 63-84.

22. George Kay, *A Social Geography of Zambia* (London: London University Press, 1967), 26-27.

23. Roberts, *A History of Zambia*, 190-94.

24. Hortense Powdermaker, *Coppertown: Changing Africa* (New York: Harper and Row, 1962), 109-12.

25. Unless otherwise specified, the discussion in this part is based on files deposited at the National Archives of Zambia (NAZ). Direct quotes are taken from the following files: NAZ/NR 3/143 md/14. Labour Department. Native Labour Conditions. Labour Supplies. Woman Power; NAZ/NR 2/27. African Welfare. General Correspondence; and NAZ/SEC 5/331. Native Labour. General Policy 1949-51.

26. "Letter to the Editor," *Central African Post*, December 14, 1950, 3.

27. Churches and missions in Northern Rhodesia never involved themselves in housing and training women domestics to the same extent that they did in the south. On South Africa, see Deborah Gaitskell, " 'Christian Compounds for Girls': Church Hostels for African Women in Johannesburg, 1907-1970," *Journal of Southern African Studies* 6 (1979): 44-69. On Southern Rhodesia, National Archives of Zimbabwe S/1561/48. Female Domestic Labour. Labour Memoranda and Minutes, 1941-1947. Report on Native Female Domestic Service, November 17, 1932.

28. Bozzoli' s account, 149-55, of the differential proletarianization of women in South Africa reckons both with the capacity of indigenous societies and of the state to subordinate women's labor. See Gaitskell et al. for an account of the different gender patterns in domestic service in South Africa. Due to a complex interplay of diverse economic and political settler motives and to the uneven displacement and increasing impoverishment of local African groups, domestic service developed predominantly as a labor sphere for women in the Cape and the Orange Free State from the time of emancipation in 1834, and in the Natal and Transvaal the gender transition from male to female was well on its way in domestic service by the 1930s.

29. As reported in the radio magazine the colonial administration made available for Africans, *The African Listener* 1, January 25,1952, 17.

30. Karen Tranberg Hansen, "Urban Women and Work in Africa: A Zambian Case," *TransAfrica Forum* 4 (1987): 9-24.

31. Hansen, *Distant Companions*, 132.

32. For example, V. W. Brelsford, "Lubamba: A Description of the Baila Custom," *Journal of the Royal Anthropological Society of Great Britain and Ireland* 63 (1933): 433-39.

33. NAZ/BS 3/3003. Prostitution and Temporary Unions of Women of Mumbwa Sub-District in Settled Areas, 1923-24.

34. Shirley Ardener, "Introduction," in *The Incorporated Wife* (London: Croom Helm, 1984), 1.

35. Emily Bradley, *Dearest Priscilla. Letters to the Wife of a Colonial Civil Servant* (London: Max Parrish, 1950), 112, 168-69.

36. Such evidence can be culled from historical accounts, biography, memoirs, and travel descriptions; for example V. W. Brelsford, *Generations of Men: The European Pioneers of Northern Rhodesia* (Lusaka: Government Printer, 1965). For details, see Hansen, 87-98.

37. Gertrude Page, *The Silent Rancher* (London: Hurst and Blackett, 1909).

38. *Ibid.*, 272, 282.

39. Barbara Carr, *Not for Me the Wilds* (Cape Town: Howard Timmis, 1965), 174-75.

40. *Ibid.*

41. This information draws on my interviews with retired colonial white householders and on anecdotal evidence, since the published literature is almost totally reticent about sexual liaisons between colonial white women and African men.

42. Hansen, *Distant Companions*, 132. If relatives who do household work in return for their upkeep were counted as servants, the total number would be much larger.

43. Central Statistical Office, *Monthly Digest of Statistics* 21, no. 23 (1985), supplement, 8.

44. One third of the employers in my survey had registered their servants.

45. Stories about women servants who usurp the place of the wife abound and are featured on and off in popular magazines and newspaper columns, among them, "Georgette, My Wife," *Woman's Exclusive* 5 (1983): 7, 9, 17, and popular Zambian columnist Kapelwa Musonda, "House Servant Outwits Owner," *Times of Zambia,* January 8, 1985, 4.

46. Bonnie B. Keller, "Marriage and Medicine: Women's Search for Love and Luck," *African Social Research* 26 (1978): 489-505; "Marriage by Elopement," *African Social Research* 27 (1979): 565-85; and Ilsa M. G. Schuster, *New Women of Lusaka* (Palo Alto, Calif.: Mayfield Publishing Corporation, 1979).

47. Keller, "Marriage," Benetta Jules-Rosette, *Symbols of Change. Urban Transition in a Zambian Community* (Norwood, N.J.: Ablex Publishing Corporation, 1981), 129-63.

48. Activities associated with sex and food preparation were in the rural societies described in the ethnographic literature from this region as surrounded by special precautions: spatial segregation by age of sleeping quarters, restrictions on women's cooking for men and handling of artifacts at the time of menstruation, and abstinence from intercourse before important celebrations and events. For examples of some of these practices, see Audrey Richards, *Chisungu. A Girl's Initiation Ceremony among the Bemba of Zambia* (London: Faber and Faber Ltd., 1951), Victor W. Turner, *The Drums of Affliction. A Study of Religious Processes among the Ndembu of Zambia* (Oxford: Clarendon, 1969), and C. M. N. White, "Elements in Luvale Beliefs and Rituals," *Rhodes-Livingstone Papers*, no. 32 (1961).

49. Laurel Bossen describes a Latin American variation on this theme involving different cultural factors than those prevalent in the Zambian case: "Wives and Servants: Women of Middle-Class Households, Guatemala City," in *Urban Life. Readings in Urban Anthropology*, ed. G. Gmelch and W. Zenner (New York: St. Martin's Press, 1980), 190-200.

BIBLIOGRAPHICAL NOTE

Further information on the nature of race relations during the colonial period may be obtained from the standard history text on Northern Rhodesia, Lewis H. Gann, *A History of Northern Rhodesia: Early Days to 1953* (New York: Humanities Press, 1964). Additional insights on the region are available in Richard Gray, *The Two Nations: Aspects of the Development of Race Relations in the Rhodesias and Nyasaland* (London: Oxford University Press, 1960); Philip Mason, *The Birth of a Dilemma: The Conquest and Settlement of Rhodesia* (London: Oxford University Press, 1958); and Dane Kennedy, *Islands of White: Settler Society and Culture in Kenya and Southern Rhodesia, 1890-1939* (Durham, N.C.: Duke University Press, 1987). For a general statement, see Anthony Kirk-Greene, "Colonial Administration and Race Relations: Some Reflections and Directions," *Ethnic and Racial Studies* 9 (1986): 274-87. Martin Chanock discusses the colonial administration's involvement in the codification of customary law in his book *Law, Custom and Social Order: The Colonial Experience in Malawi and Zambia* (Cambridge: Cambridge University Press, 1985).

Questions pertaining to class, gender, and sexuality during the colonial period are discussed by Jane L. Parpart, "Sexuality and Power on the Zambian Copperbelt, 1926-1964," in *Patriarchy and Class: African Women in the Home and the Workforce*, ed. S. Stichter and J.L. Parpart (Boulder, Colo.: Westview Press), 115-38; A.L. Epstein, *Urbanization and Kinship: The Domestic Domain on the Copperbelt of Zambia, 1950-1956* (New York: Academic Press, 1981). For more general discussions of these issues, see two papers by Ann L. Stoler: "Rethinking Colonial Categories: European Communities and the Boundaries of Rule," *Comparative Studies in Society and History* 9 (1986): 134-61; and "Making Empire Respectable: The Politics of Race and Sexual Morality in 20th-century Colonial Cultures," *American Ethnologist* 16 (1989): 634-60; and Jean and John Comaroff, *From Revelation to Revolution: Christianity, Colonialism and Consciousness in South Africa* (Chicago: University of Chicago Press, 1991).

For postcolonial political developments in Zambia, see Cherry Gertel et al., eds., *The Dynamics of the One-Party State in Zambia* (Manchester: Manchester University Press, 1984). For recent discussions of gender, see Karen Tranberg Hansen, "Negotiating Sex and Gender in Urban Zambia," *Journal of Southern African Studies* 10 (1984): 219-38; and Gisela Geisler, "Sisters under the Skin: Women and the Women's League in Zambia," *Journal of Modern African Studies* 25 (1987): 43-66. Karen Tranberg Hansen and Leslie Ashbaugh critically evaluate the development debate and performance concerning women in the southern African region with special emphasis on Zambia in "Women on the Front Line: Development Issues in Southern Africa," *Women and International Development Annual Review* 2 (1991): 205-40.

UNCOVERING THE *ZENANA*
VISIONS OF INDIAN WOMANHOOD IN ENGLISHWOMEN'S WRITINGS, 1813-1940

Janaki Nair

> Here as there [in England] the end object is not merely personal comfort but the formation of a home—that unit of civilisation where father and children, master and servant, employer and employed can learn their several duties. . . . When all is said and done also, herein lies the natural outlet for most of the talent peculiar to women. . . . An Indian household can no more be governed peacefully, without dignity and prestige, than an Indian Empire.
>
> F.A. Steel and G. Gardiner,
> *The Complete Indian Housekeeper and Cook*
> *(1902)*

The growth of feminism in the past two decades and the emergence of women's history as a field have produced a desire not only to establish that women too have a history, but also that they took part in the well known moments of human history.[1] A relentless search for new areas of enquiry into women's pasts has left few stones unturned. If attempts have been made to recover the role that women played in revolutionary moments of human history, some liberal feminist historians have also asserted a place for women in other domains traditionally held "masculine," such as imperialism.[2] The nostalgia for the Raj, whose multiple cultural productions mark an acknowledgement of the end of empire and arises from the complexities of postcolonial race relations in Britain, has amply prepared the ground for an easier recovery of the roles of English women in India in support of such a contention.[3] As a result, colonialists' writings, a long critiqued source in nationalist or marxist scholarship, have, in certain feminist intellectual practices, retained a kind of credibility they had lost elsewhere.

In this paper, I will propose an alternative scheme for the reading of Englishwomen's writings on India, not in order to establish the "correctness of the representation nor its fidelity to some great original"[4] but to locate them within the production of colonial discourse on India.[5] Within such a "discourse analysis," my emphasis will be on plotting the multiple, and apparently ambiguous, ideological purposes that were served by the various representations of Indian women engendered in these writings on the Indian *zenana*.[6] Such ideological functions revealed the primary economic role that India played as Britain's colony but must also be revealed in terms of "the exigencies of domestic—that is European—and colonialist politics and culture."[7] The "family" and the "empire" were not the homologous structures that Steel and Gardiner suggest they were: the idealized family as represented in the writings I examine below served as a means not only to critique the colonized but emerged as a response to the "threats" to the English family posed by the women's movement. The correspondence of these representations of Indian women with English feminist discourse of the period must also be traced. Implicit in this analysis, too, is a critique of some of the most recent instances of the recuperation of Englishwomen's roles in India.

Englishwomen were rare in India during the period of the East India Company, especially in the seventeenth and eighteenth centuries. By the time direct governance was assumed in 1857, and as larger areas of the Indian map came under British rule, there was a gradual shift in the control of intercourse between English men and Indians, and the colonial regime actively began discouraging officials from marrying indigenous women.[8] The separate and superior nature of the master race began to be emphasized, a separateness that could not be established without replicating the English home, which, therefore, necessitated the presence of English women. By their very sense of leisure, made possible by retinues of Indian servants, these women could communicate an ambience of gentility. They could also, and even more importantly, provide the sexual services that had been met by Indians in the past.[9] This also helped maintain the "purity of the race." By the middle of the nineteenth century, following the opening of the Suez Canal, which considerably shortened the passage to India, regular "cargoes" of British women were offloaded from "fishing fleets" at Bombay, terms entirely in keeping with India's role as supplier of raw materials for Britain.

There could obviously be no simple transference of life-in-Britain to colonial India. Apart from the physical impossibilities of such an enterprise, Englishwomen became part of a complex grid of power, constantly reconstituted, which blurred more familiar distinctions. To begin with, there was the need to assert "femininity" in order to buttress the masculine nature of the colonial project. The British, deeply disturbed by the "androgyny" of Indian men, had to stifle any sign of weakness in order to make their rule plausible; the admission of a native patriarchal order would only empower the colonized male. Thus, by characterizing the entire Indian race as feminine—that is, weak—colonial ideology put (British) patriarchy in the service of imperialism. Especially after the revolt of 1857, which made the Indians appear far more treacherous to the colonial regime, the public assertion of English femininity had undeniable advantages in accentuating the "dubious masculinity" of Indian men.[10]

The repeated assertion of what was properly female as opposed to male not only ignored cultural difference but implied an acceptance by Englishwomen of their inferior role as the female (colonized) Other.[11] Englishwomen's perceptions of the violation of the codes of "nature" were innumerable. Fanny Parks, wife of a customs collector, finally saw a *zenana* after four years in India and was disappointed it was not as "ladylike" as a gathering of Englishwomen.[12] Even the martial races were no exception to the "feminization"; Helen MacKenzie, wife of an army officer in the northwest, wrote that Hasan Khan nursed his sickly wife, dressed, and even gossiped like a woman![13] Mary Carpenter, a no-nonsense educationist who was invited by the Government of India to propose a scheme for female education recorded with dismay that "the sight of women employed as ordinary labourers—as porters toiling under heavy burdens is most repulsive . . . the degrading employments they are compelled to undertake seems to destroy the sense of feminine propriety.[14] Worse yet, she said were the feminine tasks that men performed, washing, needlework and "numberless light tasks," [15] all of which rendered Indian women unfit to perform the duties of nature. It was their public and willing acceptance of their role as breeders for race and nation that Englishwomen would uphold before the Indians.

The importance of racial difference in India overwhelmed class divisions: the ruling race had to seal the ranks, distasteful as it was to a number of the men and women of the colonial regime. All the British in India were, thus, committed to live in "a manner well above the station from which they had sprung in England."[16] This in turn meant the erasure of class differences between Indians: even high-class women of the *zenanas* of Nawabs and other noblemen failed to meet the critical standards of Emily Eden.[17]

Although their roles were severely circumscribed, the wilful leisure to which Englishwomen were condemned had its uses, serving by itself to emphasize the separate spheres of male and female colonialists. When they began recording in writing or painting the shocks of their first encounter with the "frontiers" of civilization, this leisure was turned to a more active purpose. Neither writing nor painting was an activity that Englishmen in India had ignored or belittled in the past. If anything, the compulsions of empire required that the unfamiliar be reduced to "an accepted grid for filtering through the Orient into Western conscious- ness,"[18] to be "preserved, contained, studied, admired, detested, pitied, mourned."[19]

To some extent, Englishwomen continued the project of "verbally depopulating landscapes." But there were some areas that Englishmen had been unable to penetrate (and here the copulative metaphor is intended) such as the dark, enclosed spaces of the *zenana* or women's quarters. Pamela Hinkson, who visited India in the late 1930s, remarked that the "home behind that curtain [the *zenana*] is an unknown world even to the British official of long experience and deep sympathy."[20] The private domain of the *zenana*, which Indian men had so jealously guarded, comprised an absence in the constitution of colonial discourse. By its very unknowability, it was a seat of sedition and intrigue,[21] as much as it was a site of ambiguous sexuality.[22]

The principal space, then, from which Englishwomen could produce new "knowledge" of the colonized was the *zenana*, to which they gained privileged access by virtue of being the same sex. In the course of the late nineteenth and early twentieth centuries, the *zenana* was brought before the public/colonial gaze, in itself "representing" (in the sense of speaking for) Indian womanhood. This increased visibility was made possible in a variety of writings, some of which retained a separate textual space (corre- sponding to the *zenana*) for Indian women.[23]

The *zenana* was confined to certain classes and regions: the upper and middle classes of north, northwestern, and eastern India,[24] or where Moghul influence had been most direct and sustained. There were large areas of India, and of course, other classes where women were far more "visible," and their exclusion from this representation of Indian woman- hood—or somewhat selective inclusion—is of interest to us here. Such "inclusions" and "exclusions" were crucial in the attempt to restore "order" in the field of shifting political and cultural forces, both in India and in England. It is to some of these forces that I shall briefly turn below.

Britain's economic interests in India were quite transparent, though the colonial regime strenuously presented a variety of noneconomic reasons for governance.[25] From the early nineteenth to the mid nineteenth cen- tury, British policy was marked by a desire to reform, reform almost with- out limit and with enthusiasm. These efforts, epitomized in the policies of Lord William Bentinck, Governor General from 1828-35, were influenced to a large extent by the twin ideas of evangelism and utilitarianism.[26] James Mill was intoxicated by the possibilities of compensating India for the mis- government of the past and saw India as a *tabula rasa* on which the British inscription would remain forever. This was what fueled the moral certitude of Macaulay's infamous Minute on Education (1835) by which India would be transformed into a Christian, English-speaking country, free of idola- try.[27]

By the middle of the century and especially after the Mutiny of 1857 (or the first Indian war of independence), the reformist impulse faded, and India gradually became the hope of reactionaries since it "attracted the person who was disturbed by the growing democratisation of English life" (although in India, too, the period was marked by slow and moderate reform). By the late nineteenth and early twentieth century, when Macaulay's brown *sahibs* had invaded the upper echelons of the Indian Civil Service and had to be excluded by various other strategies, the colonial regime had to adopt a new rhetoric and explain its mission as one of keeping peace and order, "an admission that England had abandoned her interest in giving India anything more than this."[28]

The shifts in India's role as a colony are, however, inadequate to establish the context in which Englishwomen's writings on Indian women were produced. The emerging politics and culture of Britain, challenges to the British state, especially after 1880, and how these challenges were met, contained, and overcome become crucial to our analysis, especially of how the "knowledge" of Indian women was deployed in the the emerging discourse of feminism and its critics. It is with this stereoscopic vision that I discuss successive representations of the *zenana* in the writing of Englishwomen on India.

This approach marks a difference from and is a critique of certain liberal feminist approaches to the role of Englishwomen. At a time when Third World women are writing their own histories, and the homogenous "Woman" as a subject of history is being undone, such intellectual practices appear as First World efforts to reinstate the colonized subject. In some cases, this has been done through producing as objects of investigation the history of Third World women and their testimony. But there has also been a search for "active" women of the First World: the additive strategy of this enterprise, that is, to multiply the instances of female presence in history, presumes the existence of a unified "Woman" subject and is often inattentive to the manner in which the history of the colonial period is being narrativized. The very critical voice that such historiography purports to raise here drowns out other critical voices, for example, critiques of colonialism itself. Part of this unified approach to women's history implies a celebration of women's roles, even when they belonged and contributed to the dominant, usually male, discourse. Thus Pat Barr's assessment of Englishwomen's roles in the Victorian period establishes that they, too, as wives of Viceroys, military officers, and civil officials, fulfilled the arduous task of building an empire.[29] The task of bringing "western style order out of eastern style chaos," if only by dispensing the daily rations to the "cunning" servants of the colonial household, was thus, the Englishwoman's as well as the Englishman's task.[30] Recounting Englishwomen's contributions, she hopes, will render less "masculine" the Kiplingesque attributes of imperialism.[31]

The reluctance to engage with the intersecting discourses of race, class, and gender, which persists in more recent work, obscures the location of Englishwomen within structures of power that engendered a "knowledge" of India and Indian womanhood.[32] "I have tried to right the balance, tell a small part of the women's story of India, the *private view of heart and mind*," Marian Fowler claims in a book published in 1987.[33] Fowler privileges this "private" vision as fleshing out more fully the Raj pageant.[34] By simply maintaining their "private lives" in the midst of their husband's public activities, Fowler claims that these women performed a "civilising, humanising" mission.

In contrast to Fowler's celebration of the private sphere, Mary Ann Lind focuses on the "compassionate memsahibs" active in the public spheres of charity and education who displayed "a more realistic and balanced view of Indian life than traditional memsahibs since they were involved in and committed to Indian affairs." Here too, the additive impulse triumphs over an analysis that explains the causes for and limits of the shifts in Englishwomen's roles.[35] But the clearest disregard for critiques of the colonial experience comes in Margaret Macmillan's *Women of the Raj*, in which she declares "whether it [the Raj] would have been better or worse, women were there and their story is a part of the Raj's history too."[36] Unlike Lind, Macmillan does not suggest that the colonial woman's role was anything other than "raising little empire builders of the future"[37] but claims that Englishwomen's roles went unhonored and unsung, even though it is to their credit that they "could so often love their servants and be loved in return."[38] There is little in these recent works to distinguish them from the "essentialised feminine" view of the women of the Raj in K.K. Dyson's *A Various Universe*,[39] a distinctly neocolonial and nonfeminist work.

If the liberal feminist recovery of the roles of Englishwomen in India is undertaken in order to suggest that the colonial enterprise was not entirely "masculine," there is irony in the repeated assertions of the essentially feminine roles fulfilled since they were always overwhelmed by and subordinated to the patriarchal/imperialist order. Such women as Honoria Lawrence tried not to be an obstacle to her husband's career by uncomplainingly enduring childbirth in difficult places.[40] Even a woman horrified by "the severe oppression of their sex in India" such as Annette Ackroyd, founder of the first working woman's college in London (1854), gave up all ambitions of pioneering schemes for women's education in India to become the dutiful wife of Henry Beveridge, a civil servant.[41] Indeed, as this text will indicate, even some women who were critics of patriarchy at home and of the empire itself unwittingly resorted to the formulations of earlier writers in their visions of Indian womanhood.

Such writings as I have examined above intervene to reconstitute what is continually being politically and economically dismantled. Gender was a constitutive element of colonial discourse but always "overdetermined"[42] by the ideology of race, which in the Indian context also conferred a superior class position on the English vis à vis the Indian. The copious literary productions of colonial women were themselves a sign of the intersecting discourses of race and class, continually rearticulated throughout the colonial period, but a sign whose meanings can only be unpacked within the discourse of colonialism. This implies mapping the ideological functions served by such production, not in a reductive sense but in order to perceive what is stable and persistent beneath the proliferation of meanings. The writings of colonial women, parading under the rubric of ethnography, whether in diaries, journals, or travel writing, were profoundly ideological; they require a symptomatic reading, an analysis of what was said but also left unsaid since "we always find at the edge of the text the language of ideology, momentarily hidden but eloquent by its very absence."[43]

The earliest of the writings that I have examined in this paper was written in 1813. The other writings extend over the period until 1940 and range from the journals of wives of Raj officials, camp notes of missionaries, and diaries of vicereines. There were also Englishwomen who came to India for the specific purpose of generating "information" on aspects of Indian womanhood, such as Mary Carpenter and Mary Frances Billington. I have also chosen to look at the writings of three women (of Irish descent) who formed an active part of the nationalist challenge in India. The texts that I have chosen represent only a small part of a sizable genre: my criterion for the choice of these particular texts has been the attention each has paid to the position of Indian women.[44] I have, in this analysis, excluded the entire genre of fiction.[45] For a valuable additional dimension, I have also used the recent reprint of the series *The Englishwoman's Review of Social and Industrial Questions,* one of the oldest women's journals, in which some of the colonial women's writings found an airing.[46]

In the following analysis of Englishwomen's writings, I have abandoned a unidirectional, chronological narrative in favor of a thematic discussion of the writings not only to emphasize the ambiguities in such representations but equally to emphasize that which is persistent in the ordering of the social reality of the *zenana,* and to grasp the apparent "contradictoriness" of these Englishwomen's writings. The dates in parentheses, therefore, serve only as markers of the periods of the texts chosen for each section.

The *Zenana* as Site of Reform/Change (1813-74)

As early as 1813, Maria Graham had hoped that there would be a few more examples of English Christian women in India to prove the virtues of enlightenment and reason.[47] Science had not yet entered the confines of the *zenana,* "where nature and superstition reigned supreme"; during the cholera epidemic of 1833 in north India, Fanny Parks found an unhealthy propitiation of goddesses to stave off the disease.[48] In spite of the East India Company's commitment not to meddle with the social customs and religious practices of India, the benefits of converting the mothers and educators of young Indians were undeniable and could even result in the transcendence of the only two states to which all Indians were condemned: "a state of violent action and excitement and one of perfect repose."[49] Whereas missionaries had had some success in converting Indian men, the liberating influence of Christianity could not spread through the continent until the "female influence in preventing conversion" was undermined; "there is little hope for Christianity in India," said A.U., "till the women can be reached, and if only the wives and mothers could be won, the greatest obstacles to progress and the religion would at once be swept away."[50]

However, Christianity alone could not ensure the liberation of women from the oppressive conditions in which they lived. As A.U. claimed, "native women are so accustomed to a life of inferiority and seclusion that even Christianity does not at once restore them to their true position."[51] As we have already seen, the legislative arm of the colonial regime had done its share of trying to protect women *from Indian men* with the abolition of sati in 1829 and the widow remarriage act of 1857. But legislation was rendered meaningless by the low educational levels of women. By the 1860s, the *zenana* as a site for conversion gradually yielded place to the notion of the *zenana* as a site of education, after which the undoubted virtues of Christianity would be easily recognized.[52] The new notion of the *zenana* as a site for educational reform paralleled the development of British interest in universal education as a form of social control in the late 1860s and 1870s; the earlier notion that people were born into original sin was replaced by a concept of "original ignorance."[53] As Colin Mackenzie claimed before his (Indian) troops in the Punjab, "we educate our women that they may be good wives and mothers, for a man can hardly be a good man without a good mother"; clearly, women in England could no longer be trusted "naturally" to become good mothers and wives.[54] Mary Carpenter was the epitome of unflagging enthusiasm for the possibilities of female education. Indeed, she observed, "under good female instruction, Hindoo girls are quite equal to their English sisters."[55] Echoing the domesticating/homogenizing aspirations of the British ruling class (since the discipline afforded by a school system would reduce the threat of dangerous deviants), Carpenter said that "education must coax the middle and upper classes out of the walls in which they are immured," an act which would simultaneously restrain the lower classes in India, hitherto deprived of the "refining influences" of the secluded upper classes.[56] This dangerous isolation was also useful in explaining the unacceptable "freedom" other groups of women encountered. Thus, Mrs. Mitchell expressed the same hope of a refining influence in her description of the Todas, a tribe of south India, whose women enjoyed an openness and freedom admirable in eastern women and who yet lacked the "decency," "femininity," and "self restraint" of the upper classes.[57] However, she warned, this had to be a gradual process; the dangers of premature introduction of women to general society were already evident. It was through education of women in the *zenana* that gradual change could be accomplished and Indians could be convinced of the virtues of colonialism, since, Mitchell claimed, "it seems so hard for them to believe that the only reason [for British presence] is to try to do them good."[58] Education, and especially of women, was the catalyst that would urge India along the continuum of "progress," for what the *zenana* was made to represent as a reformable space was the reminder of a dim past, one that England had long superseded.

The *Zenana* as Symbol of the Collective Past (1850-95)

An unshakeable faith in progress enabled the vision of the Indian *zenana* as a symbol of a collective past, one from which Englishwomen could easily distinguish themselves. The *Englishwoman's Review,* the first British periodical devoted to women's issues and the longest lived and most inclusive journal of its time,[59] regularly gave a fair amount of space to the position of women in various parts of the empire and the world. Mary Carpenter's researches on India received a wide audience in their rewritten versions,[60] and the books by other visitors to the subcontinent were regularly reviewed. The "Englishwoman was a very superior article,"[61] Emily Eden had claimed many years earlier, and this was something of which not only to be proud but grateful. A.U. asked Englishwomen not to shrink in horror from the unenviable situation of Indian women, but instead

> before you blame them, free denizens of happy English homes, thank god for the long ages of liberty of thought and action that have made it simply impossible for you to comprehend their bondage.[62]

Indian *zenanas* were those cavernous depths of "idolatry and superstition" that the blinding light of reason had not yet reached. The appeal for the education of women in India, the *Englishwoman's Review* claimed, corresponded exactly to an earlier need expressed in England, which had been adequately met.[63] By characterizing the Indian woman as a primitive ancestor, the women's movement was provided with an opportunity to count its blessings rather than advancing its critique of the English situation. Carpenter commented on the "vivid contrast" between woman in England and "her painful seclusion in this country"[64] while A.U. spoke of the *zenana* as "historyless" and as containing beings who "had no knowledge of the grand past or the busy present or the eternal future," more than a fond hope for the indefinite continuance of British colonialism.[65] But the signs of progress were everywhere, Mackenzie remarked, citing a teacher who said "the difference between the children of her pupils and those of uneducated mothers is very marked, not only in knowledge but in civilisation, in moral habits and the observance of decency."[66]

A similar vision of progress informed discussions of medical facilities for women in India. The Marchioness of Dufferin, vicereine from 1884-88, received wide publicity for starting a fund for supplying female medical aid to the women of India.[67] "Few people know the dreadful cruelties perpetrated by the Dhais, [Indian midwives]," said Lady Dufferin, again insisting that their methods were primitive.[68] At the time of Lady Dufferin's benevolent acts in India, we may recall, the "medicalisation" of the woman's body was proceeding in England; whereas midwifery had earlier been seen as essential for the practice of medicine, by the middle of the nineteenth century it was viewed as wholly "unscientific." Midwives were gradually elbowed out of an increasingly specialized profession presided over by male doctors.[69] Therefore, it was only a matter of time before education and increased medical attention for the women of India would enable a steady "progress towards western ways and customs," one that Frances Billington, in 1895, was willing to testify was well under way.[70]

The foremost sign of the primitive quality of the lives of Indians was "a plurality of wives,"[71] which had destroyed everything resembling domestic and family ties.[72] Yet this condemnation of the *zenana* as a polygamous, "primitive" institution was not without its ironies. In the southern states of Cochin, Travancore, and Malabar, Mitchell found other marital practices that were equally distasteful. Of her encounters with barebreasted Nair and Shanar women (who, in their very "nakedness," were an invitation to reform) she records "a strange country [where] husbands seem only to be appendages."[73] The Marimakkathayam or matrilineal tradition of the Nairs revealed the obverse of the situation of the *zenana*, an empowering of women which disrupted tidy notions of patriarchal power to which England had become accustomed. "In this sense," she continued, "one has to fight here not for woman's rights but for man's. I am afraid this state of things points to a very loose morality."[74] Such a contradiction in the essentialist conception of Indian womanhood, derived from the overarching importance given to *zenanas*, was, thereby, suppressed under the normalizing rubric of patriarchy as superior and evolved, a stage ahead of (primitive) matriliny. What, then, *was* the *zenana?* It was not quite patriarchal, since patriarchy, but of the English kind alone, ensured the continuity of race and preservation of imperial order.

There is also a trace here of "social purity" issues that marked the agitation for the repeal of the Contagious Diseases Acts in England (1869-86) by asserting the morality of monogamous female and male sexuality.[75] Perhaps the emergence of a more active female heterosexuality in the British women's movement prompted Billington, who visited India just ten years after Mitchell, to revise the latter's position to the claim that "Nayars had the most civilised marriage system in the world."[76] However, Carpenter, Mitchell, and Billington all shared the belief in progress, especially since, as Mitchell claimed, "a glimmering of light has penetrated the darkness of these homes; they see their bonds."[77] By splitting off the position of women in the colonies from the context of colonialism itself, which structured inequalities between Englishwomen in Britain and Indians, these Englishwomen took steps towards homogenising the history of "Woman."

The Zenana as the Symbol of Female Power (1880-1915)

In the 1880s and 1890s, just as Britain's position in the world economy was clearly in decline, the state was faced with formidable domestic challenges not only from democratic forces such as the labor movement and the women's movement but even from the Tory (Orangeist) rebellion in Northern Ireland.[78] The feminist movement, organized initially as a campaign to repeal the Contagious Diseases Acts[79] and to expand educational opportunities, broadened to encompass the women's suffrage movement and developed a much wider conception of women's emancipation.[80] Notwithstanding the primarily "social purity" (and separate sphere) content of the CD campaigns, and the ultrapatriotic anti-union conservatism of Evangelene and Christabel Pankhurst,[81] the women of Britain had seized the initiative in entering the public domain of politics. By their alliances with the growing socialist and labor movement, women, too, joined the ranks of the dangerous classes. Threatened internationally by the growing economic importance of Germany and the U.S.A., the beleagured British state was forced into a realignment of its political forces. In such a context, the representation of the zenana as a site of power-in-femininity added strength to antifeminist reaction.

A reinterpretation of earlier formulations on the zenana was most explicit in the triptych of texts by Billington, Steel, and Diver, although several other writings also expressed similar sentiments.[82] Billington's journalistic mission took her across the entire country and brought her in contact with the widest range of Indian women of all the authors whose writings I have examined. At the Girideh coal mines, she found women working underground to be a perfect contrast to the women of English mining towns whom she described with alliterative fury as "swearing drunken, degraded, disgraces"; the most remarkable point about the Girideh women was their "perfect gentleness and modesty," "general quiet, good order, discipline, and respect."[83] The Indian family could not be dismissed as it had earlier been because it cultivated such "praiseworthy domestic ideals" as the devoted care of husband and children. She admitted that to "speak of womanhood in the East as satisfied in the present conditions in life is always sufficient to send those of a certain school of thought into something like a frenzy," but she could not suppress the fact that the "zenana possessed a prestige and dignity" that were preferable to the "lot of Europeanised excresences" many sought to graft on to India.[84]

In 1905, Flora Annie Steel found few happier households than Indian ones where women upheld a standard of morality far higher than in England.[85] Steel's message verged on the profoundly antifeminist: the "stability afforded by the Indian household was incomparable, the highest in the world."[86] She readily admitted that this was made possible by the acceptance of an ideal quite different from the one being fashioned in the West, of a "human being who is not the equal of man, who cannot be so, since the man and women together make the perfect human being to whose guardianship is entrusted the immortality of race."[87] This is a foretaste of the eugenicist movement of the early decades of the twentieth century.[88] There were definite threats to the reproduction of the "master race," from the Divorce Act of 1857, the increased use of contraceptives, and the development of new female sexuality delinked from marriage and reproduction.[89] Young, vigorous, rapidly growing economies like Germany and the U.S.A. made the falling birth rate a serious cause for alarm.

However, we could also read Steel's plea as reflecting more closely an interest in defending a kind of "separate sphere" feminism, rather than antifeminism. This provided a dignified, public role for women that did not transgress the "natural" disabilities of her sex. The representation of the *zenana* as powerful provided a case for linking power with femininity, with the "primal natural power of her sex," without posing any challenge to the patriarchal household. The Indian woman established her chastity as an undeniably important *fact* and, by doing so, recognized the "supreme importance of her own position."[90] Far from being a "melancholy place of moping and anaemic martyrs,"[91] the *zenana* was a place where women enjoyed "selfpossession and dignity."[92]

The constant reference to alarming changes in Britain was most direct in Maud Diver's account of Indian womanhood. Diver, no critic of colonialism or racism, nevertheless chose to say:

> The advanced woman of the west is apt to conclude over hastily that the narrow hidden life of her eastern sister with its lack of freedom, its limited scope for self-development and individual action, must need constitute her a mere lay figure, a being wholly incapable of influencing the larger issues of life, whereas a more intimate knowledge of facts would reveal to her the truth that from the same hidden corner, and by the *natural primal power of her sex*, the eastern woman moulds the national character far more effectively than she could hope to do from the platform or the hustings.[93]

The pioneers of the women's movement in England, Diver claimed, wrongly rejected femininity as weakness, so that the "old world flower of gentleness" ran the risk of being trampled out of feminine character, an unnecessary loss. In the east, narrow though her sphere may be, the Indian "Queen" presided over her "kingdom" —"The Inside—a place of peace or of petty persecution."[94] "Feminine India," Hinkson remarked many years later, "wisely does not discard that femininity when she takes to affairs and politics."[95]

The *zenana*, then, was the seat of "primal natural feminine power," but what did this power imply? The contradictions that marked the nationalist discourse on social reform were portentous. Even as Behramji Malabari and M.G. Ranade were vigorously campaigning to raise the age of consent to 12 years, in the tradition of Ram Mohun Roy and K.C. Sen, they met a formidable opponent in B.G. Tilak. In 1895, Tilak drove the National Social Conference from the Congress *pandal* (awning), where it had always met since 1887, and, thereby, expressed a growing anger at the interference of the colonial regime in social questions, overreaching itself in transgressing the sacred site of the Hindu home.[96] Could the Indian nationalists be *retaining* the *zenana* (as an uncolonized space) at a time when the mark of the British Raj was everywhere? Could it, in other words, be developed as a site of resistance?

The *Zenana* as the Site of Resistance to "Civilization" (1900-1940)

There was a profound ambiguity in the image of the *zenana* as a center of female power. By stressing such power in a place that had long been dismissed as powerless and demonstrating only the urgency of change, Englishwomen successfully displaced the responsibility of the Raj for its stupendous failures and shifted it to the Indians themselves. The earlier reformist impulses had all but evaporated by the end of the nineteenth century and the continued exploitation of India as a field for capital investment was difficult to sheath in any "civilizing" rhetoric.[97] Macaulay's Indian gentleman had begun embarrassing the colonial regime by seeking greater representation in government (the Indian National Congress first met in 1885) and by writing devastating critiques of the size and scale of the "drain of wealth."[98] Crippling famines in 1876-77 that recurred in the 1890s, the proliferation of peasant and tribal unrest,[99] the drop of Indian per capita income (by Britain's own admission) to an all-time low of £ 2 (Rs.30),[100] culminated at a time when the colony at its doorstep (Ireland) was agitating for Home Rule.[101] But the failures of the British in India could at least in part be pinned on the immutable strong-holds of Indian society, which were impervious to any British effort. An obvious location of such immutability was the *zenana*. "It was not the man, that reputed tyrant, who most effectually barred the way to progress," said Diver. "It is the gentle, invisible, woman whose reserve of obstinacy, all the wild horses in the Empire would fail to move."[102] This was the unreasonable, illogical space that resisted colonization and, thus, civilization; "it is therefore within the

zenana that women must first be freed."[103] The Indian woman, more than
the men of the country, "voluntarily follow an unpractical, uncomfortable,
and unworldly wise course of literal obedience to some idealistic concept,"
said Stratford in 1922.[104]

When pressure on the Raj was mounting in the turbulent years of 1928-
29, with protests by peasants, workers, women, and even businessmen
marking the prelude to the massive Civil Disobedience of 1930-31, the
Simon Commission remarked in its report:

> No one with any knowledge of India would be disposed to underrate the
> power its women wield within the confines of the household. The danger
> is that, unless the influence is illumined with knowledge . . . its weight may
> be cast against the forces of progress.[105]

This uncolonized space could subvert the project of civilization, but its
continued existence also provided ample reason to deny the Indian people the responsibility of independence.[106] There was an early indication
that such a strategy could be successfully pursued. It was through an invo-
cation of this uncolonized space that Annette Beveridge (née Ackroyd)
had led the vociferous opposition to the Ilbert Bill in 1883. This bill, which
was a feeble attempt by Lord Ripon (Governor-General, 1880-84) to
expand the circle of collaborators in India by allowing Indian judges to
preside over cases in which English people were involved, aroused
Englishwomen in India to political action (which I have mentioned
above). Such a concession could not be granted to Indians unless they
exposed themselves more fully to the colonizing project. Beveridge's letter
to *The Englishman,* a British owned daily, in Calcutta bears quotation at
length:

> It is not pride of race which dictates this feeling which is the outcome of
> something deeper: it is the pride of womanhood. This is a form of respect
> which we are not ready to abrogate in order to give such advantages to
> others as are offered by Mr Ilbert's bill to its beneficiaries. . . . In this
> discussion . . . the ignorant and neglected women of India rise up from
> their enslavement in evidence against their masters. They testify to the
> justice of the resentment which English women feel at Mr Ilbert's proposal
> to subject "civilised" woman to the jurisdiction of men who have done
> little to redeem the women of their own races and whose social ideas are
> still on the outer verge of civilisation.[107]

This extraordinary delusion of the solidarity of women (English and
Indian) against the oppression by men (that is, the Indian man of the
English woman) concealed the actual complicity of English men and
women in India. It appears as if the subtext of female solidarity, across race
and class, could disrupt the seamless surface of imperialist discourse, but,
in fact, such solidarity was invoked only to affirm the patriarchal/colonial
order. In its report on the Ilbert Bill agitation, the *Englishwoman's Review*

chose a similar route out of the inevitable squaring up with the politics of race in the empire by a refusal to "discuss the merits or demerits of Mr. Ilbert's Bill" and by choosing instead to applaud the occasion it provided Englishwomen in India to prove "an interest in politics."[108] (In the final section below, I will discuss the significance of this remark for the expanding "opportunities" of Englishwomen in India.)

The fear that the *zenana* could, in nationalist discourse, take on "positive" attributes as a site of resistance was not entirely misplaced. The writings of three Britishwomen with nationalist sympathies anticipated the emergence of a "separate" but powerful strand in nationalist politics. Margaret Noble, who, as the disciple of Swami Vivekananda assumed the name of Sister Nivedita, wrote consistently from 1898 to 1911 of Indian life and was widely acknowledged in reviews in India, Britain, and America.[109] Rejecting the eastern-western dichotomy, as well as the medieval-modern one for women, she divided human society into communities dominated by the "civic" and communities divided by the "family" ideal.[110] The Indian woman, fully empowered by her (natural primal) position in the family, could make the transition to the wider "civic" world quite easily since the family was only a cellular form of society. The "nation" now became the "home" to which Indian women owed a duty of nurturing and caring.[111] "Let every Indian woman incarnate for us the whole spirit of the mother and the culture and protection of the homeland, Bhumia Devi," Noble said. Woman alone represented that unbroken continuity with a precolonial past through her residence in that uncolonized space, the *zenana*. Through her very domesticity, extended now beyond the "stones" and "walls" of her home to include "land and people," the Indian woman was a repository of resistance.[112]

Woman power was not, after all, alien to Indian women, said Annie Besant, for Shakti was the true power of Deva, and "in the representatives of Shakti will be the certain triumph of India in the nation and the Indian home."[113] She claimed to have tapped the reservoirs of "heroism, endurance and self sacrifice of the feminine nature" in the Home Rule Movement.[114] Separate, therefore equal, the public domain was now made safe for the entry of women in the national movement through the characterization of nation as home and woman as mother.

Margaret Cousins, writing in 1940, testified to the true genius of M.K.Gandhi in harnessing this new "mass" of Indian people:

> the revered leader Gandhiji was sufficient guarantee to the women of the righteousness of whatever new actions had to be taken by women in national life.[115]

Cousins made an earnest plea that "Indian women express the needs of the 'mother-half' of humanity" since the present world order needed "the creative and conserving qualities of women."[116] Her recognition of the economic importance of housework, the need for woman's control of her own sexuality, and for extended legal rights, all of which were radical ideas for her time, could not, however, overcome the characterization of "satyagraha" as eminently suited to "feminine character" whose "whole nature and function is to create and not to destroy."[117] Even in the writings of nationalist sympathizers, we now see, the final reliance was on the "primal," natural power of woman's biology, a power which could be summoned at will at particular historical junctures.

The *Zenana* as Uncolonized Space— Prolongation of the Colonial Project (1860-1940)

When even the illusion of permanence of the Raj had vanished, the rendering of the *zenana* as an uncolonized space was deployed to yet another advantage. The stubborn unchanging *zenana*, a trope of ultimate, irreducible difference, provided a site for the prolongation of the colonial project, which, given the circumstances, would never be accomplished. The *Englishwoman's Review* had seized upon this rendering with great enthusiasm and to the advantage of its readers: India could become a theater for the expanding energies of the Englishwoman. It periodically advertised positions in India for the educated women of Britain.[118] In 1881, it had even suggested that the segregation of women in India was a useful "prejudice" since it provided Englishwomen doctors and lawyers an opportunity to exercise their newly won skills, an opportunity largely denied them in Britain.[119] Diver had already championed India as a place that could deflect some of the (dangerous) energies of Englishwomen. "In this age of restless, nervous energy, a brave woman in search of work worth doing might do worse than devote her power to the service of India's stricken millions."[120] By the time of the Sex Disqualification Act of 1919, which allowed Englishwomen the right to enter civil service in various parts of the empire, single women were being increasingly employed in India.[121]

However, the futility of the effort in the colonies should be remembered, for small battles could be waged and won (a school started, a hospital run, a bill passed), but weighed against the twin tyrannies of "custom and tradition," said Maud Diver, "the innovations of a decade are as dust in the balance."[122] Norah Hamilton even pointed to unintended (read wasteful) uses to which skills bestowed by the British on Indians were put, that is, in nationalist agitation.[123] Hinkson also complained of the hopelessness of the task of education since "a failed BA reads newspapers to the illiterates rather than preaching the evils of suttee."[124] But this recognition of futility did not serve as a deterrent: Englishwomen were urged to share the arduous, "fruitless" tasks of governing the empire. The real price of empire was not paid by the indigenous people, who suffered the destruction of handicrafts, extraction of impossibly high revenues, blatantly racist judicial and legal systems, as well as incomplete capitalist development, to list a few of the exorbitant costs that India paid. The real price was being paid, Diver revealed, by the self-sacrificing men and women of England, so that "India's gradual movement towards mental and national awakening is the net result of countless seemingly futile, individual struggles, of daily battles, against heat, dust and cholera and that insidious inertia of soul and body that is the moral microbe of the East."[125] By thus shifting the burden of empire onto individual men and women, Diver successfully effaced the structures of power that were in place and trivialized the price paid by the colony. All of these problems, with the possible exception of cholera, were incurable and, therefore, made the colonial enterprise in India all the more admirable and allowed it to stretch indefinitely into the future. By stubbornly refusing colonization, India invited redoubled effort.

Even worse than their refusal to transform themselves—that is, willingly surrender to the process of colonization—was the ingratitude of Indian women, Hinkson felt in 1938-39. Given the incomparable challenges faced by the British in governing India,[126] the reluctance of an "ardent Congress lady" to praise British rule was unacceptable, so it was a rather triumphant Hinkson who forced her to admit that the British had abolished "suttee" for which act "alone I felt that their rule of India was justified."[127] At last, the very fatalism of which colonial discourse had been so intolerant now proved itself useful as an explanation of unmistakeable failure.

I have shown that the literary productions of Englishwomen in India, far from being random and marginal glosses or scattered observations of exotica, fulfilled a number of ideological functions as a part of colonial discourse. Indian women, in these writings, inhabited the very limits of society, the shadowy margins, now keeping out chaos and disorder, now embodying it. This "knowledge" about Indian womanhood provided alibis to deflect growing criticism of British rule in India and formed part of the efforts to contain the disruptive forces that threatened liberalism in Britain. For Englishwomen themselves, positioned in a context where their power yielded new "knowledge," the potential for developing any critique of their own subordinate status was thwarted. By making "visible" the woman of the colonies, they could successfully make "invisible" their own colonization by English men, who had appropriated their capacities for the reproduction of colonial order. Their own housewifization, enabled by the subordination of men and women in the colonies, paralleled the housewifization that was occurring in England.[128]

There were a few flashes in these women's perceptions that could have formed the basis for questioning their own status. Billington's radical revision of earlier views of the Nair family and Fanny Parks' admission that the Rule of Law, supposedly democratic in England, condemned married

Englishwomen to "eternal sati"[129] never gained enough importance to challenge the dominant colonial discourse. In even the writings of critics of empire and patriarchy, earlier characterizations of the *zenana* were far from obscured. The dark private world of the *zenana* provided some of the Englishwomen discussed with the satisfaction of belonging to the dominant race, and, therefore, to the superior class, a privilege won by the foreclosure of the troubling "woman's" question. By assuming the mantle of housewife in the public world of empire, the Englishwoman performed the crucial task of fulfilling Steel's and Gardiner's prescriptions for the maintenance of order between "father and children, master and servant, employer and employed," or the maintenance of that trinity of patriarchy, imperialism, and capitalism.

NOTES

This article bears traces of the critical voices of Cissie Fairchilds, Rajeshwari Mohan, Rosemary Hennessy, and Madhava Prasad. Several others have patiently borne its other incarnations. I remain solely responsible for the arguments developed herein.

1. In this sense, the optimism expressed by Joan Scott that historians are no longer satisfied with these two approaches may be a bit premature. See "Gender: A Useful Category of Historical Analysis," *American Historical Review*, Vol. 91, (December 1986): 1053-75.

2. Such an intention probably underlay the inclusion at the American Historical Association convention (Cinncinnati, December 1988) of a session entitled "Women in masculine domains," under which rubric the roles of women miners and of women in imperialism were highlighted.

3. The term Raj refers to the period of British rule in India, that is, 1757 to 1947.

4. Edward Said, *Orientalism* (New York, Vintage Books, 1979), 21.

5. I employ the term discourse in the sense developed by Michel Foucault in *The Archaeology of Knowledge* (New York: Pantheon Books, 1972). Following Foucault, discourse is taken not as a group of signs (and, therefore, as reducible to language) but as "practices that systematically form the objects of which they speak" (49). In this article, discourse analysis permits plotting the "identity and persistence of themes" (in the simultaneous or successive emergence of concepts, even their incompatibility) (35).

6. The *zenana* refers to the separate women's quarters in certain Hindu and Muslim homes, usually in north India. This text, however, argues that it came to represent far more than a "geographical space" within households to Englishwomen in India.

7. A.R. Jan Mohommed, "The Economy of the Manichean Allegory: The Function of Racial Difference in Colonialist Literature," in *'Race', Writing and Difference*, ed. Henry L. Gates (Chicago: University of Chicago Press, 1986), 78-106, esp. 81.

8. Margaret Macmillan, *Women of the Raj* (London: Thames and Hudson, 1988), 110.

9. Not all Englishmen were allowed this expensive privilege of importing Englishwomen. A small number of English subalterns were allowed to marry; for the others, who were thought to lack the moral and intellectual resources required for continence, supervised prostitution was arranged near the cantonments. Kenneth Ballhatchet discusses the complex politics of such arrangements in *Race, Sex and Class under the Raj: Imperial Attitudes and Policies and Their Critics, 1793-1905* (New York: St. Martin's Press, 1980).

10. Ashis Nandy, in *The Intimate Enemy: Loss and Recovery of the Self Under Colonialism* (Delhi: Oxford University Press, 1983), analyzes the profound psychological impact of colonialism on both colonizer and colonized. Francis Hutchins cites the case of John Beames, a Punjab officer who invited the wrath of John Lawrence, Governor of the Punjab, for having brought a piano with him. See *The Illusion of Permanence: British Imperialism in India* (Princeton, N.J.: Princeton University Press, 1967), 44.

11. Joan Liddle and Rama Joshi make a similar point in "Gender and Imperialism in British India," *Economic and Political Weekly*, 20 (October 26, 1985): WS 72-78.

12. Fanny Parks, *Wanderings of a Pilgrim in Search of the Picturesque* (Karachi: Oxford University Press, 1975), 59.

13. Helen Mackenzie, *Life in the Mission, the Camp and the Zenana, or Six Years in India*, 3 vols. (London: R. Bentley, n.d.), 2, 204.

14. Mary Carpenter, *Six Months in India*, 2 vols. (London: Longmans, 1868), 1, 80.

15. *Ibid.*, 1, 80.

16. Hutchins, *Illusion of Permanence*, 107. This had a useful corollary in England itself. The increasing use of the metaphor of "colony" for the place where the laboring and dangerous classes of England resided was no coincidence. The dark continent was at the East End of London, to be "discovered," "governed" and "contained." See excerpts from George Sims' "How the Poor Live," in *Into Unknown England, 1866-1913, Selections from the Social Explorers*, ed. Peter Keating (Manchester: Manchester University Press, 1976), 65-90. Lord Curzon, Viceroy in India from 1898-1905, was astonished to discover that some lower-class enlisted soldiers in India, whom he observed bathing, were the same color as he. Hutchins, *Illusion of Permanence*, 133.

17. Emily Eden, *Up the Country: Letters Written to Her Sister from the Upper Provinces of India* (London: Curzon Press, 1978), 237.

18. Said, *Orientalism*, 6.

19. Mary Louise Pratt, "Scratches on the Face of the Country, or What Mr Barrow Saw in the Land of the Bushmen," in *'Race', Writing, and Difference*, 138-62, esp.145. The most outstanding example of the encyclopaedic proportions of this enterprise was Francis Buchanan's work. Buchanan was invited by Lord Wellesley to investigate the newly acquired dominions of Mysore, Malabar, and Canara following the defeat of Tipu Sultan in the Fourth Mysore War (1799). His work was so well admired that he was invited to perform a similar task for provinces of Bengal in 1809.

20. Pamela Hinkson, *Indian Harvest* (London: Collins, 1941), 260.

21. Parks, *Wanderings of a Pilgrim in Search of the Picturesque*, 39.

22. The English conviction of Indian immorality/uncontrolled sexuality was based on three empirical certainties, child marriage, polygamy, and worship of the "phallus," all of which retained their mystery in the *zenana*.

23. See, for example, chapters on women in Mortimer Menpes' *India*, text by Flora Annie Steel (London: Adam and Charles Black, 1905); A.U.'s *Overland,*

Inland and Upland: A Lady's Notes of Personal Observation and Adventure, micrographic edition (Calcutta: Stamp Digest, 1984); Barbara Wingfield Stratford, *India and the English* (London: Jonathan Cape, 1922); and Hinkson, *Indian Harvest.*

24. Some contradictory evidence for contemporary South Asia has been suggested by Hannah Papanek in "Purdah: Separate Worlds and Symbolic Shelter," in *Separate Worlds: Studies of Purdah in South Asia*, ed. Hannah Papanek and Gail Minault (Delhi: Chanakya Publications, 1982), 3-53, esp. 42-43.

25. India successively served three major purposes in the British Empire: first as a supplier of manufactures; second as a supplier of raw materials and consumer of British manufactures; and finally as a field for the export of British capital and a strategic military outpost, especially after the First World War.

26. That such reform did not not necessarily mark an "improvement" or even an understanding of the complexities of the existing situation is argued by Lata Mani in "Production of an Official Discourse on Sati in early nineteenth-century Bengal," in *Economic and Political Weekly* 21 (April 26, 1986): WS 32-40.

27. Hutchins, *Illusion of Permanence*, viii. The minute primarily met the colonial need for a cheap pool of Indian labor to staff the imperial machine.

28. *Ibid.*, 187.

29. Pat Barr, *The Memsahibs: The Women of Victorian India* (London: Secker and Warburg, 1976), intro.

30. See especially the manual by Flora Annie Steel and G. Gardiner, *The Complete Indian Housekeeper and Cook* (London: W. Heinemann, 1902).

31. Barr, *The Memsahibs*, 197.

32. After all, the very act of writing, especially after the printing press became widespread, "was taken to be the visible sign of reason, which was valorised above all other human characteristics." H.L. Gates, "Writing, 'Race' and the difference it makes," in *'Race', Writing and Difference*, 1-30, esp. 8.

33. Marian Fowler, *Below the Peacock Fan: First Ladies of the Raj* (Ontario: Penguin 1987), 5 (emphasis mine).

34. Even when Emily Eden, sister of Lord Auckland, Governor General of India from 1836-42, declared, "I cannot abide India and that is the truth," Fowler chooses to remember her as possessed of a "serious empathy and awareness of India's unique pulse" (*Ibid.*, 62).

35. Mary Ann Lind, *The Compassionate Memsahibs: Welfare Activities of British Women in India, 1900-1947* (New York: Greenwood Press, 1988), 4. Six of the 15 women she studies did not mention "the Raj [sic], Indian politics, or Gandhi" in a period of heightened nationalist activity when women played a crucial role (*ibid.*, 107). However, see Geraldine Forbes' "From Purdah to Politics—The Social Feminism of the All-India Women's Organisations," 219-61, and Gail Minault's "Purdah Politics—The Role of Muslim women in Indian Nationalism, 1911-1924," 245-61, in *Separate Worlds*. See also Forbes' more recent "The Politics of Respectibility: Indian Women and the Indian National Congress" in *The Indian National Congress: Centenary, Highlights*, ed. D.A.Low (Delhi: Oxford University Press, 1988), 54-97.

36. Macmillan, *Women of the Raj*, 15.

37. *Ibid.*, 14.

38. *Ibid.*, 236.

39. Ketaki Kushari Dyson, *A Various Universe: A Study of the Journals and Memoirs of British Men and Women in the Indian Subcontinent, 1765-1856* (Delhi: Oxford University Press, 1978).

40. Barr, *The Memsahibs*, 66.

41. *Ibid.*, 163.

42. "Overdetermined" is used here in the Althusserian sense to suggest that gender is often inseparable from considerations of race and class, "determining but also determined by the various levels and instances of the social formation it animates." Louis Althusser, *For Marx* (London: New Left Books, 1977), 101.

43. Pierre Macherey, *A Theory of Literary Production* (London: Routledge and Kegan Paul, 1978), 60.

44. They are (in order of year of writing): Maria Graham, *Journal of a Residence in India* (Edinburgh: A. Constable and Co., 1813); Fanny Parks, *Wanderings of a Pilgrim in Search of the Picturesque*; Emily Eden, *Up the Country: Letters Written to Her Sister from the Upper Provinces of India*; Helen Colin Mackenzie, *Life in the Mission, the Camp, and the Zenana, or Six Years in India*; Mary Carpenter, *Six Months in India*; A.U., *Overland, Inland and Upland*; Marchioness of Dufferin and Ava, *Our Viceregal Life in India: Selections from My Journal, 1884-1888* (London: J. Murray, 1890); *Mrs. Murray Mitchell, In Southern India: A Visit to Some of the Chief Mission Stations in the Madras Presidency* (London: 1885); Mary Frances Billington, *Woman in India*, 2nd ed. (Delhi: Sri Satguru Publications, 1987); Flora Annie Steele, text for *India*; with G. Gardiner, *The Complete Indian Housekeeper and Cook*; Maud Diver, *The Englishwoman in India* (London, 1909); Norah Rowan Hamilton, *Through Wonderful India and Beyond* (London, 1915); Yvonne Fitzroy, *Courts and Camps in India: Impressions of Viceregal Tours, 1921-24* (London 1926); Barbara Wingfield Stratford, *India and the English*; Margaret Noble *The Complete Works of Sister Nivedita*, 5 vols. (Calcutta: Ramakrishna Sarada Mission, 1967); Annie Besant, *The India that Shall Be* (Madras: Theosophical Publishing House, 1940); *India: Bond or Free?* (London: G. Putnam's Sons, 1926); Margaret Cousins, *Indian Womanhood Today* (Allahabad: Kitabistan, 1941); and Pamela Hinkson, *Indian Harvest*.

45. See, however, Rosemary Hennessy and Rajeshwari Mohan, "The Construction of Woman in Three Popular Texts of Empire: Towards a Critique of Materialist Feminism," *Textual Practice* 3, 2 (Summer 1989), 323-59.

46. *The Englishwoman's Review of Social and Industrial Questions*, facsimile reprint, 1868-1910, advisory editors Janet Horowitz Murray and Myra Stark (New York: Garland Publishing, 1980).

47. Graham, *Journal of a Residence in India*, 115.

48. Parks, *Wanderings of a Pilgrim in Search of the Picturesque*, 281.

49. Mackenzie, *Life in the Mission, the Camp, and the Zenana*, 1, 189.

50. A.U., *Overland, Inland and Upland*, 142. Mrs. Murray Mitchell, touring the south in the early 1880s, voiced the same optimism.

51. A.U., *Overland, Inland and Upland*, 237.

52. Carpenter, *Six Months in India*, 1, 76.

53. In *The Feminists: Women's Emancipation Movements in Europe America and Australasia, 1840-1920* (London: Croom Helm, 1977), Richard Evans says that the Royal Commission report of 1858 recommended the establishment of a national system of girls secondary schools to educate middle-class girls in the new and complex tasks of household management. Charles Woods Educational Despatch in 1854 made suggestions for universal education in India and prominently featured female education.

54. Mackenzie, *Life in the Mission, the Camp, and the Zenana*, 1, 243.

55. Carpenter, *Six Months in India*, I, 107.

56. *Ibid.*, 1, 85, 188 . Gareth Stedman Jones, in *Outcast London: A Study in the Relationship between Classes in Victorian Society* (New York: Pantheon, 1984) notes the prevalence of similar attitudes among London reformers towards poorer sections. See especially, "The Deformation of the Gift."

57. Mitchell, *In Southern India, A Visit to Some of the Chief Mission Stations in the Madras Presidency*, 365.

58. *Ibid.*, 5.

59. See *ER*, intro. to index, ed. Janet H. Murray and Anna K. Clark (1985).

60. *ER* (1866-67): 316; (1868): 472; (1871): 85; (1876): 366; (1880): 107. Back in England, Mary Carpenter founded the India Association, which produced a journal aimed at educating fellow Britons about the condition of women in Britain's largest dominion. See *ER* (1871): 85.

61. Eden, *Up The Country*, 132.

62. A.U., *Overland, Inland and Upland*, 129.

63. *ER* (1890): 58.

64. Carpenter, *Six Months in India*, 1, 230.

65. A.U., Overland, *Inland and Upland*, 124.

66. Mackenzie, *Life in the Mission, the Camp, and the Zenana*, 3, 321.

67. *ER* (1889): 146.

68. *ER* (1891): 139.

69. Patricia Branca, *Silent Sisterhood: Middle Class Women in the Victorian Home* (Pittsburgh: Carnegie Mellon University Press, 1975), 63.

70. Billington, *Woman in India*, 1-12.

71. Parks, *Wanderings of a Pilgrim in Search of the Picturesque*, 390.

72. Mackenzie, *Life in the Mission, the Camp and the Zenana*, 307.

73. Mitchell, *In Southern India*, 244.

74. *Ibid.*, 198.

75. Judith Walkowitz, *Prostitution and Victorian Society: Women, Class, and the State* (New York and Cambridge: Cambridge University Press, 1980). Her excellent analysis of the CD campaigns could have been enriched by a discussion of the prior institution of such forms of sexual control in the cantonments of India, and the controversies that surrounded their repeated abolition and restitution in the presidencies throughout the nineteenth century. See Ballhatchet's *Race, Sex and Class under the Raj.*

76. Billington, *Woman in India*, 80, 112-15.

77. Mitchell, *In Southern India*, 53.

78. The economic decline between 1870 and 1914 is widely acknowledged, though the causes for this decline are debated. See Paul Warwick's "Did Britain Change? An Inquiry into the Causes of National Decline," *Journal of Contemporary History*, 20 (1985): 99-133. Warwick does not deal with the political challenges as they are dealt with in *Crisis in the British State, 1880-1930*, ed. Mary Langan and Bill Schwarz (London: Hutchinson, in association with the Centre for Contemporary Cultural Studies, University of Birmingham, 1985). Tom Nairn, similarly, develops the notion of crisis as posed by Irish nationalism and the working class in the period but neglects feminist challenges. See *The Break up of Britain: Crisis and Neo-nationalism*, second expanded edition (London: NLB, 1981). See also G.S. Jones, *Outcast London* for perceptions and responses to the laboring poor in this period.

79. Walkowitz, *Prostitution and Victorian Society*, 1.

80. Susan Kingsley Kent, *Sex and Suffrage in Britain, 1860-1914* (Princeton, N.J.: Princeton University Press, 1987). "The vote became both the symbol of the sexually free autonomous woman and the means by which the goals of a feminist culture were to be obtained." For a detailed analysis of British suffragists' discourse on women in the colonies, see Antoinette Burton, "The White Woman's Burden: British Feminists and the Indian Woman, 1865-1915," *Women's Studies International Forum* 13, 4 (July 1990): 295-308, and "The Feminist Quest for Identity: British

Imperial Suffragism and 'Global Sisterhood,' 1900-1915," *Journal of Women's History* 3 (Fall 1991): 46-81.

81. Martin Durham outlines the heterogeneity of the women's movement in this period in "Suffrage and After; Feminism in the Early Twentieth Century," in *Crises in The British State*, 179-91, esp. 185. See also, Walkowitz, "Male Vice and Feminist Virtue: Feminism and the Politics of Prostitution in Nineteenth Century Britain," *Past and Present*, 13 (Spring 1982): 79-93.

82. Billington was a journalist with the *Daily Graphic* and was assigned to investigate the position of women in India. Flora Annie Steel and Maud Diver were the wives of civil servants in the Punjab who spent long years in India and produced a number of novels on the Raj. Their writings received wide publicity in England; *The Complete Indian Housekeeper and Cook* completed 10 editions, Barr, *The Memsahibs*, 153.

83. Billington, *Women in India*, 155.

84. *Ibid.*, 176. Billington's observations of working-class women revealed an opposition to Lancashire industrialists who were clamoring for factory reform in India at that time to reduce competition from cheap Indian cloth. Low wages were not only adequate in India, she argued, but were a mark of the higher quality of life in India compared with the indignities of working class life in Britain.

85. Steel, *India*, 165.

86. *Ibid.*, 166.

87. *Ibid.*, 157.

88. See Jane Lewis, *Women in England, 1810-1950: Sexual Divisions and Social Change* (Brighton, Sussex: Wheatsheaf Books,1984), 98-99, and Jeffrey Weeks, *Sex, Politics and Society: The Regulation of Sexuality Since 1800* (London: Longman, 1981), 128-38.

89. Lewis, *Women in England*, 75-141; Frank Mort, "Purity Feminism and the State: Sexuality and Moral Politics, 1880-1914," in *Crisis in the British State*, 209-25, esp. 222.

90. Steel, *India*, 159.

91. Stratford, *India and the English*, 119.

92. Hamilton, *Through Wonderful India and Beyond*, 258.

93. Diver, *Englishwoman in India*, 100-01 (emphasis mine).

94. *Ibid.*, 168.

95. Hinkson, *Indian Harvest*, 73.

96. That this was at a time when the Hindu community in UP was actively campaigning for legislation against cow slaughter was but one of the many ambiguities that marked nationalist politics. See Gyan Pandey, "Rallying Round the Cow: Sectarian Strife in the Bhojpuri Region, 1888-1917," in *Subaltern Studies: Writings on South Asian History and Society*, Vol. II (Delhi: Oxford University Press, 1983), 60-129.

97. Through an interlocking system of export-import banks, managing agencies, and shipping companies, all of which were British owned, the benefits of external trade accrued entirely to British capital. India was the first of oriental countries to feel the impact of industrialization; yet it was never allowed to complete the transition to industrialization.

98. See Bipan Chandra, *The Rise and Growth of Economic Nationalism* (Delhi: Peoples' Publishing House, 1982) for an analysis of the critiques of moderate nationalists in this period.

99. See Ranajit Guha's *Elementary Aspects of Peasant Insurgency*, (Delhi: Oxford University Press, 1983) for an analysis of peasant and tribal movements at the time.

100. See Amiya Bagchi's, *Private Investment in India, 1900-1939* (Delhi: Orient Longmans, 1980) for the economic condition of India in 1900.

101. Stuart Hall and Bill Schwarz, "State and Society, 1880-1930," in *Crisis*, 7-32, esp. 29.

102. Diver, *The Englishwoman in India*, 120.

103. Hamilton, *Through Wonderful India and Beyond*, 259.

104. Stratford, *India and the English*, 122.

105. As quoted in Pamela Hinkson, *Indian Harvest*, 256.

106. Margaret Cousins referred to this strategy of the British many years later in *Indian Womanhood Today*, 85. See also Liddle and Joshi, "Gender and Imperialism in British India."

107. Barr, *The Memsahibs*, 186. See also Mrinalini Sinha, "The Age of Consent Act: The Ideal of Masculinity and Colonial Ideology in Late 19th Century Bengal," *Proceedings*, Eighth International Symposium on Asian Studies (Hong Kong: Asian Research Service, 1986), 1199-1214.

108. *ER* (1883): 202-04.

109. See the editor's preface to *The Complete Works of Sister Nivedita* and chronological table in each volume.

110. Noble, "The Present Position of Women," in *Complete Works*, (1968): 238 (vol. 4).

111. *Ibid.*, 369.

112. Noble, "The Web of Indian Life," in *Complete Works*, (1967): 68 (vol. 2).

113. Besant, "Women in India" (1917) in *The India That Shall Be* (Madras: Theosophical Publishing House, 1940), 254.

114. Besant, *India Bond or Free?*, 183.

115. Cousins, *Indian Womanhood Today*, 68. The "separate sphere" feminism of Gandhi was anticipated in the 1905 Congress call during the Swadeshi movement for women to keep the "hearths cold" to protest the partition of Bengal. Gandhi's spectacular success was in drawing women into the national movement (as he did the peasant masses) while keeping mass activity strictly pegged to safe levels. The symbolic shelter that he offered women in the public domain of politics enabled the easier acceptance of women in public life throughout the nationalist period and in the decades after independence.

116. *Ibid.*, 184.

117. *Ibid.*, 198-99. See also Barbara Ramusack, "Cultural Missionaries, Maternal Imperialists, Feminist Allies: British Women Activists in India, 1865-1945," *Women's Studies International Forum* 13, 2 (July 1990): 309-21.

118. *ER* (1867): 319; (1868): 482; (1877): 278-79; (1881): 515-16; (1885): 146; (1889): 146; (1890): 327-30.

119. *ER* (1881): 515-16. See Jeffrey Cox, "Independent Englishwomen in Delhi and Lahore, 1860-1947," in R.W. Davis, ed., *Victorian Religion and Irreligion* (forthcoming) for details on the opportunities afforded to women doctors by the Society for the Propagation of the Gospel.

120. Diver, *Englishwoman in India*, 104.

121. Lind, *Compassionate Memsahibs*, 19.

122. Diver, *Englishwomen in India*, 96-97. This remark was prompted by her assessment that the impact of Lady Dufferin's fund for female medical sevices in India was decidedly poor.

123. Hamilton, *Through Wonderful India and Beyond*, 259.

124. Hinkson, *Indian Harvest*, 258.

125. Diver, *Englishwoman in India*, 128-29 (emphasis mine).

126. Hinkson, *Indian Harvest*, 97.

127. *Ibid.*, 320.

128. Maria Mies, *Patriarchy and Accumulation on a World Scale: Women in the International Division of Labour* (London: Zed Books, 1986), 106.

129. Parks, *Wanderings of a Pilgrim in Search of the Picturesque*, 420.

AFRICA ON MY MIND

GENDER, COUNTER DISCOURSE, AND AFRICAN-AMERICAN NATIONALISM

E. Frances White

> Equality is false; it's the devil's concept. Our concept is complementarity. Complementarity means you complete or make perfect that which is imperfect.
>
> The man has the right that does not destroy the collective needs of his family.
>
> The woman has the two rights of consultation and then separation if she isn't getting what she should be getting.[1]

The African past lies camouflaged in the collective African-American memory, transformed by the middle passage, sharecropping, industrialization, urbanization. Few material goods from Africa survived this difficult history, but Africans brought with them a memory of how social relations should be constructed that has affected African-American culture to the present. Although the impact of these African roots is difficult to assess, few historians today deny the importance of this past to African-American culture.

But the memories I seek to interrogate in this essay have little to do with "real" memories or actual traditions that African-Americans have passed along through blood or even practices. Rather, I am concerned with the way African-Americans in the late twentieth century construct and reconstruct collective political memories of African culture to build a cohesive group that can shield them from racist ideology and oppression. In particular it is the political memories of African gender relations and sexuality that act as models for African-American social relations that will serve as this paper's focus.

Below I will focus on black nationalism as an oppositional strategy that both counters racism and constructs conservative utopian images of Afri-

© 1990 JOURNAL OF WOMEN'S HISTORY, VOL. 2 NO. 1 (SPRING)

can-American life. I will pay close attention to the intertwined discussions on the relationship of the African past to present-day culture and to attempts to construct utopian and repressive gender relations. After situating my work theoretically in the next section, I return to an examination of Afrocentric paradigms that support nationalist discourse on gender and the African past. Finally I look at the emergence of a black feminist discourse that attempts to combine nationalist and feminist insights in a way that counters racism but tries to avoid sexist pitfalls.

Throughout the essay, I choose examples from across the range of nationalist thinking. Some of this writing is obviously narrow and sexist. Other works have influenced my thinking deeply and have made significant contributions to understanding African-American women's lives. I argue, however, that all fail to confront the sexist models that ground an important part of their work. I imagine that my criticisms will be read by some as a dismissal of all Afrocentric thinking. Nothing could be further from my intentions. It is because I value the contributions of nationalists that I want to engage them seriously. Yet it is the kind of feminism that demands attention to internal community relations that leads me to interrogate this discourse even while acknowledging its ability to undermine racist paradigms. This kind of black feminism recognizes the dangers of criticizing internal relations in the face of racist attacks but also argues that we will fail to transform ourselves into a liberated community if we do not engage in dialogue on the difficult issues that confront us.[2]

African-American nationalists have taken the lead in resurrecting and inventing African models for the African diaspora in the United States. They recognize that dominant, negative images of Africa have justified black enslavement, segregation, and continuing impoverishment.[3] Accordingly, nationalists have always argued persuasively that African-Americans deny their connections to Africa at the peril of allowing a racist subtext to circulate without serious challenge. At the same time, nationalists have recognized that counter attacks on negative portrayals of Africa stimulate political mobilization against racism in the United States. The consciously identified connections between African independence and the U.S. civil rights movements and, more recently, between youth rebellion in South Africa and campus unrest in the U.S. stand out as successful attempts to build a Pan-African consciousness.

The construction of Pan-African connections can have its problems, however. At times it depends on the search for a glorious African past while accepting dominant European notions of what that past should look like. As I have argued elsewhere,[4] proving that Africans created "civilizations" as sophisticated as those in Europe and the near East has concerned nationalists too much.[5] In the process of elevating Egypt, for example, they have often accepted as uncivilized and even savage primitives the majority of Africans who lived in stateless societies but whose past deserves respect for its complex relationship to the world around it.[6]

Perhaps more importantly, the nationalist or Afrocentric construction of a political memory attempts to set up standards of social relations that can be both liberating and confining. The quotation at the beginning of this essay by the "inventor" of Kwanzaa traditions, Ron Karenga, illustrates this point. Building off conservative concepts of "traditional" African gender relations before colonial rule, he argues that the collective needs of black families depend on women's complementary and unequal roles. As I shall make clear below, Karenga has significantly modified his sexist ideas about gender relations, but the ideology of complementarity and collective family needs continues to work against the liberation of black women.

In addition, many nationalists, both male and female, remain openly hostile to any feminist agenda. In a paper arguing that black people should turn to African polygamous and extended family forms to solve the "problem" of female-headed households, Larry Delano Coleman concludes:

> The "hyper-liberated" black woman is in fact so much a man that she has no need for men, however wimpish they may be; and the "hyper-emasculated" black man is so much a woman, that he has no need for women. May each group of these hyper-distorted persons find homosexual heaven among the whites, for the black race would be better served without them.[7]

Coleman defines "the race" in a way that excludes feminists, lesbians, and gay men from community support—a terrifying proposition in this age of resurgent racism.[8]

In advocating polygamous families, Nathan and Julia Hare, the influential editors of *Black Male/Female Relationships*, link homosexuality with betrayal of the race:

> Just as those black persons who disidentify with their race and long to alter their skin color and facial features to approximate that of the white race may be found to suffer a racial identity crisis, the homosexual individual who disidentifies with his/her biological body to the point of subjecting to the surgery of sex-change operations similarly suffers a gender identity confusion, to say the least.[9]

Both the Hares' and Coleman's standards of appropriate gender relations depend on a misguided notion of African culture in the era before "the fall"—that is, before European domination distorted African traditions. These nationalists have idealized polygamous and extended families in a way that stresses both cooperation among women and male support of wives but ignores cross-generational conflict and intrafamily rivalry also common in extended, polygamous families. They have invented an African past to suit their conservative agenda on gender and sexuality.

In making appeals to conservative notions of appropriate gender behavior, African-American nationalists reveal their ideological ties to other

nationalist movements, including European and Euro-American bourgeois nationalists over the past 200 years. These parallels exist despite the
different class and power base of these movements. European and Euro-
American nationalists turned to the ideology of respectability to help them
impose the bourgeois manners and morals that attempted to control sexual behavior and gender relations. This ideology helped the bourgeoisie
create a "private sphere" that included family life, sexual relations, and
leisure time. Respectability set standards of proper behavior at the same
time that it constructed the very notion of private life. Nationalism and
respectability intertwined as the middle class used the nation state to
impose its notions of the private sphere's proper order on the upper and
lower classes. Through state-run institutions, such as schools, prisons, and
census bureaus, the bourgeoisie disciplined people and collected the necessary information to identify and control them.[10]

Often African-Americans have served as a model of abnormality against
which nationalism in the U.S. was constructed. White bourgeois nationalism has often portrayed African-Americans as if they threatened respectability. Specifically, white nationalists have described both black men and
women as hypersexual. Moreover, black family life has consistently served
as a model of abnormality for the construction of the ideal family life.
Black families were matriarchal when white families should have been
male dominated. Now they are said to be female-headed when the ideal
has become an equal heterosexual pair.[11]

As I have suggested, black people have developed African-American
nationalism as an oppositional discourse to counter such racist images.
Ironically, though not surprisingly, this nationalism draws on the ideology
of respectability to develop a cohesive political movement. The African-
American ideology of respectability does not always share the same moral
code with western nationalism. Some Afrocentric thinkers, such as Larry
Coleman, turn to Africa for models of gender relations and call for polygamy as an appropriate form of marriage between black men and women.
More crucially, black nationalists did not and cannot call on state power to
enforce their norms. Their opposition to abortion carries very different
weight from the campaign of the Christian right whose agenda includes
making a bid for control of state institutions.

It is this lack of access to state power and African-American nationalists'
advocacy of an oppressed people that gives Afrocentric ideology its progressive, radical edge and ultimately distinguishes it from European and
Euro-American bourgeois nationalism. Paradoxically then, Afrocentric
ideology can be radical and progressive in relation to white racism and
conservative and repressive in relation to the internal organization of the
black community. Clearly, nationalists struggle in a way that can deeply
threaten white racism. Both the open repression and the ideological back-
lash against nationalists indicate that their discourse strikes at the heart of
black oppression. Yet I often find too narrow black nationalist efforts to

define what the community or nation should be. In particular many nationalists attempt to construct sexist and heterosexist ideal models for appropriate behavior.

The Dialectics of Discursive Struggle

How does one prove strength in oppression without overstating the case, diluting criticism of the system and absolving the oppressor in the process? Likewise, the parallel dilemma is how does one critique the system and state of things without contributing to the victimology school which thrives on litanies of lost battles and casualty lists, while omitting victories and strengths and the possibilities for change inherent in both black people and society?[12]

Karenga has identified a key dilemma facing black scholarship: how do black scholars take into account the possibilities of liberation at the same time that they balance a sense of strength against the realities of victimization? One strategy for moving beyond this dilemma to what Karenga calls an "emancipatory Black science" is to examine the ideological battles in which black people engage, exploring both the racist discourse that they struggle against and the oppositional language constructed in the process of this struggle. As a site of ideological battles, discourses intertwine with the material conditions of our lives. They help organize our social existence and social reproduction through the production of signs and practices that give meaning to our lives.[13] Closely tied to the socio-economic and political institutions that enable oppressive relations, discourses are often reflected in a variety of forms. For example, the dominant discourse on Africa includes multilayered interventions that are knitted together from scholarly literature, fiction, art, movies, television, media, travel books, government documents, folklore, jokes, and more. The discourse that relies on these interventions creates an image of Africa that reinforces the continent's subordinate power relations to the west. Dominant discursive practice depends on more than lies and myths, although misrepresentation and deception do have roles to play in its strategy. Instead, the west's will to knowledge about Africa has been inextricably bound up with imperialist relations.

It is impossible for people's thoughts on Africa to be unencumbered by this discourse. None of us—not even Africans—can come to the study of Africa without being influenced by its negative image. Accordingly, dominant discourse attempts to blind both the oppressor and the oppressed by setting up smokescreens between people and reality. As Said argues for the Middle East, ". . . for a European or American studying the Orient there can be no disclaiming the main circumstance of his actuality: that he comes up against the Orient as a European or American first, as an individual second."[14] One way that dominant discourse sets up a smokescreen is to make arbitrary categories appear natural and normal. For example, it makes us think that race is a natural category by taking minor biological differences and infusing them with deep symbolic meanings that affect all our lives. Race, then, is a social construction that feels real to us and has significant consequences.

The popular literature that influences even nationalists is peppered with images of primitive natives confronting European civilization. These natives build huts rather than houses while in England similar looking structures are called picturesque cottages. By nature natives divide themselves into tribes while more sophisticated people form ethnic groups. These words—tribe, hut, native, civilization, and primitive—form a cluster of words that helps build a discourse on Africans that places them in a time warp outside our present time. Not surprisingly, this cluster of words has a history in the anthropological vocabulary that supported imperialism, a vocabulary that anthropology has discarded but that remains in popular usage. Many of these words can be found in Raymond Williams' 1976 *Keywords: A Vocabulary of Culture and Society* since the western discourse on Africa is as much about Europe as it is about Africa—an exploration of what Africa is and, therefore, what Europe is not.[15]

As Johannes Fabian has argued, the cluster of words surrounding Africa fixes "natives" in a time other than our own complex, contemporary time. Natives are primitive in the sense that they came first, living as western ancestors lived in a simpler age.[16] Even the word tribe suggests an earlier time since Europeans were said to have lived in them only in the distant past. *The Oxford English Dictionary* reminds us that a tribe is "a primary aggregate of people in a primitive or barbarous condition, under a headman or chief." Tribe, then, suggests a notion of ethnicity that is more fixed than social relations have ever been in Africa.

The concept of fixed, static tribes suited the interests of colonial rulers who sought to categorize and control Africans. It continues to suit the interests of white South Africans who engage in deadly ideological warfare. As long as we believe in the existence of isolated, primitive tribes, white South Africans will find a market for their racist ideology of separate development. They continue to claim that separate development protects tribes from the ravages of civilization and allows each tribe/nation to evolve from different starting points to its fullest potential. Tribe feeds off the racist cluster of words that speak to us through films ("Tarzan" and its recent imitation, "The Gods Must Be Crazy"); magazines (*National Geographic* and related PBS specials); and newspapers (*The New York Times'* reports on tribal massacres in Burundi and South Africa). The smokescreen created by words central to this racist discourse casts a thick pall over Africa.

And yet alternative voices do emerge. Unfortunately, many influential works on discourse, such as Said's *Orientalism*, have failed to account adequately for the development of the oppositional strategies that reveal contradictions in the dominant discourse. Admittedly even those who consciously reject hegemonic ideology or who appear to live unencumbered by it cannot go untouched by its power. But the existence of resistance suggests a need to recognize the interrelationship between dominant and counter discourse. I have followed Richard Terdiman's lead in focusing on the inseparably intertwined nature of hegemonic and oppositional discursive practices. In his "celebration" of counter discourse he suggests, "we might thus posit something like a Newton's Law in the discursive realm: for every dominant discourse a contrary and transgressive counter discourse."[17] More tersely: "No discourse is ever a monologue."[18]

The very nature of dominant discourse leads it to be contested by subordinate groups whose daily experiences help penetrate and demystify its hegemony.[19] This "dialectic of discursive struggle" reveals the vulnerabilities of hegemonies.[20] As part of the same dialectic, counter discourses operate on the same ground as dominant ideology. Scott argues:

> The crucial point is rather that the very process of attempting to legitimate a social order by idealizing it always provides its subjects with the means, the symbolic tools, the very ideas for a critique that operates entirely within the hegemony. For most purposes, then, it is not at all necessary for subordinate classes to set foot outside the confines of the ruling ideals in order to formulate a critique of power.[21]

As I will argue below, African-American nationalist contestation over the image of Africa often unconsciously accepts many of the terms of dominant discursive strategies, even when it attempts to move beyond the limits set by racist ideology.

In *Marxism and the Philosophy of Language,* V.N. Volosinov examines the struggles between dominant and counter discourses as a contest over ideological signs. A sign represents, depicts, or stands for something lying outside itself. It does not "simply exist as a part of a reality—it reflects and refracts another reality. Therefore, it may distort that reality or be true to it, or may perceive it from a special point of view, and so forth."[22] For Volosinov, language and words were often a starting place to understand social relations. Unlike other ideological signs,

> The entire reality of the word is wholly absorbed in its function of being a sign. A word contains nothing that is indifferent to this function, nothing that would not have been engendered by it. A word is the purest and most sensitive medium of social intercourse.[23]

Words, like all signs, evolve only on "interindividual territory," that is, between individuals. Thus, he stresses the "multiaccentuality" of the ideological sign. Caryl Emerson explains:

> Each social group—each class, profession, generation, religion, region—
> has its own characteristic way of speaking, its own dialect. Each dialect
> reflects and embodies a set of values and a sense of shared experience.
> Because no two individuals ever entirely coincide in their experience or
> belong to precisely the same set of social groups, every act of understand-
> ing involves an act of translation and a negotiation of values. It is essentially
> a phenomenon of interrelation and interaction.[24]

As Volosinov, Terdiman, and others have argued, language reflects the
struggles between dominant and dissident discourses. Hazel Carby
expresses this view: "The sign, then, is an arena of struggle . . . ; the forms
that signs take are conditioned by the social organization of the participants involved and also by the immediate conditions of their interactions."[25] In the case of interest to us, the meaning of Africa—the
ideological sign, Africa—is contested on discursive terrain. Dominant discourse assigns a plethora of negative images to Africa while those influenced by nationalist impulses in Africa and its diaspora struggle to replace
these images with their own positive meanings.

Yet as suggested earlier, this counter discourse has a double-edged
nature. In part because, as Emerson says, no two individuals "belong to
precisely the same set of social groups,"[26] counter discourse struggles
against both dominant and competing oppositional discourses. African-
American nationalists attempt to protect themselves from negative images
at the same time that they try to set the terms of appropriate behavior
within the black community. Terdiman and Scott, both of whom write persuasively about the ways counter discourse can penetrate the contradictions inherent in dominant discourse, fail to examine the significance of
alternative worldviews for the subordinated communities that project
them as a defense against oppression. Scott, for example, seems unaware
that poor men and women in the Malaysian village he studied might have
competing interests. Neither Scott nor Terdiman recognizes the ways gender intersects with class and ethnicity to form overlapping and often contradictory social groups.

The writings of certain feminists of color reveal the Janus-faced nature
of counter discourse as these women search for allies among the male-
dominated nationalist and white-dominated feminist movements. For
example, women of color offered challenges within the feminist movement that forced women to acknowledge the problems with an undifferentiated category, Woman. Many of these theorists highlighted the
complexities of human identity in recognition of the reality that women
have ethnic/race and class positions, *inter alia*, that interact with gender
and sexuality to influence their lives. Accordingly, feminists of color
pushed for a movement whose discursive practices opposed sexism and
racism simultaneously.[27] For example, Audre Lorde has asked, how does
horizontal hostility keep women from ending their oppression? She

argued that women need to celebrate their differences and use difference for creative dialogue.[28] Outside a narrow band of bourgeois or separatist feminists, few U.S. white feminists today write without giving at least token acknowledgement to Lorde's call to recognize difference.[29]

At the same time, women of color challenged their various ethnic communities to become conscious of sexism at home. Cherríe Moraga problematizes the meaning of home and community as she sensitively explores the way her education and light skin pushed her away from other Chicanos. "I grew white," she acknowledged.[30] But she also stressed that her community forced her to leave home because of her feminism and lesbianism. Feeling betrayed by a mother who accepted the ideology that males were better than females, she fled from those who told her, you are a traitor to your race if you do not put men first. She watched the rise of the Chicano nationalist movement, La Raza, alienated on the side lines. Yet she found herself increasingly uncomfortable in her nearly all-white surroundings.

Ultimately, she concluded that to be critical of one's race is not to betray it. She joined with other Chicana feminists to turn around the traditional interpretation of Malinche's life, which traces the birth of the Mexican people to Malinche's betrayal of her people. Instead, Moraga and others expose a prior betrayal of Malinche who had been sold into slavery by her own people.[31] By refusing to accept the terms of a Chicano nationalist movement that brands her a traitor because she publicly criticizes gender relations, Moraga demands a place for herself and other lesbians within Chicano communities.

It is not surprising that feminists such as Audre Lorde and Cherríe Moraga challenge both feminist and nationalist communities. As women with strong lesbian political consciences, they confront homophobia in nationalist movements. Locked in struggle against heterosexism in their own communities, it is very difficult for them to maintain an image of their communities as harmonious. Cheryl Clarke has specifically accused nationalists of increasing the level of homophobia in African-American communities during the 1960s and 1970s. She argues persuasively that homophobia limits the political struggle of African-Americans:

> The expression of homophobic sentiments, the threatening political postures assumed by black radicals and progressives of the nationalist/communist ilk, and the seeming lack of any willingness to understand the politics of gay and lesbian liberation collude with the dominant white male culture to repress not only gay men and lesbians, but also to repress a natural part of all human beings, namely the bisexual potential in us all. Homophobia divides black people as political allies, it cuts off political growth, stifles revolution, and perpetuates patriarchal domination.[32]

In *Reconstructing Womanhood*, Hazel Carby goes even further when she finds fault with some African-American feminists for failing to recognize that even their writings form part of a multiaccented counter discourse. She cautions black feminist literary critics to be historically specific when they write about black women's fiction and to recognize competing interests among African-American women. She asserts, "in these terms black and feminist cannot be absolute, transhistorical forms (or form) of identity."[33] Black feminists do not have an essential, biologically-based claim on understanding black women's experience since we are divided by class, region, and sexual orientation. Even we have multiple identities that create tensions and contradictions among us. We need not all agree nor need we all speak with one voice. As with all counter discourses, the assumption that there exists one essential victim suppresses internal power divisions. To Terdiman's "no discourse is ever a monologue," we should add, the site of counter discourse is itself contested terrain.

Inventing African Tradition

The contemporary African-American woman must recognize that, in keeping with her African heritage and legacy, her most important responsibilities are to the survival of the home, the family, and its children.[34]

It is out of the feminist tradition of challenging the oppositional discourses that are meaningful to women of color that I interrogate the significance of black nationalism for African-American women's lives. Like Sylvia Yanagisako, "I treat tradition as a cultural construction whose meaning must be discovered in present words no less than past acts."[35] As I have suggested, the traditions revealed in nationalist discursive practices are Janus-faced—turned toward struggle with oppressive forces and contesting for dominance within black communities.

This discourse can be represented by Molefi Kete Asante's writings and the journal he edits, *Journal of Black Studies.* Asante recognizes the importance of developing a counter discourse within the privileged arena of academia and has consistently published a high quality journal. He is also responsible for developing the first Ph.D. program in African-American Studies at Temple University.

The focus of his work and his journal is an Afrocentric one because it places "Africans and the interest of Africa at the center of our approach to problem solving."[36] By African, he means both people from the African continent and its diaspora. Although he has collapsed the distinction between African-Americans and Africans, he avoids the traps many nationalists fall into when they posit a simplistic, mystical connection between Africa and African-Americans. Unlike earlier nationalists who appealed to a natural, essential element in African culture, he argues that culture "is the product of the material and human environment in which people live."[37] In an editor's note introducing a special issue of the *Journal of Black Studies*, "African Cultural Dimensions," he continues:

> As editor I seek to promulgate the view that all culture is cognitive. The manifestations of culture are the artifacts, creative solutions, objects, and rituals that are created in response to nature. Thus, the manuscripts which have been scrupulously selected for this issue are intended to continue the drama of cultural discussion of African themes.[38]

Africans, he argues, have constructed a culture that stands in opposition to Eurocentric culture. He develops a convincing critique of a Eurocentric worldview. For Asante, Eurocentric culture is too materialistic, and the social science that has evolved from this culture in academe too often assumes an objective, universal approach that ultimately suffers from positivism. He argues that neither Marxism nor Freudianism escape from this shortcoming though he acknowledges that the Frankfurt School's criticisms of positivism has influenced his work.

According to Asante, the task for African-Americans is to move beyond the Eurocentric idea to a place where transcultural, Afrocentric analysis becomes possible. He cautions against using a Eurocentric mode that accepts oppositional dichotomies as a reflection of the real world.[39] His critique of the positivist tendency to split mind and body is cogent. Unfortunately, his theory also relies on a false dichotomy. Essentially, his categories, Afrocentric and Eurocentric, form an untenable binary opposition: Europeans are materialistic while Africans are spiritual; Europeans abort life while Africans affirm it.

He is quite right to recognize the existence of a protest discourse that counters racist ideology. But he denies the way that these discourses are both multivocal and intertwined. As suggested above, the dialectic nature of discursive struggle requires that counter and dominant discourses contest the same ideological ground.

This point can be better understood by examining the roots of Asante's Afrocentric thought. He consciously builds off Negritude and authenticity, philosophies devised explicitly to counter racist ideology and develop nationalist cohesion. V.Y. Mudimbe (1988) has exposed the nature of the binary opposition used by cultural nationalists of the 1930s and 1940s who explored their difference as blacks. Leopold Senghor and Aimé Césaire and other Francophone Africans and African-Caribbeans relied on the spiritual/materialistic dichotomy. Turned on its head, this is the opposition used against Africans during the late nineteenth century. As many have pointed out, this reversal of paradigms owed much to the celebration of the "noble savage" by such interwar European writers as J.-P. Sartre. Ironically western anthropologists, whom nationalists often disparage, also took an active role in this ideological "flip." It was anthropologists such as Michel Griaule and Melville J. Herskovits who revealed to western-educated intellectuals the internal coherence of African systems of thought.[40] Equally important was the cross-fertilization of ideas between Africans, African-Caribbeans, and African-Americans. As a result of these three influences, "African experiences, attitudes, and mentalities became mirrors of a spiritual and cultural richness."[41] Far from culture-less savages, Africans had built the essence of spiritual culture.

This reversal of the racist paradigms on Africa accompanied and contributed to the growth of the nationalist movements that ultimately freed the continent from formal colonial rule. The nature of African independence reflects the double-edged character of this nationalism. On the one hand, nationalism helped build the political coherence necessary to threaten European rule; on the other hand, it obscured class and gender divisions in a way that prevented them from being addressed fairly. Clearly, this nationalism shared much with a European brand of nationalism that envisioned a culture unequally divided along gender and class lines.

Similarly, Asante does little to take us beyond the positivism that he criticizes, and his schema assumes a universality as broad as the Eurocentric discourse he shuns. Moreover, the Afrocentric ideology he uses depends on an image of black people as having a culture that has little or nothing to do with white culture. This is one of its major contradictions. On the one hand, nationalists like Asante have to prove to African-Americans that Afrocentric ways are different from and better than Euro-American ways. Nationalists try to convince black people that they should begin to live their lives by this Afrocentric ideology. For example, some nationalists argue that African-Americans should turn away from materialism to focus on the spiritual needs of the black community. Yet on the other hand, Asante and others argue that black culture is already based on an Afrocentric worldview that distinguishes it from Euro-American culture. Rather than being an ideology that African-Americans must turn to, Afrocentric thought becomes inherent in black culture, and black people already live by these ways in opposition to dominant culture.

I would argue instead that African-American culture constantly interacts with dominant culture. Of course, black people do have their own ways not only because they protect themselves from penetration by white culture but also because they are creative. Nonetheless, blacks and whites all live together in the same society, and culture flows in both directions. Like the dominant culture, most African-Americans believe that spirituality has a higher value than materialism at the same time that most of these people pursue material goals. If materialism were not considered crass by dominant society, Afrocentric critique would have little value. It is also important to note the extent to which white culture is influenced by African-Americans. At an obvious level, we see black influence on white music with the most recent appearance of rap music on television and radio commercials. At a less obvious level, Afrocentric critiques compel hegemonic forces to work at covering the reality of racist relations. Far from being an ideology that has no relationship to Eurocentric thought, nationalist ideology is dialectically related to it.

What I find most disturbing about Asante's work is his decision to collapse differences among black people into a false unity that only a simplistic binary opposition would allow. The focus on similarities between Africans and African-Americans at the expense of recognizing historical differences can only lead to a crisis once differences are inevitably revealed. Moreover, his binary opposition cannot account for differences among Africans. Many eloquent African writers have warned us about the problems that came from accepting a false unity during the decolonization phase that has led to the transfer of local power from an expatriate elite to an indigenous one. Ngugi wa Thiongo, Sembene Ousmane, and Chinua Achebe would all warn us against such pitfalls.

And, of course, we cannot face sexism with this false unity, as Buchi Emecheta, Sembene Ousmane, and Mariama Bâ movingly show. Asante does tell us that along with the move beyond the Eurocentric idea, we can develop a "post-male ideology as we unlock creative human potential."[42] Yet he has nothing more to say about gender in the entire book. It is hard to believe that this gesture toward black feminists needs to be taken seriously. It is to other Afrocentric thinkers that we must turn to understand more clearly what this discourse has to say about women.

Among the most important nationalists the *Journal of Black Studies* publishes is Ron Karenga, the founder of US. Some readers will remember him for his leadership role among cultural nationalists in ideological battles against the Black Panthers in the 1960s and 1970s and for his pamphlet, *The Quotable Ron Karenga*. In *Black Awakening in Capitalist America*, Robert Allen quoted a critical excerpt from Karenga's book, exposing its position on women and influencing many young black women (including myself) to turn away from this nationalist position.[43]

Perhaps the key word in Karenga's early analysis of utopian gender relations is complementarity. In this theory, woman should complement male roles and, therefore, share the responsibilities of nation building. Of course, in this formulation, complementary did not mean equal. Instead, men and women were to have separate tasks and unequal power. Indeed, in much of Africa today, women give more to men than they get in return in their complementary labor exchange. This is not to suggest that African women are only victims in their societies; nonetheless, sexism based on a complementary model severely limits the possibilities of many women's lives.

It is important to note that Karenga has reformed his position on women. Apparently, he used the time he spent in jail during the 1970s effectively by spending much of his time studying. It is from his jail cell that he published influential pieces in *Black Scholar* and the *Journal of Black Studies*. He began to articulate more clearly a critique of hegemonic culture, showing the impact of reading Lukacs, Gramsci, Cabral, and Touré. And though he does not say so explicitly, he begins to respond to black feminist critics of his work. Indeed, I find the change in his position on women impressive. Although he remains mired in heterosexist assumptions and never acknowledges his change of heart, he drops his explicit arguments supporting the subordination of women. The new Ron Karenga argues for equality in the heterosexual pair despite his continued hostility to feminists.[44]

Unfortunately, too few nationalists have made this transition with him. Male roles remain defined by conventional, antifeminist notions that fail to address the realities of black life. For example, articles in Nathan and Julia Hare's journal, *Black Male/Female Relationships*, consistently articulate such roles. Charlyn A. Harper-Bolton begins her contribution, "A Reconceptualization of the African-American Woman" by examining "traditional African philosophy, the nature of the traditional African woman, and the African-American slave woman."[45] She uses African tradition as her starting point because she assumes an essential connection between the African past and African-American present:

> The contemporary African-American woman carries within her very essence, within her very soul, the legacy which was bequeathed to her by the traditional African woman and the African-American slave woman.[46]

She leaves unproblematic the African legacy to African-Americans as she presents an ahistorical model of African belief systems that ignores the conflict and struggle over meaning so basic to the making of history. This model assumes a harmonious spirituality vs. conflicting materialism dichotomy that grounds the work of Asante and her major sources, John Mbiti and Wade Nobles.[47]

It is a peculiarly Eurocentric approach that accepts conflict and competing interests in a western context but not in an African one. Harper-Bolton never moves beyond the mistaken notion that Africans lived simply and harmoniously until the evil Europeans upset their happy life. Ironically, as I have been arguing, such an image of Africans living in static isolation from historical dynamics supports racist ideals and practices and conveniently overlooks the power dynamics that existed in precolonial Africa like any where else in the world. In addition, her model portrays African women as a monolithic and undifferentiated category with no competing interests, values, and conflicts. The power of older women over younger women that characterizes so many African cultures becomes idealized as a vision of the elders' wisdom in decision making. It accepts the view of age relations presented by more powerful older women whose hidden agenda often is to socialize girls into docile daughters and daughters-in-law.

When Harper-Bolton turns to the legacy of slave women for contemporary life she owes a large, but unacknowledged, debt to the social science literature on African survivals in African-American culture. In particular, her work depends on the literature that explores the African roots of African-American family patterns. Writers such as Gutman, Blassingame, and Kullikoff have attempted to build off Melville J. Herskovits' early work on African survivals. This literature has been crucial for forming our understanding of black women's roles during slavery with particular reference to the African roots of these roles.

Unfortunately, this literature also shares certain problems that have clouded our understanding of this African heritage. What concerns me most are the sources that these historians use to compare African and African-American slave families. Two major sources have been used uncritically that are particularly problematic when studying African women's roles in the precolonial era. First, historians have relied on precolonial travellers' accounts written by westerners exploring the African continent. These accounts are important sources to turn to—and I have used them myself. But they must be used with great care because it is precisely at the point of describing African women and gender relations that these accounts are most problematic. Often these travellers' debates over whether or not African women were beasts of burden and whether or not African women were sexually loose spoke to debates in Europe. Rosalind Coward has explored the obsession of eighteenth and nineteenth century westerners with gender relations around the world, assuming as they did that these relations were a measure of civilization.[48] Needless to say, these travellers brought the sexist visions of their own society to bear on African gender relations, and, therefore, their writings must be used carefully.

But I am more troubled by the second major source used by historians looking for African legacies, that is, anthropological reports written between the 1930s and 1950s. My interest here is not in being a part of "anthropology bashing"—accusing it of being the most racist of the western disciplines. (Historians, after all, did not believe that Africa even had a history; they rarely turned their attention to its study until the 1960s.) But the use of anthropological accounts in the study of African history is very troubling to me. Used uncritically, as they most often are, these accounts lead historians into the trap that assumes a static African culture. Anthropology can give us hints about the past; but given the dynamic cultures that I assume Africa had in the past, these hints must be treated carefully.

Moreover, there is a particular problem in the use of these accounts for understanding African women's history. Most of the reports relied on were written in the midtwentieth century, a time when anthropologists and the colonial rulers for whom they worked were seeking to uncover "traditional" African social relations. They were responding to what they saw as a break down in these relations, leaving the African colonies more unruly and, most importantly, more unproductive than they hoped. Young men and young women ran off from the rural areas to towns, escaping the control of their elders. Divorce soared in many areas. The elders, too, were concerned with what they saw as a break down in their societies. Both elders and colonial rulers worried that young people made marriages without their elders' approval and then, finding that they had chosen partners with whom they were no longer compatible, the uncontrollable youth divorced without approval and made new, short-term marriages.

The anthropologists set out to find out what led to this "break down" and to discover the customary rules that they felt had restricted conflict in "traditional" Africa. Once again we see the concept of a harmonious Africa before colonial rule emerging. In his introduction to the seminal collection, *African Systems of Kinship and Marriage*, A. R. Radcliffe-Brown expressed this concern:

> African societies are undergoing revolutionary changes, as the result of European Administrators, missions, and economic factors. In the past the stability of social order in African societies has depended much more on the kinship system than on anything else. . . . The anthropological observer is able to discover new strains and tensions, new kinds of conflict, as Professor [Meyer] Fortes has done for the Ashanti and Professor Daryll Forde shows for the Yakö.[49]

In part, Radcliffe-Brown and his co-editor, Daryll Forde, offered this set of essays as a guideline to colonial administrators so that the colonialists could counteract the destabilizing influences of westernization. Such anthropologists obviously felt the need for a better understanding of people under colonial rule.

Not surprisingly, it was the male elders whom the anthropologists asked about these customary laws, not the junior women and men who now divorced at an increased rate. Martin Chanock points out in "Making Customary Law: Men, Women, and Courts in Colonial Northern Rhodesia" that customary law was developed out of this alliance between the colonial rulers and the elders' interests. Of course, African elders were unequal partners in this alliance. Yet since both elders and colonial rulers viewed the increasing rates of divorce and adultery as signs of moral decline, they collaborated to develop customary laws that controlled marriages. "For this purpose claims about custom were particularly well-suited as they provided the crucial and necessary legitimation for the control of sexual behavior."[50] Chanock shows the way customary laws in Northern Rhodesia represented increased concern with punishing women to keep them in control. Therefore, in many cases such as adultery what got institutionalized as "tradition" or "custom" was more restrictive for women than in the past.

It is with the concern of maintaining male control over women and elders' control over their juniors that many anthropologists of the 1940s and 1950s explored "traditional" African culture. To read their sources into the past could lead us to very conservative notions of what African gender relations were about. Yet Harper-Bolton accepts these views uncritically when she presents as unproblematic a model of gender relations that fails to question women's allocation to a domestic life that merely complements male roles.[51] And, by extension, she buys into an antifeminist ideology. She warns that rejection of African tradition leads women into two directions that are antithetical to healthy developments in African-American family life. In one direction, women can fall into loose sexual behavior by accepting Euro-American conceptions of woman and beauty. In the other direction, women become trapped in aggressiveness in the work place and rejection of motherhood. Harper-Bolton argues:

> What happened to this African-American woman is that she accepted, on the one hand, the Euro-American definition of "woman" and attempts, on the other hand, to reject this definition by behaving in an opposite manner. Her behavior becomes devoid of an African sense of woman-ness. In her dual acceptance/rejection of the Euro-American definition of woman, this African-American woman, in essence, becomes a "white man."[52]

Can Nationalism and Feminism Merge?

Not all Afrocentric thinkers need be so blatantly antifeminist. Some African-American women have attempted to combine nationalism and feminism. As black feminists have sought an independent identity from dominant white, bourgeois feminism, some have explicitly turned to Afrocentric ideology for their understanding of these gender relations. These efforts stressed that African-American women grew up in families that had roots in African experiences and, therefore, were fundamentally different from the ones described by white feminists. Such arguments recognized the need to search for solutions to sexism in black families that are based on their own experiences and history.

One of the most successful attempts to rely on Afrocentric thinking comes from a newly evolving school of thought known as African women's diaspora studies. This school of thought is represented best by *Black Woman Cross-Culturally* edited by Filomina Chioma Steady and *Women in Africa and the African Diaspora*, edited by Rosalyn Terborg-Penn, Andrea Benton Rushing, and Sharon Harley and tries to reclaim the African past for African-American women. These works have significantly raised the level of understanding of the connections among women in Africa and its diaspora. A number of the scholars published in these books have read extensively about black women around the world and have drawn bold comparisons. For them, women from Africa and the African diaspora are united by a history of "economic exploitation and marginalization manifested through slavery and colonization and . . . [in the contemporary period] through neocolonialism in the U.S."[53] Influenced by nationalist impulses, they criticize much of the earlier literature on black women for using a white filter to understand African culture. Further, they persuasively argue that too often black women are presented as one-dimensional victims of patriarchy or racism.[54] Instead, these women use African feminist theory as described by Steady to remove this white filter on African-American lives and to identify "the cosmology common to traditional African women who lived during the era of the slave trade" and who provided a common cultural source for all black women today.[55]

Steady is careful to point out that she does not want to romanticize African history as she acknowledges that tensions and conflicts existed in Africa as they did elsewhere. Unfortunately, none of these authors explores any of these tensions and conflicts, and, thus, they present an overwhelmingly harmonious picture. Nor do they clearly articulate the ways that they will unearth the cosmology of Africans living in the era of the Atlantic slave trade. Their footnotes do not reveal any sources on this cosmology that go beyond the problematic anthropological reports that give a male-biased view of the past.

While African women's diaspora studies takes us a long way, it reveals some of the same shortcomings I have criticized in the nationalist writings of Asante and Harper-Bolton. These feminists accept the ideology of complementarity as if it signified equal. They rely on a notion of African culture that is based on biased anthropological reports of a static, ahistorical Africa. Finally, they construct a dichotomy between African feminism and western feminism that depends on the Afrocentric spirituality/materialism dichotomy. Clearly, these women advocate women's equality, but they find it much easier to address racism in the women's movement than sexism in black liberation struggles. In their attempt to combine Afrocentric and feminist insights, they recognize the importance of nationalist discourse for countering the hegemonic ideology that seeks to confine African-American lives. But I would go beyond the conservative agenda that nationalists have constructed and, thus, strengthen their advocacy of a feminist discourse.

In the fine special issue of *Signs* on women of color, Patricia Hill Collins has produced one of the most persuasive attempts to combine Afrocentric thought and feminism. In the tradition of Molefi Asante, she recognizes the need to struggle for increased space within the academy for African-American scholars. Although she does not say so explicitly, I read her article in the light of the narrow-minded failure of many academic departments to take Afrocentric scholars seriously and to give African-Americans tenure. In recognition of the serious work many women's studies programs must do to make their classrooms appeal to more than white middle-class students, she tries to sensitize feminists to the worldview that their black students may bring with them to classes but that may be at odds with narrow academic training.

She may have gone too far, however, when she tries to identify an essential black women's standpoint. For Collins, the black women's standpoint has evolved from the experiences of enduring and resisting oppression. Black feminist thought is interdependent with this standpoint as it formulates and rearticulates the distinctive, self-defined standpoint of African-American women.[56] At the same time, black feminist theory intersects with Afrocentric and feminist thought.

For Collins, both Afrocentric and female values emerge out of concrete experience:

> Moreover, as a result of colonialism, imperialism, slavery, apartheid, and other systems of racial domination, Blacks share a common experience of oppression. These similarities in material conditions have fostered shared Afrocentric values that permeate the family structure, religious institutions, culture, and community life of Blacks in varying parts of Africa, the Caribbean, South America, and North America.[57]

Similarly:

> Women share a history of patriarchal oppression through the political economy of the material conditions of sexuality and reproduction. These shared material conditions are thought to transcend divisions among women created by race, social class, religion, sexual orientation, and ethnicity and to form the basis of a women's standpoint with its corresponding feminist consciousness and epistemology.[58]

Thus, the contours of Afrocentric feminist epistemology include black women's material conditions and a combination of Afrocentric and female values. Collins' Afrocentric feminist values share much with the essentialist cultural feminism of Carol Gilligan, including the ethic of caring and the ethic of personal accountability.[59]

Collins builds from the black feminist insight that black women experience oppressions simultaneously. Unfortunately, she remains mired in a false dichotomy that limits the value of this insight. For example, while she recognizes the importance of discussing class, she is unable to keep class as a variable throughout her analysis. At times, she assumes that all white women are middle class and all black women are working class. She sets up working-class black women to comment on the lives of privileged white women:

> Elderly domestic Rosa Wakefield assesses how the standpoints of the powerful [white middle class women] and those who serve them [poor black women] diverge: 'If you eats these dinners and don't cook 'em, if you wears these clothes and don't buy or iron them, then you might start thinking that the good fairy or some spirit did all that. . . . Blackfolks don't have no time to be thinking like that. . . . But when you don't have

anything else to do, you can think like that. It's bad for your mind, though'.[60]

Missing in such accounts is the position of middle-class black women and working-class white women. In Collins' view, all white women have class privilege, although she does recognize that some black women have obtained middle-class status. She admits that "African-American women do not uniformly share an Afrocentric feminist epistemology since social class introduces variations among Black women in seeing, valuing, and using Afrocentric feminist perspectives."[61] She even acknowledges that black women's experiences do not place them in a better position than anyone else to understand oppression.[62] Yet the quintessential black woman is one who has "experienced the greatest degree of convergence of race, class, and gender oppression. . . ."[63] Collins certainly does not raise the possibility that class differences may create tensions within the black sisterhood that she takes as unproblematic.

Ultimately, she falls prey to the positivist social science that she seeks to critique. She links positivist methodology to a Eurocentric masculinist knowledge-validation process that seeks to objectify and distance itself from the "objects" of study.[64] Like Asante, she recognizes many of the shortcomings with mainstream social science research such as the tendency to create false objectivity. Yet also like Asante, she falls into a positivist trap. In her case, she brings her readers back to the possibility of universal truths.

> Those Black feminists who develop knowledge claims that both [Afrocentric and feminist] epistemologies can accommodate may have found a route to the elusive goal of generating so-called objective generalizations that can stand as universal truths.[65]

Like most positivists, she never asks, "whose universal truths are these anyway?" Collins' quest for universal truth will be doomed to failure as long as she accepts as unproblematic an Afrocentric sisterhood across class, time, and geography. Her truths depend on an Afrocentric ideology that suppresses differences among African-Americans.

Like all oppositional discourses, the Afrocentric feminism of Collins, Steady, and Terborg-Penn have multisided struggles. They compete for ideological space against the dominant discourse on Africa, its diaspora, and within feminist and nationalist movements. The dialectics of discursive struggle links their work to dominant discourse and other competing oppositional voices. Both dominant and counter discourses occupy contested terrain. Afrocentric feminists may reveal an almost inescapable tendency in nationalist discourse that ties it to conservative agendas on gender and sexuality. At the same time, they reveal the strengths of nationalist ideology in its counterattack against racism.

NOTES

1. M. Ron Karenga, *The Quotable Karenga* (Los Angeles: US Organization, 1967) excerpted in Richard L. Allen, *Black Awakening in Capitalist America: An Analytic History* (Garden City: Anchor Books, 1970). This article benefited from the careful readings given it by a number of people. I especially want to thank Paulla Ebron, Evelynn Hammonds, Margaret Cerullo, Marla Erlien, and Frank Holmquist. A revised version of this article will appear in my forthcoming book, *Transformations: Race, Gender and Sexuality* to be published by Pandora Press.

2. See Cheryl Clarke, "The Failure to Transform: Homophobia in the Black Community," in *Home Girls: A Black Feminist Anthology*, ed. Barbara Smith (New York: Kitchen Table Press, 1983), pp. 197-208; Audre Lorde, *Sister Outsider: Essays and Speeches* (Trumansburg, N.Y.: Crossing Press, 1984).

3. They only need point to the racist scientific theories that AIDS began in Central Africa from people who ate [subtext: had sex with] green monkeys to prove this point. Spread by the popular and scientific media, this theory appealed to a white culture that still believes that black sexuality is out of control and animalistic. The scientific evidence contributed to the racist subtext of the anti-AIDS hysteria. See Evelynn Hammonds, "Race, Sex, AIDS: The Construction of 'Other,'" *Radical America* 20, no. 6 (1986); and Evelynn Hammonds and Margaret Cerullo, "AIDS in Africa: The Western Imagination and the Dark Continent," *Radical America* 21, nos. 2-3 (1987).

4. E. Frances White, "Civilization Denied: Questions on *Black Athena*," *Radical America* 18, nos. 2-3 (1987): 5.

5. See, for example, Cheikh Anta Diop, *The African Origins of Civilization: Myth or Reality*, trans. Mercer Cook (New York: Lawarence Hill and Company, 1974).

6. Chancellor Williams, *Destruction of African Civilization: Great Issues of a Race from 4500BC to 2000AD* (Chicago: Third World Press, 1974).

7. Larry Delano Coleman, "Black Man/Black Woman: Can the Breach Be Healed?" *The Nile Review* 2, no. 7: 6.

8. Cheryl Clarke, "The Failure to Transform," has raised similar objections in this thoughtful essay. She argues that leftist male intellectuals have helped to institutionalize homophobia in the black community. I refer to this essay in more detail below.

9. Nathan Hare and Julia Hare, "The Rise of Homosexuality and Other Diverse Alternatives," *Black Male/Female Relationships* 5, (1981): 10.

10. George Mosse, *Nationalism and Sexuality: Respectability and Abnormal Sexuality in Modern Europe* (New York: H. Fertig Publishers, 1985).

11. According to George Mosse, *Ibid.*, German nationalists defined certain people as 'outsiders' who did not live up to the norms set up by nationalism and respectability. By labeling homosexuals, prostitutes, Jews, etc. as perverts who lived outside the boundaries of acceptable behavior, nationalists helped build cohesion. Jewish men, for example, were said to epitomize all that was unmanly and unvirile. By contrast, a good, manly German looked on suspiciously at Jewish men. Many of the newly evolving negative identities and classifications fused with the stereotypes of Jews. In this way the rise of National Socialism was inextricably tied to the increase in anti-Semitism.

12. Ron M. Karenga, *Introduction to Black Studies* (Los Angeles: Kawaida Publications, 1982), 213.

13. See Richard Terdiman, *Discourse/Counter-Discourse: The Theory and Practice of Symbolic Resistance in Nineteenth Century France* (Ithaca: Cornell University Press, 1985).

14. Edward W. Said, *Orientalism* (New York: Vintage Books, 1978), 11.

15. Raymond Williams, *Keywords: A Vocabulary of Culture and Society* (London: Fontana, 1976).

16. Johannes Fabian, *Time and the Other: How Anthropology Makes Its Objects* (New York: Columbia University Press, 1983).

17. Terdiman, *Discourse/Counter-Discourse*, 65.

18. *Ibid.*, 36.

19. See James C. Scott, *Weapons of the Weak: Everyday Forms of Peasant Resistance* (New Haven: Yale University Press, 1985). Scott, however, may underemphasize the extent to which people are influenced by dominant hegemonies.

20. Terdiman, *Discourse/Counter-Discourse*, 68.

21. Scott, *Weapons of the Weak*, 338.

22. V.N. Volosinov, *Marxism and the Philosophy of Language*, trans. Ladislav Matejka and I.R. Titunik (New York and London: Seminar Press, 1973), 10.

23. *Ibid.*, 14.

24. Caryl Emerson, "The Outer World and Inner Speech: Bakhtin, Vygotsky and the Internalization of Language," *Bakhtin: Essays and Dialogues on His Work*. ed. Sary Saul Morson (Chicago: Chicago University Press, 1986), 185.

25. Hazel V. Carby, *Reconstructing Womanhood: The Emergence of the Afro-American Woman Novelist* (New York and Oxford: Oxford University Press, 1987), 17.

26. Emerson, "The Outer World and Inner Speech," 185.

27. For further exploration of these ideas, see E. Frances White, "Racisme et sexisme: La confrontation des féministes noires aux formes conjointes de l'oppression," *Les Temps Modernes* 42, no. 485 (December 1986): 173-84.

28. See Lorde, *Sister Outsider*.

29. For examples of white feminists who have been influenced by Audre Lorde's insights, see Barbara Johnson, *A World of Difference* (Baltimore and London: Johns Hopkins University Press, 1987); Teresa de Lauretis, "Feminist Studies/Critical Studies: Issues, Terms and Contexts," in *Feminist Studies/Critical Studies*, T. de Lauretis (Bloomington: Indiana University Press, 1986), 1-19; and de Lauretis, *Technologies of Gender: Essays on Theory, Film, and Fiction* (Bloomington: Indiana University Press, 1987).

30. Cherríe Moraga, *Loving in the War Years: lo que nunca pasá por sus labios* (Boston: South End Press, 1983), 99.

31. See also Gloria Anzaldúa, *Borderlands/La Frontera: The New Mestiza* (San Francisco: Spinster/Aunt Lite, 1987); Norma Alarcón, "Chicana's Feminist Literature: A Re-vision Through Malintzin or Malintzin: Putting Flesh Back on the Object," in *This Bridge Called My Back: Writings by Radical Women of Color*, ed. Cherríe Moraga and Gloria Anzaldúa (Watertown, Mass.: Persephone Press, 1981), 182-90.

32. Clarke, "The Failure to Transform," 207.

33. Carby, *Reconstructing Womanhood*, 17.

34. Charlyn A. Harper-Bolton, "A Reconceptualization of the Black Woman," *Black Male/Female Relationships* 6 (1982), 42.

35. Sylvia Junko Yanagisako, *Transforming the Past: Traditions and Kinship Among Japanese Americans* (Stanford: Stanford University Press, 1985), 18.

36. Molefi Kete Asante, *The Afrocentric Idea* (Philadelphia: Temple University Press, 1987), 8n.3.

37. Molefi Kete Asante, "Editor's Note," *Journal of Black Studies* 8, no. 2 (1977): 123.

38. *Ibid.*, 123.

39. See Asante, *The Afrocentric Idea*.

40. V.Y. Mudimbe, *The Invention of Africa: Gnosis, Philosophy, and the Order of Knowledge* (Bloomington: Indiana University Press, 1985), 75-92.

41. *Ibid.*, 89.

42. Asante, *Afrocentric Idea*, 8.

43. Allen, *Black Awakening in Capitalist America.*

44. See Karenga, *Introduction to Black Studies.*

45. Harper-Bolton, "A Reconceptualization of the Black Woman," 32.

46. *Ibid.*, 40.

47. See John Mbiti, *African Religion and Philosophy* (Garden City: Doubleday, 1970) and Wade Nobles, "Africanity: Its Role in Black Families," *Black Scholar* 5, no. 9 (1974).

48. Rosalind Coward, *Patriarchal Precedents: Sexuality and Social Relations* (London: Routledge & Kegan Paul, 1983).

49. A.R. Radcliffe-Brown and Daryll Forde, *African Systems of Kinship and Marriage* (London: Oxford University Press, 1950), 84-5.

50. Martin Chanock, "Making Customary Law: Men, Women, and Courts in Colonial Northern Rhodesia," *African Women and the Law: Historical Perspectives*, ed. Margaret Jean Hay and Marcia Wright (Boston: Boston University Press 1982), 60.

51. See Harper-Bolton, "Reconceptualization of the Black Woman," 38.

52. *Ibid.*, 41.

53. Filomina Chioma Steady, "African Feminism: A Worldwide Perspective," *Women in Africa and the African Diaspora*, ed. Rosalyn Terborg-Penn, Andrea Rushing, and Sharon Harley (Washington, D.C.: Howard University Press, 1987), 8.

54. Rosalyn Terborg-Penn, "African Feminism: A Theoretical Approach to the History of Women in the African Diaspora," *Women in Africa and the African Diaspora*, ed. Terborg-Penn, Rushing and Harley, 49.

55. *Ibid.*, 49; see also Steady, "African Feminism"; and Steady, "The Black Woman Cross-Culturally: An Overview," *The Black Woman Cross-Culturally* (Cambridge: Schenkman Publishing Co., 1981), 7-48.

56. Patricia Hill Collins, "The Social Construction of Black Feminist Thought," *Signs: Journal of Women in Culture and Society* 14, no. 4 (1989): 750.

57. *Ibid.*, 755.

58. *Ibid.*, 755.

59. See Carol Gilligan, *In a Different Voice* (Cambridge: Harvard University Press, 1982).

60. Collins, "Social Construction of Black Feminist Thought," 748-49.

61. *Ibid.*, 758.

62. *Ibid.*, 757.

63. *Ibid.*, 758.

64. Ironically she shows how difficult it is to separate out knowledge-validation processes when she argues that we have to use different techniques to study Black women than to study the powerful at the same time that much of her analysis depends on the insights of white men such as Peter L. Berger and Thomas Luckmann, *The Social Construction of Reality* (New York: Doubleday, 1966).

65. Collins, "Social Construction of Black Feminist Thought," 773.

WHOSE SATI?
WIDOW-BURNING IN EARLY NINETEENTH-CENTURY INDIA

Anand A. Yang

Intentionally interrogatory, the title of this essay emphasizes the speculative nature of my remarks regarding the phenomenon of sati. Derived from the Sanskrit term for pure or chaste (*sat*)—the very term "sati," therefore, is a misnomer—sati has come to signify both the act of immolation of a wife on the funeral pyre of her husband (in some areas a widow was buried with her deceased husband or took poison) and the victim herself rather than its original meaning of "a virtuous woman."[1] Generally, a woman was burnt together with her deceased husband, a practice termed *sahamarana* or *sahagamana* (dying together with). But if concremation was not possible, such as when a husband died in a distant place or a woman's pregnancy required that she wait till after delivery, a sati conformed to the practice of *anumarana* or *anugamana*: burning with the husband's ashes or with some other memento representing him, for example, his sandals, turban, or piece of clothing.[2]

The title also has another meaning, a double trajectory: an interrogation of the historical literature on the subject and an interrogation of sati as a practice involving women of different times, places, and backgrounds. Both lines of inquiry seek to converge on the same objective: better questions *and* answers regarding the phenomenon of sati.

Hitherto, much of the literature on sati has tended to favor an institutional approach.[3] Not surprisingly, the most familiar aspect of sati is the British campaign against it culminating in the promulgation of Regulation XVII in 1829 "declaring the practice of suttee, or of burning or burying alive the widows of Hindus, illegal and punishable by the criminal courts."[4] Viewed from this angle, the history of sati has been appropriated by some scholars to represent the beginnings of "a deliberate policy of modernizing and westernizing Indian society," as embodied in the person

© 1989 JOURNAL OF WOMEN'S HISTORY, VOL. 1 NO. 2 (FALL)

and policies of Governor-General Lord Bentinck who directed the official campaign against sati, and in the emergence of a Bengal "Renaissance" under the guiding hand of the "Father of Modern India," Raja Rammohun Roy, who acted as the Indian architect of this and other social reforms.[5]

The legislative prohibition of sati has also "become a founding moment in the history of women in modern India." To continue in the words of this scholar,

> colonial rule, with its moral civilizing claims, is said to have provided the contexts for a thoroughgoing re-evaluation of Indian "tradition" along lines more consonant with the "modern" economy and society believed to have been the consequence of India's incorporation into the capitalist world system. In other words, even the most anti-imperialist amongst us has felt forced to acknowledge the "positive" consequences of colonial rule for certain aspects of women's lives, if not in terms of actual practice, at least at the level of ideas about "women's rights."[6]

But as Lata Mani's deconstruction of the colonial discourse on sati reveals, women were neither the subjects nor the objects of this discourse, "but rather the grounds of the discourse on *sati.* . . . For the British, rescuing women becomes part of the civilizing mission. For the indigenous elite, protection of their status or its reform becomes an urgent necessity, in terms of the honor of the collective—religious or national."[7]

For the political and ideological context in which the government campaign for social reforms was waged, whether focusing on sati, infanticide, *thagi* (ritual murder), or human sacrifice, aimed at entitling the British with the right to proclaim the superiority of their own values, and ultimately, to justify their right to rule. Only they could usher in the morality they found wanting in the indigenous civilization. Consider the tenor of the following government pronouncement on sati:

> Of the rite itself, of its horror and abomination not a word need be said. Every rational and civilized being must feel anxious for the termination of a practice so abhorrent from humanity. . . . But to the christian and to the Englishman, who by tolerating sanctions, and by sanctioning incurs before God the responsibility of this inhuman and impious sacrifice not of one, but of thousands of victims, these feelings of anxiety must be and ought to be extreme. The whole and sole justification is state necessity— that is, the security of the British empire, and even that justification, would be, if at all, still very incomplete, if upon the continuance of the British rule did not entirely depend the future happiness and improvement of the numerous population of this eastern world.[8]

In part, the prevailing modes of inquiry have fashioned their own blinders because they have not until recently sought to penetrate the purdah of rhetoric imposed on sati, whether that made out of the fabric of discourse woven from the religious ideology sanctioning its practice, or that stitched together from the doctrines of policy makers and reformers seeking its abolition. In part, the peculiar emphases in the literature on sati reflect the predominant orientation of South Asian studies towards conventional political history rather than the "new" social history.[9]

No wonder the history of sati is still being written—or perhaps better stated, being revised. And the fact that its full reconstruction is only now being attempted reflects not only the biases and limitations of the historical record but also of historians. Enough has been uncovered by the new scholarship to establish, as does the discussion below of sati as "an invented and reinvented tradition," that the practice can no longer be merely ascribed to and explained away as a "tradition" rooted in an immemorial past. On the contrary, recent scholarship has treated it more as an "invented tradition" whose origins can be roughly dated and whose construction, institution, and development can be traced over historical time.

Another perspective, largely absent in the literature, is the focus on the human face of sati: neither the identities of those who committed sati, nor their reasons for seeking "virtue" in death has received much attention. A notable exception—although raising more questions than providing answers—is the work of Ashis Nandy which unequivocally states that not only did the incidence of sati rise sharply in the late 18th century because of the effects of the British presence on certain sectors of Bengali society but also that the considerable surge can be traced to the upper-caste Bengali gentry (*bhadralok*) who resorted to sati as a means of compensating for the social and cultural price they paid for abiding by the new rules established by the British system rather than the traditionally prescribed norms. According to this psychocultural interpretation, "the rite had anxiety-binding functions in groups rendered psychologically marginal by their exposure to western impact. These groups had come under pressure to demonstrate . . . their ritual purity and allegiance to traditional high culture. To many of them sati became an important proof of their conformity to older norms at a time when these norms had become shaky within."[10]

This essay will attempt to identify the faces of sati victims by highlighting their social and economic conditions and circumstances. Such a characterization intends to examine the practice of sati as part of the fabric of the local society in which the widows lived, and such a portrait seeks to draw us closer to the subjects themselves and their subjectivity in playing out their lives as satis. Because of limitations of data, however, a complete portrait of the victims is not possible; the best close-up of these otherwise invisible women can only put faces on them, faces whose features can be partially filled in by considering their act as an "option" bound by economic, social, and religious constraints.[11] The specific reasons for their sacrifice, however, cannot be fully determined from their perspective because their voices have not been preserved in historical documents; in fact, they appear largely as mute objects even in the most detailed of sources—colonial records of the early 19th century. Indeed, even their names have been "grotesquely mistranscribed." To continue in the words of Gayatri C. Spivak, "one never encounters the testimony of the women's voice-consciousness. Such a testimony would not be ideology-transcendent or 'fully' subjective, of course; but it would have constituted the ingredients for producing a counter sentence. As one goes [through] the records of the East India Company, one cannot put together a 'voice.' "[12]

In order to develop a more sharply focused portrait, this essay will rely on a local-level perspective based on data from the Bengal Presidency, an area which returned the highest reported cases of sati in British India. An extensive territory stretching across northeastern and northern India, this area (then encompassing the present-day Indian states of west Bengal, Bihar, Orissa, Uttar Pradesh [U.P.], and the new nation of Bangladesh) also represented a diversity of local contexts because it included several distinct cultural, linguistic, historical, and structural regions. Most studies regarding sati in Bengal have concentrated their attention on Bengal proper, particularly the area focusing on the metropolitan center of Calcutta—Calcutta Division reported the highest number of satis in the Presidency. This essay, however, will also consider the local contexts of sati in the Gangetic plain area in the western peripheries of the Presidency, the Bhojpur-speaking region. In the Bhojpur districts of Gorakhpur and Ghazipur in U.P., Saran and Shahabad in Bihar, and, to a lesser extent, in the premier city of the region, Banaras, the incidence of sati reached such significant proportions that only in Calcutta Division were there a greater number of cases.[13]

The Documentary Basis of Sati

Data exist to compile a portrait, albeit incomplete, of the many faces of sati in the early 19th century. As Bayly notes, "the British obsession with sati was boundless. Thousands of pages of Parliamentary papers were given up to 4,000 immolations while the mortality of millions from disease and starvation was only mentioned incidentally."[14] But these accounts "cannot be read as photographic representations of reality" because they reflected the "anxieties of the new rulers as much as of a practice of the people . . . ruled."[15]

The documentary basis for this essay is the data collected annually on sati in British India prior to its prohibition in 1829. Drawn from local-level police records, much of the information for the period between 1815 and 1829 was compiled into parliamentary papers for the scrutiny of the authorities in England. District judicial and police records, were they to exist in their entirety, of course, would offer the most comprehensive offi-

cial inventory of sati cases. Eyewitness accounts of sati can be found both
in official reports and in contemporary memoirs and travelogues.

To track the growing British interest in documenting the phenomenon
of sati is not only to comprehend the biases of the source materials but also
to see the gradual development of a policy. From Poona in western India,
from Banaras, and from Shahabad, in 1787, 1788, and 1789, respectively,
came the first official reports of widow-burning.[16] In response to the
Shahabad administrator who had informed the authorities of his intervention in a sati case because he had mistakenly thought that the practice had
been disallowed in the Calcutta area, government spelled out its initial
position on sati. Although approving his actions, government directed
him, in future, to "exert all his private influence to dissuade," but not "to
prevent the observance of it by coercive measures, or by any exertion of his
official powers."[17]

Because official documentation was only kept if a sati raised questions
relating to government policy and procedure, or to other matters requiring administrative attention,[18] systematic data do not exist for the early
years of British rule although some local officials kept records of incidents
they encountered in the course of their administrative rounds. Some sati
reports also appeared in other guises. For instance, an 1801 account of a
"desperate affray" involving several hundred armed men in Shahabad,
although filed as a record of a "heinous crime," reports not only of the
death of 16 men in the fighting but the subsequent satis of four widows.[19]

Sati surfaced again as an issue in 1803-04 when the missionary William
Carey produced reports documenting the incidence of sati in the Calcutta
area. Although appalled by the missionary accounts, and eager to prohibit
the practice, Governor-General Lord Wellesley deferred taking decisive
action in 1805 by turning the matter over for the consideration of the legal
authorities.[20]

Until the promulgation of Regulation XVII of 1829, the main principles
of the official policy on sati emanated from a directive issued by the
Nizamat Adalat (head criminal court) in 1805. In providing the
"guidance" sought by a district magistrate who had rescued a 12-year-old
girl from burning with her deceased husband, the Nizamat Adalat refused
to outlaw sati on the grounds that such a step was "impracticable at the
present time" and inconsistent "with the principle invariably observed by
the British government, of manifesting every possible indulgence to the
religious opinions and prejudices of the natives." This court also
expressed concern about stirring up "alarm and dissatisfaction in the
minds of the Hindoo inhabitants of these provinces."[21] Nevertheless, it
asked judicial officials to secure advance notice of the occurrence of a sati,
then to depute police officers to proceed personally to the site of the burning in order to ensure that the rite was performed voluntarily and not
under the influence of intoxicants or drugs, and to establish that the

"youth" or the "state of pregnancy" of a widow did not violate the norms of "tradition."[22]

In enacting these procedures, however, government invariably played its hand cautiously, consulting with its Hindu pandits before setting up any rules regulating sati. Thus, the parameters of a "legal" sati were drawn with the assistance of Pandit "Ghunesham Surmono" who informed the Court: "Every woman of the four cast[e]s (brahmin, khetry, bues, and soodur) is permitted to burn herself with the body of her husband. . . . No woman having infant children, or being in a state of pregnancy, uncleanness, or under the age of puberty is permitted to burn with her husband; with the following exception, namely, that if a woman having infant children can provide for their support, through the means of another person, she is permitted to burn."[23]

The issue of sati returned to the political limelight in 1812 when a local administrator sought instructions on "whether a magistrate ought to take any and what steps to prevent Hindoo females from sacrificing themselves on the funeral piles of their husbands."[24] The *Nizamat Adalat*'s rejoinder was to revive its 1805 statement—largely a dead letter until then, to redraft the earlier instructions into "Directions to be issued by Magistrates to the Police Daroghas," and to insert an additional proviso into the Draft specifying 16 years as the age of puberty.[25] Government also took this opportunity to remind local officials of its earlier orders enjoining them to gather information on satis occurring in their jurisdictions.

From a statistical and documentary viewpoint, systematic records begin in 1815 when annual reports on satis indicated name (of widow), age, caste, name and caste of husband, date of burning, name of police jurisdiction, and in a separate column entitled "Remarks," "any particular circumstances in the report of the police officers, which may appear to deserve notice."[26] The "Remarks" column allowed local officials to note whether or not a sati was legal by government's definition. Beginning in 1821, information was also gathered on the kind of sati committed: *sahamarana* or *anumarana*. The purpose behind this directive was to ensure that the customary and legal prohibition (first enacted in 1817) against Brahmin widows committing sati by *anumarana* was being enforced. Prior to the outright ban in 1829 the British strategy was to restrict the practice by tightening up the definition of a "legal" sati—a definition for which they invariably sought and received the sanction of their "authoritative" Indian advisers. In 1821 information on the economic backgrounds of the deceased husband was also collected; by 1824 data on husbands became a regular feature of sati reports.[27]

After the prohibition of sati in 1829, no doubt its practice did not fall into disuse entirely, although government vigilance and enforcement of severe punishments for offenders must have sharply reduced the number. Cases of sati also tapered off dramatically because the official ban on it—notwithstanding the fact that the implementation of legal sanctions was entrusted to a weak administrative infrastructure—proved to be enough of a blow to shake the foundations of an institution that enjoyed greater support in the spirit than in the actual practice; the number of widows who resorted to immolation never amounted to a sizable proportion of the population. Furthermore, the attack on sati was launched with the active cooperation of Indian reformers. Thus, in the initial years after its prohibition, as police and crime reports indicate, the numbers were quickly down to only one or two in districts where there had formerly been considerably more.[28]

Sati: An Invented and Reinvented Tradition[29]

The Vedas, the religious hymns constituting the earliest literature of the Aryans who arrived in India in the centuries after 1700 B.C., reveal no evidence of sati. The Rig Veda, however, refers to an act, appropriately termed a "mimetic ceremony" where a "widow lay on her husband's funeral pyre before it was lit but was raised from it by a male relative of her dead husband."[30] A later, and probably deliberate, mistranslation (perhaps in the 16th century) was made in order to attain "Vedic sanction for the act [of sati] by changing the word *agre*, to go forth into *agneh*, to the fire, in the specific verse."[31]

That sati was not a practice in vogue in the early Vedic period is also suggested by the occurrences of widow remarriages which, apparently, were not uncommon. Vedic texts, furthermore, indicate the existence of a system of *niyoga* or levirate whereby a widow without male heirs was allowed to marry her husband's brother, an act designed to consolidate property.[32]

Nor is sati featured in the literature that developed in the wake of the Vedas, whether the Hindu expository texts stemming from the period 1,000 to 500 B.C. or the early Buddhist literature. Sati makes an occasional appearance in the popular religious texts of early Hinduism, the epics, but these are works that developed by continuous accretion over a thousand-year period beginning in fifth century B.C.; some of the references to sati, moreover, have been attributed to later interpolations. Nor is there a clear-cut endorsement of sati in the prescriptive literature dating to the beginning of the Christian era. The codes associated with the names of Manu and Yajnavalkya, considered among the most authoritative of Hindu law books, for instance, prescribe austere and chaste lives for widows but issue no specific injunctions for them to become satis. Increasingly, however, in the first millennium A.D., for instance, in the popular texts of later Hinduism, the Puranas, sati is mentioned as an option for widows. But so is a life of asceticism; other texts of this period, however, glorified sati.[33]

The "virtue" of this practice was ostensibly defined by a religious logic that deemed a widow inauspicious for having outlived her husband—an abnormal circumstance said to have been brought about by her sinful nature in this, or a previous, life. A life of ascetic discipline could diminish the stigma with which widowhood branded her, but she was, nevertheless, considered a spiritual hazard to all around her except her own children. Closely related to this idea was the belief that an unattached woman, a woman without a husband, for instance, constituted a grave danger to her community because of the supposedly irrepressible sexual powers she possessed, a capacity which always had the potential to disrupt her ritually-prescribed life of austerity. No wonder at least one writer has considered sati "an expression of the perceived superfluity of women who were considered unmarriageable in a social context where marriage was the only approved status for women."[34] By becoming a sati, furthermore, a widow not only ended the threat she posed to the spiritual welfare of others but also reaped honor and merit—according to some religious texts enough to last 35 million years—for herself, her husband, and the families of her husband, her mother, and her father.[35]

The fact that sati is not featured in the earliest religious texts and is referred to infrequently in the later literature leading up to the Christian era is supported by historical information that tracks the first instance of sati only back to the fourth century B.C. Such a chronology also reflects the changing status of women in Indian society. Although the characterization of the Vedic Age between 1700 and 500 B.C. as a "golden age for women" is debatable, the decline in their status in the centuries thereafter is less a matter of dispute. As a recent review of the literature on women in South Asia notes, "by 500 B.C. women were increasingly assigned the same low status as *sudras*, forbidden to wear the sacred thread, and excluded from the performance of sacrifice either as priests or as partners with their husbands."[36]

But to attribute the rise of sati solely to the declining status of women— a position that eventuated ideologically in the model of a dutiful wife and of sati as the ultimate wifely act of duty—is to overstate the equation; nor does it adequately explain its uneven geographical spread. Just as sati lacked clear-cut scriptural authority, so too did the paradigm of dutiful wife that represented only one construct of the feminine in Hindu ideology and, at that, one emanating from the priestly tradition of Brahmanic Hinduism. Hinduism, "a composite of religious traditions in which diverse philosophical, sectarian, and cultic movements are loosely associated," has historically comprised two distinct ideological traditions: "brahmanic Hinduism [that] has tended to objectify and exclude women . . . [and] nonbrahmanic Hindu traditions [that] have tended to provide for full recognition and active participation by women."[37]

Furthermore, as Romila Thapar states, although the beginnings of sati can be "traced to the subordination of women in patriarchal society," changing "systems of kinship and inheritance" and "[c]ontrol over female sexuality" were also factors in the rise of widow immolation. Moreover, the "practice may have originated among societies in flux and become customary among those holding property such as the families of chiefs and kshatriyas. Once it was established as a custom associated with the kshatriyas it would continue to be so among those claiming kshatriya status as well."[38]

Principally associated with high status and rank during its early history, particularly with families of kingly or warrior (Kshatriya) status or those aspiring for such status, sati, according to another version, became more widespread during the Muslim period when invasions and conquests precipitated its development as a means of preserving the honor of Hindu women. Its rise, in this interpretation, is therefore typically linked to "wars of conquest and their inevitable toll on the women of the defeated groups."[39] But evidence exists from western and southern India indicating that women were becoming satis in appreciable numbers well before the advent of Muslim rule; in some areas, the peaks in numbers were reached in the pre-Islamic period. According to one scholar, inscriptional and archaeological sources, including sati stones erected at the sites of immolation, suggest that the practice was increasing towards the end of the first and the beginning of the second millennium A.D. This rise, moreover, occurred in areas characterized by internal conquests and competition, often involving traditional castes, newly-emergent castes, and tribal groups. In this setting, competition for status may have made upper-caste practices such as sati more prevalent. That is, sati became valorized as a practice—a practice emphasizing the subordination of women—as groups with different conceptions regarding the status of women encountered one another. Thus, widow immolation "may have been . . . a method of demarcating status."[40]

The spread of sati across caste boundaries must also have been generated by Sanskritization—the process whereby lower castes aspire for higher position by emulating the "customs, rituals, ideology, and way of life" of higher castes. Although the effect of Sanskritization is evident from the enormous range of castes who performed sati, the practice never became generalized throughout the subcontinent but was confined to certain areas: in the north, particularly to the Gangetic Valley, Punjab, and Rajasthan; in the west, to the southern Konkan region; and in the south, to Madurai and Vijayanagar.[41]

Whether its rise can be attributed to groups aspiring for Kshatriya status or of lower castes emulating the rituals of higher castes, sati clearly developed as a reinvented tradition, a tradition no longer confined to warrior widows whose husbands had died in battle. A crucial development in this regard may have been its adoption by Brahmins who, according to some religious texts, were specifically prohibited from taking up this practice.[42] Perhaps the Brahmin appropriation of this warrior practice represented yet another round in the ongoing "inner conflict of tradition" that J.C. Heesterman regards as the "pivot of Indian tradition": the "irreconcilability of 'brahmin' and 'king,' who yet are dependent on each other, for the king will need the transcendent legitimation that only the brahmin can give. But the brahmin, however much he may need the king's material support, cannot enter into relations with the king, for this would involve him in the world of interdependence—a situation that would be fatal to the brahmin's transcendence."[43] Surely, with the practice rooted in both the kingly and Brahminical traditions, its constituency must have grown rapidly across spatial and social boundaries.

Certainly, in Bengal, where sati dates back to at least the 12th century A.D., Brahmins figured prominently among its practitioners. But from very early on, as vernacular sources indicate, it was not restricted to Brahmins, but observed by both upper and lower castes.[44] Perhaps its rise in Bengal was not unrelated to the growing reliance on marriage in the period between 1450 and 1800 as "the way to sustain rank and the path to fame [for upper castes—Brahmins and Kayasths]."[45] And, as the emphasis on marriage intensified, so must have the importance of sati as its structural concomitant. Not surprisingly, Brahmins took to this practice in great numbers; so did merchants and the writer caste of Kayasths who sought to emulate the ritual observances of the Brahmins. And once elevated to new heights as a status-conferring ritual, the next step was its practice by lower—artisan and entrepreneurial—castes who saw it as an avenue for attaining prestige and status in society.[46]

A practice once tied to the warrior ideal of the Kshatriya thus became a tradition appropriated by all of society. But in the process of widening its constituency, as the evidence from Bengal shows, sati emerged as a reinvented tradition. How novel the reinvented tradition was—assuming that the old tradition really was guided by a heroic ideal—is apparent from looking at sati in its "new" context, a context in which it figures as an "option" bound by the economic, social, and religious constraints of widowhood.[47]

Sati: Subjects and Subjectivity

Abraham Caldecott, writing in 1783, stated that had he not seen a sati with his own eyes he would "have been apt to doubt the veracity of it, but the fact is so well established, and so many instances of the like nature have occurred . . . as leaves no doubt of the generality of the Practice all over Bengal."[48] A few "hard" estimates reinforce this impression of the "generality of the Practice" for the pre-1815 period. William Carey's investigations in a 30-mile radius of Calcutta in 1803-04 showed that as many as 438 widows had committed sati over a 12-month period.[49] District records can also provide some information for the pre-1815 years, but if the numbers ·for Saran are any indication, these may not be reliable. For 1812, 1813, and 1814, Saran returned one, two, and five cases—a far cry from the 15 noted for 1815 when the administrative machinery was geared to the task of collecting such information. In the magistrate's words, the police did not pay attention "to cases of this nature, and it is most probable that a small part only of those that actually took place . . . were reported."[50] Much more consonant with later statistics is the estimate for Burdwan district that 114 cases occurred in 1811-12 and 1812-13.[51] Statistical investigations conducted in Bengal at roughly this same period reported an average of 25 satis a year for Shahabad and 13 for Gorakhpur.[52]

In the 10 years between 1815 and 1824, 6,632 cases of sati were reported for the three Presidencies of Bengal, Bombay, and Madras. Of these, 5,997 (90.4 percent) occurred in Bengal.[53] In the 14 years between 1815 and 1828 (Table 1), a grand total of 8,134 cases of sati were reported for the Bengal Presidency. But as the data reveal, the practice was not uniformly observed across the region but predominated in specific areas. The division of Calcutta alone accounted for 5,119 cases, or almost 63 percent of the Presidency total, followed by Banaras, Dacca, and Patna divisions in a distant second, third, and fourth position, respectively.

TABLE 1
Sati Cases in Bengal Presidency, 1815-1828

Division:	1815	1816	1817	1818	1819	1820	1821	1822	1823	1824	1825	1826	1827	1828	Total
Calcutta*	253	289	442	544	421	370	392	328	340	373	398	324	337	308	5119
Dacca	31	24	52	58	55	51	52	45	40	40	101	65	49	47	710
Murshidabad	11	22	42	30	25	21	11	22	13	14	21	8	9	10	260
Patna†	20	29	49	57	40	42	69	70	49	42	38	43	55	55	689
Banaras	48	65	103	137	92	93	114	102	121	93	64	70	49	33	1153
Bareilly	15	13	19	13	17	20	15	16	12	10	17	8	18	10	203
Total:	378	442	707	839	650	597	654	583	575	572	639	518	517	463	8134

Source: Compiled from Great Britain, Parliament, *Parliamentary Papers* (hereafter *PP*), *1821, 1823, 1824, 1825, 1826/27, 1830;* Amitabha Mukhopadhyay, "Sati as a Social Institution in Bengal," *Bengal Past and Present* 76 (1951): 106.

* Includes the numbers for the Orissan "districts" of Cuttack, Khurda, Puri, and Balasore, which then formed part of Calcutta division. The totals for these districts varied from 9 in 1815 to a high of 45 in 1825.

† The tallies for Gorakhpur have been retained in the Banaras totals although that district was transferred to Patna Division in 1824.

Further geographical breakdown of these figures show (Table 2) that sati was practiced throughout the districts of Calcutta division, but unevenly elsewhere. In the predominantly Muslim Dacca Division in east Bengal, it was primarily confined to Dacca City, Tipperah, and Bakarganj—areas with large Hindu populations; in Banaras, the highest incidence was in Ghazipur and Gorakhpur; and in Patna Division, in Saran and Shahabad. Indeed, 90 percent of the total cases reported for the Presidency occurred in the nine jurisdictions of Calcutta Division (which included Cuttack at this time) and the above-mentioned areas of east Bengal, U.P., and Bihar.

TABLE 2
Sati Cases in Districts of Bengal Presidency, 1815-1826

Presidency Division:	1815	1816	1817	1818	1819	1820	1821	1822	1823	1824	1825	1826	Average
Burdwan	50	67	98	132	75	57	62	40	45	56	63	45	**66**
Hughli	72	51	112	141	115	93	95	79	81	91	104	98	**94**
Jessore	7	13	21	23	16	25	31	21	14	30	16	3	**18**
Jungle Mehals	34	39	43	61	31	18	39	24	27	16	9	11	**29**
Midnapur	4	11	7	22	13	12	6	16	15	22	22	15	**14**
Nadia	50	56	85	80	47	59	59	50	59	79	60	44	**61**
Suburbs of Calcutta	25	40	39	43	52	47	39	43	46	34	48	35	**41**
24-Parganas	2	3	20	31	39	26	33	25	21	22	26	20	**22**
Cuttack†	9	9	14	11	33	33	28	27	30	24	30	45	**24**
Dacca Division:													
Dacca City	4	6	18	25	15	18	26	9	14	7	18	12	**14**
Tipperah	20	7	13	22	21	17	11	6	9	6	8	4	**12**
Bakarganj	no figures available				6	3	3	18	11	23	63	45	**21**
Patna Division:													
Saran	12	16	25	23	10	11	15	12	7	12	15	10	**14**
Shahabad	4	9	14	25	17	19	39	36	30	18	20	22	**21**
Banaras Division:													
Banaras City	13	12	16	15	18	11	12	10	18	16	17	15	**14**
Ghazipur	8	15	27	43	26	34	35	48	55	33	21	19	**30**
Gorakhpur	14	23	24	50	23	32	44	28	32	17	9	22	**26**

Source: Compiled from *PP, 1821, 1823, 1824, 1825, 1826/27, 1830.*

Notwithstanding the bold arguments of Ashis Nandy, little evidence exists to suggest that a considerable surge in incidence of sati occurred beginning in the late 18th century. That sati increased with the coming of the British rests on a statistical inference for which Nandy can muster little evidence other than to refer to a few contemporary observations to that effect. Not only is the pre-1815 data scanty, but even the usable "hard numbers" are fraught with problems. Although sati was by its very nature a public act—for "virtue" in that practice lay in part in exposing it to the gaze of a crowd—the emerging colonial government simply did not possess the administrative apparatus to extend far into any locality and, certainly, not to maintain a regular presence in the interior. Furthermore, with much of the personnel of the incipient Raj lodged in cities, and in a major town or two in localities where there were no cities, reporting was only as good as the administrative infrastructure. In short, the inherent biases built into the system of reporting favored better coverage for towns than countryside, and, not surprisingly, nowhere was official representation better than in the heart of the emerging empire—Calcutta. Indeed, in some districts, away from metropolitan centers, local officials did not even make their first visit into the interior until 1815![54]

The social geography of sati (see Table 2) also indicates that the practice was not confined to the Calcutta area, but also prevailed in such districts far removed from the seat of the Presidency as Ghazipur, Gorakhpur, Saran, and Shahabad. Furthermore, to consider sati as an urban-based phenomenon centered on Calcutta ignores the sizable territorial dimensions of Calcutta Division. Nandy's critics have rightly noted that even Raja Rammohan Roy's family village "which may nowadays feel like 'greater Calcutta' . . . is about sixty miles away as the crow flies, and before the railway age, when that distance took many hours to traverse, it was considered quite another area."[55]

To explain the higher incidence of sati in the Calcutta area, Nandy offers a cultural analysis emphasizing that city's close integration into the British system and its urban-ness, characteristics he contrasts with other parts of India where the practice was less common. Thus, he concludes that "the rite was prevalent among passive people and not among the 'bold and manly' type," an assertion which prompts him to emphasize "the difference between the exposed easterners [Bengalis], feeling increasingly impotent ritually, and the unexposed northern and western parts of India, still mainly outside direct British rule and yet undisturbed in their traditional life style. It was also noticed by others that there had been only one instance of the wife of a dead Indian soldier of the colonial army committing sati."[56] In elaborating on why he considers only one case of sati by a sepoy's wife "crucial," Nandy writes:

> given that (1) traditionally sati had been associated with the so called martial races, (2) the British Indian Army was drawn almost entirely from these races, and (3) the earlier epidemics of sati (such as the one in Rajasthan towards the end of the Mughal period and the one in South India during the decline of the Vijayanagar kingdom) had a clear kshatriya (martial or princely caste) connection. Offset these against the facts that Bengal did not have a proper kshatriya caste and that the region was marginal to mainstream Hinduism, and one is forced to conclude that the eighteenth century epidemic of sati was not a pure product of traditions and that it drew upon a different configuration of political, cultural and psychological forces.[57]

The post-1823 sati reports, which contain information on the profession of deceased husbands, however, do not support the assertion that only one dead sepoy's wife committed sati. Since the "martial races" recruited into the Bengal Army were drawn not from the heart of the Presidency but from the Bhojpur region, it is in the data for those areas that the best prospects lie for finding cases of sati among the widows of sepoys. The information for Shahabad—a district which supplied a considerable number of men for the military—does not disappoint. Names of sepoy widows who burnt themselves appear repeatedly on its sati rosters: in 1824 Mussamut Dela, wife of Naik Tiwari, Brahmin, and M. Somerin, wife of Sahi Rai; in 1825 Nagbansi, wife of Adhir Singh, Rajput, Jethun, Brahmin, wife of Bissambhar Ojha, and Hisabea, wife of Raghubans Rai, Bhumihar Brahmin; in 1826 Musst. Fakania, Rajput, Musst. Dhupia, Rajput, and Musst. Abhi Lakhi, Brahmin.[58]

Nandy may be right, however, in insisting that sati was rooted in a different tradition in the region of Bengal focusing on Calcutta. Certainly, the notion of sati in the Bhojpur region seems to have had much of a "kshatriya connection" as evidenced not only in the roster of victims above but also in the above-mentioned account of a "desperate affray" in Shahabad in which 16 men were killed and four widows committed sati subsequently. Consider also the place of pride given to the tradition of sati in the Choudhary family, a Patna family of Bhumihar Brahmins with a long history of military service.[59]

Some scholars have also sought to relate the high incidence of sati (and female infanticide) in Bengal to the extreme hypergamy of the higher castes (*kulinism*), the practice whereby women of high castes had to marry men of equivalent or higher status. Presumably, this practice so restricted the pool of appropriate bridegrooms that a few eligible high caste males were able to accumulate many, often young, wives for whom the demise of their husband left no choice but for them to commit sati. The evidence regarding the geographical distribution of sati in Bengal, however, offers little conclusive proof because rates of sati were higher in the west than in the east (more in Calcutta than Dacca division), whereas kulinism was more predominant in the east than in the west.[60]

Another argument has been to relate the high incidence of sati to the existing system of law in Bengal, the *Dayabagha* school of law. In contrast to the *Mitakshara* school of law, the *Dayabagha* school allowed widows greater access to their deceased husbands' property for support although it did not favor their rights of inheritance. Whereas this "might have encouraged heirs to do away with widows or to pressurize them into suicide" and may therefore explain the "numbers of satis in Bengal by comparison with other parts of India . . . it hardly explains the great variation of incidence between the different districts and cities of Bengal."[61]

Some correspondence can be established, however, between incidence of sati and mortality rates: "There is no doubt that the rite was a primitive Malthusian means of population control in famine-ridden Bengal. Previously, high mortality rates and prohibition of remarriage of widows had helped the society to limit the number of mothers to below the level of available fertile women. However, at times of scarcity, these controls became inadequate and . . . the widows at certain levels of consciousness seemed 'useless' drags on resources."[62] But if sati were "a Malthusian form of population control, stimulated by a series of crop failures and widespread famines," as G. Morris Carstairs notes, "it would surely have resulted in higher rates among the poorer castes, less well protected against starvation, than among the gentry."[63]

Much more significant is the correlation between changing rates of sati and shifts in mortality rates due to epidemics. Consider especially the increase in numbers of sati during peak years of cholera epidemics: in Bengal this occurred in 1817 and 1818 when cholera had a devastating effect on mortality rates (see Table 1). The close correspondence between the geography of the epidemic and sati rates in affected districts further demonstrates this correlation. Note that the unusual rise in cases of sati in 1817 and 1818 was registered primarily in Calcutta Division—in and around Calcutta, Burdwan, Jessore, Nadia, and 24-Parganas—precisely those areas that were also the most seriously afflicted by cholera.[64] In other parts of the Presidency, too, where increases, although not on a par with those for Calcutta Division, were registered for 1817 and 1818, local officials attributed the rise "to the mortality occasioned by the epidemic."[65] Much the same conclusion was reached by the Banaras magistrate who plotted the rise in sati cases in his city in 1823, 1824, and 1825 with the "extreme sickness and mortality" of those years.[66] Similarly, the noticeable increase in satis in Dacca Division in 1825, especially in Bakarganj (see Table 1), was attributed "to the excessive mortality which occurred in the district, owing to the prevalence of cholera morbus."[67]

According to an official report in 1824, the annual death rate in the Bengal Presidency (total population 50 million people) was one in 33, that is, approximately 1,500,000 people. A sixth of this total, or 250,000, represented the number of Hindu women who became widows. Rounding out to 600 the figure for those who burned themselves that year, the number of immolations only constituted 0.2 percent of the overall number of widows.[68] By this calculation, the incidence of sati in Hughli, the district consistently reporting the highest number of cases in British India, added up to 1.2 percent.[69]

Perhaps Banaras provides the best illustration of the limited incidence of sati, especially when the practice of sati is viewed against a backdrop of that city's reputation as a place to which "large numbers of elderly people . . . [came] specifically to die . . . and so achieve immediate salvation."[70] Thus, the Banaras magistrate noted with surprise—and in an obvious ethnocentric manner—that only 125 cases had occurred in the nine years between 1820 and 1828.

> Benares is one of the most sacred homes of Hinduism . . . in it the bigotry of the people is nurtured . . . it is peopled by the wealthiest and most scrupulous of Hindus . . . inhabited by crowds of every description of religious enthusiasts, the place where every Hindu is anxious to die, and the resort of all classes of rank of all ages, more especially those whose earthly career is drawing to its close. . . . At such a place then it would be expected the performance of this most inhuman rite would be frequent,

and that its frequency would be in proportion to the peculiar sanctity of the spot, a sanctity immemorially acknowledged.[71]

The practice of sati, in short, was not only peculiar to certain regions of the subcontinent, but within those particular areas, taken up by only a small fraction of the widows. Although difficult to verify because the data say little about kinship ties between satis, this restricted scope of the rite probably indicates, as many scholars suspect, that it was a practice that must have been a tradition only in certain lineages.[72] The Choudhary family of Patna, for instance, honor and worship, "along with their family gods," two satis, wives of one of their ancestors who "immolated themselves on the funeral pyre at their Patna house on hearing of the death of their husband on the battlefield. . . . It is still believed that the lineage which was threatened at that time with extinction continues through their blessing."[73]

Another aspect of the identity of sati victims in the early 19th century that explains the phenomenon better is their caste and economic backgrounds. Contrary to the conventional wisdom regarding the high caste status of sati victims, a different portrait emerges from a close examination of the detailed information. Of the 575 cases reported in 1823, 234 were Brahmins (41 percent), 35 Kshatriyas (six percent), 14 Vaishyas (two percent), and 292 Sudras (51 percent).[74]

That this configuration of nearly even representation of both high and low castes was not uncommon is also borne out by the figures for individual districts. Of the 52 victims in 24-Parganas in 1819, 20 were Brahmins, 10 Kayasths, and two Vaidyas, and the rest comprising such low castes as Sadgope, Jogi, Kaivarta, Kansari, Suri, and Ahir (Goalla). The 141 cases enumerated for Hughli district in 1818 reveal a similar composition: other than 40 Brahmins, 26 Kayathas, and four Vaidyas, the remaining 71 were of the lower castes.[75] The diversity of caste backgrounds of sati victims also shows up clearly in the details regarding the Bhojpur districts of Ghazipur, Gorakhpur, Saran, and Shahabad. While Saran's numbers include a disproportionately higher percentage of high caste women among its satis, the figures for the other three districts conform more closely with those for the rest of the Presidency. But in Saran, too, lower-caste women followed the practice. Noticeably present among the 168 satis in that district between 1815 and 1826 are two Harijans (Untouchables): in 1816 Punbosia Chamar, the wife of Jodhi, and in 1818, Dukhni Chamar, the wife of Dohari. Such diversity in the caste composition of sati victims certainly does not authenticate Nandy's characterization of sati as the expression of a rudderless upper-caste Bengali gentry seeking to anchor themselves in a period of flux by resorting to the "traditional" practice of sati.

The caste backgrounds of satis in Banaras city, however, add up to a different picture. An overwhelming majority were upper caste, particularly Brahmins. In 1821 all 12 satis were upper caste (11 Brahmins and one

TABLE 3
Caste Composition of Sati Victims in Bhojpur Districts, 1815-1826

	1815	1816	1817	1818	1819	1820	1821	1822	1823	1824	1825	1826
Ghazipur Upper Castes	2	7	13	19	14	17	13	16	32	25	13	13
% of total	(25)	(46)	(48)	(42)	(50)	(50)	(37)	(34)	(54)	(75)	(61)	(68)
Gorakhpur Upper Castes	8	16	14	28	14	16	24	15	18	14	7	16
% of total	(57)	(69)	(58)	(56)	(60)	(50)	(54)	(53)	(56)	(82)	(77)	(72)
Saran Upper Castes	8	12	11	3	6	7	12	9	6	6	12	6
% of total	(73)	(63)	(79)	(57)	(60)	(64)	(80)	(75)	(86)	(50)	(80)	(60)
Shahabad Upper Castes	1	5	9	13	9	11	20	21	18	10	13	12
% of total	(25)	(56)	(64)	(52)	(50)	(58)	(51)	(58)	(60)	(55)	(65)	(55)

Source: Compiled from *PP, 1821, 1823, 1824, 1825, 1830.*

Rajput); only in 1816 and 1820 did the proportion fall below 70 percent (66 and 63 percent, respectively). No doubt, the caste profile for this city is skewed by the fact that people from other areas of the subcontinent converged on it to die there. Not surprisingly, then, many "foreigners" stand out among the roster of sati victims, including such typically Bengali names as Biswas, Mukherjee, Chakravarty, Bhattacharya, and Banerjee, as well as the well-known Maratha name of Joshi and even a "Moorleedhur," identified as a former resident of Nepal.[76]

A different light on the practice of sati is also cast by analyzing the ages of its victims. Whereas many studies have tended to emphasize the young ages of widows in any given year, almost half of them were 50 and over, and two-thirds 40 years and more (see Table 4). In 1818, out of 839 cases 123, or 14.6 percent, were 70 and over; but only 98, or 11.6 percent, aged 25 or under. The overwhelming majority, as in other years, were 40 years and more. As the official report concluded in presenting these statistics, "a great proportion of these acts of self-devotion have not taken place in youth, or even in the vigor of age; but a period when life, in the common course of nature, must have been near its close."[77]

Almost every district also yields examples of women who had not only reached a ripe old age but who immolated themselves long after their husbands' demises. To draw on illustrations from Ghazipur's 1822 cases: 60-year-old Jhunia committed sati 15 years after her husband passed away; 70-year-old Karanja 40 years after her husband's death; 80-year-old

TABLE 4
Age Composition of Sati Victims in Bengal Presidency in 1825 and 1826

	0-19	20-29	30-39	40-49	50-59	60-69	70-79	80-89	90-99	100+	Total
1825	17	98	104	122	110	112	46	26	3	1	639
% of total	(2.7)	(15.3)	(16.3)	(19.1)	(17.2)	(17.5)	(7.2)	(4.1)	(.5)	(.1)	100%
1826	20	104	70	77	84	81	53	24	3	2	518
% of total	(4)	(20)	(13.5)	(14.9)	(16.2)	(15.6)	(10.2)	(4.6)	(.6)	(.4)	100%

Source: Compiled from *PP, 1830,* vol. 28, pp. 113-18, 208-13.

Bhujagan 25 years after her husband's death, and 70-year-old Hulasi immolated herself on the funeral pyre of her son, 16 years after her husband Niamdhar Tiwari had died.[78] Equally striking are the cases from other Bhojpur districts: Lagni burnt herself at the age of 90, 25 years after the death of her husband; Namao ascended the funeral pyre at the age of 80 following the absence of her husband, presumed dead, for a period of 15 years.[79]

Such characteristics of its victims suggest that sati was a form of ritual suicide[80] conditioned at least in part by personal considerations. The economic conditions of many widows further underscores this coloring. Data collected on satis from 1822 onwards reveal that many widows came from impoverished families. Of the 40 cases reported for Burdwan in 1822, only three or four of the deceased "left any considerable property . . . the greater proportion were in a state of poverty." Similar observations were filed for other districts that year: Hughli's 79 satis followed 25 husbands who had died in "opulent circumstances, thirteen in middling, and forty-one in poor circumstances"; Bakarganj's 18 cases involved only five deceased husbands who were "in respectable circumstances, all the rest died indigent."[81]

The high representation of poor widows who took their lives after the demise of their husbands is again borne out by the statistics for 1823. Hughli's 81 cases involved 37 husbands who were "poor, sixteen in middling, and twenty-four in opulent circumstances"; Jessore's 14 incidents involved six husbands in "good [condition], three in middling, and five in bad circumstances"; Jungle Mehals' 27 cases included 10 said to be "poor, the rest were generally in moderate circumstances"; and "the greater part" of the 31 cases in Cuttack "appear to have been in low circumstances."[82]

Much the same conclusions regarding the advanced age and impoverished conditions of sati victims emerges from the information collected for 1826 when almost every district report turned in full details on these subjects. Burdwan's report on 45 satis referred to women who "generally speaking . . . have attained mature ages, and their deceased husbands to have been in low circumstances"; Hughli's 98 cases evoked the observation that the "greater proportion of the husbands appear to have been in poor or middling circumstances"; Nadia's 45 "female sacrifices . . . [involved] parties . . . for the most part . . . in poor circumstances; and the widows were, generally speaking, of an advanced age."[83]

Furthermore, even in the best of circumstances, the practice of sati was shaped by other considerations. For it existed in a milieu in which widowhood was regarded as the final and lowest stage in the life of a woman, a stage sometimes termed "cold sati."[84] In other words, a widow was regarded as "a marginal entity in society":

She was not allowed to wear the insignia of her active married state, that is, her clothes and her jewelry, but wore rags. In some cases her hair was shorn. She was not permitted to partake in family meals, could only sleep on the ground and in all ways was kept separate from the active social world of the living. She was treated by the family and the rest of society as unclean, and polluting, and her marginality was enforced by these pollution taboos. She was expected to devote the rest of her life to asceticism and worship of the gods, especially Siva, and her dead husband.[85]

Thus, viewed from the perspective of widows in early 19th-century India, the "option" of becoming a sati was not only conditioned by their economic and social circumstances but also by the "virtue" they earned in gaining long-term spiritual rewards for themselves and their families and by the deliverance they attained by closing out their lives as the "symbolically dead,"[86] a role to which they were consigned. As an alternative to life as a "cold sati," a life of marginal existence and symbolic death that was made more precarious for many by advancing age and poverty, self-immolation was an act of ritual suicide that terminated their "after lives" of certain misery as widows.[87]

NOTES

This a much traveled essay that has benefited from many readings and suggestions. An excerpt from an earlier version appeared in *Manushi* 42-43 (1987): 26-29.

1. This essay follows the now common usage of the term to refer to both the act of widow burning as well as the woman victim. To differentiate between the two, some writers use suttee, the Anglicized term for sati, to refer to the practice and sati to the victim. E.g., see V.N. Datta, *Sati: A Historical, Social and Philosophical Enquiry into the Hindu Rite of Widow Burning* (New Delhi: Manohar, 1988), 1. See also Datta, *Sati*, 2, regarding the prevalence of widow immolation in other parts of the world.

2. Edward Thompson, *Suttee* (Boston: Houghton Mifflin, 1928), 15; Upendra Thakur, *The History of Suicide in India: An Introduction* (Delhi: Munshiram Manoharlal, 1963), 141-42.

3. E.g., see Thompson, *Suttee*; R.K. Saxena, *Social Reforms: Infanticide and Sati* (New Delhi: Trimurti Publications, 1975); Amitabha Mukhopadhyay, "Sati as a Social Institution in Bengal," *Bengal Past and Present* 76 (1951): 99-105.

4. "Sati: Regulation XVII, A.D. 1829 . . .," in *The Correspondence of Lord William Cavendish Bentinck, vol. 1: 1828-1831*, ed. C.H. Philips (Oxford: Oxford University Press, 1977), 360.

5. John Rosselli, *Lord William Bentinck: The Making of a Liberal Imperialist, 1774-1839* (Brighton: Sussex University Press, 1974), 208-14; Rajat K. Ray, "Introduction," in *Rammohun Roy and the Process of Modernization in India*, ed. V.C. Joshi (Delhi: Vikas, 1975), 1-20.

6. Lata Mani, "Contentious Traditions: The Debate on Sati in Colonial India," *Cultural Critique* (1987): 119-20.

7. *Ibid.*, 153. British attitudes towards sati were also characterized by a "deep ambivalence." See Veena Das, "Gender Studies, Cross-Cultural Comparison and the Colonial Organization of Knowledge," *Berkshire Review* 58 (1986): 68.

8. "Government circular on sati addressed to military officers," Nov. 10, 1828, in *Correspondence of Bentinck*, 91.

9. Hanna Papanek, "False Specialization and the Purdah of Scholarship—A Review Article," *Journal of Asian Studies* 44 (1984): 127-48. A significant departure from the conventional modes of interpretation is the work of Lata Mani (cited in notes 6 and 47).

10. Ashis Nandy, "Sati: A Nineteenth Century Tale of Women, Violence and Protest," in *Rammohun Roy*, ed. Joshi, 174-75.

11. See Helena Znaniecka Lopata, ed., *Widows*, 2 Vols. (Durham: Duke University Press, 1987), for a study emphasizing the significance of the social context of widowhood in shaping the "after life" of widows in positive or negative ways. Also see Betty Potash, ed., *Widows in African Societies: Choices and Constraints* (Stanford: Stanford University Press, 1986) for an anthropological analysis of the lives of widows and their options, choices, and strategies.

12. See Gayatri C. Spivak, "Can the Subaltern Speak? Speculations on Widow-Sacrifice," *Wedge* 7/8 (1985): 120-30 for a provocative discussion of the "muting" of subaltern women in the colonial discourse.

13. On the Bhojpur region, see Gyan Pandey, "Rallying round the Cow: Sectarian strife in the Bhojpur Region, c. 1888-1917," in *Subaltern Studies II: Writings on South Asian History and Society*, ed. Ranajit Guha (Delhi: Oxford University Press, 1983), 60-129. See also Robert I. Crane, ed., *Regions and Regionalism in South Asian Studies: An Exploratory Study* (Duke University, Monograph and Occasional Paper Series, Monograph No. 5, 1967).

14. C.A. Bayly, "From Ritual to Ceremony: Death Ritual and Society in Hindu North India since 1600," in *Mirrors of Mortality: Studies in the Social History of Death*, ed. Joachim Whaley (New York: St. Martin's Press, 1981), 174.

15. Das, "Gender and Colonial Knowledge," 69.

16. Great Britain, Parliament, *Parliamentary Papers* (hereafter *PP*) (Commons), *1821*, vol. 18, 3-22.

17. *Ibid.*, 22.

18. See, e.g., Magistrate, Nadia, to Secty., Judicial, Oct. 30, 1803, Bengal Criminal Judicial Consultations, Nov. 5 to Dec. 29, 1803, Nov. 3, no. 10.

19. Collector, Shahabad, to Board of Revenue, Sept. 29, 1801, Bengal Revenue Consultations, 1801, Sept. 2 to Oct. 29, 1801, Oct. 22, no. 13.

20. Thompson, *Suttee*, 61.

21. Acting Register of the Nizamat Adalat (N.A.) to Secty., Judicial, June 5, 1806, in *PP, 1821*, vol. 18, 27.

22. Police officers were also ordered to submit information on sati cases in their monthly reports to the magistrates, *ibid.*, 28.

23. In the four-fold division of Aryan society, Brahmins or priests, constituted the highest order followed by Kshatriyas or warriors, Vaishyas or merchants and artisans, and Sudras or serfs. According to this pandit, if a woman reneged on her intention to commit sati before pronouncing the *sankalpa*, or resolution to die, she faced no punishments. However, if she had already announced her *sankalpa* and performed other ceremonies but refused to ascend the funeral pyre, then her decision could only be rectified by her "undergoing a severe penance." "Question to the Pundit the Nizamut Adawlut," in *ibid.*, 28-29.

24. Magistrate, Bundelkhand, to Register, N.A., Aug. 3, 1813, *ibid.*, 32.

25. Register, N.A., to Chief Secty., March 11, 1813, *ibid.*

26. *PP, 1821,* vol. 18, 44.

27. *PP, 1823,* vol. 17, 7-26; *PP, 1824,* vol. 23, 76; *PP, 1825,* vol. 24; *PP, 1826/27,* vol. 20. A column entitled "Profession, and Circumstances of the Husband" was added to the 1824 report.

28. Commissioner, Patna, to Secty., Judicial, Oct. 15, 1834, Bengal Criminal Judicial Consultations, Jan. 26 to Feb. 9, 1836, Jan. 26, no. 22.

29. This section draws on the highly suggestive and provocative ideas of Eric Hobsbawm, "Introduction: Inventing Traditions," in *The Invention of Tradition,* ed. Hobsbawm and Terence Ranger (Cambridge: Cambridge University Press, 1983), 1-14.

30. Romila Thapar, "In History," *Seminar* 342 (1988): 15. See also the other essays in this important and informative special issue on sati.

31. *Ibid.* Whether or not sati was referred to and endorsed by the Vedas is a subject of some disputation. See, e.g., Datta, *Sati,* 2-3.

32. Thapar, "In History," 15; A.L. Basham, *The Wonder that was India* (New York: Grove Press, 1959), 186-87.

33. P. Thomas, *Indian Women through the Ages* (Bombay: Asia Publishing House, 1964), 217-24; Datta, *Sati,* 3-4; Benoy Bhusan Roy, *Socioeconomic Impact of Sati in Bengal and the Role of Raja Rammohun Roy* (Calcutta: Naya Prokash, 1987), 1-2; Thapar, "In History," 15-16.

34. Dorothy Stein, "Burning Widows, Burning Brides: The Perils of Daughterhood in India," *Pacific Affairs* 61 (1988): 465; and her "Women to Burn: Suttee as a Normative Institution," *Signs* 4 (1978): 253-68; and Richard Lannoy, *The Speaking Tree: A Study of Indian Culture and Society* (London: Oxford University Press, 1971), 114-18, regarding the belief that women have a greater need of sexual satisfaction than men.

35. Thakur, *Suicide in India,* 126-45; Basham, *Wonder that was India,* 186-88.

36. Barbara N. Ramusack, "Women in South and Southeast Asia," in *Restoring Women to History* (Bloomington: Organization of American Historians, 1988), 4. Sudras were said to be the servants of the three higher orders.

37. Sandra P. Robinson, "Hindu Paradigms of Women: Image and Values," in *Women, Religion and Social Change,* ed. Yvonne Yazbeck Haddad and Ellison Banks Findly (Albany: State University of New York Press, 1985), 183. See also Susan S. Wadley, "Women and the Hindu Tradition," *Signs* 3 (1977): 113-25.

38. Thapar, "In History," 15.

39. Vina Mazumdar, "Comment on Suttee," *Signs* 4 (1978): 273. See also Sanjukta Gupta and Richard Gombrich, "Another View of Widow-burning and Womanliness in Indian Public Culture," *Journal of Commonwealth and Comparative Politics* 22 (1984): 255-56 for an argument that Hindu emphasis on the chastity of women was reinforced under Muslim rule because Muslim rulers posed a threat to the purity of Hindu women and because Muslim culture placed an even higher premium on chastity as "virtually the sole repository of family honor."

40. Thapar, "In History," 16.

41. Mukhopadhyay, "Sati in Bengal," 100; Kenneth Ballhatchet, *Social Policy and Social Change in Western India 1817-1830* (London: Oxford University Press, 1957), 291. See also Ray, "Introduction," 3-5 regarding the "spread of sati as a Sanskritizing rite"; and M.N. Srinivas, *Social Change in Modern India* (Berkeley: University of California Press, 1969), 6 for a standard definition of Sanskritization.

42. Thapar, "In History," 17.

43. *The Inner Conflict of Tradition: Essays in Indian Ritual, Kingship, and Society* (Chicago: University of Chicago Press, 1985), 15.

44. Mukhopadhyay, "Sati in Bengal," 99-101; Zakiuddin Ahmad, "Sati in Eighteenth Century Bengal," *Journal of the Asiatic Society of Pakistan* 13 (1968): 149-50; Thompson, *Suttee,* 15-43.

45. Ronald B. Inden, *Marriage and Rank in Bengali Culture: A History of Caste and Clan in Middle-Period Bengal* (Berkeley: University of California Press, 1976), 82.

46. Bayly, "From Ritual to Ceremony," 175; Thapar, "In History," 17.

47. No wonder the practice in the 18th and 19th centuries is often seen as an involuntary act, more akin to murder than ritual suicide. E.g., Datta, *Sati,* 216-19. Note also that in the 19th-century debate over sati the British followed legal and Brahminical precedents and ignored the multivocal nature of the discourse on sati. See Lata Mani, "Production of an Official Discourse on Sati in Early Nineteenth Century Bengal," *Economic and Political Weekly* 21 (1986): 32-40.

48. Caldecott to Pettet, Sept. 14, 1783, Caldecott Manuscript, Eur. Mss. D. 778, India Office Library and Records, London.

49. S. Pearce Carey, *William Carey* (London: Hodder & Stoughton, 1923), 209.

50. Acting Magistrate, Saran, to Acting Suptd. of Police, Lower Provinces, Feb. 20, 1819, Saran District Records, Letters Issued, 11-4-1816 to 17-6-1819, Bihar State Archives, Patna.

51. Magistrate to Register, N.A., Dec. 18, 1813, *PP, 1821,* vol. 18, 37.

52. Francis Buchanan, *An Account of the District of Shahabad in 1812-13* (Patna: Patna Law Press, 1934), 213; Montgomery Martin, *Eastern India,* vol. 2, *Bhagalpur, Gorakhpur* (1838; reprint ed., Delhi: Cosmo Publications, 1976), 475.

53. Mukhopadhyay, "Sati in Bengal," 105. These numbers do not include satis occurring in such areas as Punjab and Rajasthan that were then territories not completely under British control but where the practice was prevalent. On Rajasthan, see Saxena, *Social Reforms,* 57-147. On sati in Bombay Presidency, see Ballhatchet, *Social Policy in India,* 275-91.

54. Anand A. Yang, *The Limited Raj: Agrarian Relations in Saran District, India, 1793-1920* (Berkeley: University of California Press, 1989); Basudeb Chattopadhyay, "The Penetration of Authority in the Interior: A Case-study of the Zamindari of Nakashipara, 1850-1860," *Peasant Studies* 12 (1985): 151-69. See also Nandy, "Sati," 174-75.

55. Gupta and Gombrich, "Another View of Widow-burning," 254.

56. Nandy, "Sati," 175.

57. Ashis Nandy, "Cultures of Politics and Politics of Cultures," *Journal of Commonwealth and Comparative Politics* 22 (1984): 265.

58. Wherever possible, I have attempted to correct the "grotesquely mistranscribed" names. Compiled from *PP, 1826/27,* vol. 20, 108; *PP, 1830,* vol. 28, 30, 93-100, 189-91. The 1830 identifications of sepoy widows also lists Musst. Una of Ghazipur and Musst. Gurua of Kanpur. See also Buchanan, *Shahabad,* 153 for an estimate that at least 4,680, and as many as 12,000 men from Shahabad were serving in the military in 1812-13.

59. "A Short History of the Chaudhary Family, Patna City (translated from the Hindi of Pandit Rampratap Pandey)," in Babu Ramgopal Singh Chowdhary, *Select Writings and Speeches of Babu Ramgopal Singh Chowdhary* (Bankipur: Express Press, 1917), ii. Bhumihar Brahmins, a dominant landholding caste in the region, sometimes termed Kshatriya Brahmins, have historically valorized their military and kingly identities. See M.A. Sherring, *Hindu Tribes and Castes* (1872; reprint ed., Delhi: Cosmo Publications, 1974), 39-54.

60. Gupta and Gombrich, "Another View of Widow-burning," 256; Mukhopadhyay, "Sati in Bengal," 108. Infanticide is said to stem from the same dynamic

because the dearth of men of appropriate status also meant that high castes were faced with the dreadful prospect of raising unmarriageable daughters.

61. Bayly, "From Rituals to Ceremony," 174. Such pressures have also been cited as reasons why many satis in Bengal should be seen as involuntary, i.e., as murder. E.g., see Ahmad, "Sati in Bengal," 161-63.

62. Nandy, "Sati," 171, goes on to argue that large-scale scarcities occurred in Bengal, such as the disastrous famine of 1770, after a period of about 150 years of relatively famine-free existence.

63. "Ashis Nandy on the Inner World," *Journal of Commonwealth and Comparative Politics* 22 (1984): 259. Perhaps this was another dynamic in the generalization of the practice across social and economic lines.

64. James Jameson, *Report on the Epidemick Cholera Morbus* (Calcutta: A.G. Balfour, 1820), 3-32, 167-74.

65 Magistrate, Patna, to Suptd., Police, Dec. 21, 1818, *PP, 1821*, vol. 18, 233.

66. Robert Hamilton to Captain Benson, March 1, 1829, in *Correspondence of Bentinck*, 175. For a similar trend in western India, see Ballhatchet, *Social Policy in India*, 275.

67. "Extract from . . . suttee report . . . for the year 1825," *PP, 1830*, vol. 28, 26.

68. "Mr. Harington's Minute," with Governor-General's Dec. 3, 1824, *PP, 1825*, vol. 24, 11.

69. I have used an 1822 population estimate of 1,239,150. See Durgaprasad Bhattacharya and Bibhavati Bhattacharya, eds., *Census of India, 1961: Report on the Population Estimates of India (1820-1830)* (New Delhi: Government of India, 1963), 71.

70. Bayly, "From Ritual to Ceremony," 161.

71. Hamilton to Benson, March 1, 1829, *Correspondence of Bentinck*, 172.

72. Elizabeth Leigh Stutchbury, "Blood, Fire and Meditation: Human Sacrifice and Widow Burning in Nineteenth Century India," in *Women in India and Nepal*, ed. Michael Allen and S.N. Mukherjee (Canberra: Australian National University Monographs on South Asia No. 8, 1982), 41.

73. "History of the Chaudhary Family," in *Writings of Chowdhary*, ii.

74. *PP, 1825*, vol. 24, 153.

75. Mukhopadhyay, "Sati," 108-9. Although upper-caste victims comprised approximately half the total number of satis in most districts, in proportion to the percentage of high to low castes in the overall population, they, of course, constituted a substantial proportion. Interpolating on the basis of the systematic census data of the late 19th century, one can assume that high castes typically represented eight to 20 percent of the total population of most Bengal districts, their numbers standing higher in Bihar than in Bengal proper.

76. E.g., see *PP, 1821, 1823, 1825*. Nearly eight percent of the population of Banaras, a center of pilgrimage, were Marathas in 1820. See Bayly, "From Ritual to Ceremony," 164-65.

77. "Remarks . . . for the year 1818," May 21, 1819, *PP, 1821*, vol. 18, 222. For a different emphasis—on the youth of the victims—see Gupta and Gombrich, "Another View of Widow-burning," 256.

78. *PP, 1825*, vol. 24, 67-70.

79. *PP, 1821*, vol. 18, 166-68.

80. For a discussion of sati as suicide and particularly Durkheim's views on this subject, see Raj S. Gandhi, "Sati as Altruistic Suicide," *Contributions to Asian Studies* 10 (1977): 141-57; Arvind Sharma, "Emile Durkheim on Suttee as Suicide," *International Journal of Contemporary Sociology* 15 (1978): 283-91.

81. *PP, 1825*, vol. 24, 76-77.

82. *Ibid.*, 140-41. For a different profile, see the details regarding the 46 cases from the suburbs of Calcutta where the majority of the deceased husbands of satis were said to have "been in good [economic] circumstances" (141).

83. *PP, 1830*, vol. 28, 138-39.

84. Susan Hill Gross and Marjorie Wall Bingham, *Women in India* (Hudson, Wisconsin: GEM Publications, 1980), 30.

85. Stutchbury, "Widow Burning in India," 37; Stein, "Women to Burn," 254-55.

86. See Lina M. Fruzzetti, *The Gift of a Virgin: Women, Marriage, and Ritual in a Bengali Society* (New Brunswick: Rutgers University Press, 1982), 103-7 for an excellent discussion of the present-day status of the widow. Also Manisha Roy, *Bengali Women* (Chicago: University of Chicago Press, 1975), 146-47.

87. Nor have the conditions and ideologies favoring sati completely disappeared in 20th-century India. Thousands were present at the recent burning of 17-year-old Roop Kanwar, a bride of eight months, who immolated herself on her husband's funeral pyre in Rajasthan on Sept. 4, 1987. For the literature— and some shocking pronouncement—on this incident, see, e.g., the special issues of *Manushi* 42-43 (1987); *Seminar* 342 (1988); and *Economic and Political Weekly*, Nov. 7, 1987, and Nov. 14, 1987.

BIBLIOGRAPHICAL NOTE

Perhaps the best entry into the literature is via the writings responding to the sensational Deorala sati of 1987. Two useful points of departure are "Sati: A Symposium on Widow Immolation and Its Social Context," *Seminar* 342 (Feb. 1988), and the special double issue of *Manushi* 42-43 (Sept.-Dec 1987). These special issues of two leading Indian journals are important considerations not only of the historical, religious, and cultural contexts of the practice but also of its present-day ideological and social resonances. They can also be read as interventions in the debate that erupted in the wake of the Deorala incident. Romila Thapar's "In History" piece in *Seminar* is especially valuable; also notable is the *Seminar* bibliography of "Further Reading" (pp. 49-52).

An instructive contrast to the current scholarship is Edward Thompson's *Suttee: A Historical and Philosophical Enquiry into the Hindu Rite of Widow-Burning* (Boston: Houghton Mifflin, 1928). The centerpiece of this book—as with much of the early work dating from the pre-1970s period (the rest is mostly in the form of journal articles)—is the colonial campaign leading up to the promulgation of Regulation XVII of 1829, which declaired sati "illegal and punishable by the criminal courts." In this old political history version, the outlawing of sati is characterized as emerging from the encounter between the modernizing and westernizing forces of British rule and the traditional society of India, an encounter that also ushered in the beginning of modern India and modern Indians as epitomized by the life and career of the Indian architect of this and other social reforms, Raja Rammohun Roy.

Although drawing on this frame of analysis, Ashis Nandy's "Sati: A Nineteenth Century Tale of Women, Violence and Protest" (in *Rammohun Roy and the Process of Modernization in India* [Delhi: Vikas, 1975], 168-94) represents one of the first systematic attempts to raise new and provocative questions regarding this practice. His argument rests on a psychohistorical and sociological explanation for the ostensible rise in incidence of "widow burning" in the late eighteenth and early nineteenth centuries.

Similarly concerned with explaining the phonomenon of sati within its larger contexts (economic, social, cultural, religious, and psychological) are a number of recent studies: V. N. Datta, *Sati: A Historical, Social and Philosophical Enquiry into the Hindu Rite of Widow Burning* (New Delhi: Manohar Books, 1988); Arvind Sharma with Ajit Ray, Alaka Hejib, and Katherine K. Young, *Sati: Historical and Phenomenological Essays* (Delhi: Motilal Banarsidass, 1988); Dorothy K. Stein, "Women to Burn: Suttee as a Normative Institution," *Signs* 4 (1978): 253-73, and "Burning Widows, Burning Bridges: The Perils of Daughterhood in India," *Pacific Affairs* 61 (1988): 465-85; Elizabeth Leigh Stutchbury, "Blood, Fire and Mediation: Human Sacrifice and Widow Burning in the Nineteenth Century," in *Women in India and Nepal*, ed. Michael Allen and S. N. Mukherjee (Canberra: Australian National University, 1982); and the chapter in this volume.

In part the new angles on sati have been opened up by close readings of the colonial discourse. As Lata Mani ("Contentious Traditions: The Debate on Sati in Colonial India," *Cultural Critique*, 1987, 119-56) and Gayatri Spivak ("Can the Subaltern Speak? Speculations on Widow-Sacrifice," *Wedge* 7/8 [1985]: 120-30) demonstrate by deconstructing this discourse produced by colonial rulers acting in conversation with Indian reformers and religious elites (Brahmins), the aims and intentions underlying the words and actions of British rulers have as much, if not more, to do with issues of colonial knowledge and power as with a concern for social reform.

More nuanced readings of religious texts have also led to breakthroughs. No longer can the contradictory messages regarding sati conveyed by different "sacred" texts be ignored; nor can the new inscriptional and archeological evidence about its precolonial past. Indeed, much of the recent literature suggests that the colonial practice of sati was an "invented tradition" that enlarged its constituency and developed over time.

Better answers to questions regarding who committed sati and why—especially in the colonial period for which the most systematic documentary evidence exists—are also beginning to appear. Although with differing emphases, the recent studies noted above all seek to establish its constituencies and contexts that were shaped by variations in patriarchal practices and in regional and local cultures and traditions, and by class, caste, and demographic factors.

II

Women as Activists

THE DEBATE ON WOMEN'S LIBERATION IN THE IRANIAN CONSTITUTIONAL REVOLUTION, 1906-1911

Janet Afary

The origin of the Iranian women's movement is often traced to the 1906-1911 Constitutional Revolution. Yet a close study of the archives demonstrates that the substantial scope of this movement has not been fully recounted. We have read much about the involved women's enthusiastic commitment to the nationalist cause, but not enough about their equally strong commitment to fighting patriarchal traditions. We have come to think of them as activists, but not as thinkers and intellectuals in their own right. We have known about their appreciation for constitutionalism, but not about their criticism of its political and social shortcomings. If we attempt to situate the dialectics of the women's movement within the history of the revolution as a whole, we begin to gain a greater appreciation for the critical self-consciousness developed among the women's liberationists of that era, and perhaps we also begin to redefine the meaning of the Constitutional Revolution itself.[1]

Contemporary research on the history of social movements in early twentieth-century Iran has not taken adequate advantage of one of the richest available sources, the newspapers of the Constitutional Revolution. In contrast, the classic studies of the two early scholars of the Constitutional Revolution—Edward G. Browne's *The Persian Revolution* (1910) and Ahmad Kasravi's *History of Constitutionalism in Iran* (1951)—were based on extensive research on the major periodicals of the period. Browne, who wished to demonstrate to the Western world the unprecedented achievements of this technologically underdeveloped land during the revolutionary process, drew on *Habl al-Matin*'s editorials in his discussion of the 1907 Anglo-Russian Alliance, an agreement which had partitioned Iran into a northern and a southern sphere of influence of the two Powers with a "neutral zone" in between. He also left behind his unique translation and compilation *The Press and Poetry of Modern Persia* (1914), which documented the many newspapers of the constitutional period in brief. Kasravi, on the other hand, was concerned with the internal developments of the revolution and the clash between the secular and the religious wings of the movement. He drew extensively on the newspaper of the Tabriz Provincial Council, the *Anjuman,* documenting the accomplishments of this body. Kasravi detailed the acrimonious debates between the Tabriz Provincial Council and the parliament over the 1907 Supplementary Laws to the Constitution. These laws altered the theretofore secular constitution of December 1906 by giving a committee of clerics veto power over the pronouncements of the parliament.[2]

Both Browne and Kasravi, however, were concerned with issues which dominated the political scenes of their time, namely, the clash between the nascent Iranian nationalism and the growing power of Western imperialism, and the debates over the constitution and political reform in the country. While both men took note of women's participation as an indication of the emancipatory nature of the movement, neither writer was overtly interested in the details of this movement. The young American financial advisor Morgan Shuster in his *The Strangling of Persia* (1912) discussed the women's societies in some detail, in part because he had been aided by them in his daily political affairs on a number of occasions.[3]

Eighty years later, however, in coming across a number of letters, articles, reports, and editorials from the archives of this period by activist women and men, one cannot help but gain a new appreciation of women's contributions to the revolutionary movement. When viewed from the prism of the last two decades of research on the history of the women's movement globally, the general characterization that some women supported the Constitutional Revolution hardly tells the whole story. In trying to weave the women's discourse into the history of the period, rather than treating it apart from the men's discourse, we realize how some women activists began to develop a consciousness of themselves and their demands as well as an awareness of the many obstacles confronting them.

Some of the activist women became critical thinkers who, though they supported the new parliament, confronted the male leadership on social and political issues, and spoke against the inaction of the delegates. Without any institutional support, a number of women created a network of associations, schools for girls, and hospitals, and contributed enthusiastically to the political debates in the country. Some challenged the conservative wing of the clerics (*ulama*) in the daily papers, even though at times they found it necessary to draw justification from religious texts in order to press for their rights. During the Second Constitutional Period of 1909-1911, several women affiliated with the influential social democratic tendencies raised issues which are considered feminist demands today, such as critiques of easy male divorce and polygyny. We shall also look briefly at some of the male supporters of the women's movement, among them journalists, delegates to the parliament, and political activists, whose efforts on behalf of women's rights, though never backed by the constitutional government, helped place the question of women's liberation on the political agenda.

On August 5, 1906, a coalition of intellectuals, merchants, clerics, and craftsmen, through a series of strikes and sit-ins, forced Muzaffar al-Din Shah to sign a royal proclamation giving the nation the right to a parliament (*Majlis*), which opened on October 7, 1906, and a constitution, which was ratified on December 30, 1906. The electoral laws of September 1906 granted limited franchise to the nobility, clerics, landowners, merchants, and middle-class guilds, from which all classes of women were explicitly excluded, as they were in practice.

After the formation of the parliament, however, a more significant and direct expression of grassroots democracy manifested itself in two forms: the local councils called *anjumans* (an old Persian name meaning a place of gathering), and the newspapers which became the conduit between the anjumans and the parliament. The September 9, 1906, electoral laws had called for the formation of local anjumans to monitor the election process. But in addition to these official societies, a large number of popular anjumans were spontaneously formed throughout the country. Likewise, a new type of journalism had emerged in the course of the movement. Many writers and poets found the old literary styles and forms, such as the *qasideh* and the *ghazal*, incoherent or insufficient for the new political and social demands the revolution had brought forth. Instead they turned to daily conversational language, satire, and folk songs, through which they reached a mass audience.[4] Between 1905 and 1911 over two hundred periodicals began publication, many of which became well known for their remarkable literary expression.[5] Among these were *Anjuman*, the newspaper of the Tabriz Provincial Council (1906-1908); *Majlis*, organ of the parliament (1906-1908); *Habl al-Matin* (The Firm Cable), which became the most influential paper of the years 1907-1908; the socialist paper *Sur-i Israfil* (Trumpet Call of Israfil), renowned for its satirical columns by Ali Akbar Dihkhuda (1907-1908); *Musavat* (Equality), which gained a reputation as a supporter of civil rights, including the rights of the minority Zoroastrian community, between the years 1907 and 1909; and the social democratic paper *Iran-i Nau* (New Iran), which was the organ of the Democratic Party in 1909-1911.

At the beginning of the twentieth century, a variety of factors had laid the ground work for the increased political and social participation of women. The mid-nineteenth-century Babi movement, which had called for religious reforms, particularly changes in the treatment of women in society, and included the leadership of the brilliant female theologian and poet Tahireh Qurrat al-Ain (1814-1854), was brutally suppressed.[6] But

Babi doctrines continued to capture the imaginations of many intellectuals who wrote about the necessity of social change; among them were Mirza Aqa Khan Kirmani and Shaikh Ahmad Ruhi, who wrote against women's subjugation in family and society and condemned the practice of veiling. Other male intellectuals also raised their voices in defense of women's rights. Malkom Khan and the north Azerbaijani playwright Mirza Fath Ali Akhundzadeh had been strong advocates of greater freedom for women and promoted the issue of women's education as well as an end to polygyny. I'tisam al-Mulk, editor of the journal *Bahar* (Spring) in Tabriz, introduced many Azerbaijanis to significant works of European literature and was father of the renowned woman poet Parvin I'tisami. He translated the Egyptian Qasim Amin's famous treatise on women's emancipation, *Tahrir al-Mar'a*, which appeared under the title *Education of Women* (Tarbiyat-i Nisvan) in 1900.[7] Many exile papers such as *Akhtar* (Star) in Istanbul, *Qanun* (Law) in London, *Habl al-Matin* (Firm Cable) in Calcutta, and *Surayya* (Pleiades) and *Parvarish* (Fostering) in Egypt, published articles on behalf of women's education and greater social and political freedom.[8] The Russian Revolution of 1905 also played a significant role in radicalizing a segment of the population. The Organization of Social Democrats (Firqehyi Ijtima'iyun Amiyyun), founded in 1905 among Iranian migrant workers and merchants in Russia, kept close ties with both the Muslim social democratic Himmat Party and the Baku and Tiflis committees of the Russian Social Democratic Workers' Party.[9] The Organization of Social Democrats would open branches inside the country after the revolution, known as the Anjumans of the Mujahidin, and call for a radical program of social reform.

The protests against the tobacco concessions of 1890-91, which included mass demonstrations in Shiraz, Tabriz, Mashhad, Isfahan, and Tehran, gave Iranians, including women, a taste of victory through sustained mobilization. Women of the royal harem put aside their waterpipes and refused to follow Nasir al-Din Shah's order on the use of tobacco, while others who played a visible part in these protests called for removal of the Shah.[10] News of the growing women's-rights movements in both Europe and Asia had also elicited a greater questioning of the traditional patriarchal society in Iran. The stage was thus set for a new phase of social and political participation by women which would take shape during the course of the Constitutional Revolution.

Women protesters were present from the earliest stages of the movement.[11] They facilitated the strikes and sit-ins, lent their moral and financial support to the constitutionalists, and even defended them physically against the forces of the Shah. In this early stage of the movement, some women emerged as strong defenders of clerics who had sided with the constitutionalist cause. During the sanctuary held at the Shah Abdul Azim Mosque, a number of women, fully veiled as was the tradition at the time, reportedly created human barricades and protected the striking clerics against the armed government forces.[12] In the summer of 1906, during the sit-ins of the constitutionalists at the British legation, several thousand women gathered to join the strikers, whereupon the British ambassador intervened in order to dissuade the men from allowing the women to join.[13]

After formation of the parliament in October 1906, women began to organize around the two major political issues of the period, the plan to form a national bank to lessen Iran's dependency on foreign loans, and the prohibition against the use of foreign textiles. The liberal cleric and secret Babi sympathizer Sayyid Jamal al-Din Isfahani's appeal from the pulpit to both men and women to pledge money for the creation of the new bank was greeted enthusiastically.[14] A large number of women parted with their jewelry, some women workers turned in their wages, while some of the more affluent lent their inheritances. Newspapers of the period often printed the names of these women, both to give them credit and to embarrass the wealthy male members of the community who had not been so forthcoming. *Majlis*, organ of the parliament, reported in November 1906 that "widows were turning in their earrings and bracelets" to help accumulate the necessary capital for the establishment of the bank, and that "each was competing against the other" in order to make the highest contribution.[15] Similarly, a great number of women became involved in the movement to wear indigenous fabrics and stop purchase of imported European textiles. It was argued that the boycott of European textiles would free the nation from its dependence on European manufacturers and merchants. In Tabriz, women's meetings were organized around this issue. Those who gathered pleaded with others "to wear their old clothes for some time," hoping that in the near future the nation would begin to produce its own textiles.[16]

The budding of a critical consciousness can be detected even at this early stage of the national movement. Women as active campaigners in the ban against foreign commodities resented the pressure by some men who began to interpret the ban against foreign products as control over women's clothing. The Tabriz Anjuman wrote about the "barbarous and self-interested conduct" of some men who cursed and harassed women in the streets and bazaars because these women had worn elegant evening chadors or high-heeled shoes. They insisted that it was the opposition campaign against foreign goods, and not what women chose to wear, that had to be the focus of attention in the movement.[17]

It was not long before the participation and politicization of women in the national movement took on the added dimension of addressing women's issues and creating women's anjumans and schools. The first step was an appeal by an anonymous woman writer to Sayyid Muhammad Tabataba'i, the prominent proconstitutionalist cleric in the parliament, on behalf of female education and social participation. It was published in *Majlis* on December 30, 1906, the very day the constitution was signed by the Shah. In her letter, the writer argued that Iran had fallen behind the caravan of civilization because women were denied an education. She demanded that the newly formed government act responsibly and take steps to create schools for girls as it had done for boys. The response of the *Majlis* revealed the strong bias among the constitutionalists against women's political participation. The author of the letter was told that women were entitled to a limited concept of education, one which prepared them for the "raising of children, home economics, preserving the [family] honor and other such sciences that deal with the issue of morality and means of livelihood of the family," but were advised, in no uncertain terms, to keep out of politics and affairs of the government, which were considered a "prerogative of the men."[18]

Instead of waiting for the male leadership to offer them institutional support, a number of women became active themselves. At a meeting in early 1907, a resolution was passed calling for education of women and the abolition of extravagant dowries. By 1910 a women's journal called *Danish* (Knowledge) had appeared. In this period fifty girls' schools were established in Tehran, and a women's congress on education was held in April of that same year.[19]

Formation of the new schools was closely tied to the activity of the women's anjumans, which continued to operate without official permission. There were about a dozen women's anjumans in Tehran, and their activities were coordinated by a central committee. There was also an information center where "someone was always in attendance to answer questions and explain matters to any interested woman."[20] One of the first such societies was the Anjuman for Freedom of Women (Anjuman-i azadi zanan), formed in early 1907 after the ratification of the December 30, 1906, constitution.[21] The bi-weekly meetings of this group were attended by both men and women. Fathers and brothers would accompany daughters and sisters, husbands would join wives, while unaccompanied men and women were prohibited from participating. It seems that the involvement of relatives was required as a means of protecting the association against charges of indecency, although such a precaution was, as we shall see, of little help. Anjuman for Freedom of Women was primarily an educational forum. Meetings were held in a remote flowershop and garden outside the city of Tehran so that the event would draw less attention. Women, who were the only speakers in this anjuman, gave public lectures on social and political issues related to women's lives, followed by open discussion. By itself this was an astonishing achievement. Women, whose voices until then could be heard only by their closest relatives, were now orators on politics, feminism, and revolution. News of the gatherings eventually reached the conservative clerics in the bazaar, whose reaction can be guessed. An angry mob marched toward the secret meeting place of the anjuman. A young Armenian man saved the day, however, by rushing to the meeting place and sounding an alarm to the audience, who then fled in great haste before the mob reached the hall.[22]

Among the participants in this anjuman were the two daughters of Nasir al-Din Shah, Taj al-Saltaneh, whose memoirs reveal a strong socialist as well as feminist tendency, and Eftekhar al-Saltaneh. Mary Wood Park Jordan, an American Presbyterian missionary woman, also participated in the meetings. Several women who became prominent feminists in the 1920s, such as Sadiqeh Daulatabadi and Shams al-Muluk Javahir Kalam, were also members of Anjuman for Freedom of Women.[23]

There were other active anjumans in this period. The Secret Union of Women (Itihadiyeh-yi ghaibi-yi nisvan) spoke on behalf of the poor in the country and challenged the delegates to the parliament. An open letter of the Secret Union of Women, as we shall see, revealed a strong religious dimension within the group as well.[24] The Anjuman of Women (Anjuman-i nisvan) petitioned the first parliament for the recognition of women's anjumans.[25] The Anjuman of Ladies of the Nation (Anjuman-i mukhaddarat-i vatan), which began its activities in 1910, included a number of prominent women, closely associated with the constitutionalist leaders, who played a critical role during the December 1911 demonstrations.[26] The women's anjumans were by no means limited to Tehran. In Azerbaijan such societies had been formed as early as the fall of 1906. The French journal *Revue du monde musulmane* reported that by February 1907, 150 women had organized themselves into a society for combating "old traditions which are prejudicial and contrary to progress."[27] The women of Isfahan who formed the Council of Women of Isfahan (Hay'at-i nisvan-i Isfahan) were also very active during the protest demonstration of December 1911.[28] Collective letters on behalf of women of Qazvin and Sangalach were also sent to the newspapers, pointing to the existence of similar societies in small cities. Nor were the anjumans limited to Tehran. In Turkey, exiled Iranian women formed the Welfare Anjuman of Iranian Women Residing in Istanbul (Anjuman-i khayriyeh-yi nisvan-i iranian-i muqim-i istanbul). This organization made financial contributions in support of the civil war of Tabriz in 1908-1909.[29] From Ashkhabad in Russia, which included a large number of Iranian immigrants, residents closely followed the efforts on behalf of women's education in Iran. Among them was the woman poet Shams Kasma'i, who demanded that women's schools be opened throughout Iran, and suggested that they teach both new sciences and professions such as medicine, dentistry, surgery, and midwifery.[30]

The anjumans included single and married women working together. Some came from the royal family, such as the two daughters of the earlier monarch Nasir al-Din Shah, Eftekhar al-Saltaneh and especially Taj al-Saltaneh, who became a member of Anjuman for Freedom of Women (1907). Some came from families who were sympathetic to the revolution and used their resources to help finance new schools and orphanages. Daurat al-Mu'ali (d. 1924), a member of Anjuman of Ladies of the Nation

(1910), was a pioneer in establishing girls' schools. Her father was Nasir al-Din Shah's personal physician, and he had used his privileged position to establish a number of boys' schools in the years before the revolution. Daurat al-Mu'ali would likewise open the Ladies' School (Madrasah-yi mukhaddarat) of Tehran and would appeal to a number of educated women in her family to help teach in the school.[31]

Some members of the anjumans belonged to the families of clerics, in which many girls did receive an education at home. Safiyeh Yazdi, a member of Anjuman for Freedom of Women and also a pioneer in women's education, was the wife of a leading cleric (Mujtahid), Muhammad Husain Yazdi. Yazdi was one of the five clerics in the first parliament who were given the authority to review all legislation presented to that body according to the 1907 Supplementary Laws. However, unlike Shaikh Fazlallah Nuri and other conservative clerics, Yazdi supported the idea of women's education and encouraged his wife's actions. Safiyeh founded the Iffatiyeh school for girls in 1910 and gained a following for her outspoken lectures on women's issues.[32]

Some of the women came from Babi families, where a basic principle of the new religion was education and socialization of women. Sadiqeh Daulatabadi (1881-1961), whose father was the most important Azali Babi theologian in Isfahan, was both a member of the Anjuman for Freedom of Women and secretary for Anjuman of Ladies of the Nation. In 1918 she opened the first girls' schools in the city of Isfahan. In subsequent years she established the Women's Association of Isfahan and began publication of the weekly *Women's Voice*. In 1927, after several years of study at the Sorbonne, she returned to Iran and became the first woman to appear unveiled in European attire on the streets; it was a daring act for which she was subjected to much abuse and harassment. Her last will summed up the lifelong struggle of this eighty-year-old ardent feminist against the practice of veiling, declaring, "I do not want a single veiled woman to participate in my funeral, and I will never forgive women who visit my grave while wearing a veil."[33]

Several American Presbyterian missionaries, as well as women graduates of the American school, were also active in the anjumans. The question of equality of women was one of the educational principles of the Presbyterian missionaries. In many Asian countries they were the first to open schools for women and to use the services of women doctors, nurses, and teachers. As mentioned earlier, Mary Wood Park Jordan, who accompanied her husband, Samuel Jordan, to Iran in 1898, participated in the meetings of the Anjuman for Freedom of Women. Jordan would remain a strong advocate of women's rights throughout her teaching years in Iran. Her male students would recount how they had to memorize and write a composition on the statement "No country rises higher than the level of the women of that country."[34]

Some members of the women's anjumans crossed the barricades, as their fathers and brothers were prominent opponents of the revolution; among them was the daughter of the governor of Gilan, Sardar Afkham, who was killed by the revolutionary Mujahidin during their takeover of Rasht in 1909. There were also those who joined the movement with little education and no family support. Mahrukh Gauharshinas (1872-1938) had to fight both at home and in public in order to continue her activities. Through her life story we learn that in Tehran a revolutionary women's anjuman was formed whose members made a lifetime commitment to attain the goal of women's emancipation, no matter what the obstacles. Group members wore a special ring which they had designed themselves. On the ring was an engraving of two clasped hands, presumably to signify the women's solidarity with one another. Mahrukh started the Progress (Taraqqi) Girls' School in Tehran in 1911 without informing her husband. Even when he did find out and accused her of disgracing the family, Mahrukh continued her activities. She went on to introduce coeducation in her elementary school and solicited male constitutionalists to teach in the secondary school.[35] Despite the efforts of these women and many others, government-sponsored public schools would not be opened in the country until 1918.

At the beginning of the revolution, women activists had emerged as vocal supporters of those members of the clerics who had joined the constitutionalist cause. Later, however, some of the clerics, including Shaikh Fazlallah Nuri, became both anticonstitutionalists and outspoken critics of women's education, calling schools for girls un-Islamic and unleashing a campaign of public harassment of both students and teachers. In his journal *Lavayeh*, Shaikh Fazlallah echoed the principal points of these clerics against not only constitutionalism but also all that was deemed a product of foreign ideology and, therefore, detrimental to the tenets of religion and rule of the clerics. The subject of women's education and women's unveiling was related to the constitution's call for equal rights among all men, religious minorities as well as Muslims. It was argued that such rights would increase the danger of intermarriage between non-Muslim men and Muslim women, and therefore bring about the loss of honor which accompanied it for the whole nation.[36]

The opposition of Shaikh Fazlallah and others was challenged by women in a number of ways. Some appealed to the conservative clerics and theological students to give up their steadfast enmity toward women's education and cited verses from the Quran as justification. In the journal *Musavat*, a group of women who called themselves Supporters of Education for the Oppressed Women of Iran addressed a letter to the theological students. These clerical students, who had been supporters of the constitutional cause, had nevertheless spoken out against women's emancipation. The drafters of the letter argued: "Are we not, the oppressed female population of Iran, human beings like yourselves? Are we not partners and participants in the general rights of humanity with you? Do you consider us only voiceless, and load-carrying animals, or do you also recognize us as human beings? We ask for your sense of justice. Until when shall we be excluded from the command, 'the search for knowledge is the responsibility of all Muslim men and women?' "[37]

The opponents of women's education, they argued, had no basis for their attacks, since there were no male workers or teachers in the schools. The editors of *Musavat* also appealed to the Anjuman of the Union of Theological Students to end their enmity toward women and to recognize the fact that they were supported by many men. "Since three-fourth of the nation is appealing to you," *Musavat* insisted, the women's calls must be heeded.[38]

Other women were much more indignant and openly attacked the clerics. In August 1907 an anonymous woman wrote a letter to *Sur-i Israfil* supporting a series of essays in that journal which critiqued the limitations of thought imposed by the clerics. We must not underestimate the power of the reactionary clerics and think that the whole nation as "awakened," she warned. Even those who had joined the movement could easily be swayed by the likes of Shaikh Fazlallah, since he had accused the constitutionalists of having Babi reformist sentiments: "About Shaikh Fazlallah, all know that said person has excited such sedition and are aware of the extent to which he has agitated people. Until now, most people rich or poor, old or young, were supporters of the sacred National Consultative Parliament, and were in unison with all sisters and brothers. Now allegations are raised that people have joined the Babi cause and that with their leaders they want to harass the aforementioned Shaikh or want to sell out Islam."[39]

A month later, *Habl al-Matin* published a polemical letter by a woman who challenged the theological premise of Shaikh Fazlallah's religious order (*fatwa*) against women's education. The idea of God promoted by Shaikh Fazlallah was truly an evil one, she wrote. This God was said to have created woman in the form of a human being but then prohibited her from advancing in the realm of human civilization. This "unmerciful God" had put greater responsibility on the shoulders of women, asking them to obey not only God but also "fathers and husbands," while men were required to obey only God and no other. Moreover, women were given no remuneration for this excess responsibility and burden. The God of Shaikh Fazlallah was unacceptable to women. There was much difference, she argued, "between our God who has mandated knowledge for women, and your God who has prohibited knowledge for them and proclaimed it against religion and faith." She insisted that Shaikh Fazlallah had expressed such extreme carelessness and negligence in his religious rulings that he should be removed from the bench.[40] The opponents of the new schools claimed that they were concerned with women's loss of honor, she continued. But it seems that they had forgotten how the little girls who attended the "worthless" traditional schools (*maktabkhaneh*) were often sexually molested by the male relatives of the instructor (*mullabaji*). Instead the new schools not only provided women with a decent education but also protected them from such advances. Nor had the opponents of women's education given any thought to the lives of the many destitute, illiterate, and widowed women, with little means of support, who ended up as beggars and prostitutes. "With such vast differences and the clarity of the issue, I beg for your justice, what irreligious person would prescribe the traditional schools [*maktab*] but issue a religious prohibition against the new schools [*madrasah*]?"[41]

Some of the anjumans criticized the delegates to the parliament. General disillusionment toward the parliament was obvious by the fall of 1907. The Secret Union of Women published an open letter to the delegates demanding their resignation unless immediate reform measures were adopted. "We spend our dear life, day and night, reading the newspapers to see what the National Consultative Parliament has said, what it has done." We read it all, only to conclude that fourteen months after the revolution, the parliament has done nothing for the nation, the writers insisted. Thousands of petitions had been read, and everyone was promised that, "God willing, the day after tomorrow an appropriate response will be given." But this "day after tomorrow" never arrived! The assembly had not taken even one or two small steps of reform to please the nation, and people were asking themselves, "If we wanted the Shah and the ministers to run the affairs of the nation," then why all this trouble for a revolution? The Secret Union of Women then asked that women be given the opportunity to run the affairs of the government for a period of forty days. During this period they intended to select new representatives and ministers, and to begin a program of national reorganization which proposed radical measures to feed the poor and end all forms of autocracy.[42] But the letter also revealed the ambivalent attitude of at least some women's anjumans toward the clerical leadership, who continued to be both feared and respected. The Secret Union of Women tried to exempt the clerics by condemning only the secular wing of the parliament, while sympathizing with the clerical leadership within the assembly. This approach was adopted at a time when most of the clerics inside the parliament were unsympathetic to the social reforms proposed by the left-wing delegates.

During the Second Constitutional Period of 1909-1911, women's activities became public and increased significantly. Open forums on a variety of social and political issues, among them rights of women, were organized. Bibi Khanum Vaziroff, head the Maidens' School, invited women to attend regular meetings at her house for coffee and a few rounds of waterpipe, as well as political discussions, on weekends: "Any one of the sisters who wishes to lecture will be allowed and permitted to do so. I will be speaking on the advantages of constitutionalism and the disadvantages of autocracy."[43]

Conferences and plays were held for women as fundraisers for the movement; the money thus collected went for the establishment of schools for orphan girls, adult education programs, and women's hospitals.[44]

Several intellectual women now began to openly question the prevalent male supremacism of the Muslim and Iranian culture and addressed the previously taboo issues of polygyny and frequent divorce. The memoirs of Taj al-Saltaneh, daughter of Nasir al-Din Shah and member of Anjuman for Freedom of Women, are one of the more lengthy documents to have survived from this period. In 1914 she wrote openly of her forced marriage at the age of thirteen, her husband's subsequent extramarital affairs, and her own secret abortion. She also recounted her response to a questionnaire which was distributed among sympathetic women in the period 1908-1909 by an Armenian social democrat from the Caucasus named Ba'i Anuf. He had asked them to express their views on the merits of constitutionalism and its relation to women's issues.

When Taj al-Saltaneh was asked to define the "social connection between women's unveiling and the nation's progress," she addressed the issues of veiling, prostitution, and arranged loveless marriages among the poor and the more affluent members of society. She argued that among the urban working class, the meager income of the man was never adequate to cover all the expenses of his family, a family which typically included several women in the house—wife, mother, daughters, sisters, and often nieces. Many women in these families turned to prostitution in order to support themselves. But if the veil was removed, Taj al-Saltaneh argued, and women earned an honorable living, then the whole family could live in comfort and dignity.

Among the wealthy classes, she said, the relationship between men and women was alienated and distant. Couples married without mutual love and sought emotional fulfillment outside marriage. Men, who traditionally married for social position and wealth, turned to mistresses for companionship, and spent their time away from wife and family, drinking and socializing. The wives, who felt no affection for their husbands and were lonely, threw extravagant parties, bought expensive furniture, clothing, and jewels, and hired many women companions and servants. But "if women were unveiled and, as in all civilized nations, men and women could see each other, want each other, and join in a permanent union of love," then would this not be preferable to a life spent alongside mistresses and companions? she asked.[45]

In 1909 a series of essays entitled "The Journal of a Woman Scholar" were published in the social democratic paper *Iran-i Nau*, organ of the influential Democrat Party. The Democrat Party was the minority faction in the parliament, and shared in the formation of a government in the year 1910. The anonymous writer, who signed her articles under the female pen name of Tahireh, condemned polygyny and easy male divorce and wrote of the predicament of both women and men in unhappy marriages. She also tried to convince her readers of the merits of an educated wife and mother and insisted that the key to the nation's progress was the advancement of its women, since educated mothers would be able to raise more enlightened citizens and therefore a stronger nation.[46] The male community's "whimsical" treatment of women had to be changed. Instead of helping to create strong bonds of friendship, love, and mutual respect with their wives, men went out after what their eyes desired. They felt no loyalty toward their wives, and when they were advised to remain faithful, their answer would be, "God has made it easy for us so that if a woman was not to our liking we could divorce her and take another as wife," or else they would argue that "since the nation [*tayafeh*] of women are like female slaves, we can take several wives. In the end one of them will be to our liking." Tahireh responded to these and similar arguments with a bitter sense of indignation and anger. She questioned how there could be such "ignorance, such cruelty toward one's fellow human beings! Would any man like it if his wife took several husbands? Impossible!"[47]

To those who argued that Muslim men, according to the law, had the right to practice polygyny, she responded in the tradition of many women liberationists in the nineteenth and twentieth centuries in the Middle East, arguing that the Prophet Muhammad had stipulated that such a man must treat all his wives equally. But then, she added, this was an impossibility. No man could treat two women justly. The cowives despise one another, and no matter how a man treats one wife, the other will always be resentful. Thus the Prophet's stipulation had meant to demonstrate the near-impossibility of such an arrangement, Tahireh insisted. To carry this line of argument further was to call for major reform in marriage laws, but this was almost a heretical proposal at the time. She thus took refuge in the argument that if a woman was educated and accomplished, if she provided a healthful atmosphere in the house, then perhaps the man would be encouraged not to exercise his right and would prefer the peace and tranquility of a monogamous marriage.[48]

Women often did not form long-lasting emotional ties with their husbands. "This house and this husband are temporary," a woman was always told, and when a marriage did not work, one looked for another man. Mothers advised their daughters, she writes, thus:

> My beloved girl! Think of yourself. Never form strong emotional ties to these unfaithful men. Try hard so that your husband never becomes wealthy and rich. The minute his single shirt becomes two, he will take another wife and make your life miserable. At the least, dear one, think of your future and make him pay you. This way, in your miserable days, you will have some savings, and when you go to visit the fortune teller mulla who gives prayers for good luck, you will not be ashamed; or if you end up in a divorce, when you go to your next husband's house, at least, you are not empty-handed.[49]

Having usurped all privileges in life and deprived women of all blessings such as education, travel, and science, these same men nevertheless had the audacity to proclaim that "the women in our nation are still not worthy of any education."[50] But where did you examine "our lack of potential," Tahireh asked. When did you ever open a school for us? Find teachers for us? Provide the means for our education, so that our lack of potential and talent became known to you?[51]

The absurdities men uttered about women's so-called lack of intelligence, strength, and potential were not to be bothered with, she concluded. In truth, women not only were men's equal but were stronger than men in many ways:

> The almighty God has created us equal with men, and indeed some of our powers are greater than those of men. For example, no man can bear a child, but we women can. Our loyalty and love are many times greater than that of a man. In intelligence and acumen we surpass the men. In strength and hardiness we are greater because no man will tolerate for a minute the many injuries, troubles, and miseries we women suffer through. Therefore, we are in no way less than the men. So why is it that we have been called the lowest of creatures and the cause of infamy for our dear homeland?[52]

Some male constitutionalists, such as the writers of *Iran-i Nau*, argued on behalf of women's social and political participation in society. In addition to the articles by Tahireh, lectures by young graduates of the newly formed girls' schools were often printed in the paper. On a few occasions *Iran-i Nau* also addressed the issue of prostitution and the conditions under which women abandoned their homes. Prostitution was a direct result of women's lack of education and financial desperation, *Iran-i Nau* argued. A report entitled "Don't Fight with Your Wives" discussed the insecure life of a married woman, Batul Khanum, who lived in constant fear of abandonment by her husband, and thus became an easy pawn for schemes by a woman broker. Batul Khanum, whose marriage was on the rocks, was told by the broker, "Your husband is tired of you and no longer loves you. I feel sorry for you and have been thinking of a solution to your problems. . . ." Batul Khanum turned her jewelry over to the broker, who promised to find her a solution if she left home. Her story turned out to have a "happy ending," since after days of being abandoned, Batul Khanum's husband located her, the broker was arrested, and the jewels were returned.[53]

Journalists, poets, and even delegates to the parliament also emerged as vocal supporters of women's rights. The social satire of Ali Akbar Dihkhuda, editor of *Sur-i Israfil* (1907-1908); the support of the representative Vakil al-Ru'aya, who petitioned the first parliament on behalf of the women's anjumans and the second parliament for recognition of women's suffrage; and the poetry of Iraj Mirza did much to place the question of women's liberation on the political agenda.

The Tiflis-based Turkish-language satirical paper *Mulla Nasr al-Din*, which began publication in 1906, had initiated a radical critique of women's subjugation in traditional Muslim societies. The cartoons and stories singled out women's segregation, polygyny, and wife beating. Dihkhuda, editor of the left-wing weekly *Sur-i Israfil* in Tehran, shared *Mulla Nasr al-Din*'s sentiments on this issue. In his columns Dihkhuda often exposed the hypocrisy of the male community, including the clerics who preached one set of beliefs and norms of behavior to women and practiced quite another themselves. He would not hesitate to write of his opposition to the practice of veiling in a satirical poem:

> Times a hundred I've told you your project will fail,
> O Kably
> While half the nation are wrapped in a veil,
> O Kably[54]

Dihkhuda's columns referred to the harsh treatment of women by fathers and husbands, child marriages, loveless marriages, and polygyny. He accused the semiliterate low cleric (*akhund*) of taking advantage of his religious position and turning his bureau in the mosque into a brothel. In one of Dihkhuda's columns, the akhund had married for wealth, had entered into a number of temporary marriages, and was so shameless in conduct as to have spent the last penny of his wife's dowry.[55] Likewise, Dihkhuda denounced the delegates to the parliament who had refused to lend their support to the creation of new educational and social institutions for women, even as women continued to organize societies and establish schools. "What is the reason that our women have organized several times and presented petitions to the parliament and members of the cabinet pleading to receive permission to form new schools and anjumans of women, and each time, our representatives and cabinet members not only did not support them but indeed opposed them?"[56]

In August 1907 when a group of destitute widows whose pensions had been postponed for months staged a sit-in at the Artillery Square near the parliament, the journal *Habl al-Matin* spoke out on their behalf. *Habl al-Matin* had published women's letters on major social and political issues from time to time. This time, however, the journal devoted an editorial to the plight of the poor women of Tehran, writing: "The most miserable and innocent people of the world are Iranian women, especially the residents of large cities, and particularly the women of Tehran, to whom every door of refuge is closed. . . ."[57]

These women, *Habl al-Matin* continued, had neither an education nor a profession from which to make a living and so were completely dependent on their husbands for their daily bread. Because of this precarious life, they accepted their husbands' abuses and obeyed all their petty wishes. Still, "the unjust men act as if they do not consider women human beings." The very men who wished to be viewed as generous and open-handed in the public realm, were evil and mean-spirited with their wives. They treated women miserably and considered wife beating "an essential component" of their relationship. Moreover, the moment a man's business prospered, he forgot his "long-time bedfellow" and sought a younger companion. The editorial, which was titled "The Most Dishonored People," argued that the nation, by virtue of its treatment of women, had allowed itself to become a shame and disgrace. *Habl al-Matin* pledged to open a donation fund for the women squatters in the Artillery Square if the ministers and the wealthier members of the community refused to help these women immediately.

The women's anjumans were extremely receptive to the articles which called for their support or addressed issues relevant to them. When *Iran-i Nau* reported the plight of a young slave girl, women immediately offered their help. Slave trade had officially been banned in the country for many years, but the practice continued, though to a lesser extent than in the previous centuries. A young woman slave repeatedly, and unsuccessfully, had tried to escape when she was offered for sale by her wealthy owner, and as a result she was severely punished. Upon learning of her story, three women came to the offices of the newspaper and offered to buy the slave woman's freedom, while the owner was publicly humiliated in the paper for his actions.[58] On yet another occasion when a slave woman ran away from her owner's house, leaving behind a small child, *Iran-i Nau* protested, writing, "We are amazed that in the twentieth century and at a time when people in our nation are struggling for political freedom and sacrificing their lives, human beings are being sold as if they were animals."[59]

The Second Constitutional Period of 1909-1911 came to an end in December 1911. The Russian government, which considered the reform measures carried out by the parliament an interference with its colonial interests in Iran, gave an ultimatum to the parliament in November 1911, with the full support of the British government. The letter of ultimatum called for the removal of the American financial advisor, Morgan Shuster, and the political subordination of the constitutional government to the two Powers in accordance with the 1907 Anglo-Russian Convention. As the delegates deliberated the issue of closing down the parliament, women in Tehran and Isfahan, among others, helped organize a successful boycott of foreign goods and services. A large demonstration of several thousand women, principally organized by Anjuman of Ladies of the Nation, was held on December 1, 1911, outside the parliament. The participants called upon the delegates to resist the foreign ultimatum and followed their actions with a stream of telegrams to European governments and appeals to other women including the British suffragettes.[60]

The parliament, which would not accept the Russian ultimatum, was closed down by a coup d'etat a few weeks later. But the women's actions remained in the collective memory of the nation, and this memory was revived during the 1978-79 revolution by a new generation of young feminist participants, who often referred to the origins of the Iranian women's movement in the Constitutional Revolution, even though the many dimensions of this movement were yet unknown.

A close study of the Constitutional Revolution reveals that once its initial goals, the establishment of a parliament and a constitution, were reached, the diverse coalition of intellectuals, clerics, merchants, and craftsmen which helped bring about the August 1906 revolution faced new contradictions from within. When a number of social and political issues, such as the question of women's education, were placed on the agenda of the assembly, some of the participants, including conservative clerics such as Shaikh Fazlallah Nuri, abandoned the movement and joined the opposition. In turn, women activists who had supported the movement since its inception channeled their efforts into the creation of women's anjumans and educational institutions. Often they found its necessary to confront the conservative clerics, who strongly opposed their actions, though some remained ambivalent in their treatment of the clerics and the role of religion in their lives. But the delegates to the parliament also came under attack by the activist women for not undertaking major reforms in the country. During the Second Constitutional Period of 1909-1911, the anjumans and the intellectual women whose voices could be heard in the leading journals of the period began to question more openly some of the traditional patriarchal relations which predominated between men and women at home. Throughout the years of the revolution, a number of male intellectuals, both within the parliament and outside it, emerged as vocal supporters of women's rights. Journalists turned pages of their newspapers over to women writers and columnists. They devoted editorials to the subject, and challenged delegates to the parliament to recognize the women's anjumans and support them in their social and cultural activities. Although the revolution came to an end in December 1911, the women's activities hardly stopped. The creation of schools and other institutions for women continued through the war years. A second wave of the women's movement began in the aftermath of the Russian Revolution of 1917, when feminists and Marxist intellectuals who had come of age during the Constitutional Revolution, such as Sadiqeh Daulatabadi, Muhtaram Iskandari, and Avetis Sultanzadeh, helped create a variety of forums through which the women's quest for emancipation would continue.

For the most part, however, both male and female advocates of women's rights subscribed to the position that greater educational and social opportunities for women strengthened family ties. In their belief that a woman's "sexual promiscuity" stemmed from her ignorance and lack of education, the early advocates of women's rights in Iran were similar to European feminists of the eighteenth century such as Mary Wollstonecraft, who had also tried to convince the male community of the merits of an educated woman, who supposedly remained even more loyal to traditional family values. Such assumptions were widely shattered when in the post-World War II period greater economic, educational, and professional opportunities for Iranian women, albeit within the constraints of an absolutist monarchy, came to challenge the Islamic family laws and acceptable social and sexual practices, especially for women. By the time of the 1979 revolution, many clerics and reform-minded intellectuals would argue that greater economic and employment opportunities, as well as westernization, had led to a vast increase in "promiscuity" and "looseness" among women, and they began to call for a return to traditional Islamic laws. On the other hand, since the 1979 revolution many Iranian feminists have come to the realization that they can no longer eliminate the issues of sexuality and needed religious reforms from their political discussions, that the question of women's liberation cannot be reduced to greater education and work opportunities alone. Furthermore, there is a realization that on many issues there can be no compromise with traditional Islamic values, these including the veil, polygyny, and divorce. This makes the task of women's liberation in the Middle East even more challenging, as there is a greater awareness that the struggle for secularization of politics, feminism, and radical social and economic change will have to be carried out all at once and specifically by women themselves.

NOTES

I would like to thank Beth Baron and Nikki Keddie, who read the earlier drafts of this essay and made many valuable suggestions. I am, however, solely responsible for any shortcomings.

1. Some of the earlier studies of this period which introduced the subject were Badr al-Muluk Bamdad, *From Darkness into Light: Women's Emancipation in Iran*, trans. and ed. F. R. Bagley (Smithtown, N.Y.: Exposition Press, 1977). This book, and its earlier Persian edition *Zanan-i Irani az Inqilab-i Mashrutiyat ta Inqilab-i Sifid* (Iranian Women from the Constitutional Revolution to the White Revolution) (Tehran: Ibn Sina Press, 1968), were among the first biographical studies in Iran to reveal new information about women leaders in that movement. Mangol Bayat-Philipp, "Women and Revolution in Iran, 1905-11," in *Women in the Muslim World*, ed. Nikki Keddie and Lois Beck (Cambridge: Harvard University Press, 1978), 295-308, discussed, among other issues, the debates on women's suffrage by male constitutionalists in the parliament in 1911. Huma Natiq in her "Nigahi bi Barkhi Nivishtiha va Mubarizat-i Zan dar Dauran-i Mashrutiyat" (A Look at Some of the Writings and Struggles of Women in the Constitutional Period), *Kitab-i Jum'eh* 30 (1979): 45-54, unearthed the writings of the late nineteenth-century activist Bibi Khanum as well as those of Taj al-Saltaneh, the Qajar princess who was involved in the women's societies. Abdulhusain Nahid, *Zanan-i Iran dar Junbish-i*

Mashruteh (Iranian Women in the Constitutional Movement) (Tehran: n.p., 1981), was reprinted by Iranian feminists in Germany, and focused on the history of women's revolutionary activities in the late nineteenth and early twentieth centuries. See also my "On the Origins of Feminism in Early 20th-Century Iran," *Journal of Women's History* 1, no. 2 (Fall 1989): 65-87.

2. E. G. Browne, *The Persian Revolution of 1905-1909* (Cambridge: Cambridge University Press, 1910); and Browne, *The Press and Poetry of Modern Persia* (Cambridge: Cambridge University Press, 1914). Part one of this book, an annotated bibliography of the constitutional newspapers, was compiled by Mirza Muhammad Ali Khan Tarbiyat and includes material contributed by H. L. Rabino, the scholar and British vice-consul in Rasht at the time. Ahmad Kasravi, *Tarikh-i Mashruteh-yi Iran* (History of Constitutionalism in Iran) (Tehran: Sipihr Publications, 1984).

3. William Morgan Shuster, *The Strangling of Persia* (New York: The Century Company, 1912), 191-99.

4. Yahya Aryanpur, *Az Saba ta Nima* 2 (From Saba to Nima) (Tehran: Kitabha-yi Jibi, 1972), 78; Jan Rypka, *History of Iranian Literature* (Dordrecht, Holland: D. Reidel Publishing Company, 1968), 362-65.

5. Browne, *The Press and Poetry*, 26.

6. A recent and comprehensive discussion of Qurrat al-Ain appears in Abbas Amanat, *Resurrection and Renewal: The Making of the Babi Movement in Iran, 1844-1850* (Ithaca: Cornell University Press, 1989), 295-331.

7. Aryanpur, *Az Saba ta Nima* 2, 113.

8. Abdulhusain Nahid, *Zanan-i Iran dar Junbish-i Mashruteh*, 25-28.

9. See Tadeusz Swietochowski, "Himmat Party: Socialism and the Nationality Question in Russian Azerbaijan, 1904-1920," *Cahiers du Monde Russe et Sovietique* 19 (1978): 119-42.

10. Nikki R. Keddie, *Roots of Revolution* (New Haven: Yale University Press, 1981), 66-67; Nahid, *Zanan-i Iran dar Junbish-i Mashruteh*, 30-36.

11. One of the earliest warnings to Muzaffar al-Din Shah was handed to him by a woman, Mrs. Jahangir, the aunt of Mirza Jahangir Khan Shirazi, editor of *Sur-i Israfil.* As the Shah descended from his carriage, she cut through the circle of his guards and handed them what seemed to be a petition. In fact this was a letter of warning to the Shah from the Revolutionary Committee of Tehran, threatening him that were he not to set up a "parliament of the representatives of the nation to spread justice as in all civilized nations of the world," he would be killed. According to Malikzadeh, who recounts the story, Mrs. Jahangir's house was a meeting place for the revolutionaries throughout the years of the revolution. She lost both her son and her nephew, Mirza Jahangir Khan, during the 1908 coup, at which time her residence was turned into an arms reservoir for the constitutionalist fighters. See Mahdi Malikzadeh, *Tarikh-i Inqilab-i Mashrutiyat-i Iran* 2 (History of the Iranian Constitutional Revolution) (Tehran: Ibn Sina Press, n.d.), 61-64.

12. Nahid, *Zanan-i Iran dar Junbish-i Mashruteh*, 55-58.

13. The letter containing this information is reprinted in Isma'il Ra'in, *Anjumanha-yi Sirri* (The Secret Anjumans) (Tehran: Tehran Mussavar Press, 1966), 98-99.

14. Pari Shaikh al-Islami, *Zanan-i Ruznameh-nigar va Andishmand-i Iran* (Journalist and Intellectual Women of Iran) (Tehran: Maz Graphics Press, 1972), 71-72.

15. *Majlis* 2 (27 November 1906): 4.

16. *Anjuman* 41 (9 February 1907): 4.

17. *Anjuman* 11 (1906), quoted in Mansureh-yi Rafi'i, *Anjuman* (Tehran: Nashr-i Tarikh-i Iran, 1983), 118.

18. *Majlis* 6 (30 December 1906): 3.

19. *The Times* (13 August 1910): 3.

20. See Clara Colliver Rice, *Persian Women and Their Ways* (London: Seeley, Service & Company, 1923), 271.

21. Bamdad, *From Darkness into Light*, 30-31.

22. *Ibid.*

23. For a list of some of the members of this group, see *ibid.*, 30.

24. *Nida-yi Vatan* 70 (2 October 1907): 3-4.

25. *Majlis* 72 (14 March 1908): 2.

26. Bamdad, *From Darkness into Light*, 34-35.

27. *Revue du Monde Musulman* 2 (1907): 213.

28. *Iran-i Nau* 120 (19 December 1911): 4.

29. *Musavat* 28 (7 February 1909): 7.

30. See *Iran-i Nau* 54 (31 October 1909): 4.

31. See Fakhri Qavami, *Karnameh-yi Zanan-i Mashhur-i Iran az Oabl az Islam ta 'Asr-i Hazir* (Report of Famous Women of Iran from before Islam to the Present Time) (Tehran: Kitabha-yi Jibi, n.d.), 128-31.

32. Fakhri Qavami, *Karnameh-yi Zanan*, 141.

33. Pari Shaikh al-Islami, *Zanan-i Ruznameh-nigar*, 88-99; and Qavami, *Karnameh-yi Zanan*, 140.

34. Quoted in Yahya Armajani, "Sam Jordan and the Evangelical Ethic in Iran," in *Religious Ferment in Asia*, ed. Robert J. Miller (Lawrence: University Press of Kansas, 1974), 33.

35. Bamdad, *From Darkness into Light*, 45-47, and Qavami, *Karnameh-yi Zanan*, 140.

36. *Lavayeh-i Aqa Shaikh Fazlallah* (Petitions of Shaikh Fazlallah Nuri), ed. Huma Rizvani (Tehran: Nashr-i Tarikh-i Iran, 1983), 27.

37. *Musavat* 18 (22 March 1908): 5-6.

38. *Ibid.*

39. *Sur-i Israfil* 7 & 8 (1 August 1907): 4-5.

40. "Letter of One of the Women," in *Habl al-Matin* 105 (1 September 1907): 4-6.

41. *Ibid.*

42. *Nida-yi Vatan* 70 (2 October 1907): 3-4.

43. *Iran-i Nau* 150 (7 March 1910): 1.

44. For a study of theatre in this period, see also Jamshid Malikpur, *Adabiyat-i Namayash-i dar Iran: Dauran-i Inqilab-i Mashruteh* 2 (Theatrical Literature in Iran: The Period of the Constitutional Revolution) (Tehran: Tus Publications, 1983).

45. *Khatirat-i Taj al-Saltaneh* (Memoirs of Taj al-Saltaneh), ed. Mansureh Ittihadiyeh Nizam Mafi and Sirus Sa'dvandian (Tehran: Nashr-i Tarikh-i Iran, 1983), 101-102. See also Shireen Mahdavi, "Taj al-Saltaneh, an Emancipated Qajar Princess," *Middle Eastern Studies* 23, no. 2 (April 1987): 188-93.

46. *Iran-i Nau* 65 (13 November 1909): 3. The name Tahireh immediately brings to mind the famous nineteenth-century Babi woman leader Tahireh Qurrat al-'Ain, and thus the possibility that the writer who adopted this pen name was also a Babi.

47. *Iran-i Nau* 65 (13 November 1909): 3.

48. *Iran-i Nau* 67 (18 November 1909).

49. *Iran-i Nau* 78 (30 November 1909): 2-3.

50. *Ibid.*

51. *Iran-i Nau* 84 (8 December 1909): 3.

52. *Iran-i Nau* 92 (18 December 1909): 4.

53. *Iran-i Nau* 59 (6 November 1909): 2-3.

54. *Sur-i Israfil* 17 (20 November 1907): 7. English translation appears in Browne, *Press and Poetry of Modern Persia,* 181. Kably is an abbreviation for Karbala'i, one who has made a pilgrimage to Karbala, and is a common prefix to men's names.

55. *Sur-i Israfil* 28 (6 May 1908): 7-8.

56. *Sur-i Israfil* 31 (22 June 1908): 7.

57. *Habl al-Matin* 103 (29 August 1907): 1-2.

58. *Iran-i Nau* 45 (20 October 1909): 2; and *Iran-i Nau* 46 (26 October 1909): 2.

59. *Iran-i Nau* 98 (26 December 1909): 2-3.

60. See Afary, "On the Origins of Feminism," 77-81.

CHRISTIANITY, FEMINISM, AND COMMUNISM
THE LIFE AND TIMES OF DENG YUZHI
(CORA DENG)

Emily Honig

Unlike the twentieth-century Chinese women whose lives Western readers know the most about—the revolutionary martyr Qiu Jin, the writer Ding Ling, and Mao Zedong's controversial wife Jiang Qing—Deng Yuzhi (known to her Western friends as Cora Deng) considered herself neither a feminist nor a revolutionary. She described herself as first and foremost a Christian, yet as head of the Labor Bureau of the Young Women's Christian Association (YWCA), she played a major role in organizing women to participate in the Chinese communist revolution of the 1920s-1949. She exemplifies a group of urban, educated Chinese women who equated Christianity with social activism and international sisterhood. Their quiet, understated contribution to the Chinese revolution has been largely ignored in studies that have focused instead on workers and peasants, the two groups the Chinese Communist Party (CCP) most explicitly tried to organize.

This essay explores the relationship between Christianity, feminism, and communism in Deng Yuzhi's life. In spite of her own retrospective emphasis on her Christian identity, she devoted much of her life to instilling a working-class and feminist consciousness among women factory workers. Defining, juggling, and sometimes manipulating the Christian, communist, and feminist elements of her identity was a major theme in her career.

The integration of Christianity, feminism, and communism might at first seem paradoxical. Although liberation theologians in Latin America have insisted upon the compatibility of Christianity and communism, in the context of Republican-period China their synthesis seemed unlikely. The missionaries who went to China sought converts to Christianity, not Marxism. Instilling a revolutionary ideology was not their mission; nor did the Church encourage people to get involved in the revolutionary movement. Deng Yuzhi was by no means the only Christian sympathetic to communism, for individuals such as Wu Yaozong (Y. T. Wu) devoted much of their careers to establishing the potential connections. Deng, however, added a concern with women's issues to the amalgam.

Feminism and Christianity might seem as unlikely a combination in Republican-period China as Christianity and communism. A major aspect of the missionary enterprise in China was the establishment of girls' schools, yet their aims were limited. On the one hand, they attacked what they perceived as the most oppressive aspects of Chinese women's lives, such as footbinding and arranged marriages. Moreover, they provided young women an opportunity for education that in some cases made it possible for them to have professional careers. Yet the vision of gender roles that they advocated was one based on traditional Western values: a woman might have a career, but she should be a responsible housewife as well.[1] The cultivation of "Christian feminists" was not the goal. Although the YWCA night schools that Deng Yuzhi directed technically belonged to the missionary effort in China, their message to women was far more radical, and feminist, than that of the more typical missionary schools Deng herself had attended.

Although feminism and communism might not at first seem incongruous, their union has been as troubled in China as in other countries experiencing socialist revolution.[2] Particularly after the 1920s, most women who joined the Chinese Communist Party (CCP) or who were sympathetic to the communist movement subordinated their feminist principles to the "larger" goals of the revolution. The few who did not, such as Ding Ling, were silenced.

Deng Yuzhi, then, represents an unusual amalgam in the history of the Chinese revolution. Yet, as we shall see below, to describe Deng as a "Christian feminist communist" is far too simplistic. In fact, what is most striking about her is that she never fully identified with any one of these appellations: although sympathetic to the aims of the CCP, she never joined or called herself a communist; she devoted most of her career to women's work, yet never called herself a feminist; and although she calls herself Christian, her life has been a remarkably unreligious one. As we shall see, during different periods of her life Deng has drawn on—while never entirely subordinating herself to—each of these ideologies and structures to define a vision of politics that is her own.

What emerges is that although she was a Christian from childhood, attended missionary schools and college, and devoted her life to working for a Christian missionary organization, the YWCA, Christianity was not a prominent component of Deng's identity until the 1940s. A commitment to creating a feminist and working-class consciousness was far more salient. In the 1940s, however, as her work and convictions drew her closer to those of the CCP, the articulation of a Christian identity became a way of protecting and maintaining her own agenda. Ironically, only after Liberation in 1949 did Christianity become central to her identity.

In exploring the relationship between Christianity, feminism and communism in Deng Yuzhi's life, this essay draws on archival materials from the YWCA, Deng's own published writings, and interviews with her friends and colleagues. The primary source, however, is an extensive oral history that I conducted with her in 1985. I first met Deng Yuzhi in 1979, when I was beginning research on the history of women cotton-mill workers in Shanghai. For the two years I was in Shanghai, we met almost every week, to discuss my research and her past, and to share opinions about China's present. Her passion for recalling the past, as well as her extraordinary memory, made me determined to record her life history. By 1985, she, too, was unmistakably anxious to tell her life story to herself, and had set up a tape recorder of her own for that purpose.[3]

Like any historical inquiry, an oral history is inevitably shaped by the period during which it is recorded. Had Deng told her life stories immediately after Liberation in 1949 or during the Cultural Revolution (1966-76), it might have included the same events, but it would have been colored by a different tone and interpretation from her account in 1985. The year 1985, nearly a decade after the end of the Cultural Revolution, was a relatively relaxed time. Relations between Chinese and foreigners were far looser and freer of restrictions than they had been even five years earlier, when I first got to know Deng Yuzhi. The mid-1980s were also a period of political liberalization and openness to the West. Prior to the mid-1980s, Deng might well have been reluctant to record her life history at all, fearful she might say things considered politically "incorrect." She certainly would not have told her story to a foreigner. The general admiration of the West that was popular in the mid-1980s most likely made her feel freer to speak about the time she spent abroad and her affiliation with a Western missionary organization. The YWCA, after all, was being revived in China in the 1980s, and Deng was playing a central role in that work.

Politics was not the only factor shaping the version of her life that Deng related in the mid-1980s. At the age of eighty-five, she had resolved much of her past, and had a deep investment in presenting her life as non-conflictual. Thus, at points when one might expect emotional or political conflict, her account is conspicuously straightforward.

A Christian Education

As with many of her contemporaries, Deng Yuzhi's Christian identity did not represent a process of individual deliberation and conversion, but rather the continuation of a family tradition begun by her grandmother. This "tradition," however, began only after her parents died. They had never been Christians and had raised Deng and her sisters in a manner considered progressive for its time. While they were alive, Deng's early experiences resembled those of a number of women who became well-known revolutionaries.

Deng was born in 1900 in the Hubei city of Shashi. At the age of eight she moved with her family to Changsha, where her father had received an official appointment. Changsha was the political, cultural, and educational center of Hunan, a province which from the 1890s was reputed for its radicalism.[4] When she arrived there, Deng joined the ranks of the relatively small number of Chinese women who had the opportunity to attend school. Not until 1906 had government-sponsored schools for girls been established in China, and even then, their mandate was to educate girls to become "good wives and mothers."[5] (Although missionary schools had opened several decades earlier, they did not gain legitimacy among gentry families until the early twentieth century.)[6] Unlike some girls, such as Xie Bingying, who had to threaten suicide or stage a hunger strike to overcome their parrents' conviction that going to school violated codes of proper female conduct,[7] Deng, her sister, and her sister-in-law were enthusiastically enrolled in the Zhounan Girls' Middle School by her parents. "My parents wanted to send us to a modern school because the atmosphere in Changsha was very progressive at that time," Deng recalled. "My father was a strict Confucian, but he was very progressive on social issues. He was one of those people who cut off their queues, and he had joined the Anti-Footbinding Society."[8]

Of the schools in Changsha that admitted women, Zhounan was particularly known for its progressivism. Well before the May Fourth Movement of 1919—when all aspects of women's traditional status were challenged—Zhounan students stood out for their public defiance of traditional female roles. At the time of the 1911 Revolution, which replaced the dynastic system with a republican form of government, Zhounan students were conspicuous for their bobbed hair and for appearing in public unescorted, thereby appalling older women.[9] Had Deng stayed at Zhounan, her future might have been more like that of her schoolmates Xiang Jingyu, Cai Chang, Ding Ling, and Yang Kaihui (Mao Zedong's first wife), all of whom became active in the CCP.

Deng unwittingly moved into a different, more religiously oriented, social world when her parents died in the early 1910s. From then on she was raised by her grandmother, a devout Buddhist who had become a Christian through contact with missionaries at the Yale Hospital in Changsha where Deng's father was treated for tuberculosis. Deng attributes her grandmother's conversion to the help provided by missionaries:

> There was a Bible woman from the hospital who came to our house every day, to try to help us, comfort us, and help with losing the breadwinner. I think one reason my grandmother was converted was that the church was a place where you could go for help with all of your problems. They were

> very friendly there and would do anything to help you. . . . Christianity
> was much better organized [than Buddhism]. After my grandmother was
> converted, she went to church every Sunday and took us along.

More influential than attending church services, however, was her
grandmother's decision to send Deng to a missionary school once she
graduated from Zhounan. This undoubtedly reflected her grandmother's
Christian identity, even though Deng ascribes the switch to her own desire
to learn English.

The move from Zhounan to the missionary-sponsored Fuxiang School
for Girls marked a major turning point in Deng's life. Although it was not
her decision or desire to attend a missionary school, she immediately identified potential advantages (such as learning English, and thereby gaining
a familiarity with the West). Moreover, almost as soon as she moved to
Fuxiang, she found a niche—the YWCA—through which she could keep
alive, within a missionary environment, the progressive political values she
most likely acquired at Zhounan.

Upon entering Fuxiang, she became involved with the social service
committee of the YWCA, which provided the link between Christianity and
social activism that became central to her life's work. "I wanted to do
something helpful for people—to serve, not just be served," she recalls.

> I had caught that idea from my childhood, listening to all those sermons
> about how people should be good to others, like Good Samaritans. So
> religion did have some positive effect on me which lasted my whole
> life—not believing in God, but those ethical elements about how to live a
> life useful to others. That's why I joined the social service committee of
> the YWCA.

At this point in her life, Christianity was obviously not her most powerfully
held conviction. She knew she wanted to "serve others," yet her ideas
about whom to serve and how were vague, and she had not yet begun to
focus on women or workers. The YWCA suited her needs well.

The YWCA was not typical of missionary organizations in China. Even in
the U.S. and England, where the YWCA was first formed in the 1880s, spirituality and religion were subordinate to an emphasis on social work and
the enhancement of women's opportunities. Although when the YWCA
was established in China in the 1890s it devoted most of its initial energies
to recruiting high-school students (the number of female college students
was still too small), its programs always aimed to educate schoolgirls about
the problems of the urban poor.[10] Other missionary groups sometimes criticized the YWCA's emphasis on social work, charging that it was "not pay-
ing sufficient attention to religious pursuits and [was] in danger of losing
'its identity in church and community.' "[11] For Deng, however, this is what
made the YWCA compelling—there was not a time in her life after

Fuxiang (except during the Cultural Revolution of the 1960s) when she was *not* engaged in YWCA work.

The Challenge of May Fourth

As for many members of her generation, the May Fourth Movement in 1919 represented Deng's initiation into politics. When news reached Beijing of the Versailles Peace Conference proposal to cede parts of Shandong Province to Japan, students immediately mobilized massive demonstrations. They demanded that the Chinese delegation refuse to sign the treaty, called for the resignation of the pro-Japanese ministers in the government, and organized a boycott of Japanese goods. Almost immediately, these protests spread to campuses throughout China.

As president of the Student Self-Government Association at Fuxiang, Deng not only chaired meetings of the student body but played a major role in organizing students to participate in the political demonstrations of 1919. That spring and summer, like students throughout China, she and her classmates took to the streets, making speeches and visiting shopkeepers in an attempt to persuade them to join the boycott of Japanese goods. It was the first time that she had to confront, and mediate, the potential conflict between religious and political convictions; it was also the first time she had to confront women's issues, albeit in the very personal context of her own marriage.

For students at a missionary school such as Fuxiang, the decision to take a political stand had to be considered in the context of religious beliefs. Deng did not find it difficult to identify a Christian basis for participation in the May Fourth Movement, but her views were not shared by all her classmates. "Not all the students at Fuxiang joined the movement," she recalls.

> There was a small group who thought that we did not need to show our patriotism. There was a religious debate about it. There were these people who put all their hopes for change in God. But there were also people who thought that we not only had to have faith in God, but also to live in accordance with God's will. Since God does not want people to be exploited or suppressed by others, we thought that fighting for national survival was carrying out God's will. This internal debate went on for a month. We looked down on those who didn't join.

This belief in the relevance of Christian values to contemporary political struggles underlay almost all of Deng's future work.

The May Fourth experience affected Deng's ideas not only about the potential fusion of Christianity and social activism, but about women's roles as well. The May Fourth Movement made all previously prescribed social relationships subject to debate among the urban educated elite, as

Confucianism and Confucian social organization were seen as the cause of China's inability to defend itself against Western imperialism. The traditional family system and women's roles in it became emblematic of everything corrupt about Confucianism; family revolution became "the center of revolutionary politics."[12] Some of the most famous writings of the time concerned the status of women. For example, one of Mao Zedong's earliest essays, "A Critique of Miss Zhao's Suicide," described how a young woman expressed her rejection of an arranged marriage by slitting her throat while riding in a sedan chair to the marriage ceremony. Henrik Ibsen's play *A Doll's House* was translated, widely published, and performed; the central figure, Nora, became a symbol to Chinese women of women's emancipation. In a speech to students at a Beijing women's college entitled "What Happens After Nora Leaves Home?" China's preeminent writer Lu Xun dealt with the problem of women's achieving individual liberation in an oppressive society.[13] New publications such as *New Youth* (*Xin qingnian*) and the *Ladies' Journal* (*Funü zazhi*), filled with accounts of women's tragic experiences as virtuous widows or child daughters-in-law, were read and passionately discussed by Deng and her classmates.

The radical views of women's roles were more than abstract ideals for students at missionary schools, as many of their teachers were single women determined to establish their own careers and support themselves. Ironically, these women, who might have been caricatured as "old maids" or "spinsters" in their own countries, in many ways exemplified May Fourth ideals.[14] "I saw all those teachers at Fuxiang living independently," Deng recalled.

> They earned their own salary and were free to use their money however they wanted. Some of them—both Chinese and American— were not married. No! No one thought it was odd that they were single. People respected them because they could earn their own living. That was the atmosphere in Changsha during those early days of the New Culture Movement. People wanted to be independent, and so did I.

In fact, refusing to marry was highly unusual in China at this time. According to one survey, less than one woman in a thousand in rural China never married, although the number was slightly higher in urban areas.[15] Nevertheless, inspired by the example of her teachers, Deng became determined to "support myself and not depend on a father, husband, or son." Like many of her classmates, she had no intention of marrying.[16]

The radical May Fourth values that Deng adopted during her high-school years met their first major challenge when she graduated. Her hope of going on to college was suddenly dashed when her grandmother informed her that her marriage, long ago arranged by her parents, was to take place immediately. Although arranged marriages were typical in China at that time, Deng belonged to the first generation of Chinese women who were committed to challenging the practice. Unlike some of her contemporaries, Deng was not resisting an arranged marriage for the sake of a mate she had freely chosen herself. Instead, she desperately wanted to remain independent, continue her education, and pursue a career—all of which she assumed marriage would preclude.

It was therefore only after extracting a promise that her husband's family would permit her to attend college that she acquiesced to the marriage. The marriage agreement also stipulated that the husband's family permit Deng to practice Christianity and not force her to engage in ancestor worship—a requirement issued by her grandmother. Although being able to maintain a Christian identity was not crucial to Deng, it ultimately provided her a rationale to escape an undesirable marriage. When her husband's family forced her to worship their ancestors, forbade her from attending church (which had never been particularly important to Deng), and refused to allow her to continue her education, Deng seized her belongings and fled, seeking refuge at Fuxiang, where she had planned to study an additional year of English in order to pass the entrance exam for Jinling College.

Despite attempts by her husband's family to lure her back from Fuxiang, Deng finished the year of English, then moved to Nanjing to begin Jinling in 1920. Jinling, at that time, was one of a handful of colleges open to women, and had been the first, in 1919, to have women graduates.[17] It was a small missionary college—there were scarcely more than one hundred students and five or six faculty members at the time Deng attended—and therefore very personal.[18] So, for example, when during her sophomore year Deng's husband, his relatives, and eventually a lawyer came to insist on her return, Jinling's president, Matilda Thurston, intervened in Deng's defense, arranging to send her to Shanghai.[19]

Learning about the Working Class

For the ten years following her flight to Shanghai in 1921, Deng Yuzhi's life was fragmented: she spent two years in Changsha working for the YWCA, two years back at Jinling finishing her undergraduate education, two more years working for the YWCA, and finally a year in England studying at the London School of Economics. Despite the many changes, however, her interest in understanding and analyzing the lives of workers continued to grow.

Perhaps most influential in triggering Deng's interest in the Chinese working class was her friendship and working relationship with Maud Russell, a YWCA secretary from the U.S. who had been in China since the mid-1910s. Deng first met Russell when she returned to Changsha in 1922, to help her grandmother care for her brother's children while he was studying in England. Maud offered her a job in the Student Department of the YWCA. This represented not only Deng's first YWCA job but also a turning point in the development of her political thinking. Nearly sixty years later, she made a birthday tape to send to Maud, who lived in New York after her return from China in the late 1940s, single-handedly publishing the *Far Eastern Reporter* from her apartment on Riverside Drive. In it, Deng recalled how Russell had been the first to introduce her to revolutionary ideas.

> Maud taught me to read something about revolution. She helped me study English and asked me to study with her a book called *Dialectical Materialism.* (laughs) I had very poor English then, and there were so many big words in that book. I had to use a dictionary all the time in order to find out the real meaning. Whatever little knowledge I had about socialism at that time was started by my contact with Maud, and her helping me read those famous books about social revolution.

Perhaps unbeknownst to Deng was that when Russell first went to China in the mid-1910s to work for the YWCA, she saw herself as a Christian missionary, not a communist; it was the experience of living in China, and working with people such as Deng, that radicalized her thinking and made her a Marxist, committed to socialist revolution in China.[20] Many considered Russell, along with Lily K. Haass and Talitha Gerlach, to represent the "radical" faction among the foreign YWCA secretaries. (Lily Haass was at one point criticized by the YWCA board for recruiting so many radicals or communists, to which she replied, "But they are the best students in China!")[21]

Russell introduced Deng not only to radical ideas that were becoming increasingly popular in China at that time, but to the workers' movement as well. Although an organized labor movement had existed in China since the early twentieth century, it had become particularly active and powerful during the early 1920s, as the CCP devoted most of its efforts to organizing urban workers to lead the revolutionary effort. Understanding the lives and struggles of workers was therefore a major concern of both Chinese and foreign radicals.

It was in this context that analyzing workers' lives became one of Deng's major interests, and when she returned to Jinling in 1924, she decided to major in sociology. She was encouraged by Mary Treudley, Jinling's sociology teacher, known for her philosophy of relating religious education to contemporary social problems. It is not coincidental that Deng chose Treudley as her advisor; she had identified the faculty member whose understanding of the relationship between religion and politics resembled hers at that time. Treudley's avowed purpose in going to China was "putting *all* I have into a constructive program for putting Christ into daily human life."[22] Yet she passionately believed in training her students to observe and analyze social problems surrounding them. "Every Sunday the girls visit in the homes of our neighbors," Treudley reported, "and out of these visits come some of the problems that give point to our discussion of poverty."[23]

Based on one of these expeditions, Deng wrote one of her first surveys of a group of urban poor—a report on a children's home in Nanjing that had been visited by her sociology class in 1925.[24] The next year, for her graduation thesis, she conducted a survey of the handicraft tapestry industry in Nanjing—the precursor, in some ways, of the more substantial study of women factory workers in Shanghai that formed the basis of her master's thesis at New York University, in 1941.

Deng graduated from Jinling determined to become a teacher—an aspiration shared by many of her classmates and fueled by the severe shortage of qualified teachers to staff the growing number of girls' schools in China. Before she could implement this plan, however, she was once again recruited by Maud Russell to work for the Student Department of the YWCA—but this time she would be based in Shanghai.

Deng's tenure as a student secretary represented the one time during the 1920s when she was not focused on workers, yet this interest was never far in the background, and her desire to pursue it caused her to change jobs. As student secretary she had to focus more on the religious aspects of the YWCA's program than at any other time in her career. At the Wuhan Student Conference in 1926, for example, Deng "led morning devotional hours," as well as a discussion on the "relation of government and mission school students."[25] Deng recalled that when, in 1926-27, she traveled to Fujian to meet with the YWCA Students' Associations,

> We would meet with the cabinet and they would report on what they had done during the semester. They would ask us to lead their prayers and help them to study the Bible and discuss some problems they found in their work. We thought of it as casework: each person could come and have a talk with us about how to *zuo ren*—what we live for.

Ultimately, however, the emphasis on religion dissatisfied Deng, and she became increasingly restless with her job as secretary in the Student Department. Her frustration coincided with a concerted attempt by the Labor Bureau to lure her away from student work in order to direct its program of worker education. "It was a very big decision for me to switch to the Industrial Department," Deng recalled.

> Just going on year after year doing the student work—reading Bibles, making speeches like sermons—was not really what I wanted. I was still interested in teaching, so I was going to leave the YWCA and find a teaching job.

In other words, doing "social work" was far more important to Deng than a commitment to the YWCA or to Christian service. Just as she was about to leave the YWCA, another secretary told her about the possibility of working directly with factory girls—work that would involve teaching. "[She] knew that I was more interested in social problems than the religious aspect of the YWCA work."

In 1928 Deng began a year as a trainee in the Labor Bureau of the YWCA, headed at the time by Lily K. Haass. During this time she had the opportunity not only to acquaint herself with the programs for women workers run by the Labor Bureau, but also to develop her interest in economics. "In 1928 I started writing a book, *Women and Money*," she recalled.

> I had read books like Bernard Shaw's *The Intelligent Women's Guide to Capitalism and Socialism*, or something like that, and we had discussed it in our discussion group. I thought that in Chinese society there was such a big gap between the poor and the rich. . . . Inside rich people's homes food was spoiling, while poor people were lying on the streets as corpses. We saw them every day—people dying of hunger and cold. As I went through the factories I saw the terrible living conditions and the long hours, the child labor, and all that. I was so impressed by the injustice. Then I tried to describe why women were not able to earn their own living, why they were subject to oppression in the home as well as the factory. . . .
>
> I had the book all drafted out, but it was stopped before I finished it. I had shown it to the general secretary, Cai Kui, and she said, "Your writing is not good enough." I don't really think that was the reason, because you can always correct it. As I think back, I believe she thought I was too radical.

Although her first writing project was aborted, she had the opportunity to pursue her interest in women's economic status when she was sent, in 1929, on a YWCA scholarship to study labor economics at the London School of Economics.

By the time Deng returned to China in 1930, she had an expertise in economics that was unusual for a Chinese woman at that time. She had also developed a commitment to working with women workers. On the surface, it seems that Deng's integration of Christian beliefs, a concern with women's issues, and the working class was compatible with the YWCA, that the YWCA provided an almost perfect niche for someone such as Deng. A closer look, however, reveals that Deng already had views that differed from the YWCA's—as exemplified by her recognition that her book *Women and Money* was "too radical." The differences, and the ways in which Deng developed her own vision, become particularly evident in the years during which she directed the Labor Bureau. The bureau, we shall see, provided a structure within which she could do the work she wanted.

The Labor Bureau

When Deng returned to China from England in 1930, she became head of the YWCA Labor Bureau. (Her appointment represented a commitment of the YWCA to appoint Chinese, rather than foreigners, to leadership positions.)[26] For the next twenty years, she devoted herself to developing a program of education for women workers—the work for which she is best known.

Ever since the early 1900s, when the YWCA began a program in Shanghai—China's largest industrial center—it had been concerned with the plight of women workers, who represented nearly two-thirds of the city's workforce.[27] Initially, the YWCA's industrial program had focused on attracting women mill workers to sing, crochet, learn to read, and engage in Bible study, with the hope of "developing workers who would carry on Christian work."[28] This goal of conversion and training literate homemakers, as we shall see, was very different from Deng's aim of developing what can be described as a working-class feminist consciousness.

The program was sporadic until the early 1920s, when the association requested that someone with expertise in industrial problems be sent to China to assist in formulating a plan for industrial work. The appointment in 1921 of Agatha Harrison represented the beginning of a shift away from a concern with Christian education. When interviewed for the job, Harrison was "very frank in saying that she is not a member of any church, although she has a very definite faith." She was asked "point blank whether she approved of the taking of Christianity to non-Christian countries and she replied that she was not sure, but that probably she would become sure on seeing the need for it on the spot. She would not be willing to take a Bible class."[29] After arriving in Shanghai, Harrison organized a campaign against child labor, which became the focus of the YWCA Labor Bureau's work for several years.

The Labor Bureau did not completely abandon its efforts to work with women themselves, and during the mid-1920s set up pilot programs for popular education in several working-class districts of Shanghai.[30] This was a period when the Chinese Communist Party, founded in 1921, was actively organizing workers to join unions and participate in strikes, causing at least some members of the Labor Bureau to advocate a greater emphasis on educating women workers. As Lily Haass explained to a YWCA board that was less than enthusiastic about this shift, "The labour movement is the big factor in the future of our economic society and [it] makes all the difference in the world what that labour movement thinks. If we wish to help to create that thinking we will need to do it where the workers are. This does not mean that we care any less about public opinion or legislation."[31]

The shift to a program of worker education that emphasized politics more than religion culminated in Deng Yuzhi's directorship of the Labor Bureau. It would be misleading, however, to view Deng as simply continuing a preexisting trend, for she designed a program that represented a significant departure from that of the past, one that represented her growing sympathies with the goals of the Chinese Communist Party. The YWCA

Labor Bureau, we shall see, provided her a structure through which she could contribute to the organizing of the communist revolution, without having to join the Party or subordinate her work to its dictates.

Under Deng's leadership, the Labor Bureau established night schools for women workers in China's major industrial centers. The purpose of the schools was ostensibly to teach women literacy, but Deng designed a program that, couched in the rhetoric of Christian values, aimed to help them understand their position—as women and as workers—in China's social-economic system. To those who still expressed concern that the program represented too great a departure from the goals of missionary work, Deng replied:

> Some centres have Sunday Schools for the girls, other have Christmas services and parties, but the most important religious work done is through the secretary's personal contact with the girls. . . . The result of coming into touch with people who try to live a Christian life in all relations is a mighty factor in our religious work with workers, whose lives are in action more than in thought. Then day in and day out what the secretary does to help the girls in their one hundred and one personal and home problems; friendship with boys, friendship between girls, adjustment of marriages, the right kind of philosophy of life, enlarging their interest in life, are all religious work without fixed forms, and they represent the most important part of our work among industrial girls, for these give to us, as well as to the workers themselves, the permanent values of life.[32]

The notion of engaging in "religious work without fixed form" was extremely useful to Deng in justifying social and political work that might otherwise have been abhorrent to the YWCA.

In the curriculum Deng developed, students spent two years taking basic courses in writing, arithmetic, geography, history, and current events, followed by a third year of elective courses about industrial problems, trade unionism, and labor legislation. Teachers supplemented the text required by China's ruling party, the Guomindang, with one Deng had helped them edit themselves. This text, according to one of the teachers, explained "what imperialism was, how to be patriotic, why workers were oppressed, and why workers' lives are so inferior to those of the capitalists."[33] Classroom activities often encouraged women to become activists. For example, allegedly teaching letter writing, one of the teachers familiarized students with the factory law of the Shanghai Municipal Council and then had them write letters to the council reporting conditions in the factories where they worked that did not conform to the law.[34] The schools also taught women such practical skills as public speaking and singing that would enable them to participate more actively in the labor movement. The large number of night-school students who became activists in the labor movement attests to the program's success.[35]

While teaching women to understand (and ultimately to work to change) their position in the social and economic system was the major goal of the curriculum, Deng also saw the night schools as an arena where women workers could understand current political problems. By the 1930s, increasing Japanese aggression in China loomed as the major political issue. Teachers at the YWCA schools therefore organized discussions of Japanese imperialism, taught the students patriotic songs, and encouraged them to participate in the National Salvation Movement. Deng herself wrote a pamphlet for students, entitled *Zhongri quanxi* (Relations between China and Japan). At the same time, people such as Agnes Smedley, an American journalist who had close relations with leaders of the CCP, were invited to speak to the students about the attempts by the Communist Party to resist Japan and to organize a radically new type of society in Yanan.

The 1930s were a time of severe political repression, when suspected communists were systematically arrested and executed by the CCP's rival, the Guomindang. Deng recognized that the YWCA provided an almost unique forum for political activity. The police were not likely to challenge meetings held by foreigners, she observed. "And of course we were Christians, so they shouldn't suspect us of doing things like being communists!" Deng was, in a certain sense, manipulating both the police and the YWCA, engaging in work that neither would have wholly sanctioned.

Christianity and Communism

The radical curriculum as well as the number of activists graduating from the YWCA schools attracted the attention of the Chinese Communist Party. It had been less than successful in its own attempts to organize women workers during the 1920s; following the coup of 1927, when the Guomindang attacked the CCP-organized labor movement in Shanghai, the communists' efforts at labor organizing went completely underground. Thus, despite its earlier condemnation of the YWCA's religious orientation, the CCP, beginning in the 1930s, saw the YWCA Labor Bureau as an organization through which it could work to establish contact with women workers.

Deng's relationship with the CCP was complex. When, in the early 1980s, she was asked by a British friend why she had never joined the Party in the 1930s, she instantly replied, "But I was a Christian, so how could I have been a communist?" The question implies a degree of religiosity that hardly characterized Deng's life at this time. One cannot help but wonder whether she drew on her Christian identity to separate herself from the CCP and as an excuse never to confront the decision to join. Why she preferred not to join the Party remains unclear. Perhaps she anticipated that her feminist concerns would be coopted; at a minimum she knew that in joining the Party she would have to subordinate her own agenda.

Even if she never joined the CCP, she rarely disguised her sympathies for its beliefs and political aspirations. At the YWCA's student conference in summer 1933, for example, she assisted Maud Russell in teaching a course called "Christianity and Communism."

> We discussed what the October Revolution brought to Russia, how they were living, what their educational system is. We approached it from the Christian point of view—like we are all equal before God, should not have money as the incentive. Service should be the goal; serving people should be our aim. And that goes together with the communist idea of serving the general masses. Of course there was this idea of class struggle. I don't remember how Maud put it, but she did give us the sense that capitalism, the exploitation system, was bad. I shared her views at the time.

Throughout the 1930s, Deng continued to emphasize the benefits of socialist and Communist revolution at workers' conferences sponsored by the YWCA. At a conference in the late 1930s, for example, the themes for discussion included "world unemployment" and "capitalism, socialism, and communism."[36] Deng was never concerned with analyzing the relationship between Christianity and communism in a precise way. Instead, her work reflected, and sometimes foreshadowed, the endeavors of individuals such as Y. T. Wu to articulate the compatibility of Christianity and Marxism or communism.[37]

Perceiving the CCP as embracing the same Christian values in which she believed, Deng did not object to, but rather cooperated with, CCP attempts to influence women workers through the night schools. Moreover, she developed an argument that this was compatible with the goals of the YWCA, all the while knowing that not all YWCA staff members would agree. "The YMCA and YWCA are not churches," she explained. "They are social organizations with membership among the masses. So we got in touch with the more progressive groups, including the underground communist group. They wouldn't tell you they were communists, but they would appear as patriotic workers. That we would welcome." Thus, she helped the Party arrange to send its members (including Jiang Qing) to teach at the schools. She also enlisted the help of Party cultural workers, such as the composer Tian Han, in helping the night-school students produce skits that had an unmistakably revolutionary message. One such skit, "Where to Go?" depicted poverty-stricken peasants who left their rural homes in search of work. In the city they were abused by supervisors in the factories, their children had to work in silk filatures, and they were frequently unemployed.

> So, where should they go? At the end of the play was the idea that they had to go and struggle to have a better society. But it was not stated so

clearly. We might have raised suspicions from the local authorities there who were already suspecting that perhaps we had communists among our students. So we tried not to make it so clear-cut that they must overthrow the capitalist system. The play didn't say it in those words, but it was in the conversations of the characters. We left it to the students and the audience to make their own conclusions about where to go.

Thus, although Deng never joined the Party, her work directing the night schools contributed in an indirect but crucial way to the growth of a communist-influenced workers' movement in China.

The understated contribution of the night schools to the Chinese revolution, including the special role played by Deng Yuzhi, was acknowledged by the CCP in several ways. In the late 1930s, when the CCP had formed a united front with the Guomindang in order to fight Japan, Zhou Enlai and Deng Yingchao both met with Deng to enlist her support in the communist-organized resistance movement. In addition to her work in the night schools, communist leaders undoubtedly saw Deng as a link to both women's and religious organizations. From Deng's perspective, the CCP represented values and engaged in struggles (such as resisting the Japanese) in which she believed. "What held us together," Deng recalled,

was that we wanted to be an independent country managed by our own people. That was in accordance with the communist idea of a free China as well. So on those terms we worked together. As far as religious beliefs are concerned, they were atheists and we had our own beliefs. They didn't ask us to become atheists and we didn't ask them to become Christians. Zhou Enlai made it very clear to us, "You go on with your own religious activities and we are atheists. But we won't bother you. That's your freedom."

The Guomindang had observed Deng's importance as well, and the wife of its leader, Madame Chiang Kai-shek, was dispatched to recruit Deng to work with the Guomindang-sponsored women's patriotic movement. Explicit refusal would have been dangerous; it was only because Lily Haass quickly arranged for Deng to go to the U. S. in 1939—to publicize the Chinese war effort and to study for a master's degree at New York University—that she was able to evade Madame Chiang's overtures.[38]

Christianity and Liberation

Deng Yuzhi's importance to the Communist revolution was again recognized when the CCP prepared to assume power in 1949, at the end of the Civil War with the Guomindang. Having been invited by Deng Yingchao to participate in meetings to establish the All-China Federation of Women, Deng traveled clandestinely to Beijing. Once there, she was also asked to join the newly formed People's Political Consultative Council (PPCC). And when the CCP declared its final victory over the Guomindang on October 1, 1949, Deng was invited to join other government officials standing on the viewing platform at Tiananmen Square with Mao Zedong, celebrating the founding of the People's Republic.

Deng's affiliation with the CCP placed her in controversy within the YWCA. On the one hand, her political views and experience made her the most likely person to head the China YWCA after 1949. Cai Kui, who had been the general secretary of the China YWCA since the mid-1930s, resigned, recognizing the lack of support for her among the younger, more progressive secretaries.[39] In a confidential letter to the general secretary of the World YWCA, Cai Kui expressed her confidence that "Deng is the best person we have available to lead the association and to represent us to outside bodies."

> She sees very clearly what the YWCA can do in these times and really understands the new China in general outline more clearly than many of us, so that she sees how to apply the YWCA to the situation. She also has conviction about the YWCA and speaks out in its support, sometimes managing to convince those among our younger staff who feel our whole future lies in complete identification with the Democratic Women's Federation. Few others can do this for they either do not see the issues clearly or else do not have the confidence of the younger group. Cora has the confidence of the staff and of many of the committee members, and in this she holds a unique position. I hope you will not let past prejudices come in the way of your staff in co-operating with her, nor let her different approach to things influence the place of the China YWCA within the world's family.[40]

Not everyone in the YWCA was convinced by Cai Kui, however. The "past prejudices" to which she alluded concerned Deng's "radical" reputation. "Deng is as erratic as ever," complained one YWCA secretary in China, "goes the 'whole hog' but insists that she is Christian, not Communist."[41] Another declared that she was "much distressed if it is true that Deng is to be GS [general secretary]—surely our National Committee folks aren't that stupid! It'll be wrangling, wrangling, wrangling!!!"[42] Yet a third worried that Cai Kui's replacement by Deng Yuzhi would undermine the efforts of the YWCA "to hold to its Christian ideals."[43] These concerns notwithstanding, however, Deng was appointed to the post.

Perhaps ironically, Deng's Christian identity became more pronounced in her tenure as general secretary throughout the decades following Liberation. This may have been partly because the CCP treated her as a representative of Christian and religious people in China. It was as a Christian that she was appointed to certain government organizations, such as the religious federation; even her appointment to the state-sponsored All-China Federation of Women reflected the Party's desire to include representatives of Christian women. When she was invited to attend the Third World Peace Conference in Warsaw in 1953, she was to represent Chinese Christians.

Perhaps unwittingly, Deng became a spokesperson for the interests and rights of Chinese Christians. For example, when she was invited to Beijing in 1949 to participate in the founding of the PPCC, she joined other religious leaders in attempting to ensure that the newly established government would protect religious freedom. "At first," she recalled,

> the Common Program stated that people are free to have faith. But faith meant faith in communism, not religious faith. Various religious groups carried on a discussion before the PPCC met. In our Christian groups we had discussions, too. All of us came to the conclusion that there must be a separate clause in the Common Program protecting freedom of religious belief. We got it. That shows the communists were very wise, and could really work with the people. We were quite moved.

While working to represent the interests of Chinese Christians to the CCP, Deng also represented the CCP to religious organizations, including the YWCA. She frequently found it necessary to defend the CCP to YWCA officials outside of China, who were deeply suspicious of the ability of the Chinese YWCA to adhere to the organization's principles. For example, at a meeting of the World YWCA in India in the fall of 1950, she encountered what she found to be a surprising degree of suspicion and hostility from other foreign representatives. Certain that Christianity and communism were contradictory and incompatible, they feared that the Chinese YWCA had become communist. She repeatedly explained that "we were a women's organization doing work from the Christian angle, according to Christian purpose, and according to our own program line."

At first glance it might seem that Deng's increased emphasis on the religious/Christian aspects of the YWCA was simply an expression of the new role she was placed in after the Communist Party assumed power. Yet scattered evidence suggests that her personal identification as a Christian also intensified in the years following Liberation. For example, in November 1950, when making what for her was an extremely difficult decision to violate the wishes of the World YWCA and attend the World Peace Conference in Warsaw, she wrote the following to an American YWCA colleague:

> I thought hard and I prayed hard for wisdom from God to help me make a right decision. Yesterday I made the decision to go. There may be problems and difficulties, but most of the actions we take have problems and difficulties. However, I have faith in God and His hand will lead me through all the way. So, please pray for me. . . .[44]

The expression of faith in God is striking, for it is conspicuously absent from all her previous personal letters as well as her recollections. Nor is it coincidental that these sentiments were articulated shortly after Liberation.

The private and public expressions of her Christian identity suggest a change in the meaning of that identity wrought by Liberation. Before 1949, Deng defined and articulated a sense of purpose through a commitment to social change and revolution, particularly for women. While she believed this commitment embodied her Christian values, those values did not define the struggle in which she engaged, and she rarely spoke or behaved in ways that indicated they were central to her identity. As she had to affiliate more closely with the CCP in the years before Liberation, however, she became more outspoken about her Christian identity, perhaps to establish a boundary between herself and the Party. Once the Communist Party won political power, it was her Christian identity that defined her individual agency and the arena for struggle in which she could engage. In this context, it is not surprising that she expressed religious convictions in ways that seemed discontinuous with her past.

The relationship of Deng's Christian, feminist, and communist identities from the early 1950s through the present is beyond the scope of this essay. It is also more difficult to analyze, for besides her own recollections, few sources about her thinking and activities exist. As a member of a number of government bodies (the All-China Federation of Women, the People's Political Consultative Council, as well as the national federation of religious organizations), as general secretary of the China YWCA (not director of its Labor Bureau, which was disbanded in 1952), and as the subject of criticism for her religious affiliation during a number of political campaigns, Deng defined, juggled, and continued to manipulate her Christian, feminist, and communist identities in a context radically different from the pre-1949 past.

NOTES

Research for this project was funded by the National Endowment for the Humanities and the History of Christianity in China Project sponsored by the Luce Foundation. I am grateful to Robert Entenmann, Licia Fiol-Matta, Christina Gilmartin, Gail Hershatter, Carmalita Hinton, and Marilyn Young for comments on earlier versions of this essay.

1. For a discussion of missionary education for women, see Jane Hunter, *The Gospel of Gentility: American Women Missionaries in Turn-of-the-Century China* (New Haven: Yale University Press, 1984).

2. For a discussion of the relationship of feminism to socialist revolution, see Sonia Kruks, Rayna Rapp, and Marilyn B. Young, eds., *Promissory Notes: Women in the Transition to Socialism* (New York: Monthly Review Press, 1989).

3. The oral history was conducted in English, by Deng's choice. (In conversation, we had always alternated between Chinese and English.) Possibly she simply enjoyed speaking English, or perhaps she felt it afforded a kind of privacy from neighbors or whoever else might listen to the tapes, even though she was ordinarily

remarkably unconcerned with the potential risks of talking to a foreigner with no "official" approval.

4. For a discussion of Changsha's radicalism in the early twentieth century, see Joseph Esherick, *Reform and Revolution in China: The 1911 Revolution in Hunan and Hubei* (Berkeley: University of California Press, 1976), 6; Jonathan Spence, *The Gate of Heavenly Peace* (New York: Vintage Press, 1981), 125.

5. Hunter, 25.

6. Elisabeth Croll, *Feminism and Socialism in China* (New York: Schocken Books, 1978), 51.

7. Yi-tsi Feuerwerker, "Women as Writers in the 1920's and 1930's," in Margery Wolf and Roxane Witke, eds., *Women in Chinese Society* (Stanford: Stanford University Press, 1975), 156.

8. Unless otherwise cited, all quotations of Cora Deng are from the oral history I conducted in 1985.

9. Edward H. Hume, *Doctors East, Doctors West: An American Physician's Life in China* (New York: W. W. Norton and Co., 1946), 159.

10. Alice Drucker, "The Role of the YWCA in the Development of the Chinese Women's Movement, 1890-1927," *Social Service Review* (Sept. 1979): 424-30.

11. *Ibid.*, 430.

12. Judith Stacey, *Patriarchy and Socialist Revolution in China* (Berkeley: University of California Press, 1983), 76.

13. For a discussion of these writings, see Jonathan Spence, *The Search for Modern China* (New York: W. W. Norton and Co., 1990), 304-305, 317-19.

14. For a discussion of single women missionaries in China, see Hunter, 52-89.

15. George W. Barclay, Ansley J. Coale, Michael A. Stoto, and T. James Trussell, "A Reassessment of the Demography of Traditional Rural China," *Population Index* 42, 4 (1976): 610.

16. For a discussion of the tendency of women who attended missionary schools to resist marriage, see Hunter, 248-50.

17. Nancy Boyd, *Emissaries: The Overseas Work of the American YWCA, 1895-1970* (New York: The Woman's Press, 1986), 66.

18. Edited letters of Matilda Thurston, Sept. 27, 1925. China Records Project, Yale Divinity School, New Haven, CT.

19. Edited letters of Matilda Thurston, March 17, 1922. China Records Project, Yale Divinity School, New Haven, CT.

20. Interview with Maud Russell, New York, Sept. 1989.

21. *Ibid.*

22. Application to teach at Jinling College, 1921. China Records Project, Yale Divinity School, New Haven, CT.

23. Mary Treudley, "At Work in a Social Laboratory" (Dec. 1, 1927): 3. China Records Project, Yale Divinity School, New Haven, CT.

24. Deng Yu-dji, "The Ping Erh Yuen (A Report on the Children's Home visited by Sociology 41, October, 1925)," *Ginling College Magazine* 2, 1 (Dec. 1925): 31-37.

25. Maud Russell, "Wuhan Student Conference," Feb. 5-8, 1926. World YWCA Archives, Geneva, Switzerland.

26. Drucker, 430.

27. Emily Honig, *Sisters and Strangers: Women in the Shanghai Cotton Mills, 1919-1949* (Stanford: Stanford University Press, 1986), 24-25.

28. May Bagwell, "An Account of the Industrial Work of the Shanghai YWCA, 1904-29," in *A Study of the YWCA of China, 1891-1930* (n.p., n.d.), 221-22. World YWCA Archives, Geneva, Switzerland.

29. Letter to Grace Coppock, Dec. 8, 1920. World YWCA Archives, Geneva, Switzerland.

30. Bagwell, 225.

31. Lily Haass to Mary Dingman, Jan. 5, 1928. World YWCA Archives, Geneva Switzerland.

32. Cora Deng, "The Industrial Work of the YWCA in China," Nov. 29, 1934, 32. World YWCA Archives, Geneva, Switzerland.

33. Interview with Zhang Shuyi, Beijing, May 16, 1980.

34. Interview with Zhong Shaoqin (Helen Zhong), Beijing, May 17, 1980.

35. For a more detailed discussion of the curriculum at the YWCA night schools, see Honig, 219-24.

36. Lily K. Haass, "The Social and Industrial Programme of the YWCA in China," May 9, 1939. World YWCA Archives, Geneva, Switzerland.

37. On Wu Yaozong, see Stephen Endicott, *James G. Endicott: Rebel Out of China* (Toronto: University of Toronto Press, 1980), 224-26.

38. Lily K. Haass to Sarah Lyon and Bessie Cotton, March 4, 1938. YWCA National Board Archives, New York.

39. Interview with Yao Xianhui, Oct. 16, 1989. According to Yao, who was a YWCA secretary herself in the mid-1930s, Cora Deng and Cai Kui were the two most likely candidates to replace Ding Shuching when she died. Although Deng played a more prominent role in the YWCA at that time, the board preferred Cai because she was not as overtly progressive as Deng. Yao believes that Deng's and Cai's views were fairly similar, but that once she was appointed general secretary, Cai became more moderate, placing greater emphasis on Christianity than social action.

40. Tsai Kwei to Helen Roberts, Dec. 17, 1949. World YWCA Archives, Geneva, Switzerland.

41. Letter from Florence Pierce to Leila Anderson, Oct. 3, 1949. YWCA National Board Archives, New York.

42. Leila Anderson to Florence Pierce, Dec. 9, 1949. YWCA National Board Archives, New York.

43. Letter from Quaker missionary in Shanghai, June 26, 1950. World YWCA Archives, Geneva, Switzerland.

44. Cora Deng to Miss Barnes, Nov. 15, 1950. World YWCA Archives, Geneva, Switzerland.

BIBLIOGRAPHICAL NOTE

The classic work on women in China is *Women and the Family in Rural Taiwan* (Stanford: Stanford University Press, 1972) by the anthropologist Margery Wolf. Although it is based on fieldwork conducted in the 1960s, it remains the best introduction to Chinese women's role in the family.

Students interested in women during the late imperial period should begin with the symposium published in the February 1987 issue of the *Journal of Asian Studies*, which includes "Widows in the Kinship, Class, and Community Structures of Qing Dynasty China" by Susan Mann; "Concepts of Pregnancy, Childbirth, and Infancy in Ch'ing Dynasty China" by Charlotte Furth; and "Ideology and Sexuality: Rape Laws in Qing China" by Vivian Ng. A portrait of the life of a poor peasant woman during the Qing can be found in *The Death of Woman Wang* by Jonathan Spence (New York: Penguin Books, 1978). Changes in women's status during the Qing as well as the emergence of male "feminists" are discussed in Paul Ropp, "The Seeds of Change: Reflections on the Condition of Women in the Early and Mid Ch'ing" (*Signs* 2, 1 [1976]: 5-23), and Joanna Handlin, "Lu K'un's New Audience: The Influence of Women's Literacy on Sixteenth-Century Thought," in Margery Wolf and Roxane Witke's volume *Women in Chinese Society* (Stanford: Stanford University Press, 1975).

A much greater variety of personal accounts are available to study the lives of Chinese women during the first half of the twentieth-century. The medical missionary Ida Pruitt's two oral histories, *A Daughter of Han: The Autobiography of a Chinese Working Woman* (Stanford: Stanford University Press, 1967) and *Old Madam Yin* (Stanford: Stanford University Press, 1979), are poignant accounts of working-class and upper-class women, respectively. *Autobiography of a Chinese Girl* by Hsieh Ping-ying is an excellent account of the childhood and schooling of a woman who was part of the May Fourth generation. The lives and ideas of women with revolutionary ideas can also be explored through fiction. The short stories of China's best-known woman writer, Ding Ling, are collected in Tani Barlow, ed., *I Myself Am a Woman: Selected Writings of Ding Ling* (Boston: Beacon Press, 1989). These stories should be read in conjunction with Xiao Hong's semi-autobiographical novel *Market Street: A Chinese Woman in Harbin* (Seattle: University of Washington Press, 1986).

Several historical studies describe Chinese women during the early twentieth century, emphasizing the effects of urbanization and industrialization. *Sisters and Strangers: Women in the Shanghai Cotton Mills, 1919-1949* by Emily Honig (Stanford: Stanford University Press, 1986) is a social history of urban women workers. Marjorie Topley's article "Marriage Resistance in Rural Kwangtung" (in Wolf and Witke, eds., *Women in Chinese Society*, pp. 67-88) analyzes the effects of the silk industry on women's marital relationships. The vast number of women who worked as prostitutes is discussed in Sue Gronewald, *Beautiful Merchandise: Prostitution in China, 1860-1936* (New York, 1982).

Much of the literature on Chinese women in the twentieth century focuses on their role in the communist revolution. Two overviews of the subject are Ono Kazuko, *Chinese Women in a Century of Revolution, 1850-1950* (Stanford: Stanford University Press, 1989), and Elisabeth Croll, *Feminism and Socialism in China* (New York: Schocken Books, 1980). The most important interpretive accounts of women's role in the CCP-organized revolution are Kay Ann Johnson, *Women, the Family, and Peasant Revolution in China* (Chicago: University of Chicago Press, 1983), and Judith Stacey, *Peasant Patriarchy and Socialist Revolution in China* (Berkeley: University of California Press, 1983).

ON BEHALF OF WOMEN
AND THE NATION

FUNMILAYO RANSOME-KUTI
AND THE STRUGGLES FOR NIGERIAN
INDEPENDENCE AND WOMEN'S EQUALITY

Cheryl Johnson-Odim

Funmilayo Ransome-Kuti's name is well known throughout the West African nation of Nigeria. When she died in April of 1978, various newspaper headlines attested to her historical significance: "The Voice of Woman Is Dead,"[1] "Defender of the Rights of Women: Eulogy on the Soul of Funmilayo Ransome-Kuti."[2] Over a period of several days, long eulogies appeared in a number of leading Nigerian newspapers in which her personal life and her life's work were chronicled.[3] Ransome-Kuti was a significant figure during a critical era in Nigeria's history—the mid-1940s to the early 1960s—the heyday of the nationalist and anticolonial movements and the struggle for Nigeria's independence. The fact that she was a woman, a leader of women, and a feminist made her star even brighter. No other Nigerian woman of her time ranked as such a national figure or had the international exposure and connections of Ransome-Kuti. In fact, in all of West Africa, only a few other women had comparable international links.[4] Throughout her active adult life, Ransome-Kuti espoused a global perspective. She sought to wed a gender, race, and class analysis in her activism in the anticolonial struggle and on behalf of the rights of women. Although deeply engaged in the political sphere, she did not consider herself a politician but rather a human rights activist. Although clearly a leader of women and a feminist, she constantly championed the poor and disenfranchised of both sexes. In a country and at a time in which ethnic allegiance often rivaled allegiance to the nation, she was among a handful of nationalists who struggled to organize across ethnic and class lines. For all these reasons she often defended beleaguered positions and constantly felt herself under attack. While she enjoyed the steady support of a progressive husband, she had few close friends. In many quarters she suffered the reputation of being stubborn and difficult, of not being a team player, and of seeking to be a one-woman show. At one point she believed her life to be in danger, and at another she recorded nightmares in her diary.[5] Yet Funmilayo Ransome-Kuti consistently rose to the challenge of her life. During one public speaking engagement, she quoted an African proverb which symbolized her life's philosophy: "A carrier must first of all bend down to take his load before another person can help him to put it on his head."[6] Activist, educator, wife, mother—she fulfilled many roles.

Funmilayo Ransome-Kuti was born on October 25, 1900, in Kemta district, Abeokuta, Nigeria. Her parents were Yoruba by ethnicity and Christian. Her grandparents had been captured by Portuguese slave dealers after Britain had outlawed the slave trade. The British recaptured them from the Portuguese and settled them in Sierra Leone, from where they made their way back to Nigeria. Both of her parents had also been born in Abeokuta, and though a world traveler herself, except for a few years immediately following her marriage, she too would be a lifelong resident of Abeokuta. She attended mission schools in Abeokuta, being the first female to attend the Abeokuta Grammar School, and in 1919 her parents sent her to Britain to further her education. Originally christened Frances Funmilayo, while in England she had experiences with racism that caused her to drop the name Frances, and from then on she used and was known only as Funmilayo. In 1922 Ransome-Kuti returned from England and almost immediately became principal of a girls' school in Abeokuta. In 1925 she married the Reverend I. O. Ransome-Kuti, an Anglican minister and a founder in 1931 of the Nigerian Union of Teachers (NUT), one of the early protonationalist and multiethnic organizations in Nigeria. Between 1925 and 1932, the Ransome-Kutis relocated to Ijebu-Ode, a town near Abeokuta, where the Reverend Ransome-Kuti was principal of the Ijebu-Ode Grammar School and Funmilayo Ransome-Kuti began her first civic project, the organization of literacy classes for adult women. In 1931 the Ransome-Kutis returned to Abeokuta, where Mrs. Ransome-Kuti founded a nursery school. In 1942 she organized the Abeokuta Ladies' Club (ALC), a group of educated Nigerian women concerned mostly with charitable work.

Ransome-Kuti had a woman friend who was illiterate and not a member of the ALC. The friend was a trader who often traveled to Lagos. In 1944 she confided to Ransome-Kuti that she was fascinated by reading. She mentioned how she often bought newspapers on her trips to Lagos and stored them for the day when she would learn how to read. Now she asked Ransome-Kuti to teach her. Funmilayo Ransome-Kuti organized a literacy class which began with six women but expanded rapidly. It was in the context of these classes and the network which began to emerge that she later confided she discovered the degree of women's inequality and began seriously to question the colonial order, whether it was embodied in the British presence itself or in Nigerian representatives of British power. It was also these classes that brought her to the attention of the market women and through which she gained their trust.

In 1944 several market women complained to Funmilayo Ransome-Kuti that they were being abusively forced to supply government soldiers with food and to pay exorbitant taxes. The general conscription of food and service from colonial populations was standard British policy during World War II. In addition the taxation of women, inaugurated by the British, had long been considered onerous, unjust, and foreign. In Abeokuta, British policy was to rule indirectly through the traditional ruler, the *Alake*. In a later reflection, Ransome-Kuti would remark about the struggle against the *Alake* Ademola: "I didn't really attack Ademola, I attacked imperialism. Those Europeans were using him against his people. . . . I was attacking Europeans indirectly and they know it."[7] The *Alake* Ademola had, with the protection and encouragement of the British, assumed powers far outreaching those normally held by his office. The *Alake* was appointed head of what was known as the Sole Native Authority System (SNA), the ultimate governing power in Abeokuta. In increasing and strengthening the *Alake*'s powers, the British made it easier for them to rule through him. In the 1930s in the assessment of taxes and the levying of rates for items such as water usage, the *Alake* had often incurred the wrath of his people. There had been several protests against him.

In 1940s the British required the *Alake* to supply food for Nigerian soldiers active in the war effort. The market women accused the *Alake* of abusing this directive by forcing them to sell him food for less than the market price while he later collected a larger amount when he resold to the British. The women traders reported that the *Alake* stationed policemen in major markets and on trading routes, who confiscated the traders' produce. They also complained that in the process of collecting taxes, the policemen often beat women or stripped them naked, ostensibly to assess whether they were old enough to pay.

With strong support from her husband and members of the NUT in Abeokuta, Ransome-Kuti undertook to aid the market women by helping them draw up petitions and swear out official complaints. Also, the Abeokuta Ladies' Club passed resolutions calling upon the government to improve sanitation and medical care, provide playgrounds for children, and support literacy classes—all things they felt should be done in return for women's taxation. These early efforts were largely ignored by the *Alake* and the British, though they were chronicled in several newspapers in the capital city, Lagos.[8]

By 1946, building upon a small nucleus of the Abeokuta Ladies' Club, the market women, and contacts made through the literacy classes and early protest efforts, Ransome-Kuti founded the Abeokuta Women's Union (AWU) to replace the ALC. The change in name signified not only growth in numbers but a commitment to political purposes as well. Among the avowed objectives of the AWU were (1) to unite women; (2) to promote social, economic, and political rights and interests of women; and (3) to cooperate with all organizations seeking and fighting genuinely and selflessly for the economic and political freedom and independence of the people. The AWU immediately began a fierce campaign against the SNA and the *Alake.*

The women pursued their protests for several years, building up to the climactic resignation of the *Alake* in January 1949. By that time the AWU was approximately twenty thousand women strong. In 1947 and 1948 the women had employed a number of strategies to achieve their goals of an end to women's taxation, the resignation of the *Alake,* and the reform of the Sole Native Authority System, including the appointment of women (chosen by themselves) as members of the SNA's Executive Council. In one petition the women wrote: "Inasmuch as women pay taxes, we too desire to have a say in the management of the country, because a taxpayer should also have a voice in the spending of the taxes."[9] Besides circulating petitions and swearing out official complaints, the women under Ransome-Kuti's leadership publicized their cause by writing to newspapers, the colonial secretary's office, and the governor. The AWU hired attorneys and accountants to audit the public records of the SNA, and several of the women, including Funmilayo Ransome-Kuti, refused to pay their taxes. Several women went to jail and/or were fined. Once, in order to travel to England (see below), Ransome-Kuti paid her own fine, and once, when she was prepared to put it to the test by going to jail (and 5,000 women waited outside the courthouse, claiming they would go with her), some anonymous person paid her fine.

The women's protests climaxed in November and December of 1947 when they held vigils several days long outside the *Alake*'s palace, also the headquarters of the SNA. Up to ten thousand women slept and ate outside the palace, singing derisive songs ("O ye men, vagina's head will seek vengeance. . . . Anyone who does not know Kuti will get into trouble. . . . White man, you will not get to your country safely") and not allowing anyone in or out. Within weeks the *Alake* and the British district officer sought to meet with the representatives of the AWU, hinting that there was the possibility of some women appointees to the SNA. However, they stipulated that Funmilayo Ransome-Kuti must not be one of the representatives. The women found this unacceptable, and again thousands of them demonstrated outside the palace. By June 1948 the *Alake* appointed a special committee of men and women to investigate the AWU's complaints, suspended female taxation, and agreed in principle that women should be represented in the SNA, then he left town for a cooling-off period. By now, however, the women were unprepared to support a lasting peace until the *Alake* abdicated. Even after the formation of an interim council to replace the SNA, the appointment to this body of four women executives of the AWU (including Ransome-Kuti), and the abolition of tax on women, the women were adamant that the *Alake* resign. Finally, on January 3, 1949, he did. The market women declared a holiday, and the AWU published a pamphlet that chronicled the story of their protest and even quoted from the American Declaration of Independence on the rights of the governed. Newspapers all over Nigeria headlined the event, and Ransome-Kuti achieved a lasting fame in the national spotlight. In ensuing years, when taxation on women was reimposed and the *Alake* Ademola reclaimed the throne, she continued to struggle for women's rights and against colonialism at the head of her new organization, the Nigerian Women's Union, which sprouted branches all over the country, organizing women across class and ethnic lines. In the 1950s, the NWU branch in Abeokuta operated a weaving cooperative, ran a maternity and child welfare clinic, and conducted literacy classes.

In 1947, in the midst of the women's protest, Ransome-Kuti was drawn from the national into the international limelight when she accompanied a National Council of Nigeria and the Cameroons (NCNC) delegation to England. The NCNC was among the early nationalist political parties. Founded in 1944 by Nnamdi Azikiwe, by 1946 the party had a large following and a newspaper, the *West African Pilot.* In Abeokuta, among the first to join the party were Ransome-Kuti and her husband, the Reverend I. O. Ransome-Kuti. An educator by profession, the Reverend Ransome-Kuti had considerable international experience as a result of his travels on behalf of the Nigerian Union of Teachers. He had a number of British friends who were prominent in anti-imperialist circles in England. Many of them had been introduced to him by his boyhood friend Ladipo Solanke, who was now resident in England and who was founder of the militant, anticolonial, and pan-Africanist West African Students' Union (WASU). Funmilayo Ransome-Kuti was also a close friend and frequent correspondent of Solanke. One of the people with whom the Reverend Ransome-Kuti had struck up a cordial relationship on a 1939 visit to England was Arthur Creech-Jones, who was deputy secretary of state for the colonies between 1947 and 1950 and was the founding chair in 1949 of the Fabian Colonial Bureau. The bureau's aims were to formulate proposals for self-government in the colonies, prepare data on colonial issues for members of Parliament, and generally propagate an anticolonial policy. When Creech-Jones visited Nigeria in 1944 as a member of the Elliot Commission on Higher Education, he met Funmilayo Ransome-Kuti, and beginning in 1945 she maintained a lively correspondence with him and his wife, Violet. Thus, in 1947, when the NCNC resolved to send a delegation to London to protest the limits (vis-à-vis Nigerian independence) of the newly proposed Richards Constitution, and when Azikiwe editorialized in the *West African Pilot* that there should be a woman member of the delegation, Funmilayo Ransome-Kuti was an obvious choice to be among those considered. The NCNC's first choice of a woman was Madam Alimotu Pelewura, leader of the Lagos market women and well respected for her political battles in Lagos in the 1930s against women's taxation and for their enfranchisement. Pelewura, however, was old and sick. The next obvious choice was Ransome-Kuti, at the very moment deeply embroiled in the struggle against the *Alake*. Besides the national attention this had brought her, NCNC insiders knew she was well known to Creech-Jones, the newly appointed deputy colonial secretary.

The 1947 NCNC delegation was very poorly organized. The strong-willed leader Azikiwe was frequently accused of elitist behavior and was not known for possessing a consultative style of leadership. The delegation spent two months in London, and unfortunately Parliament was in summer recess much of that time, reflecting poor planning on the part of the delegation leadership, mostly Azikiwe. Ransome-Kuti was publicly critical of Azikiwe and was among those who most vociferously objected to his attitude and methods. She was quick to notice that while everyone else was in moderately priced accommodations, Azikiwe stayed at an expensive hotel. Her criticisms created considerable ill will between her and Azikiwe and would affect her political relationship with the NCNC in the future.

Still, undeterred and determined not to squander the opportunity, Ransome-Kuti resolved to use the time in London to contact women's organizations. She began by contacting her friends the Creech-Joneses. Violet Creech-Jones lined up engagements for Ransome-Kuti. The secretary himself assigned a woman from his office to arrange an itinerary for her.

Ransome-Kuti also made her own plans. She contacted the director of the BBC secretariat, Mary P. Ussher, to attempt to arrange an appearance, but was told they had just concluded a series on women all over the world. She was invited to address the London Women's Parliament Committee. She also addressed a reception of women journalists, the London National Federation of Young Farmers Clubs, the National Federation of Women Institute, and the National Union of Townwomen's Guilds. She visited several factories and daycare centers, the Association of Country Women of the World, and the National Council for Maternity and Child Welfare. At one factory, Mitcham Works, Ltd. in Surrey, she arrived at 11 A.M. to address the workers and did not leave until closing at 5 P.M. On September 20, 1947, the lord mayor of Manchester held a reception for Ransome-Kuti where she spoke about the problems of women in Nigeria and the Cameroons.[10]

While in London, Ransome-Kuti stirred up a great deal of controversy as the result of an article she wrote which appeared in the August 10, 1947, issue of the *Daily Worker*, newspaper of the British Communist Party. She was asked to write about the conditions of Nigerian women. Under the title "We Had Equality 'Til Britain Came," she argued that colonialism had severely marginalized women in the political and economic spheres and in addition oppressed them with unjust taxes and yet denied them the right to vote. She said women in Nigeria suffered under "slavery—political, social and economic" and asked the help of British women in ending such exploitation. The article was reprinted in several Nigerian newspapers, and there was immediate reaction in the capital city of Lagos and Ransome-Kuti's hometown of Abeokuta. The *Alake* denounced the article. The Nigerian Women's Party, an organization of elite women in Lagos, was also embarrassed by and very critical of Ransome-Kuti's remarks. However, the Lagos Market Women's Association and the Abeokuta Women's Union held mass meetings in which they supported Ransome-Kuti's statement, and organized a huge reception for her when she arrived back from London. Later, in defending what she wrote, Ransome-Kuti stated, "The true position of Nigerian women had to be judged from the women who carried babies on their backs and farmed from sunrise to sunset. . . . not women who used tea, sugar and flour."[11]

During the trip, Ransome-Kuti was approached by members of the British branch of the Women's International Democratic Federation (WIDF). the WIDF had been founded in Paris in December 1945. It was among a number of international socialist organizations inspired by the Soviet Union in the aftermath of World War II. The stated aims of the WIDF were to unite women regardless of race, nationality, religion, and political opinion, so that they might work together to win, implement, and defend their rights and the rights of children to life, well-being, and education; win and defend national independence and democratic freedoms; eliminate apartheid, racial discrimination, and fascism; and work for peace and universal disarmament.[12] In the immediate postwar period, many British liberals, laborites, pacifists, and anticolonialists were members of such organizations. African and Indian students as well as other anticolonialists from the colonies were also attracted to the anti-imperialist positions of such organizations. It would not be until the 1950s, when the cold war became more pronounced, that affiliation with such organizations would carry the label "communist sympathizer" and the taint attached to it.

It is not surprising, given her friends in the Fabian Colonial Bureau and her own ideological positions, that Ransome-Kuti would be attracted to the aims and program of the WIDF. Shortly after she met with them, the executive committee of the secretariat of the WIDF met in Stockholm and set up a special commission to investigate the conditions of women in Africa and Asia. The commission reports were presented to the Second World Congress of Women for Peace, meeting in Budapest in December 1948, and shortly thereafter were published in a WIDF book, *The Women of Asia and Africa: Documents*. Funmilayo Ransome-Kuti authored the report on Nigeria, part of which had already been published a month earlier in the WIDF Information Bulletin no. 33 of November 1948.

Ransome-Kuti continued a frequent correspondence with various WIDF members and committees after her return to Nigeria. Initially, she seems to have been cautious in responding to their invitations to become a member and to attend various international conferences, even consulting her friend Ladipo Solanke about how she should view the WIDF. Her uncertainty may have reflected a number of things. The WIDF was anxious to involve women of color in its activities, and Ransome-Kuti may have been suspicious of the organization's anxious courting. She also likely felt the need to tread cautiously given the furor over her *Daily Worker* article. Having spent little time with WIDF members, she may have felt unsure of the organization's purposes and reputation. At this early date Ransome-Kuti had little international political experience or exposure, and she often relied on and trusted Solanke's advice in these matters. In 1948 she wrote to the WIDF requesting information on how the Nigerian Women's Union (NWU) could become involved with the organization. She reevaluated this position, though, and in 1952, in response to an article in the London-based *Journal of the Royal African Society* which stated that the NWU was affiliated with the WIDF, she wrote a letter saying in part, "I shall be grateful indeed to know where you received your information. . . . Our organization is not affiliated with *any organization in the world, not even in Nigeria here . . .*" (original emphasis). She resolved her dilemma by becoming personally active with the WIDF but keeping the NWU independent.

In April 1952 she attended the WIDF-sponsored Conference on the Defense of Children, which was held in Vienna. After this conference Ransome-Kuti was interviewed by Sheila Lynd of the *Daily Worker*. On May 14, 1952, the article appeared under the title "Nothing Dismays Mrs. Kuti," and Ransome-Kuti was quoted on her feelings after the Vienna conference: "Surely it will help towards peace and understanding for so many to meet without thinking of colour, religion and position and pool ideas about the welfare of children. When I go back I shall tour Nigeria reporting what I saw and heard there. Then I shall call the leaders of the movement together and we shall draw up our proposals to the government based on the resolution about the Child's rights to health and education." In June 1953 she attended the WIDF World Congress of Women in Copenhagen, at which she was elected a vice-president of the organization. In 1954 the WIDF published a book, *That They May Live: African Women Arise*, in which Ransome-Kuti authored a one-page report on Nigeria and which carried a photograph of her with a caption stating, "She conducts tireless action in defense of women's rights."

In 1956 Ransome-Kuti traveled to China on a ticket purchased by the WIDF. This trip attracted international attention, and on May 28, 1956, the *Times* of London carried an article about communist indoctrination of Africans, citing Ransome-Kuti's affiliation with the WIDF as an example. The following year when she applied for renewal of her passport to go to London for health reasons, her request was denied. She had in fact been warned previously that this might happen if she continued to travel to countries with communist governments. The government refused her passport in the belief she intended to travel to East Berlin and that the Federation of Nigeria had to be protected from "communism and communistic ideas." They later further stated that it had been thought Ransome-Kuti was the "innocent victim of communist schemes," but that the government now believed her relationship with the WIDF was proof of her intent to "indulge in communist activities."[13] Ransome-Kuti immediately mobilized her forces to challenge the government's action. First, a delegation of the Nigerian Women's Union visited the prime minister. They accused the government of "red hunting" and asked for renewal of Ransome-Kuti's passport. Shortly thereafter three major Nigerian newspapers, the *Daily Service, Daily Times,* and *West African Pilot,* all carried editorials and articles supporting Ransome-Kuti's right to travel wherever she pleased. The Nigerian Trade Union Federation and the Nigerian Students' Union of Great Britain also criticized the government's action. Several of Ransome-Kuti's high-profile friends in England wrote expressing concern.

Ransome-Kuti held a news conference at which she denied being a communist and ridiculed the government's charges that her travel to communist countries was evidence of her desire to make Nigerians communists. She inquired whether the Nigerian prime minister's visits to Egypt and Saudi Arabia were evidence of his desire to Islamize Nigeria.[14] She also sent a long letter of protest to the prime minister and forwarded copies to the British secretary of state for the colonies, the governor general of Lagos, the assistant secretary of immigration, and the United Nations. Despite all the furor, the government did not change its position, and Ransome-Kuti's passport was not renewed until after independence in 1960. In 1961 she traveled to Budapest, and in 1962 and 1963 to Moscow. She also traveled to Bulgaria, East Berlin, Hungary, Israel, and Poland. In the midst of the turmoil over her passport, she was invited to attend a women's conference held in San Francisco in 1959, but the United States government denied her a visa. In an interview with this author in August 1976, Ransome-Kuti remarked, "All our big men and women now travel to China and Russia; I suffered for their freedoms." So much had changed after independence that Ransome-Kuti was able to accept science equipment from the Soviet Union for her Abeokuta Grammar School, and in 1969 two women Soviet science teachers taught at the school.

Ransome-Kuti was not a member of the Communist Party, nor did she ever profess communism. She did, however, hold to socialist ideals at both the public and the personal levels—which she admirably integrated. She felt that the state owed basic things to every human being—education, decent food and shelter, adequate medical care, and all the freedoms associated with full participation in the governing process. It is unknown whether she ever read Rousseau or Locke, but she certainly subscribed to the ideal of the social contract. She *had* read and quoted the American Declaration of Independence (see above). She held strong convictions about women's equality with men, and in a May 1975 interview in *New Breed* magazine she stated that she believed in women's liberation.

On the personal level she was remarkably consistent with her public political positions. One informant who knew the Ransome-Kutis well, Olisa Chukura, characterized their marriage as "an egalitarian relationship out of its time" and complimented the Reverend Ransome-Kuti as the "most democratic man I have ever known." Although she was the wife of an ordained minister, Ransome-Kuti held unorthodox views on organized religion. In a May 5, 1978, eulogy in the *Punch* she is quoted as having earlier stated: "I believe in my God. You could be a pagan and be godly. As far as I can see, if you don't think of cheating people you are godly and if there is any paradise you will get there. Many pastors as I see them will end up in hell. I will see God in the sort of life I lead, not because I go to church every Sunday." At the school which she and her husband ran in Abeokuta, they and their four children regularly took their meals with the boarding students, and the Ransome-Kutis' sons were taught to cook just as their sister was.

Ransome-Kuti's political maneuvering was also characterized by its prag-matism. In her struggles she sought support from diverse ideological sources and often performed a delicate balancing act in seeking to main-tain her right to independent political thought and action. In 1952, when Abeokuta women were tear-gassed while demonstrating against the pay-ment of water rates, she sought condemnation of the incident from the WIDF and the British Women's International Association (BWIA); the lat-ter expressed concern about whether Ransome-Kuti was a communist. On Ladipo Solanke's advice, Ransome-Kuti wrote to the BWIA, assuring them she was not a communist and that the Nigerian Women's Union was not affiliated with the WIDF. She mentioned nothing of her own relationship with the WIDF.

Ransome-Kuti also traveled throughout Africa, maintaining especially close links with women's organizations in Algeria, Egypt, and Ghana. In September 1960 Kwame Nkrumah, president of Ghana and well-known pan-Africanist, invited her to attend the inaugural ceremony of the Ghana women's movement. She also attended women's conferences in the Afri-can nations of Dahomey (now Benin), Guinea, Liberia, and Togo. Among her personal papers are also a number of letters from and reports on activ-ist black women in South Africa.

In addition to her international activity, Ransome-Kuti continued to be active in Nigerian politics. In 1951 she was a candidate for election to the Federal House of Assembly, the Egba Division, but was defeated. Very few women were qualified at the time to vote, as taxation was a qualification. Following her defeat, Kuti authored an article in *West Africa* magazine titled "Women Should Play a Bigger Part in the Elections."[15] She criticized the electoral system, which she considered hard for people to understand and unsuitable for such a new electorate. Criticizing the lack of participa-tion by women due to the tax requirements, Kuti also maintained that "corruption reared its ugly head in the election." She added: "Women are earnestly praying for the day when there will be universal adult suffrage, so that once again they can assist the men to do things properly, as they did in the days of the Dahomeyan war, and other crises in Egbaland."

A few months later she wrote a letter to the editor of *West Africa* in which she outlined some of the demands of the NWU "for changes in Nigeria to ensure democracy and justice in our politics."[16] Among the demands were universal adult suffrage, abolition of the electoral college, and allocation of a definite proportion of representatives to women. She added that "peaceful demonstrations are the national expression of the people against oppression—they should not be interfered with by the police in any part of Nigeria."

In August 1953 she organized a conference in Abeokuta of representatives of several women's organizations in Nigeria. Although the NWU already had branches in most major cities of the east, south, and north of Nigeria, her desire was to forge an alliance between active women's groups. An organization, the Federation of Nigerian Women's Societies (FNWS), emerged from the conference. Ransome-Kuti was elected president of the FNWS, and the conference passed several resolutions regarding female political activity. Three of the most important resolutions were a call for universal adult suffrage, the use of symbols for illiterate voters, and the adoption of a quota system which would ensure that a certain percentage of regional and federal council seats would be allocated to women.

In the 1950s Ransome-Kuti remained an active member of the National Council of Nigeria and the Cameroons (NCNC). She was president of its Western Nigerian women's wing and treasurer of its Western Working Committee. By now she and the NCNC leader, Nnamdi Azikiwe, were not the closest of friends, both because of their strong-willed personalities and as a result of the fallout from the 1947 Richard's Constitution delegation.

In 1959 Ransome-Kuti desired to run for a seat in the Federal House of Assembly. Initially her candidacy was supported by the Abeokuta NCNC secretariat, and she was slated to be its official candidate. The NCNC national executive committee, however, wished to run a Mr. J. Akande and prevailed upon the Abeokuta secretariat to also back Akande's candidacy. Ransome-Kuti alleged it was because they said she "could not be controlled." A vigorous debate ensued between Ransome-Kuti's and Akande's promoters. Infuriated when the NCNC refused to sponsor her as an official party candidate, Ransome-Kuti ran as an independent. With her decision to run as an independent and the consequent splintering of the NCNC supporters, neither she nor Akande stood a change of winning. The NCNC lost the election totally, and Ransome-Kuti was expelled from the party. She accused the NCNC of wanting to use women "for their own benefit" and resolved to form her own political party. The party was called the Commoners' People's Party (CPP), and she later stated that she meant it to be only Abeokuta-based and that its main aim was to get women elected to local office and give them control over their own local affairs. For a while the party allied itself with another disgruntled Abeokuta element, but the CPP had little to offer the alliance. The party lasted only a little over a year. Its main contribution to the political scene seems to have been its desire to focus attention on the problems of the poor and disenfranchised, to whose welfare Ransome-Kuti always felt herself dedicated.

In a 1961 article in the *Journal of Human Relations*, Ransome-Kuti continued to articulate her political philosophy.[17] She proclaimed literacy to be the "weapon of liberty" and recalled that when she had visited a Chinese women's adult education class, she had been extremely impressed because even when visitors entered the room, the women were so absorbed in their lessons that they barely took their eyes from their books. She continued to make several proposals for the newly independent Nigeria, suggesting that Nigerian doctors analyze the vitamins and minerals contained in common Nigerian fruits and vegetables and advise women as to which combination of these provided nutritionally balanced meals. She exhorted Nigerian women to urge the government to encourage cooperative farming and counseled them not to forget their sisters in other parts of Africa: "When any section of African people is still in slavery, no independent section can be truly happy." True to her word, when the Sharpeville massacre of pass-law protesters occurred in South Africa, she was in contact with the ANC representatives in Algeria and vehemently denounced the incident.

Ransome-Kuti was admired by Nigerians from all over the country, both men and women. Even Nigerians abroad, such as the militant West African Students' Union in Britain, wrote to her with praise and support. Perhaps the supreme compliment of love, trust, and admiration came from an Enugu woman who wrote in May 1948: "Even the veiled children in their respective mothers' wombs, though inarticulate, nod approval of your deeds."[18]

Ransome-Kuti spent her life in active pursuit of gender equality and recognition of the rights of ordinary people to have their basic needs met. She fully acknowledged the fact that she would have accomplished little, great as her commitment was, had not tens of thousands of women supported her and shared her sacrifices.

In 1966 Nigeria experienced its first military coup, and except for a brief period in the early 1980s under President Shehu Shagari, military rule has characterized government in Nigeria from 1966 to the present. This fact severely circumscribed civilian political activity, though Ransome-Kuti remained active as an educator. The 1960s also saw a number of national and international honors bestowed upon her.

In 1965 the government awarded her membership in the Order of the Niger for her contributions to the nation. In 1968 she received an honorary doctorate of laws from the University of Ibadan (Nigeria), after which she wrote the vice chancellor, saying in part that the degree was "proof of your telling me I am not alone in my struggle." In 1969 she appeared in the *International Women's Who's Who.* That same year she was appointed chairman of the Western State Advisory Board of Education and wrote in her letter of acceptance, "May I never let womanhood down." In 1970 she was awarded the Lenin Peace Prize by the Supreme Soviet of the USSR, and the Soviet ambassador to Nigeria, A. Romanov, wrote to her that the prize was "in recognition of your noble activities for many years in promoting friendship and mutual cooperation between Nigerian and Soviet peoples." He enclosed a letter of congratulations signed by the chair of the Soviet Women's Committee, Valentina Nikolaeva-Tereshkova.[19] There were many less well known honors.

In February 1977 soldiers attacked the Ransome-Kuti family residence in Lagos to harass the Ransome-Kutis' musician son, Fela, known for his music replete with political messages, including criticism of the military and the ruling junta.[20] Ransome-Kuti was visiting, and soldiers threw her from a second-story window. At the time she was seventy-seven years old, and many observers believe she never fully recovered from the physical injuries and psychological trauma of the attack. A little more than a year later, on April 12, 1978, she died in Lagos. On Friday, May 5, a motorcade bore her body to Abeokuta, where all markets and shops were closed for the day. She lay in state at the grammar school named after her husband, who died in 1955, before she was interred in a vault with him. A plethora of newspaper articles hailed Ransome-Kuti as a "progressive revolutionary," a "pan-Africanist visionary," and an "anti-imperialist."[21]

Within Nigeria, Ransome-Kuti's name will forever be associated with the rights of women and social, political, and economic justice for the exploited and oppressed. She could easily have converted her class privilege into personal gain and comfort but chose rather to practice what she preached by integrating her personal life and the political causes she espoused. Yet she was very human. Her political style was not particularly diplomatic, and once she made up her mind, she rarely changed it. She was not a "team player" with unconditional loyalty to anything or anyone other than her principles; she was always willing to buck the tide, even to lose, rather than compromise a stand to which she was wedded. She sometimes found it difficult to perform the proverbial balancing act of women activists with families and was criticized as being more dedicated to public than to private life. Each of her children, however, shares a vision of her as stern and disciplined but loving, and each has been profoundly affected by her commitment to the poor and dispossessed, her sense of patriotism, and her pan-Africanism. Her eldest son remarked in a 1981 interview, "We were brought up along with the school children [at his parents' school in Abeokuta] and we learned to live amongst the people. My parents were always involved with the community, and my mother always fought for the rights and development of women as persons in their own right."[22]

Funmilayo Ransome-Kuti was seen as a leader of Nigerian women, and consequently we must see in her life not only the individual but also some of the thinking of the collective womanhood which supported her. No list of important women political activists of the twentieth century is complete without her name.

NOTES

This essay is drawn from a book-length biography of Funmilayo Ransome-Kuti (co-authored with Nina Mba) which is in process. The author's research was begun in 1976, at which time she had a series of interviews with Ransome-Kuti over a period of six months and worked in the Ransome-Kuti papers, which were then in boxes in the basement of her home in Abeokuta, and are now housed at the University of Ibadan Library in Nigeria. Other important sources of information are the Reverend I.O. Ransome-Kuti's papers (also at the University of Ibadan Library), the Ladipo Solanke papers (at the Gandhi Memorial Library at the University of Lagos), the Egba Native Authority archives (at Abeokuta), the *Daily Worker* (London), and the *Daily Service, Daily Times,* and *West African Pilot* (all in Nigeria).

1. *Daily Times,* April 14, 1978.
2. *Daily Times,* May 5, 1978.
3. *Daily Times,* April 14 and 18 and May 5, 1978; *Sunday Times,* April 16 and May 7, 1878; *Punch,* May 5, 1978; *Sunday Punch,* May 7, 1978.
4. Adelaide Casely Hayford and Constance Cummings-John of Sierra Leone, and Mabel Dove of Ghana.
5. Diary in Funmilayo Ransome-Kuti (FRK) papers, which are at the University of Ibadan in Nigeria.
6. In a speech she made on education in 1948, FRK papers.
7. *New Breed Magazine,* May 1975, pp. 23-31.
8. See, for instance the *Daily Service* of October 12 and November 12, 1945.
9. *Daily Service,* July 8, 1946.
10. See correspondence in FRK papers dated September 4, 1947, from Mary P. Ussher, director BBC Secretariat; August 29, 1947, from Freda Gimble, organizer, London Women's Parliament Cte.; and copy of her speech given at Kristen Hall, Lagos, on October 17, 1947, when delegation returned from London.
11. *West African Pilot,* September 2, 1948.
12. Constitution of WIDF in Northwestern University Deering Library. The WIDF is still active.
13. Correspondence and other material relevant to the passport dispute can be found in the FRK papers. See also the *Daily Times,* December 21, 1957, and January 2, 1958; *West African Pilot,* December 30, 1957; and *Daily Service,* March 4, 1958. See also Nigeria Federal House of Assembly debates for March 3, 1958.
14. See *Daily Service,* March 4, 1958.
15. *West Africa,* November 3, 1951, p. 1015.
16. *Ibid.,* May 31, 1952, p. 490.
17. *Journal of Human Relations,* Autumn 1961, pp. 68-72.
18. Letter in FRK papers from S. I. Oguntoyinbo.
19. Copies of correspondence in FRK papers.
20. Ransome-Kuti was especially close to this son and in 1976 had gone along with him in effecting a name change from Ransome-Kuti, by dropping the British Ransome and substituting the Yoruba Anikulayo. She also had three other children: Obikoye Ransome-Kuti, an internationally renowned pediatrician; Dolupo Ransome-Kuti, a registered nurse; and Bekolari Ransome-Kuti, a physician and human rights activist.
21. See *Sunday Times,* April 16, 1978, and *Daily Times,* April 18, 1978.
22. *Daily Times,* August 29, 1981.

THE VOICES OF DORIA SHAFIK

FEMINIST CONSCIOUSNESS
IN EGYPT, 1940-1960

Cynthia Nelson

> Neither the life of an individual nor the
> history of a society can be understood
> without the understanding of both.
>
> —C. Wright Mills,
> *The Sociological Imagination*

This paper is a prelude to a much larger project that would attempt to understand the linkage between biography and history—between the life of Doria Shafik and the historical moment in which she lived and died. As Dilthey has suggested:

> There is no one "meaning of life," but only the meaning which individuals have perceived in, or attribute to their own lives in terms of certain ideas or values. Each life has its own focal point or points, around which it is more or less consistently organized and only in terms of these can it be understood. (Dilthey 1961, p. 85)

The rationale for the choice of Doria Shafik for such a project rests on my long-term interest in the relationship of feminist movements to the broader issues of social transformation.

I first became acquainted with one voice (the aesthetic) of Doria Shafik nearly two years ago when I received a gift of five volumes of her poetry.[1] Through the reading of this poetry— despite its Egyptian roots in the desert and the Nile; despite its confrontation with a history that was not mine; despite its own unique biographical trajectory—I discovered a voice that touched me by its paean to human solitude. From those poems I wanted to know more about Doria Shafik.

Despite a growing interest in and literature on feminism and feminist movements in Egypt and the Middle East (Ahmed 1982), I was surprised by the lack of material on the feminist struggles of the 1940s and 1950s. It almost seemed that the history of the feminist movement in Egypt leaped from the period of Huda Sha'rawi (1920s and 1930s) to Jihan Sadat or Nawal El Saadawi of the 1970s and 1980s. Yet when one examines the available historical evidence—the Egyptian press, journals, and articles during that period; her own numerous publications in Arabic, French, and English; her name in five major Middle East and international editions of *Who's Who*—we discover "a woman who, with her life and struggle, was *not* an ordinary event in Egyptian life" (Abd al-Qadir 1975).

This apparent "conspiracy of silence," both on a very visible struggle and the woman who personified it, has further increased my desire to recover this voice through which we might understand her own experience within an important time of change and transformation in Egyptian society.

I begin with a short biographical sketch of her early life until the eve of the Second World War. Then I follow with a brief yet broad sweep of the dominant historical trends of the period. This will lead us into an examination of her feminist activism centered around the issue of *full political rights for women* during the period of 1945-1957.

I do not intend to reconstruct a personality (although an understanding of her ideas and values is important to an understanding of her actions), but rather to present a series of "voices" that spoke out on issues that she considered central to her *self* and *the historical moment* in which she lived.

The Voice of Autobiography: Reflections on Childhood

"My life began with the First World War . . . and since, every day of my existence has been a struggle." Thus begins the very first sentence of her memoirs.[2] As we read on, we learn that although she was born in Tanta, she passed her early childhood in Mansura where her father held a post as engineer. Her mother belonged to an "old upper-bourgeoisie Egyptian family which had lost most of its fortune." She was the third of a family of six children. She idolized her mother, although it was her father more than anyone who recognized and encouraged her precocious intellectual talents. "My father came from a less well-known family. But such a social inequality was widely compensated for by his high intellect and impeccable morality."

She was sent to a kindergarten run by Italian nuns. At the age of eight she was sent to live with her grandmother in order to go to the French mission school at Tanta, where her own mother had been educated. Her mother died of a heart attack when Doria was only eleven—an event that marked her for life:

> That day remains in my memory as a profound and incurable wound, a wound so huge that it marked, with its desolation, the whole of my life . . . and as an outlet for my despair. I concentrated all my energy into study . . . the result was that I progressed so rapidly that after some time I found myself in the same class as my elder sister. (Memoirs)

When her father was transferred to Alexandria, she entered the French mission school there. She loved the sea as it reminded her of the Nile:

> I would spend hours watching the sea. Its immensity—bestowing upon me a sort of presentiment of the Absolute—conveyed to my sensibility the "aesthetic emotion" which has played so great a role in my personality's formation. . . . Looking at the Mediterranean . . . I was discovering "Great Nature" in its immeasurable and profound Beauty . . . whispering to my heart . . . echoes of universal Harmony. All such evocations being incarnated in an irreducible "aesthetic feeling." (Memoirs)

Even at this very early age she was determined to continue on for her university education in Paris. She prepared herself through independent study, took the two matriculation examinations at age sixteen, brilliantly placing second in the whole country. Her sights were on the Sorbonne and the study of philosophy, but financial support was a barrier.

It was at this point in her life that she attracted the attention of Huda Sha'rawi, the great feminist leader of the 1920s and 1930s. Doria wrote her a letter explaining her situation, and immediately Sha'rawi sent a telegram inviting Doria Shafik to Cairo. Her father willingly accepted her plan and permitted her to go to Cairo to meet the famous Egyptian feminist. Her memoirs on this meeting are most insightful:

> She welcomed me with such charm and simplicity that she immediately won my heart. I found in her a warmth that resembled that of a mother . . . a mother who would take my hand and guide me towards my future. . . . She saw how moved I was and did everything to make me feel at ease. . . . "I am happy to see you are so smart," she said; "I am pleased that a girl of your standard will represent Egypt abroad." "Then you think my departure is possible?" I asked. "Why not? Tomorrow someone will speak about you to the Minister of Education." She saw so much emotion and gratitude on my face that she asked me: "Why this ardent desire to study abroad?" . . . I was near to tears. She noticed it and, without waiting for the answer, quickly changed the subject. . . . She spoke to me about the causes which led her towards the Path of "Feminism." She related the unhappiness she had experienced within the harem—when, newly married, she was almost a prisoner in her own home. For the first time I realized that this lady—rich, beautiful, having everything—*had suffered*; that there must be some "values" beyond the material ones. . . . LIBERTY . . . the profound reason for her "feminism." I left the palace with a great quietness of the Soul . . . *convinced that nothing really worthwhile can be accomplished without suffering.* Such an example it was, illustrating how

the *Will of a Woman* can supersede the *Law*. An example which was to remain in my memory and my heart, leading me in my struggle and, later—when the social oppression often happened to be too heavy on my shoulders—conveying courage and hope.

Doria left for Paris in 1930 at the age of sixteen to begin her studies at the Sorbonne. During her first months there she wrote an essay later published in *L'Egyptienne*,[3] entitled "Does Woman Have the Right to Philosophize?" In this essay we begin to hear the strains of her feminist consciousness awakening. She obtained both her *License* and *Doctorat d'Etat* in philosophy, writing two theses for the latter degree—*L'Art pour l'art dans l'Egypte antique* (the major thesis) and *La Femme et le droit religieux de l'Egypte contemporaine*, both published in France in 1940. While in Paris she met and married the man she loved (her cousin), who was also studying for his doctorate in law. On the eve of the Second World War she returned to Cairo.

Before turning to the feminist voice of Doria Shafik and her involvement in the political struggle for women's rights, I should like to draw attention to certain historical trends unfolding in Egypt at the time of her return from France.

Historical Trends in Egypt

During the 1930s, the Second World War, and after, there was a growing disillusionment with quarreling politicians and a power-hungry monarchy, which evolved into an antagonism to constitutional government in general and to its European origins in particular. A radicalism to the right of xenophobic nationalism and religious fanaticism set in, which made it possible for the Muslim Brotherhood to attract hundreds of thousands of followers beginning in the late 1930s, from both the dispossessed urban masses and the permanently poverty-stricken rural population. In April 1944 Sayyid Qutb founded a journal called *Firaq al-ikhwat al-muslimat*, in which he advocated equal rights for women in education, arguing that illiteracy was against Islam. Education would bring civilization and the regeneration of Islam, but this would be with women constituting the major educational force in the home. He did not believe women should work outside the home, arguing that in the pre-Islamic period, *al-jahiliya*, when women had equality, there was utter chaos in society. Islam needed educated women to bring up educated children. By 1947 an organization called the Headquarters of the Muslim Sisters was formed, giving recognition to women's place in the Muslim Brotherhood movement. Fifty branches were set up all over the country with some 5,000 lay preachers. The organization was dissolved in 1948.

There were other factors which favored this new radical conservatism in Egyptian society and politics. The attack of the modernists on tradition was short-lived. As a contender for power with an Islamic restoration in view, the Muslim Brotherhood was the only militant political organization in Egypt in the thirties and forties to embrace the theocratic ideal of Islamic government and to seek by violent and other means to attain it. Another extremist group emerged in the thirties, *Misr al-fatat*, founded by a lawyer, Ahmad Husayn, in 1933. It became a political party in 1938 and published its own newspaper. It emphasized the importance of religious belief and morality, and advocated more education for women since they produce the future heroes. A third trend, preaching return to the early principles of Islam as laid down by the prophet, was the *Salafiya* movement. Its adherents were the religious disciples of Mohammad 'Abdu, led by Rashid Rida (d. 1935), who headed a movement whose basic teachings reverted to strict Islamic orthodoxy (Vatikiotis 1969).

Throughout this period of the thirties and forties the *Salafiya*, the *Misr al-fatat*, and the Muslim Brotherhood agitated against foreign schools and the activities of Christian missions and missionaries, and attacked the work of European orientalists. Terrorist activities were the main tactics of the Muslim Brotherhood during the late forties. When the regime could no longer conceal its utter failure in the Palestine war of 1948-49, a *general condition of sedition was generated in Egyptian politics which lasted for the next three years and laid the seeds for the 1952 revolution.*

How might we describe the feminist activism of Doria Shafik during this period? How does her feminist consciousness reflect the broader social and political turmoil, and conversely how is the broader social and political turmoil reflected in her feminism? How shall we assess the historical role of Doria Shafik in the unfolding of feminist consciousness in Egypt? Answers to these questions must be tentative, as we have only begun to discover and analyze the sources.

The Voice of Feminism and Political Action: *Bint al-Nil*

Although Doria Shafik started her professional career as a teacher in Alexandria College for Girls and the Sania School, after obtaining her Ph.D. she was considered for the post of professor at the Faculty of Letters of Cairo University. However, the Dean of the Faculty opposed her nomination, claiming that he could not "assume the responsibility of having such a beautiful woman on his staff." She then found another job as Inspector of the French Language in the Ministry of Education. But her independent spirit soon ran counter to the demands of bureaucracy, and she left the job with the government. She then turned to journalism and founded three women's magazines, including the well-known feminist journal *Bint al-Nil* (Daughter of the Nile).

Bint al-Nil, founded in 1945 in association with Dr. Ibrahim 'Abdu, was the first post-World War II feminist journal published in Arabic. Although there were others that had started earlier (*Al-Misriya* in 1925, *Fatat al-Sharq* in 1906, and *L'Egyptienne* in 1925), they had all ceased publication after 1939. *Bint al-Nil* continued to be published monthly until 1957 when Nasser ordered its closure for reasons that we shall discuss later. It is during this period and through the pages of *Bint al-Nil*, as well as her public protests, that we can follow the feminist thought and actions of Doria Shafik.

An examination of the early editorials shows that Shafik simultaneously displayed cautious religious conservatism and outspoken admiration for women's participation in political struggle. To illustrate these parallel strands of thought, I cite from some of the early editorials of *Bint al-Nil*.[4] In 1946 she wrote:

> Legislation to achieve equality will take away from woman privileges she has long enjoyed, and will also burden her with tasks and responsibilities. . . . I do not think we are unaware that equating women with men will deprive a women of her rights of being supported by her man, because such equality will leave behind a chaotic home as a problem will arise in our homes: Who is responsible for the home—the man or the woman? (January 1946, p.1)

> Safia Zaghloul, a pioneer and an example to be followed, was the first Egyptian woman to go out into the street. But into which street? *The street in which there was the sweet struggle for the nation.* (March 1946, p. 1)

> In Palestine I was fascinated by the role women play, not only in social life but also in political life as well. You find each woman beside the man struggling for the nation. And when circumstances required or the conditions became difficult, she would stick to him like the Arab villages stick to the mountains of the nation. The Palestinian woman gives every visitor the idea that there is a real feminist movement in Palestine and that this movement has its weight and value in the life of the country. This movement is neither pretentious nor empty, for women there read as men read because education for them is something sacred. I admire Palestine, and my admiration will increase as time goes on, because these people have nurtured the great religions in their cradles, and they have illuminated the world with their religious monuments, and they have created a fine public image of Arabism. Their struggle is an Arab struggle, and the Palestinians will never be humiliated nor overrun by invaders; nor shall westerners raise their flags over them as long as their struggle is such a struggle. (April 1946, p. 1)[5]

In 1948 we notice a change of tone in her editorials on equal rights, suggesting another consciousness emerging which saw women's emancipation linked to sharing the same opportunities as men:

> I was hesitant in advocating such rights, yet I see that women's staying away from public life is causing tragedies that I have no doubt *will not be dealt with or abolished without our true participation in public affairs.* And this will

not be achieved unless we have a share in making decisions and solving
dilemmas. (February 1948, p. 1)

The conditions in the country during this period were such that one
could speak out more freely, and the outrage felt throughout the country
over the Palestine war was echoed in the pages of *Bint al-Nil.*

The war that is going on between the Arab countries and the Jewish gangs
in Palestine is neither political nor religious . . . but it is a kind of Ameri-
can-Russian colonialism. (June 1948, p. 1)

It is also during this period, 1948, that she formed the Bint al-Nil Union,
whose avowed goal was to obtain full political rights for women, in the
belief that the basis for true liberation was for women to be equal to men
in these rights. The plan for this movement was adumbrated in the second
thesis she wrote for the Ph.D. at the Sorbonne, *La Femme et le droit religieux
de l'Egypte contemporaine,* which was a kind of plea leading to the conclusion
that Islam was not opposed to the complete emancipation of women. The
Bint al-Nil Union became affiliated to the International Council of
Women (ICW) under the name of National Council of Egyptian Women,
and Doria Shafik was elected to the Executive Committee of the ICW.[6] It
was during her participation in the international meetings that she visited
Paris once again and had her first two collections of poetry accepted for
publication by Pierre Seghers.

The primary purpose of the Bint al-Nil Union at its very beginning was
to claim the rights of women by stressing that the Egyptian Constitution of
1923 proclaimed the equality of the sexes. She felt that the two draft laws
restricting polygyny and altering divorce, introduced into Parliament as a
result of Huda Sha'rawi's movement, had not received consideration
because there were no women sitting in the legislature: "If women were
sitting in Parliament, such projects would long since have been enacted."

It was with this single-minded objective in view that she launched her
"movement" in 1948. The first political action directed toward the
achievement of this objective came on 19 February 1951, when she organized a demonstration that led to the seizure of Parliament by women:

A thousand women forced the gates of the Parliament, overpowered the
guards, amidst cries of "Down with Parliament without women"; "This
Parliament does not represent the whole nation"; "Women's place is next
to yours." The disturbance went on for three hours, preventing legislators
from proceeding with their work. The President of the Chamber sent a
message complaining that this mode of action was not compatible with
oriental customs. The reply was: "It is high time that we rid ourselves of
the very heavy burden of these customs." He then sent for the leaders of
the demonstration, who were taken to the Pharaonic Hall, where no
woman had ever before entered. Only when the President of both Cham-

bers had promised to lend their support to our feminist demands did the demonstrators disperse. (Memoirs)

A few days later Doria Shafik had to appear in court, where she was accused of having instigated the demonstration. Hundreds of Bint al-Nil supporters came to the hearing, which almost turned into another demonstration. The judge quickly decided to adjourn the hearing indefinitely.[7]

This public act provoked outrage among the Islamic conservatives, who openly accused her of trying to destroy the unity of Islam and corrupt the Muslim social structure. The Head of the Union of Muslim Associations in Egypt[8] cabled His Majesty King Faruk:

> Recently an adventurous movement has begun which defies the limits set by God and dares to challenge Islamic beliefs, thus creating a serious danger to the nation. This devilish movement is made up of women who are not attached to their homes and do not carry out family duties such as taking care of their husbands and children. They are inspired by imperialistic foreign influences which are moving against our religion and social system. Our reputation will be ruined, as this movement proclaims principles that are obviously contradictory to Islam—that is, the restriction of divorce and polygyny. Therefore, the general association of the Islamic Organizations of Egypt requests His Majesty: 1) to abolish women's organizations that call for participation in politics; 2) to force Muslim women to return to their homes and tables with the necessary legal codes to protect them from corruption; and 3) to strictly impose the veil.

Doria Shafik's response:

> I have never known of a cause opposed by such insults, attacks, lies, and silly thoughts as the cause of women. Only its opponents have been heard. And people listen to them as if they alone were the leaders of guidance and the minarets of right religion. The makers of these anecdotes have closed their eyes to the facts. The education of girls at a university is a fact; the employment of women in public service is a fact; and women's constitutional rights is a problem that will be solved in spite of the opposition, the meetings, the insults and accusations, because it is a logical and fair cause, supported by the merciful and generous religion of Islam. Our cause is destined ultimately to be achieved, in spite of their futile objections!!! (Memoirs)

In 1951 Doria Shafik formed a political party, also named Bint al-Nil. Meanwhile the different activities of the Bint al-Nil Union were growing. Centers for combating illiteracy among adult women were being established in increasing numbers; training centers were set up to provide young men and women in the provinces an opportunity to learn productive skills; and a labor office was set up to help find jobs for rural women coming to the city (Shafik 1952). Eager to prove equality to men in every respect, the Bint al-Nil Union formed its own all-woman military unit. Two

hundred young women were given military training, and many of them
wanted to fight in the Canal Zone side by side with their brothers.[9] As she
recalled in her memoirs:

> I wondered if there was a way of meeting their enthusiasm without
> exposing them to danger. They were not yet fully trained and experienced
> in warfare. An idea came to me on 22 January 1952. One of our young
> nationalist leaders, president of the National Party, had recently given a
> lecture at the Bint al-Nil Club in Cairo. The title of the lecture was "The
> Fight of Indian Women." The lecturer related the sequences in the great
> struggle of Indian women, who had fought side by side with men in the
> movement for liberation from foreign occupation in India. . . . Ending his
> lecture looking at me, he said: "The only way to gain all your rights is to
> fight for national liberation, just as Indian women have done." So I
> proposed that a demonstration against foreign domination need not
> necessarily involve bloodshed. It could be done locally as a symbolic
> gesture. We could stop one of the British banks in Cairo from working for
> one day. It would be a demonstration against colonialism in the field of
> economy.

So with her 200 young recruits she surrounded the entrances to
Barclay's Bank and managed to prevent the employees from entering.
Those who were already inside and wished to leave were allowed to do so.
This dramatic gesture created a popular response and crowds gathered
around the bank, many wanting to storm it and destroy it, a consequence
of her action that Doria Shafik had not anticipated:

> I had intended this as a simple symbolic gesture to prove that women are
> not only asking for political rights but actually performing acts of national
> importance—women's freedom being linked to national freedom. I had
> not expected such crowds or growing violence. (Memoirs)

On 26 January 1952, "the tragic, smoking ruins were all that was left
that evening of the centre of Cairo, all that was left of a regime and a society, all that was left of the relationship between the people and authority"
(Lacouture 1958, p. 105). The last days of January were spent in an atmosphere of anger and anguish, in which mob rule had supplanted legal
power. Doria Shafik was not unaware of the implications of these events for
her cause:

> I was getting more and more conscious that Freedom is one entity—Free-
> dom of Women being inseparable from Freedom of the Nation. I was
> convinced that there would be no free women in an occupied country,
> and no occupied country with free women. (Memoirs)

The next opportunity for a public stand came during the general elections of March 1952, in which Doria Shafik attempted to offer her name as
a candidate in the district of 'Abdin, in order to challenge the electoral law

denying women the right to vote. While recovering from an appendectomy, she submitted her letter of candidacy with the required deposit. She recalled:

> Meanwhile hundreds of women from the poorer classes came to the clinic with long lists of names (thumb prints) giving me their votes for the coming election. This turned into a public demonstration, drawing the attention of the press, for the Minister of the Interior had returned my letter of candidacy, saying he did not have my name on his list, and therefore I could not be nominated. (Memoirs)

The July 23 Revolution took place, and Doria Shafik and the Bint al-Nil Union turned their attention to intensifying their reform activities. It was not until March 1954 that Doria Shafik, impatient with the lack of government acceptance of the demands for full political rights for women, decided to take direct action. But this time she decided to act alone. As she related in her memoirs:

> In March 1954 when a Constitutional Assembly was formed, whose function it was to adopt or reject the new Egyptian constitution, there was no mention in the newspapers that women would take part. I was disappointed. I had been sure since the Egyptian Revolution that its leaders would in time realize a second revolution, no less important than the first: that of giving women a say in the laws of the country. I felt women's rights were in danger. Lacking women, the Assembly might adopt a constitution in which women's rights were not guaranteed. . . . *I decided to play the last card. I decided to go on a hunger strike to death for "women's full political rights."*

With this in mind and on the day that it was announced in the newspapers that the Constitutional Assembly would convene without women represented, Doria Shafik entered the building of the Press Syndicate at twelve o'clock noon to begin her hunger strike—but not before she had carefully planned her strategy. She had gone to her office without telling her family what she was planning to do, and had prepared the following statement in French, English, and Arabic and had it sent to President Naguib, the Revolutionary Command Council, 'Ali Maher (President of the Constitutional Committee), the President of the Council of State, the Rector of Al-Azhar, prominent members of the ulema, eminent Egyptian personalities, and the Egyptian and foreign press and news agencies:

> Today at noon I will start a hunger strike to death in the Press Syndicate building in order to gain full political rights for women. I protest against the formation of a Constitutional Assembly without women's representation. I will never agree to be ruled by a constitution in the preparation of which I had no say. (Memoirs)

After eight days in which this act drew international as well as national attention, the added participation of fourteen other women in Cairo, and a similar strike by the Bint al-Nil Union in Alexandria, the government finally acceded to the demands. The Governor of Cairo, who was sent as a representative of the government, told the strikers: "I am charged by the government to inform you that the new Egyptian constitution will guarantee women's full political rights." Doria Shafik persisted and asked that this be put in writing. "But, Madame Shafik, I cannot ask the government to put this in writing. It is impossible." "Then," she said, "you put in writing what you have been sent to announce." The Governor agreed and the strike ended.[10] The women by this time had been transported to the hospital. As Doria Shafik recalled the experience:

> I was happy. I had my girls and my husband near me. I had a written promise for women's political rights. . . . I had gone through the greatest experience of my life. My hunger strike had brought me in touch with the ABSOLUTE!!! (Memoirs)

And as she was to write later in the journal *Bint al-Nil*:

> My hunger strike was not a feminist demonstration relating only to women's rights. . . . The international press as a whole received it with what it implied of meanings greater and more profound even than the rights of women . . . the strength of the democratic trend and the rooting of a new popular consciousness in Egypt . . . the consciousness that could tolerate no longer to be patient about rule with no parliament, no constitution, no freedom. (*Bint al-Nil*, April 1954)

The dream for which she experienced the "Absolute" did not materialize. It wasn't until the Egyptian Constitution of January 1956 that women achieved the vote, but an electoral law limited this right to vote to those women who formally applied for it and thus presumably had to be educated, a condition not required of men (Lacouture 1958, p. 109; Vatikiotis 1969, p. 387).

Doria Shafik continued to protest these halfway measures. She filed a *Procès Verbal* stating:

> The Bint al-Nil Union refuses to accept a fragment of the political rights of the Egyptian woman, since that would be in contradiction with its own Bylaws demanding that the Egyptian women acquire the totality of their rights.[11]

During the latter 1950s and within the larger arena of Egyptian political life, when Nasser's regime was consolidating its power, the issues of women's rights and feminist consciousness were subsumed into the goals and aspirations of the new socialist state. Political parties and feminist unions were superseded by a larger state-controlled system. Both internally and externally Egypt was passing through the agonies of a *society in transition*, with the redefining of its manifest destiny, the attempt at union with Syria, the First Suez War, the nonaligned movement, the rise of Arab Socialism all contributing to an increased intolerance of dissent and opposition.

Within this historical context Doria Shafik took her final public, symbolic stance—not for women's rights, not for national liberation, but for that abstract ideal of human freedom for which her poetic soul hungered.

On 6 February 1957 she walked into the Indian Embassy, after having announced to President Nasser, the Egyptian and international press and news agencies that she was going to "hunger unto death as a protest against the infringement of my human freedom on two fronts—the external and the internal: 1) the Israeli occupation of Egyptian land, and 2) the onset of dictatorship that is leading Egypt into bankruptcy and chaos."

This was the ultimate symbolic gesture—the final outcry. For after that Doria Shafik disappeared from public life. Nasser had her put under house arrest, closed down the Bint al-Nil Union, including the journal, and ordered her name forever banned from public print. Her former comrades in the Bint al-Nil Union forced her resignation, and they, along with all other women's associations, publicly denounced her as a traitor to the revolution.

Conclusion

This brief and all too sketchy exposition has been an exercise in biography and history in an attempt at historical understanding through the understanding of the individual person. In sharing the "voices" of Doria Shafik, I have tried to let you hear them in the context of her own historical moment, not ours. For me the unrelenting message of these "voices" is that they are but one voice that believes it is on a mission—the struggle for the Absolute. For me the evidence suggests that her struggle for full political and constitutional rights for Egyptian women was far more the natural and inevitable expression of her own inner commitment to human freedom, propelling her forward to her ultimate destiny—like some heroic character in a Greek tragedy—than it ever was a consciously articulated, systematically developed, and logically consistent feminist ideology. And it is perhaps for this reason that she may appear, to contemporary feminists, to be naive, unsystematic, and ineffectual in achieving fundamental change in the status and condition of women.

As we have seen, her feminist struggle began in the mid-1940s with the voice of cautious conservatism, much in the vein of her predecessor, Huda Sha'rawi. She advocated, quite as carefully as her mentor, a balance between Islamic teaching and feminist reform. Throughout she remained scrupulously correct and loyal in her attitude toward Islam, never consciously trying to separate her feminist activity from the principles of the Muslim religion as she understood that religion. In this early period (1945-

1951) there is no doubt that Doria Shafik believed she was furthering the fundamental aims of the earlier feminists, which linked women's rights to broader social and political issues.

In 1951, with the storming of the Parliament and the increasing attention she and the Bint al-Nil Union were attracting both nationally and internationally, we begin to hear her speak more of women's freedom and national freedom as a single entity. But we also sense that she was becoming more conscious of some historical mission that she should fulfill. And we begin to sense a *self* becoming more conscious of *itself* as a force for change. This is particularly symbolized in her 1954 hunger strike and suggests a break with the earlier movement. At this point Doria Shafik and her struggle appear to have been less connected to the dominant trends of social and political change occurring in Egypt: yet she was unyielding in her perseverance for complete and unequivocal political rights for women. But the public arena in which she could carry out her symbolic gestures was becoming narrower, and the perceived violation of her transcendent idea of human freedom propelled her toward her final, solitary stance.

After 1957 the voice of Doria Shafik was directed inward and is available only in her extensive memoirs and her poetry, some of which is contained in those marvelous five volumes with which I began my search. That she has *not* been recognized by a later generation (whatever their views of her role in the unfolding of feminist consciousness in Egyptian history) is an issue that leads us into the sociology of knowledge, one that we cannot address at this time. Suffice it for me to end with a quotation from Emma Goldman:

> The real revolutionist—the dreamer, the creative artist, the iconoclast in whatever line—is fated to be misunderstood, not only by her own kind, but often by her own comrades. This is the doom of all great spirits; they are detached from their environment. Theirs is a lonely life—the life of the transition stage, the hardest and most difficult for the individual as well as for a people. (Falk 1984, p. ix)

NOTES

1. The five volumes of poetry are: *Larmes d'Isis* and *Avec Dante aux enfers* (in four parts), published by Pierre Fanlac, Paris, 1979. In the dedication of these poems, Pierre Seghers, friend and publisher of her first volume of collected poetry in 1948, describes Doria Shafik as follows:

> Inhabited by that exalted flame that makes men tremble and consumes them, Doria Shafik, poet of interior thorns and hidden treasures, wakeful soul of the solitary guardian—the fortress of conscience and humanity was always threatened—Doria, as the great fire of bramble crackling at the

edge of the sand, or a felucca under its triumphant sail on the Nile, illuminated herself with her torches, while over her hung a mortal reddening shadow that the river was slowly carrying away. But where?

2. Over the years of house arrest and then self-imposed seclusion, Doria Shafik wrote her memoirs. They are unpublished and remain with her daughters along with other private papers. It is due to their trust and confidence that I was allowed access to these papers.

3. *L'Egyptienne* is the name of the feminist journal, started by Huda Sha'rawi and Ceza Nabaraoui, that was published from 1925 to 1939. Its main objective was: "To disseminate information abroad about the Egyptian woman as she is in our days . . . and to enlighten European public opinion about the true political and social situation in Egypt."

4. In a personal interview with Dr. Ibrahim 'Abdu, I was told that it was he who wrote the editorials in Arabic, because her Arabic in the early years was not strong. She would outline in French the main ideas that she wanted to get across, and then these would be translated into Arabic. When questioned, he admitted that he would often "tone down" Doria Shafik's ideas. This raises the question as to whose voice we are really hearing in those early editorials. He said that after 1948, when one could speak out more freely on these issues, Doria Shafik stressed more political subjects and *Bint al-Nil* expressed more directly its criticisms of government, King, and politics. She began to give more emphasis to the idea of freedom, and the children's magazine *Katkout* also focused on that subject (Personal interview, 31 March 1985).

5. These are Doria Shafik's impressions after a three-day trip to Palestine at the invitation of Ouly Abul Huda, President of the Feminist Solidarity Society in Palestine.

6. The fact that there were many women's associations in Egypt at this time suggests that there might have been competition and conflict. In several articles written in *La Bourse Egyptienne* and *Le Journal d'Egypte* that I have yet to obtain, there seems to have been a confrontation with another major feminist union over *Bint al-Nil*'s subsuming other unions under its aegis.

7. Doria Shafik, although married to a very prominent lawyer, deliberately chose women lawyers to defend her at this trial.

8. The particular groups represented in this association include: Muslim Brotherhood, Azhar Ulema Front, Association of the Mosque Ulema, Legal Society, Truthful Brothers, Pilgrims Propaganda, Piety and Guidance, and Pilgrimage Supporters.

9. After the abrogation of the Anglo-Egyptian Treaty of 1936 in October 1951, Egyptian partisans started guerilla attacks against the British forces in the Suez Canal Zone. This "Battle of the Canal" came to its height on 19 January 1952. On that day, for the first time the Egyptian commandos made a bold attack—in broad daylight and almost in battle formation—on the British garrison at Tel el-Kebir. The British retaliated on 25 January with an attack on an Egyptian police barracks, in which fifty Egyptians were killed and one hundred wounded.

10. This was the period when Naguib and Nasser were struggling for political control of the revolution. Naguib was officially the president when Shafik's strike began, and it was he, not Nasser, who sent the Governor of Cairo with the message. After Nasser took over power, that governor was dismissed.

11. Between the hunger strike of 1954 and the statement on women's rights in the January 1956 constitution, Doria Shafik had accepted invitations from several feminist organizations in Europe, Asia, and America to speak about the situation of Egyptian women. This resulted in a book entitled *Rihlati hawal al-'alam*.

A month before her trip she was told that it would be preferable that her talks in the U.S. be given in English. At that time she spoke only French and Arabic. But in the course of that month she managed by determination and perseverance to learn English.

REFERENCES

Abd al-Qadir, Muhammad Z., Nahnu al-Nur. *Al-Ahram*, 22 September 1975.

Ahmed, Leila, Feminism and Feminist Movements in the Middle East. In *Women and Islam*, ed. Azizah al-Hibri. Oxford: Pergamon Press, 1982.

Dilthey, Wilhelm, *Pattern and Meaning in History: Thoughts on History and Society*. New York: Harper and Row, 1961.

Falk, Candace, *Love, Anarchy, and Emma Goldman*. New York: Holt, Rinehart and Winston, 1984.

Lacouture, Jean, and Lacouture, Simonne, *Egypt in Transition*. New York: Criterion, 1958.

Mills, C. Wright, *The Sociological Imagination*. New York: Grove Press, 1961.

Vatikiotis, P. J., *The Modern History of Egypt*. London: Weidenfeld and Nicolson, 1969.

PUBLISHED WORKS OF DORIA SHAFIK

1940 *L'Art pour l'art dans l'Egypte antique*. Paris: Paul Geuthner.

1940 *La Femme et la droit religieux de l'Egypte contemporaine*. Paris: Paul Geuthner.

1944 *La Femme nouvelle en Egypte*. Cairo: Schindler.

1945 *Tatawwur al-nahda al-nisa'iya fi Misr* (Development of the Renaissance of Women in Egypt), with Ibrahim 'Abdu. Cairo: Maktabat al-Tawakul.

1948 *La Bonne Aventure* (Collected Poetry). Paris: Pierre Seghers.

1952 *L'Esclave Sultan* (novel).

1952 Egyptian Feminism. *Middle East Affairs* 3 (August): 233-38.

1953 *Al-Kitab al-abyad li huquq al-mar'a al siyasiya* (The White Book on the Political Rights of Women). Cairo: Matba'at Misr.

1954 *L'Amour perdu* (Collected Poetry). Paris: Pierre Seghers.

1955 *Rihlati hawal al-'alam* (My Trip Around the World). Cairo: Al-Matba'a al Sharqiya.

1955 *Al-Mar'a al-misriya min al-farawna ila al-yawm* (The Egyptian Woman from the Pharaohs Until Today), with Ibrahim 'Abdu. Cairo: Matba'at Misr.

1979 *Larmes d'Isis* (Collected Poetry). Paris: Pierre Fanlac.

1979 *Avec Dante aux enfers* (Collected Poetry, 4 vols.). Paris: Pierre Fanlac.

EMBATTLED ADVOCATES
THE DEBATE OVER BIRTH CONTROL IN INDIA, 1920-1940

Barbara N. Ramusack

Despite voluminous literature about the promotion of family planning in India after 1947, little attention has been given to the debate over this issue before independence. There is evidence of a Hindu Malthusian League in Madras in 1882,[1] and population issues were mentioned in the controversy about the origins of Indian poverty during the closing decades of the 19th century. It was, however, only in the early 1920s that Indian men initiated a sustained public discussion about the need for birth control and attempted to establish institutions to provide information on contraception. Under the leadership of Rani Lakshmibai Rajwade, who had received her medical education in Bombay and Great Britain, and the All India Women's Conference (AIWC), Indian women quickly joined the public discourse that peaked during the mid-1930s. Foreigners also entered the debate as propagandists, most notably Margaret Sanger, as links to international organizations and as medical providers of limited contraceptive information.

This essay will analyze gender as a key factor in the effort to promote contraception in India during the two decades from 1920 to 1940. How were Indian men and women similar and dissimilar in their advocacy of reproductive control? What rationales did they advance for their support of birth control? What types of plans did they seek to inaugurate? Were their programs directed to particular classes, regional areas, or religious groups? What kinds of associations did they form to institutionalize the extension of reproductive control? Were some proponents more willing than others to ally themselves with foreign individuals, groups, or programs? To appreciate the arena in which both Indian and foreign advocates of birth control functioned, one must also survey the opposition to their positions. What were the legal, political, social, economic, and moral

© 1989 JOURNAL OF WOMEN'S HISTORY, VOL. 1 NO. 2 (FALL)

constraints on the practice of contraception? Who were the most important individuals and groups who argued against birth control? Here again,
did gender make a difference? What reasons were utilized to support a
negative stance? Is it possible to assess their impact in countering the supporters of birth control?

During the 1920s and 1930s, Indian society experienced many crucial
developments, including the emergence of Mahatma Gandhi as the overarching leader of the nationalist struggle for independence; the intensifi-
cation of personal identification with communal groups based on
religious or caste affiliations; and the emergence of regional and national
women's organizations. Thus, to provide the broader context, the public
discussion of contraception will be related to the evolution of Indian
nationalism, to the rise of communal groups in the political sphere, and to
the development of women's associational activity.

In this exploratory analysis, it is important to emphasize the scattered
and limited nature of the sources presently available. Among most elite
and nonelite categories of Indian society during much of the 20th century,
personal sexuality was considered an inappropriate topic for discussion in
sexually mixed public groups or even between husbands and wives.[2] A few
pioneering men and women wrote books and articles on sexuality and on
the general need for contraception, but almost no one publicly declared
that they themselves practiced contraception. Indian men and women discussed sexual issues in private among their own gender groups, but the
written records of their discourses are sparse. Much of the information
currently accessible is filtered through the reporting of foreign observers.[3]
Because scholars must be cautious in their use of this material, my conclusions may sound irritatingly tentative.

Terminology and definitions are also problematic. Although many
Indian speakers used the term birth control, they did not explicitly
espouse the orientation of the birth controllers in the United States, who
initially wanted to enable women to control their reproductive functions
in order to gain personal autonomy and improved economic conditions.[4]
Therefore, it seems more appropriate to use the term reproductive control in this essay except where the more precise meaning of birth control
is intended or where that term is used by the speakers themselves. Finally,
this account will not seek to determine the effectiveness of actual programs but, rather, to analyze the content of the discourse, which has continuing implications for policymakers, bureaucrats, and women activists.

Early Pioneers in India

As was the pattern with other social reform movements affecting
women, such as female education and widow remarriage, Indian and Brit-

ish males were the first advocates of reproductive control in India. They were usually administrators, statisticians, or social scientists, especially economists, who were influenced by Neo-Malthusian and eugenic theories. There were no legal prohibitions on the dissemination of information on or the practice of contraception in India, but questions about the morality of contraception were found to varying degrees in all Indian religious traditions. The male vanguard was most active as propagandists establishing the necessity for and morality of reproductive control. Census studies, which had been conducted decennially since 1881, provided increasingly sophisticated data that some interpreted to indicate disturbing rates of population growth and evidence of poor health and economic misery among that expanding population. P.K. Wattal's *The Population Problem in India: A Census Study*, published in 1916 and in revised versions in 1934 and 1938, was one of the first monographs to raise the need to limit population as an issue of public policy in India.[5]

Wattal was soon joined by two Marathi Hindu social reformers who firmly established Bombay, the second largest city in India, as the leading center of the discussion over reproductive control. R.D. Karve, whose father founded the S.N.D.T. Women's University in 1916, led the transition from theoretical arguments on the need for reproductive control to efforts to enable people to practice it. After studying the subject for 15 years and gathering information during a tour of Europe in 1920, Karve started supplying information and appliances related to contraception in 1921 in Bombay. He soon lost his position as professor of mathematics at Wilson College in Bombay because of his advocacy of contraception and so devoted himself full time to this cause. In his first book, *Morality and Birth Control* (1921), he argued that contraception was, indeed, morally acceptable. N.S. Phadke, a professor of philosophy and a novelist in Marathi, also began to champion contraception during the early 1920s. He was among the first Indians to correspond with Margaret Sanger and to publish in her journal, the *Birth Control Review*. In 1924, he reflected his economic orientation by urging that "We must keep our population proportionate to our resources . . . and so guide and control [procreation] that our progeny will not contain even a single 'unwanted' child."[6] Phadke established the Bombay Birth Control League, which soon languished as the philosopher lost his teaching position. Forced to seek employment in Nagpur and then the princely state of Kolhapur, Phadke inadvertently spread propaganda beyond the metropolitan area of Bombay.[7] In the princely states, which were scattered over two-fifths of the territory of India, Indian rulers were internally autonomous, while the British exercised tight control of their external relations, defense, and communications. Princely states could either be areas of progressive social and political reform or of conspicuous autocracy, depending on the orientation of an individual ruler.

Two other associations were also founded in the 1920s. In 1927 to the southwest of Bombay, and still in the Marathi cultural area, the Sholapur Eugenics Education Society sought to educate the general public "to recognise the responsibility of parenthood" and to further "measures or tendencies, such as opening Mothers' Clinics, as would prevent the diminution of superior types or the multiplication of the inferior."[8] This group enunciated more clearly than others its eugenic orientation but sought to promote birth control as eugenicists increasingly came to do in England during the 1920s. Dr. A.P. Pillay, its honorary medical director, would emerge during the 1930s as a significant advocate of reproductive control in Bombay city.

Across the southern half of India on the eastern coast in Madras there was a revival of Neo-Malthusian sentiments that had first emerged in the 1880s. The Madras Neo-Malthusian League, founded by some elite Tamil Brahmins, sought to spread knowledge of reproductive control and to give medical assistance on hygienic contraceptive methods to married people "who desire to limit their families or who are in any way unfit for parenthood."[9] Neo-Malthusian and eugenic doctrines were intermingled in the ideology of its members. This group published a propaganda journal, *Madras Birth Control Bulletin*, and sold various contraceptives.[10] These two associations, which sought reproductive control for the economic and eugenic improvement of the Indian populations, helped to lay the groundwork for a subsequent shift from women's health issues to family planning as the justification for a program of reproductive control.

Margaret Sanger had initially come to know of the movement for reproductive control in India through male leaders such as Phadke, Karve, and Pillay. During the mid-1920s, she temporarily opened another channel to India through Agnes Smedley, a political and social radical who had briefly worked in the birth control movement in New York. Attracted to Indian nationalism during World War I through contact with Lala Lajpat Rai, a Punjabi nationalist then in exile in New York, Smedley went in early 1921 to Berlin where she lived intermittently with Virendranath Chattopadhyaya, a Bengali in exile because of his sympathies with terrorism and communism.[11] In 1924, Smedley urged Sanger to recruit physicians in India as propagandists and to promote birth control "for child and racial betterment," using Japan rather than the west as an example. Sanger was receptive to these suggestions, since she had increasingly sought to spread access to contraception in the United States through an alliance with the medical profession. She had also served as mentor for Baroness Ishimoto, a leader in the birth control movement in Japan.[12]

Smedley further cautioned Sanger that in India "it is better not to stress the woman freedom viewpoint until you have a foothold" when she propagandized for birth control.[13] Sanger and many western women who used the term birth control initially meant that women should choose the timing and number of pregnancies through contraception. Women were to be the initiators; contraception and not continence was to be the method; and the objectives were to include greater personal control for women over their health and economic situation. Thus, Smedley clearly indicated that she perceived a need to underplay certain implications of birth control for an Indian audience because of a possible unreceptivity to increased personal freedom for Indian women. Smedley's rhetoric, which emphasized the amelioration of children and the "race," could be accepted by eugenicists who sought to improve the physical and intellectual quality of the population by urging the "fit" to procreate and the "unfit" to limit their progeny. She also indicated the need to avoid controversy by citing an Asian rather than a western model at a time when the nationalist struggle in India had achieved new power during the first non-cooperation movement lead by Mahatma Gandhi in 1920-22.

Mahatma Gandhi Speaks on Birth Control

In 1920, Gandhi had advocated suspending procreation through *brahmacharya*, which referred to the student stage of male Hindu life when one was to study the ancient Vedas and to practice continence, until India became free.[14] By 1925, the expanding public discussion on birth control provoked Gandhi to elaborate his views on the subject. He agreed "there can be no two opinions about the necessity of birth control. But the only method handed down from ages past is self-control or *Brahmacharya*." For him, sexual union was meant for progeny and not for pleasure, so "it is still worse for a person to indulge his animal passions and escape the consequences of his acts" through the use of artificial means of contraception.[15] To Gandhi, one could not escape the karma or consequences of sexual union. A few weeks later, Gandhi added that women would reject artificial methods as inconsistent with their dignity. Such methods would increase the appetite for sex and would result in the dissolution of the marriage bed.[16] Gandhi's views stimulated much discussion in the Indian press, with R.D. Karve being his major antagonist.

Sanger's first confrontation with Gandhi occurred in the pages of *Birth Control Review* in response to his 1925 articles. In an editorial, she thanked him for stimulating discussion and proclaimed that

> sexual expression is one of the most profoundly spiritual of all the avenues of human experience, and Birth Control the supreme moral instrument by which, without injury to others nor to the future destinies of mankind on this earth, each individual is enabled to progress on the road to self-development and self-realization.[17]

Sanger challenged Gandhi on his own ground of the spiritual value and goal of the sexual act and of contraceptive methods. Although she did not raise the issue of women's rights, she clearly indicated that birth control should bring greater autonomy to both women and men.

Gradual Involvement of Women—Foreign and Indian

Although women were to be the prime target group for the use of contraceptive methods, it is remarkable that little effort was made to involve Indian women in the organizational and propaganda work during the 1920s. This inconsistency was apparent to some. In 1926, Mary Winson, a member of the National Council of the American Birth Control League, was traveling as a tourist and met N.S. Phadke in Bombay. She was impressed by the absence of legal restrictions on the dissemination of contraceptive information but later wrote that "the Birth Control Movement will always be lacking in proper perspective until the educated women of India join it wholeheartedly; throwing off false ideals of modesty in which they have been educated."[18] Winson's assessment is based on limited observation, but Phadke himself reported that there was not one woman on the executive committee of the Bombay Birth Control League. As late as June 1929, Justice V. Ramesam, a vice-president of the Madras Neo-Malthusian League, advised Sanger that

> we believe that Dr. [Muthulakshmi] Reddy herself does not know much about the reasons for birth control. We are not aware of any organization of Indian women interested in considering the problems that would be raised in a Birth Control Conference.[19]

Reddy was a physician in Madras who was active both in women's organizations and in electoral politics as the first Indian woman member of a provincial legislative assembly.[20] Ramesam told Sanger to invite some Indian man already in Europe as the Indian representative to a forthcoming international conference on birth control. Thus, although Sanger tried to incorporate Indian women into the international discourse, she was counseled by Indian men that only they were qualified to discuss the issues. Still, on a more private level, there were Indian and foreign women in India who were interested in birth control, but they were not yet publicly visible.

So far it has been possible to locate only one source that documents what elite or nonelite, urban or rural Indian women were thinking about the evolving debate over reproductive control during the 1920s. Ruth F. Woodsmall, an American working for the International YWCA in western Asia, toured India during the cold weather months of December 1930 through March 1931 as a member of the Laymen's Foreign Mission Enquiry. Her specific responsibility was to interview missionaries, British officials, and Indian leaders on the present and future activities of Christian missionaries with Indian women. During the course of over 100 interviews, four women spoke of requests for information on reproductive control from Indian women. Thus, the sample is narrow, but it indicates that some Indian women were interested in contraception.

Mrs. Murray Titus, working in Budaon, United Provinces, reported that

> again and again women who have been burdened by frequent or constant child bearing many of whom suffer miscarriages, have come to me begging me to tell them something or to give them something that would release them from this slavery, especially when they get to be about 35 to 40 years of age and are already overburdened with numbers of little children clinging to their skirts, for whom they are unable to provide properly.[21]

These sentiments were echoed by Miss E.W. Maconachie, working in Pathankot, Punjab, who said that women "come and beg me to do something to let them have no more children. *They just get worn out.*"[22]

In Bombay, Mrs. Gates, who ran Bowker Hall, a social settlement house, advised that "birth control is a question which is beginning to be discussed" even though there was "a good deal of opposition to Birth Control from Catholics and Hindus."[23] Dr. Mrs. D. Devanesan, the Lady Superintendent of the Child Welfare Scheme of the Health Department in Madras, confirmed the opposition of some Hindus. She related that

> in my annual report for 1928 I wrote a note about the need of birth control; the effect of too constant child-bearing upon both mother and children; the amount of abortion, and the great values to society if birth control knowledge could only be given to poor people. But in the council meetings they have made a lot of trouble over this. One man who was the leader of the opposition made a long speech and said it was against the Hindu religion.

The municipal council then passed a resolution "telling us that our job was only to see that healthy babies were born and that we should have nothing to do with birth control."[24]

Dr. Devanesan is representative of Indian women physicians who were becoming interested in reproductive control based on their professional experiences. When Agnes Smedley had sent a list of 18 people in India to whom Sanger should write, she included the names of nine women, most of whom were physicians and some from minority communities, especially Jews and Parsis.[25] Several of these women would emerge as major leaders in the campaign by local and national women's organizations, chiefly the All India Women's Conference and the Bombay Presidency Women's Council, to obtain the dissemination of information on contraception in public clinics. Their principal rationale would be that reproductive control would improve the health of children and mothers.

The All India Women's Conference (AIWC) and Birth Control

The AIWC began as a one-time conference to outline an appropriate curriculum and system of education for girls. Its organizers tried to ensure grass-roots representation from across India by asking local organizations to debate the issues and then to elect representatives to a national session at which they would present the views of the sending groups on the various resolutions. At their first session in Poona in 1927, the women quickly decided that they could not reform education in isolation from the general social and economic situation of women. Consequently, they resolved to form a permanent organization and to meet annually. In order to include all women, the AIWC was to eschew overtly political issues since they were seen to have the most potential for divisiveness. Concentrating on the improvement of the social condition of women through such measures as raising the minimum age of marriage and establishing a women's college in New Delhi, the founders of the AIWC advocated what Geraldine Forbes has called social feminism. They accepted their roles as wives and mothers and carefully sought to integrate their goals with the nationalist struggle for independence from Britain.[26]

At the sixth session of the AIWC in Madras in December 1931, Rani Lakshmi Rajwade, a practicing physician before her relatively late marriage to a general in the Marathi-ruled princely state of Gwalior south of the United Provinces, proposed the following resolution:

> In view of the immense increase in the population of the country and having regard to the poverty and the low physical standard of the people, this Conference is in favour of appointing a committee of medical women to study and recommend ways and means of educating the public to regulate the size of their families.[27]

It is not yet possible to determine why she raised this issue in 1931 and not earlier, but the release of the preliminary report of the Census of 1931 and of the testimony given to the Age of Consent Committee, which had investigated the issue of raising the age of consent for sexual relations, appear to be possible causes.[28] Rajwade's initial arguments were similar to those of such male pioneers as Wattal and Phadke, but she concluded by urging that mothers should have the opportunity to limit their families. Dr. Mrs. Malini Sukhtankar from Bombay seconded the resolution, citing appalling infant mortality figures.

In the liveliest debate ever heard at the AIWC, members took sharply opposing positions. The main supporters were younger social activists such as Lakshmi Menon, a lawyer practicing in Lucknow, and Renuka Ray, a volunteer social worker from Calcutta who had obtained some of her education in London. Echoing the earlier sentiments of Mary Winson, Ray argued that Indian women "should tear the veil of false modesty and prejudice if they wanted the race to be full of vigour, health and happiness."[29] Ray later would comment in her memoirs that the press criticized women from respectable families who propagandized for reproductive control since that was not considered decent work for them. As in much of the social feminism of the AIWC, Ray saw the activism of women as furthering nationalist goals, in this case the prevention of the deaths of mothers and children.[30]

The opponents were mainly the religiously orthodox, including single women such as Khadijah Begum Ferozuddin, a Muslim professor at Government College for Women in Lahore, and Miss Ouwerkerk, a Dutch, Christian missionary teacher in Trivandrum, the capital of the southern princely state of Travancore. The few Muslim women who spoke publicly on this issue viewed contraception as prohibited by Islam, although contemporary scholars generally agree that the Qur'an does not specifically prohibit fertility control but is strongly pronatalist.[31] Many missionaries, especially Catholics, were strong critics. Although Khadijah and Ouwerkerk used religion to justify their opposition, their unmarried status might have influenced their attitude. They did not articulate it, but their lack of involvement with childbearing might have made them less sympathetic to pleas for contraception. Some Indian women, such as Muthulakshmi Reddy, proposed the Gandhian ideal of self-control. Reddy, however, indicated the need for a comprehensive approach to improving the health of women and children. She called for an extension of maternity and child welfare centers that would also educate men to the duties of fatherhood, since mothers often suffered because fathers were irresponsible. After Rajwade's resolution was defeated—it attracted only seven affirmative votes—Reddy secured the passage of a substituted resolution calling for education in mothercraft and fathercraft.

Rajwade and her allies spent 1932 organizing support for reproductive control among the regional constituent units of the AIWC. The 1932 session of the AIWC was held at Lucknow near Rajwade's base in Gwalior. There Mrs. Vimala Deshpande introduced the following resolution that outlined the future parameters for the debate on birth control within the AIWC:

> This conference feels that on account of the low physique of women, high infant mortality and increasing poverty of the country, men and women should be instructed in methods of Birth Control in recognised clinics. It calls upon all municipalities and local bodies to open such centres and invites the special help of the medical authorities toward the solution of this important problem.[32]

This statement indicates some of the contradictions within the program of these elite women to promote contraception. First, they recognized the existence of high infant mortality but did not grasp that such rates were a powerful factor in influencing couples, particularly those in lower economic classes, to have as many children as possible to insure that some would survive to provide for their parents in their old age.[33] Although an increasing population might impoverish a nation over the long term, in the short term children could be economic producers for their family units. Second, because most Indian women, including the activists of the AIWC, accepted the primacy of their roles as wives and especially as mothers, there was a considerable effort to avoid promoting contraception as a means of preventing the birth of children. Thus, the improved health of mothers and children was to be the paramount rationales. Third, the concrete objective was to provide for the dissemination of information through public health clinics that were supported by municipal councils where Indian members were in the majority. The clientele of these clinics were poorer women who were not likely to be members of the AIWC.

Rameshwari Nehru, a Kashmiri Brahmin who had been the one Indian woman member of the Age of Consent Committee that had recommended in 1929 to increase the minimum age of consent for sexual relations for wives to 15, highlighted key class issues. Agreeing with opponents that self-control was best but that few could practice it, she argued that the rich were already using artificial contraception and that "it is the ignorant and the poor who have not such means at their disposal who are crushed under the weight of frequent births and who need our guidance and advice."[34] Nehru's remarks illuminate that the elite, urban-based women of the AIWC sought to secure the transfer of contraceptive information through public clinics to nonelite women who were not represented within the AIWC. This orientation was significantly different from most of their resolutions that tended to focus on matters of immediate concern to their own membership such as education, the franchise, and changes in marriage and divorce laws.

None of the spokeswomen for birth control within the AIWC provided any indication in their speeches or letters on how they ascertained that nonelite women desired information on contraception. They might have assumed that their audiences would know about their possible contacts with servant women or nonelite women through volunteer social work. Alternatively, the AIWC members themselves might have been utilizing contraception and have believed that nonelite women would want information on it. There are no indications that the AIWC leaders had access to material such as the interviews of Ruth Woodsmall that suggested that some poorer women wanted contraceptive information. In any case, the AIWC and other educated women remained vulnerable to the charge from Gandhi and other opponents of birth control that they were not representative of the nonelite, especially village women, on the issue of contraception.

At Lucknow in 1932, the advocates of reproductive control were better prepared than they had been at Madras, and their resolution passed with only seven dissenting votes. The AIWC would continue to vote on a resolution calling for the provision of contraceptive information through public clinics until 1940 and to urge its constituent units to undertake propaganda promoting the legitimacy of the use of contraceptives. As a voluntary organization, the AIWC was able to educate public opinion on a controversial topic that a colonial government decided to ignore and Indian politicians sought to avoid. During the early 1930s, when Gandhi defied the British with widespread civil disobedience, colonial administrators did not want to alienate politically conservative Indian allies who might oppose the spread and use of contraceptive information as contradicting their interpretation of religious texts and traditions or their familial arrangements.[35] Indian politicians did not want to consider possibly divisive social issues as they increasingly confronted challenges from religious groups, most notably Muslims, for a separate political existence and from nonelite groups such as the scheduled castes and tribes for greater political representation. Although the AIWC was significant as an all-Indian association, its effectiveness as a propaganda group would be limited. Composed of elite women, its annual meeting and central officers had only personal influence with its constituent units.

During 1933, the Central Provinces (South) Constituency of the AIWC in Nagpur, a major industrial and political center, found it difficult to secure places to meet and then to attract women to discuss birth control in public.[36] Resolutions on birth control were passed in the south at Salem in Tamilnadu and in the north at Agra but were defeated in Andhra in the midsouth and in Lahore, the capital of Punjab. Sources presently available do not indicate why there were these regional differences. Local units were even more divided than the annual sessions. As they were the groups who could most appropriately lobby with municipal councils and provincial legislatures to introduce information on contraception as a service of public health clinics, the impact of the AIWC on political institutions and politicians would be attenuated. The influence of the AIWC was further diffused since birth control was only one of many issues that it addressed. More specialized organizations soon joined the campaign.

The Crest of the First Wave of the Birth Control Movement: Associations, Clinics, and a Journal

Parallel to the discussions within the AIWC, Indian male social reformers and some physicians formed new institutions to disseminate information on and means of contraception in India. In late 1934, Dr. A.P. Pillay, who had moved from Sholapur to Bombay, founded *Marriage Hygiene,* a quarterly journal. At first a collection of editorial notes, book reviews, and extracts from other journals, *Marriage Hygiene* quickly developed an international network of contributors. H.G. Wells acclaimed it as the leading journal in English, and Norman Himes, the early and authoritative historian of contraception as well as its American editor, said that it was the only scientific one on its subject.[37] Even though it carried several contributions from Joseph Spengler from Duke University, early issues were seized by U.S. Customs because they allegedly contained information on contraception and, thus, were in violation of the Comstock law that forbade dissemination of contraceptive information through the U.S. mails.

Pillay also organized the Society for the Study and Promotion of Family Hygiene in December 1935. Its title reflected that its aims were "to increase happiness in marital and family relationships and to ensure a general improvement of the human race."[38] The Society was to foster research, to educate especially through its journal and a series of classes on elementary sexology and marriage hygiene, and to give contraceptive advice through clinics to married women who needed it. Sir V. Ramesam from Madras was to be the first president and Margaret Sanger the vice-president, while Pillay was the organizing secretary. The Management Committee included British and Indian physicians, academic supporters such as P.K. Wattal and Professor Gyan Chand, the president of the All-India Economic Conference, and one woman, Dr. Ruth Young, the British director of the Government of India's Maternity and Child Welfare Bureau.

It is not clear why women supporters of reproductive control in the Bombay area were not involved with this Society. Dr. Young, who was based in New Delhi, was a cautious advocate. In a controversial and influential article in *Marriage Hygiene,* she made the key distinction not frequently articulated that "birth control as a means of population control is what appeals to some people, birth control as a personal matter, to others" and affirmed that "women should have the right of deciding the number of children they wish to have and the spacing of these children." In her assessment of the problems confronting the proponents of contraception, she claimed that most Indian women were not asking for contraceptive information even though they might want release from childbearing. Young's assertion about the lack of demand might indicate that Indian women were more willing to express their interest in contraception to private individuals and physicians, such as the Christian missionaries interviewed by Woodsmall, rather than those employed by the government. However, since the sample is so small, it is impossible to make any conclusive assessment. Dr. Young also argued that no one method of contraception was appropriate for all cases and that the lack of medical women prevented the effective delivery of contraceptive technique. Pillay viewed Young's statement of problem areas as opposition and commented in an editorial note that her "pessimism about the future of birth control seems ununderstandable, unless it is attributed to a subconscious hostility to the movement, because of its 'moral' implications."[39] Pillay seemed to imply that her status as a single woman might be the basis for that subconscious hostility. Ironically, Kingsley Davis, whose 1951 book on the population of South Asia remains a basic reference, cited Young's article as the one piece of evidence for his conclusion that Indian women were not interested in contraception during the 1930s.[40] Still, Young raised valid points that remain current obstacles to the effective practice of contraception in India, such as the inadequacy of the available methods and of the number of female physicians.

The other woman prominently involved with the Marriage Hygiene Society was Lady Cowasji Jehangir, a Parsi who had long been active in maternal and infant welfare work in Bombay. She chaired the committee that organized and supervised the two clinics that the Family Hygiene Society operated. On May 19, 1935, the first clinic opened for two afternoons a week in the Parel cotton mill area in Bombay, where family and community controls would be weaker than elsewhere since many of the textile workers were migrants.[41] Jehangir made a public plea to the medical profession and employers of female labor for their assistance in acquainting "the poor married women with the work of the Clinic which is solely run for the maternal welfare of women." She asserted that "the available statistics prove that unless spacing of children is resorted to by these women, their health and hence their efficiency are bound to suffer materially."[42] The Family Hygiene Society was an elite group operating clinics for a nonelite clientele who were not represented among its membership. By August 1936, the Parel Clinic was operating every afternoon, and the number of women advised was 107, 75 percent of whom had four pregnancies and 55 percent of whom had six or more pregnancies.[43] The Society started a second clinic on December 14, 1936, at the Parakh Hospital on Sandhurst Road.

Across India in Calcutta, the largest city of the British Empire, there was a similar effort to provide an institutional base for reproductive control. In response to the visit of Edith How-Martyn, an English associate of Sanger, in early 1935, Colonel Owen Berkeley-Hill, a retired member of the Indian Medical Service and an active contributor to *Marriage Hygiene*, formed the Women's Welfare Society with a group of associates. They started a birth control clinic in June 1935 at Dufferin Hospital, but the Hospital would not allow the clinic to advertise so it attracted few clients. By September 1936, the Women's Welfare Society decided to operate an independent clinic in rented facilities under the direction of Dr. Margaret Neal and to broaden its scope to include contraception, child guidance, vocational guidance, and sex hygiene. This action was reflected in a change of its name to the Marriage Welfare and Child Guidance Association. The independent clinic of this Association, which did not accept women with incomes over 200 rupees, was active until 1942 when it closed as the Japanese invasion of Burma threatened Calcutta.

In contrast to the Bombay society that seemed to be dominated by men, the Calcutta organization had more female participation.[44] Although three Bengali women were officers, Mrs. Soudamini Mehta, a prominent Gujarati who was secretary of the group, has reminisced that few AIWC women joined the association because many did not want to offend Gandhi on this issue.[45] Other women who were marginal to Calcutta society were more active. Mrs. Neuta Ghosh, a Polish Jew married to a Bengali, functioned as treasurer.[46] At the 1935 meeting of the All India Women's Conference in Trivandrum, Neuta Ghosh would share a room with two other women from Calcutta, Shudha Mazumdar, a Bengali social worker, and Anna Bose, an American married to a Bengali. Another more famous American woman would also travel from Calcutta to Trivandrum to propagandize for birth control for Indian women.

Foreign Women as Propagandists: Margaret Sanger and Edith How-Martyn

In late November 1935, Margaret Sanger, the self-proclaimed coiner of the term birth control, steamed into Bombay harbor. Having overshadowed many of her coworkers in the birth control movement in the United States for almost two decades, Sanger was ready to redirect her considerable energy and talents to a new arena where fresh triumphs might be won for the birth control cause. The previous year, Edith How-Martyn, one of the first English feminists to support actively the birth control movement by joining the Neo-Malthusian League in London, had propagandized about birth control in India. She attended the annual session of the All India Women's Conference at Karachi, a port city on the Arabian Sea, and then toured India for two months. In response to the reception accorded to How-Martyn and possibly because of her own disappointment at her inability to secure a change in the Comstock law, Sanger had sought an invitation to attend the 1935 AIWC meeting. The American woman felt that such an invitation was necessary since Indians should not think that "we are imposing this idea [birth control] upon them." Sanger's personal objectives are reflected in her appraisal that an Indian tour would

> inspire our own women here, have a great influence on government officials, would impress legislators as well as women's groups in Egypt, Persia and other countries. . . . Altogether it would make the Indian women, by comparison, with their vision and foresight seem 100 years ahead of the rest of the world [and] put to shame most of the other women's organizations that are timid and fearful and afraid of their shadows.[47]

Her intermediary with the AIWC was Margaret Cousins, whom she had met in New York in 1932. An Irish feminist long resident in India, Cousins had been a key organizer of the All India Women's Conference. Well aware of the controversial nature of the topic and its American prophet and of the determination of Indian women to define their own agenda, Cousins arranged that Rani Lakshmibai Rajwade, the honorary secretary of the AIWC and an early proponent of reproductive control, would ask the Standing Committee of the AIWC to consider an invitation for Sanger even though Cousins herself would be present at the meeting.[48]

Upon her disembarking, Sanger was greeted by a delegation of Indian doctors and social workers led by How-Martyn, who had once characterized herself as the porter for Sanger in the international movement for birth control, and A.P. Pillay. In Bombay, Sanger immediately set to work addressing a wide range of public audiences and giving to medical groups specialized lectures on contraception accompanied by demonstration films. She lobbied British officials such as Lord Brabourne, the governor of Bombay, who advised Sanger that he and his wife were sympathetic toward birth control but could not become publicly involved because of the volatile political situation and religious controversies.[49] She inspired the *Bombay Chronicle*, a nationalist newspaper, to hold a prize competition for essays on birth control and, thus, expanded the number of publicists and their access to the press.[50]

After spending three weeks crisscrossing India, Sanger arrived in Trivandrum in late December 1935. Here she encountered an unexpected opponent. After How-Martyn and Cousins had assured her that Maharani Sethu Parvathibai, the Regent of Travancore who was to preside over the AIWC, was favorably inclined toward birth control, the Maharani tried to persuade Sanger not to speak in favor of the birth control resolution at the AIWC. Early on the morning of the scheduled debate, the Maharani urged Sanger to campaign instead for the suppression of brothels, a less controversial topic. According to Shudha Mazumdar, Catholic nuns had organized the local accommodations for AIWC members under the direction of Miss D.H. Watts, an Anglo-Indian Catholic, who served as the social secretary to the senior Maharani Parvathibai and as governess to the junior Maharani Lakshmibai. Strongly opposed to birth control, the nuns had distributed leaflets against the practice in the rooms of the conference attendees.[51] In order to avoid a sharp break with the Catholic women who were a major element in the educational system of Travancore, the Maharani stayed at home on December 31, 1935. She deputed Mrs. Rustomji Faridoonji, a Parsi stalwart in the AIWC, to preside with specific instructions to allow two opponents of birth control to speak for every supporter.[52]

When the discussion of the resolution on birth control at the AIWC began, the press was excluded as they had been at earlier such debates because of the nature of the topic. Misses Watts, Ouwerkerk, Rosemeyer, Gomes, and Mrs. P. Thannu Pillai from Travancore led the opposition. Their major arguments were that birth control led to race suicide and immorality. Sanger reported that one supporter pointed out that it was the unmarried women who seemed to know the most about the passions of men in and out of marriage. After the audience laughed at this anomaly, the remaining unmarried speakers stressed that brothers and other family relationships were the basis for their knowledge.[53] The advocates of contraception generally emphasized health considerations: that birth control was really birth spacing and not birth prevention; that two year intervals between births would reduce the high rates of maternal and infant mortality; and that the masses needed access to contraceptive information since they found it difficult to practice continence. Dr. Mrs. Malimbai Sukthanker pointed out that the men on the Bombay Municipal Council had defeated a resolution on the establishment of public birth control clinics and so women continued to suffer. By implication, the AIWC had to help themselves and their voiceless sisters on this issue. The proponents carried the day 82 to 25, and the local Catholic group withdrew from the AIWC.[54] Lakshmi Menon, an outspoken young lawyer then practicing in Lucknow in northern India but originally from Trivandrum, claimed that

> Mrs. Sanger's presence was invaluable. . . . The popular misapprehensions that birth control means birth prevention, and that artificial aids to control natural processes are either inherently wrong, or not elsewhere practised in personal or social life were ably answered by her.[55]

Sanger's role at the AIWC was less significant than her propaganda work before and after the closed meeting. Her most publicized activity in India, attracting space in Indian newspapers and the *New York Times*, was her pilgrimage to Wardha, the remote site of Mahatma Gandhi's village ashram in central India, in early December 1935. Earlier in the year, Margaret Cousins had told her that "Mahatma Gandhi is the greatest stumbling bock to the B.C. movement in India. . . . But women go ahead in spite of him and then he gives in and learns."[56]

Mahatma Gandhi and Margaret Sanger Debate Birth Control

After 20 years of intense political activity in India, Gandhi was once again focussing primarily on social reforms that would create the basis for a renewed Indian society in an independent state. His basic doctrine of *satyagraha* postulated that one must grasp truth and then nonviolently resist evil wherever one encountered it. In order to practice *satyagraha*, one must control one's bodily passions, whether for sex, food, or intoxicating drinks. Birth control for Gandhi meant abstinence. When he began his conversation with Sanger, his premise was that women must deny their husband's sexual demands when they would endanger their health or produce too many children, since he wanted women "to learn the primary right of resistance." Dedication to truth or a code of ethics involved the sacrifice of health and ease, since there were "things more precious than life and well-being." Gandhi affirmed that "with me God is truth. I would sacrifice everything, even India, for the sake of truth." Then he claimed that he had

> known tens of thousands of women in India, their experiences and their aspirations. I have discussed it with some of my educated sisters but I have questioned their authority to speak on behalf of their unsophisticated sisters, because they have never mixed with them. The educated ones have never felt one with them. But I have. They have regarded me as half a woman because I have completely identified myself with them.[57]

Raising the issue of class, Gandhi thus questioned the right of the educated, elite women who were members of the AIWC and foreign women, such as Sanger to argue about the desire of poor, especially village, women for access to artificial means of contraception. Class differences made communication difficult, but Gandhi ignored that the AIWC and Sanger had their initial focus on public health clinics in urban areas. Gandhi also underestimated the tenacity of the social ideal that a wife was to be subservient to her husband in all ways, including matters of sexual intercourse.

A persistent antagonist, Sanger continued her discussions with Gandhi for a day and a half. When she left Wardha, she thought that she had secured two concessions from Gandhi, namely that

> he does not necessarily imply life-long celibacy for the mass but rather the regulation of their sex functions so that they shall not waste or exhaust their vital force through sexual intercourse and . . . he is willing to concede that the "safe period," after scientific study, may be the answer.[58]

Mahadev Desai, the private secretary to Gandhi, commented that "as Mrs. Sanger was so dreadfully in earnest Gandhiji did mention a remedy which could conceivably appeal to him. That method was the avoidance of sexual union during the unsafe period. . . ." Gandhi preferred such a method since it included some element of self-control. Desai wondered whether Sanger did not advocate it because it would eliminate the need for birth control clinics and her own propaganda work,[59] but Gandhi and Desai were more optimistic about the rhythm method than were many who had utilized it.

Undaunted by Gandhi's adverse response to their message, Sanger and How-Martyn tirelessly spoke in a variety of public arenas. As Sanger had formed an alliance with the medical profession in the United States dur-

ing the 1920s, she and How-Martyn particularly courted the medical profession in India. They stimulated the All-India Medical Conference to pass
its first resolution on contraception in December 1935 and made overtures to female medical missionaries who frequently practiced as gynecol-
ogists and obstetricians because Indian women generally would not visit a
male physician. Cousins claimed that Sanger's

> most important influence will be felt amongst the medical
> organisations. . . . She showed them a biological film illustrating her
> subject which raised it from the field of propaganda into the realm of
> science.
>   Her private demonstrations of contraceptive technique to groups of
> women and separate groups of men were unique in Indian history, and
> she has left 50 demonstration gynaeplaques and a large quantity of
> medical supplies.[60]

Dr. Rose Beals, who had worked for over 30 years at the American Marathi
Mission Hospital in Wai near Poona, testified that the Sanger gynaeplaque
that illustrated the female reproductive organs was helpful in her birth
control work with village women.[61]

In a pamphlet on their tour, "Round the World for Birth Control,"
Sanger wrote that in India she and How-Martyn held a total of 105 meetings, 32 before medical organizations, with Sanger addressing 64 and
How-Martyn 41. They traveled independently, with Sanger covering 10,000
miles and How-Martyn 6,500. They entered many political and cultural
spheres and stopped at major British Indian political centers such as Bombay, Calcutta, Madras, Lucknow, Allahabad, and Delhi, at isolated sites
such as Wardha, and capitals of princely states, most notably Mysore,
Hyderabad, and Baroda. When they left India for southeast Asia and
China, Sanger and How-Martyn thought that they had made a significant
impact on the debate over birth control in India. As mentioned earlier,
such Indian women leaders as Lakshmi Menon had made positive assessments. The Family Hygiene Society in Bombay was grateful for Sanger's
bringing foam powder to its notice as an inexpensive contraceptive but
hoped that her next visit would be longer to ensure that birth control clinics would actually be established in major cities.[62]
Sanger would not return to India until 1952, when her Indian collaborators would be Dhanvanthi Rama Rau and Avabai Wadia who became the
postindependence leaders of the family planning movement in India.
Edith How-Martyn returned to India for two more tours and in 1936-37
reported that there were 20 clinics throughout India and 40 other places
such as maternal welfare centers where information on contraception
could be obtained.[63] The limited statistics that are available indicate that
these birth control clinics had difficulties attracting poorer women. In
1937, Lady Cowasji Jehangir argued for graphic posters, especially in the

form of slides at movie theaters, to inform illiterate women.[64] Margaret
Cousins, who was a sympathetic observer, reported that at the Baby Clinic
in Trivandrum

> they have been pressing the Birth Control propaganda & equipment
> (free) on the poor mothers. They find the response most disappointing
> with the poor but the middle class women are mopping it up & buying
> pessaries in the chemist's stores quite bravely.[65]

It was becoming apparent that propaganda by elite associations and the
establishment of a few clinics would not attract nonelite women to the use
of contraception. Efforts to expand the number of clinics would eventually
be stymied by political forces beyond the influence of voluntary associations.

The Campaign for Reproductive Control Ebbs

Women's groups and single-issue associations such as those in Bombay
and Calcutta that advocated providing information on contraception in
public clinics encountered strong opposition from Indian male members
of municipal councils. In May 1935, the Delhi Municipal Committee
debated a proposal to open a birth control clinic, but the resolution won
only five affirmative votes. The debate revealed how opponents would uti-
lize religious, communal, and medical reasons. In Islam, there was no one
central body that issued an overarching theological position on contraception, but Muslim members alleged that it was against the Qur'an. Asaf Ali,
a prominent Muslim nationalist who accepted this interpretation, argued
that such a clinic would not force Muslims or any other group to practice
contraception. Using communal grounds, a Hindu protested that if
Muslims were allowed to propagate then Hindus would be reduced to a
minority if they practiced contraception. One member satirically inter-
jected that the Hindus who constituted a majority of 80 percent could then
obtain minority rights currently accorded to the Muslims. One Hindu physician member alleged that the nature of the female body demanded that
she must bear a child every three years, but he never mentioned what the
consequences were for young Hindu widows who generally were not permitted to remarry.[66]
Most governmental bodies were equally reluctant to provide information on contraception in publicly supported institutions. On February 4,
1937, the Bombay Municipality rejected a proposal to operate such clinics
in municipal hospitals on grounds similar to those enunciated in Delhi.
Contraception was against religious precepts; it fostered immorality;
Muslims would soon outnumber Hindus; it was medically dangerous. Just
a few days earlier on January 28, the Bombay Presidency Women's Council

had voted in favor of such clinics in "poverty stricken areas."[67] The vote in the Bombay municipal council was much closer than in Delhi with the proposal losing by only four votes, but women's groups, voluntary associations, and foreign propagandists such as How-Martyn, who was then in India on her third tour, had minimal leverage with governmental bodies.

Some princely states were more forthcoming. Dr. Mrs. M. Ratnamma Isaac, a physician in Mysore state service, proudly pointed out to AIWC members that Mysore was the first state to have birth control clinics in three large state hospitals, establishing them in 1930.[68] Mysore had a long-standing reputation as a socially and politically progressive state, but its example was not emulated by many other princely states.

Although the rhetoric in favor of AIWC resolutions on birth control clinics increasingly emphasized the rights of women as mothers to information on reproductive control, the AIWC as an organization seemed to recede from a central focus on birth control. It concentrated on lobbying with Indian legislators, who now controlled provincial ministries and had more informational power in the central government under the 1935 Government of India Act, for legal reforms regarding women's rights. Many of its constituent units worked on local projects or suffered from apathy or the impact of communal tensions as growing numbers of people viewed their religious affiliation as their primary group commitment. It became difficult to schedule half-yearly meetings of the executive committee and annual sessions of the memberships. Many of its stalwarts were fully involved in political struggles. The Quit India movement of 1942, in which the Indian National Congress demanded that the British leave India immediately, disrupted its operations since several AIWC officers, including Vijayalakshmi Pandit, its current president and the sister of Jawaharlal Nehru, were jailed.

Some individual AIWC members persevered as articulate champions of reproductive control, although they encountered indifference or scorn. Alexandra Datta, a Scottish woman married to a Bengali Christian, became the organizer for the Family Planning Association in 1938 and pointed the way to the next phase of women's involvement in the 1950s in the campaign for reproductive control.[69] Rani Rajwade, who first raised the issue in 1931 within the AIWC, remained in the front line in a new arena. She chaired the Subcommittee on Women of the National Planning Committee (NPC) appointed by the Indian National Congress in 1938. The Subcommittee issued an interim report in 1940 that endorsed reproductive control,[70] but it aroused opposition from a key Muslim member, Begum Shareefah Hamid Ali. Shareefah had been a member of the Bombay Family Hygiene Society during the 1930s and an active officer of the AIWC, but by 1940 she argued that contraception and other proposed measures such as the liberalization of divorce laws were immoral and anti-family.[71] The written record is frustratingly silent on why she had come to oppose reproductive control that had been one of the goals of the Bombay Society.

Kamaladevi Chattopadhyaya, the first organizing secretary of the AIWC and an outspoken member of the Socialist wing of the Indian National Congress, was another unwavering advocate of birth control. In a rebuttal to Mr. Satyamurti, a conservative Congress member of the Madras Legislative Council, she declared that birth control was "the sacred and inalienable right of every woman to possess the means to control her body and no God or man can attempt to deprive her of that right without perpetrating an outrage on womanhood."[72] Her rhetoric sounds contemporary, but it is difficult to know the meaning of these words in the context of the 1930s. Kamaladevi briefly reports on the campaign in the 1930s in favor of birth control in her two memoirs but does not mention her own role and activities.[73] Still, her social radicalism had negative political consequences for her. Margaret Cousins, who was her mentor and coworker in the AIWC, indicated that Kamaladevi paid "for her championship of Birth Control and Social Reforms by being denied inclusion in the Working Committee of the Congress." Cousins was "not surprised at the Old Guard" but she was "deeply disappointed at Jawaharlal [Nehru] and the young Socialists."[74]

Most Congress leaders continued to avoid any discussion of reproductive control, probably because of Gandhi's known position, the divisive nature of the topic, and their own religious and social conservatism. The only Congress leader to mention birth control in a presidential address was Subhas Chandra Bose, the popular Bengali leader who was the principal rival of Jawaharlal Nehru. In his speech at Haripura in February 1938, Bose contended that it was "desirable to restrict our population until we are able to feed, clothe and educate those who already exist," but he offered no specific proposals for implementation. Bose would soon be maneuvered into the political wilderness because of his challenge to Gandhi, who had selected Nehru as his political heir.[75]

The debate over the need for reproductive control through contraception in India stagnated during the 1940s. The conjunction of a world war that disrupted daily routines and communications and the final stage of a nationalist struggle demanding immediate independence pushed birth control and most social reform issues to the background. The already precarious existence of private birth control clinics could not withstand a shift in loyalties to winning independence or supporting the war effort. The AIWC became a paper organization as officers were jailed, annual meetings postponed, and constituent units hardly functioned.

Foreign collaborators were cut off from India. Sanger bided her time in the United States; How-Martyn emigrated to Australia; Cousins suffered a stroke in 1943. War-time conditions precluded a full census in 1941, so firm statistical indicators were denied to the advocates of reproductive control. Finally, communal tension between Muslims and Hindus increased as the Muslim League proclaimed the separate state of Pakistan as its overriding goal in 1940. Indian politicians and British officials were even more hesitant to undertake polemical social initiatives. When P.N. Sapru, a Liberal Party member, introduced a resolution calling for the "popularization of birth control and establishment of clinics" in the Council of State in March 1940, the Government of India remained neutral and made no effort to implement it, even though it passed by nine to eight.[76]

Conclusion and Continuities

The debate over birth control that occurred in India from 1920 to 1940 reflects significant differences but also some similarities among Indian women and men advocates. First, Indian men and women were the prime movers. Men such as Wattal, Karve, and Pillay were the early champions. They wanted to reduce birth rates for nation-building goals: to ameliorate the economic conditions in India and to enhance the health of the Indian population. As in earlier reform movements, the Indian men who first called for reproductive control were aware of western theories. They appropriated Neo-Malthusian and eugenic arguments but shaped them to their own visions of a strong Indian nation. They appealed to other elite Indian males through books and journals with arguments about the political, economic, and, to a lesser extent, the personal benefits of exercising reproductive control. A few, most notably Karve and Pillay, established clinics to deliver contraceptives. Their efforts to include elite Indian women in their groups or to survey nonelite women about their desire for knowledge about contraception were minimal. Karve worked with his wife, and Pillay appears, from photographs, to have employed women physicians and nurses at his clinics in Bombay and did collaborate with Lady Jehangir. But others such as Ramesan did not think much of women's knowledge of birth control or attempt to bring them into leadership positions.

Indian women became major participants in this movement much more quickly than in the 19th-century movements promoting widow remarriage or female education. Their more rapid response reflects their growing experience in the public arena in both social reform and political activity and their willingness to risk some degree of public censure. First, educated Indian women provided leadership in the propaganda campaign, and some Indian women physicians gave credible medical justifications for contraception. Second, women's associations, especially the All India Women's Conference, gave women a collective voice. Their plea was muted and perhaps distorted since they excluded the press from their discussions of contraception, but it was uttered despite vocal opposition.

Indian women activists began with the rhetoric of their male counterparts, but they emphasized health issues as their main rationale for promoting contraception. They urged that knowledge of contraception be restricted to married women and promoted it as an aid to physically and mentally healthy families. As was happening in Great Britain during the 1920s, Indian women defined birth control as birth spacing to produce healthier babies and mothers, in order to counter the premise that birth control was birth prevention. This appeal reflected their acceptance of motherhood as the primary occupation of Indian women, and it simultaneously supported the nationalist goal of creating a new and better Indian society. It also served implicitly to answer critics, especially Gandhi, who claimed that contraception was immoral. Careful spacing of children, furthermore, should not affect existing population ratios among religious or ethnic communities since more children should survive. Thus, communal political groups should not be alarmed. By the late 1930s, a few Indian women related birth control to greater autonomy for women, but they were in a definite minority.

Both Indian men and women focused on programs designed to extend information on contraception to nonelite women. All appeared to assume that elite women had access to such knowledge, but demographic research on elite women has yet to determine when their rates of fertility began to decline. Neither Indian men nor women indicated how they had ascertained the desire of nonelite women for contraception, but there are gender differences in their arguments. Men generally stressed economic and eugenic rationales. Women cited their common roles as wives and mothers in an attempt to overcome the class divisions with nonelite women. The latter might have also functioned as surrogates. Elite women might have felt more comfortable arguing for the legitimacy of and need for more women to adopt contraception in order to justify privately their own use of it. Educated Indian women might have also been influenced by the examples of Margaret Sanger and Marie Stopes, who opened birth control clinics in lower-class neighborhoods to provide for women who could not consult private physicians.

Class, however, was a problematic issue for both genders. Indian men and Indian women supporters of contraception during these two decades give no public indication of understanding that high infant mortality rates meant that reproductive control might be viewed as counterproductive by the lower-class women whom they meant to help. Poor women had to produce as many children as possible to ensure that some would survive to provide for them in their old age. An effective reproductive control program had first to address such broad health issues as improving infant mortality rates. An even more difficult issue was the lack of control that most poor women could exercise over their own sexuality. Urban clinics would have served women who were more removed from some family controls, such as that exercised by a mother-in-law, than were village women, but urban women were still supposed to defer to their husbands in most decisions, including the frequency of sexual relations.

There were no significant gender differences in the willingness to collaborate with such foreigners as Sanger and How-Martyn, who were not part of the official establishment. Sanger gave Indian male pioneers the opportunity to achieve legitimacy abroad through the pages of her journal and by participation in various international conferences. She provided data from her clinical records and some limited funds. Sanger and How-Martyn functioned most effectively in the Indian context as propagandists. It was difficult for Indian women in particular to be effective publicists for reproductive control in a society where divine sexual acts were prominently depicted in sculpture and painting but personal sexuality was not frequently discussed between husbands and wives and by either group in public. Sanger, because of her notoriety, could attract and address public audiences that Indian women would have found painful to confront. The American woman, however, could evoke controversy and then leave India without having to suffer the social or political repercussions that Indian women might have had to face.

Equally important was the role of Sanger and How-Martyn in stimulating action and bringing together indigenous groups who would have to form the institutions needed for any long-term accomplishments. They could provoke professional groups such as the All India Medical Association to give some attention to a topic they had avoided until 1935. How-Martyn could help the Society for Marriage Hygiene to organize a conference on population. Indian male advocates of reproductive control appeared to be more comfortable working with foreign women, who could be viewed possibly as asexual or at least as coworkers without interfering in kinship networks and obligations. Thus, these foreign women could be bridges between Indian women and these male-dominated, single-issue associations. Still, these foreign women could neither formulate policies nor provide the sustained work necessary to maintain and to extend contraceptive programs. Indian men and women undertook those long-term efforts.

Sanger and How-Martyn understood the importance of engaging Gandhi in public debate on this topic and of attempting to change his position. Indian women found it difficult to dispute openly with the supreme leader of their independence movement and the man who had done more than anyone else to bring them and other underrepresented groups into the political arena. Sanger could badger Gandhi until he made the concession of the rhythm method, which was significant in the context of the 1930s and would be the initial method advocated by the Health Ministry after independence. Margaret Cousins, who was a known admirer of Gandhi but not his protege, could popularize the reconciliation of Gandhi's call for self-control with the use of contraception as a temporary measure until all could practice continence. This compromise would be cited in the National Planning Committee Report on Women.

Since there were no legal prohibitions on the dissemination of information on contraception or the use of contraceptive devices in India, the first stage of the reproductive control movement did not have to focus on legislative changes. But it did confront other formidable obstacles. Because of his political and moral stature, Gandhi strongly reenforced the critics who deemed contraception to be immoral. Opponents who used religious rationales were bolstered by growing communal tensions between Hindus and Muslims, which made numbers count in any final political settlement. The independence struggle made suspect appeals to western theories and examples. It also rendered Indian politicians and British officials reluctant to undertake any initiative on this controversial topic.

Voluntary associations, whether they were single-issue oriented as the Marriage Hygiene Society or umbrella ones such as the AIWC, had to educate public and official opinion and to create essentially pilot projects. Itinerant foreign proselytizers were welcome to join this enterprise, but Indian men and women had been the initiators. Their debates and the clinics established were few in number and reached very restricted segments of the population, but they are important for what they reveal as problems that later government-sponsored programs would confront. First, how was the target population to be determined? Would men be in control of the sexuality of women? Elite women or nonelite women? Or a coalition of men and women from all economic groups? Second, what would be safe, inexpensive, effective, and easily used contraceptives? Third, who would deliver contraceptive information and devices—physicians, female or male; midwives; paraprofessional health workers; or political or social organizations such as neighborhood or village units? Fourth, what type of organization would be most effective—comprehensive maternal health clinics or specific "birth control" clinics? Fifth, what goals were to be assigned which priorities—the well-being of the nation; the family; children, men, and women? Finally, what should and would be the role of the consumers of this service—women and men—in planning the programs for reproductive control? These questions are still being asked, and acceptable answers remain elusive.

NOTES

The initial version of this essay was presented at the Regional Conference for Asia on Women and the Household in New Delhi, January 27-31, 1985. I am particularly indebted to Dr. Kamala Gopala Rao, the commentator on our panel, for her insightful remarks. Others who have provided most helpful criticisms on subsequent drafts are Antoinette Burton, Ellen Chesler, Dagmar Engels, Geraldine Forbes, Richard Soloway, the South Asia Regional Seminar sponsored by Duke

University, and various anonymous readers. I am also most grateful for support of my research from the National Endowment for the Humanities in 1979; the Fulbright-Hays program of the U.S. Department of Education in 1981-82; the Excess Foreign Currency Grant Program of the Smithsonian Institution in 1985; and the Taft Faculty Fund of the University of Cincinnati in 1985. The National Humanities Center provided the time and tranquillity necessary to undertake two major revisions during 1986-87.

1. Rosanna Ledbetter, *A History of the Malthusian League, 1877-1927* (Columbus: Ohio State University Press, 1976), 192.

2. An insightful analysis of the contradictory position of village women for whom sexual intercourse is enjoined but ritually polluting and a shameful matter is in Patricia Jeffery, Roger Jeffery, and Andrew Lyon, *Labour Pains and Labour Power: Women and Childbearing in India* (London: Zed Books, 1989), especially 28-31.

3. Meredith Borthwick cites a Christian woman missionary, a Bengali woman, and a Bengal man as sources on the prominence of sexuality in conversations among elite Bengali women in *The Changing Role of Women in Bengal 1849-1905* (Princeton: Princeton University Press, 1984), 18-19.

4. Two basic sources on the birth control movement in the United States are Linda Gordon, *Woman's Body, Woman's Right: A Social History of Birth Control in America* (New York: Viking and Penguin, 1976), and James Reed, *From Private Vice to Public Virtue: The Birth Control Movement and American Society Since 1830* (New York: Basic Books, 1978).

5. P.K. Wattal, *The Population Problem in India: A Census Study* (Bombay: Bennett, Coleman, 1916).

6. N.S. Phadke, "Birth Control in India," *Birth Control Review* 8, No. 4 (April 1924): 107.

7. While serving as professor of mental and moral philosophy at Rajaram College in Kolhapur, he published *Sex Problems in India* (Bombay: D.B. Taraporevala Sons & Company, 1927).

8. Aims and Objectives of the Sholapur Eugenics Education Society, Handbill, Sanger Collection, Library of Congress (LC), Container (C) 25, Reel (R) 17.

9. Madras Neo-Malthusian League (For Human Welfare through Birth Control) Objects, Handbill, Sanger, LC, C25, R17.

10. Norman E. Himes, *Medical History of Contraception* (Baltimore: Williams and Wilkins, 1936), 123-24. Himes incorrectly gives 1929 as the founding date of the Madras League.

11. Agnes Smedley, *Battle Hymn of China* (New York: Alfred A. Knopf, 1943), 8-22, and Janice R. MacKinnon and Stephen R. MacKinnon, *Agnes Smedley: The Life and Times of an American Radical* (Berkeley: University of California Press, 1988), 69-133 for Smedley's life in Germany and 98-99 and 114-15 for her contacts with Sanger.

12. Baroness Shidzue Ishimoto, *Facing Two Ways: The Story of My Life* (Stanford: Stanford University Press, 1984), 183, 220-30. Agnes Smedley introduced Ishmito to Sanger in New York in 1920, and then the Baroness served as her hostess in 1922 in Japan where Sanger was allowed to enter on the condition she would not speak publicly about birth control.

13. Smedley to Sanger, June 1924, Sanger, LC, C14, R10.

14. Mohandas Karamchand Gandhi, *Birth Control*, edited and published by Anand T. Hingorani (Bombay: Bharatiya Vidya Bhavan, 1962), 112-15 from *Young India*, 13 October 1920.

15. *Ibid.*, 1-2 from *Young India*, 12 March 1925.

16. *Ibid.*, 4 from *Young India*, 2 April 1925.

17. *Birth Control Review* 9, No. 9 (September 1925): 244.

18. *Ibid.* 10, No. 6 (June 1926): 208.

19. V. Ramesam to Sanger, 10 June 1929, Sanger, LC, C25, R17.

20. In her *Autobiography*, Reddy makes no mention of reproductive control but praises the virtue of continence in her discussion of her work to abolish the legal basis for the institution of *devadasis* or temple dancers, some of whom had been coerced into prostitution-type relationships. *Autobiography of Dr. Mrs. S. Muthulakshmi Reddy* (Mylapore: Printed at M.K.J. Press, 1964[?]), 146-47.

21. Interview dated 11 March 1931, Ruth V. Woodsmall Collection, Sophie Smith Collection (SSC), Box (B), B, File (F) 4.

22. Interview dated 28 March 1931, *ibid.* Italics in original.

23. Interview dated December 1930, *ibid.*

24. Interview dated 2 December 1931 but it must be 1930, *ibid.*

25. Smedley to Sanger, not dated but the letter must be from late June or early July 1924, Sanger, LC, C14, R10.

26. Geraldine H. Forbes, "From Purdah to Politics: The Social Feminism of the All-India Women's Organizations," in *Separate Worlds: Studies of Purdah in South Asia*, ed. Hanna Papanek and Gail Minault (Columbia, Mo.: South Asia Books, 1982), 219-44, and Geraldine H. Forbes, "The Indian Women's Movement: A Struggle for Women's Rights or National Liberation?," in *The Extended Family: Women and Political Participation in India and Pakistan*, ed. Gail Minault (Columbia, Mo.: South Asia Books, 1981), 49-82.

27. All India Women's Conference (AIWC), Proceedings of Sixth Session, Madras, 1 January 1932, p. 81a at the Margaret Cousins Library, AIWC headquarters, New Delhi. There is no complete record of the speeches and discussions of the AIWC meetings since volunteers took them down. Speakers were asked to supply copies of their speeches, but they rarely did so. The bound proceedings, which are available in New Delhi, generally did not include the speeches delivered in Indian languages in their original versions or in English translations.

28. I am indebted to Dagmar Engels for her insights on the impact of the Age of Consent testimony, which was only gradually released to the public, although the Report of the Committee was published in 1929.

29. AIWC, Proceedings of the Sixth Session, Madras, 1 January 1932, 85.

30. Renuka Ray, *My Reminiscences* (New Delhi: Allied Publishers, 1982), 82-83.

31. Nadia H. Youssef, "The Status and Fertility Patterns of Muslim Women," *Women in the Muslim World*, ed. Lois Beck and Nikki Keddie (Cambridge, Mass.: Harvard University Press, 1978), 87-88, and Basim F. Musallam, *Sex and Society in Islam* (Cambridge, Mass.: Cambridge University Press, 1983), especially 10-27.

32. AIWC, Proceedings of Seventh Session, Lucknow, 30 December 1932, 90.

33. A sensitive discussion of the continuing impact of high infant mortality rates is in Jeffery, Jeffery, and Lyon, *Labour Pains and Labour Power*, 178-206.

34. AIWC, Proceedings of Seventh Session, Lucknow, 30 December 1932, 94-95.

35. In "Sex, Marriage and Social Reform: Bengal in the 1920s," a paper presented at the Ninth European Conference on Modern South Asian Studies, Heidelberg University, 9-12 July, 1986, 24-25, Dagmar Engels has argued that the British focused on public health rather than sexual aspects of social reform legislation to avoid alienating conservative supporters during the 1920s.

36. Annual of Central Provinces (South) Constituency of AIWC, Annual Reports from the Constituencies, 1933, 33 at the AIWC Archives in New Delhi.

37. Wells was quoted in "Marriage Hygiene: An Appeal," *Indian Social Reformer* 47, No. 10 (November 7, 1936): 156. Himes, *Medical History of Contraception*, 124.

38. *Marriage Hygiene* 2, No. 2 (November 1935): 116.

39. *Marriage Hygiene* 2, No. 1 (August 1935): 37-42.

40. Kingsley Davis, *The Population of India and Pakistan* (Princeton: Princeton University Press, 1951), 227.

41. Personal communication from Dagmar Engels.

42. *Indian Social Reformer* 47, No. 1 (5 September 1936): 9.

43. *Marriage Hygiene* 3, No. 1 (August 1936): 3.

44. Pamphlet, "Marriage Welfare and Child Guidance Association" (Calcutta: n.p., November 1936), Sanger, SSC, B115, and How-Martyn to Sanger, 17 September 1935, Sanger, LC, C25, R17. (Sanger's papers are divided between the Library of Congress and the Sophie Smith Collection at Smith College.)

45. Margaret Sanger commented on Soudamini Mehta in *Margaret Sanger: An Autobiography* (New York: W.W. Norton, 1938), 472-73. I am indebted to Aparna Basu for sharing with me in January 1986 her mother's (Soudamini Mehta) reminiscences about propaganda work for birth control in Calcutta during the 1930s.

46. Neuta Ghosh to Anasuya Kale, 10 November 1936, in P.B. Kale, *Anasuyabai ani Mi* (Anasuya and I) (Nagpur: P.B. Kale, 1962), 262.

47. Sanger to Cousins, 10 May 1935, Sanger Collection, LC, C25, R17.

48. Cousins to Sanger, 6 and 27 August 1935, *ibid.*

49. Sanger to Gerda S. Guy, 30 November 1935, Sanger, LC, C26, R17.

50. Ten prize essays were published in two issues of the *Bombay Chronicle* on 11 and 19 January 1936.

51. I am indebted to Geraldine Forbes for her notes from an interview in Calcutta in July 1972 with Shudha Mazumdar and her summary of Mazumdar's typed notes for a second volume of memoirs. Several people repeated this information about the opposition of the Catholic nuns to me during a visit to Trivandrum in December 1981. Miss Watts is described in Charles Allen and Sharada Dwivedi, *The Lives of Indian Princes* (London: Arrow Books, 1986), 24.

52. Letter No. 3 from Sanger to friends and family, 2 January 1936, Sanger, SSC, B88, F894.

53. *Ibid.*

54. N.N. Mitra ed., *Indian Annual Register*, Vol. II (July-December 1935): 361-63.

55. *Marriage Hygiene* 2, No. 3 (February 1936): 330.

56. Cousins to Sanger, 11 February 1935, Sanger, LC, C25, R17.

57. "Gandhi and Mrs. Sanger Debate Birth Control," *Asia Magazine* (November 1936), reprint in Florence Rose Papers, SSC, Box 39.

58. Sanger to Maurice Newfield, 4 December 1935, Sanger, SCC, B115, F1144.

59. *Harijan* (25 January 1936): 398.

60. "Margaret Sanger in India" by an Onlooker who was Margaret Cousins, *Stri Dharma* 19, No. 4 (May 1936): 118.

61. Rose F. Beal to Sanger, 3 January 1936, Sanger, LC, C26, R17.

62. *Marriage Hygiene* 2, No. 4 (May 1936): 380-81.

63. Edith How-Martyn, "Birth Control in India: Third Tour 1936-37" (London: Printed by George Standring, April 1937), Fawcett Library, London, Pamphlet Collection, 312.12 (54), 4-5. Also available at Sanger, SSC, B115, no folder.

64. Lady Cowasji Jehangir, "Maternal Welfare Work in Bombay," *The Asiatic Review* 33 (October 1937): 759-67. I am grateful to Geraldine Forbes for this reference.

65. Cousins to Sanger, 8 May 1935, Sanger, LC, C25, R17.

66. *Indian Social Reformer* 45, No. 39 (25 May 1935): 609-10.

67. *Marriage Hygiene* 3, No. 3 (February 1937): 244-45.

68. AIWC, Proceedings of Seventh Session, Lucknow, 30 December 1932, 95-96.

69. "Birth Control Worldwide, October 1938-September 1939," 3, Fawcett Library, Pamphlet Collection, 312.12 (00).

70. National Planning Committee Series, *Woman's Role in Planned Economy: Report of the Sub-Committee, Chairwoman, Rani Lakshmibai Rajwade*, ed. by K.T. Shah (Bombay: Vora, 1947), 175. The report argued for limitation of families "in the interests of the children, the parents as well as the nation."

71. Shareefah Hamid Ali to Jawaharlal Nehru, 1 April 1940, Nehru Papers, Nehru Memorial Museum and Library, New Delhi, I, 37, 1937.

72. Kamaladevi Chattopadhyaya, "Reactionary All Along the Line. Satyamurti Strays from Politics to Birth Control," n.d., 2-3, Sanger, SSC, B115, F1145. Although this article is undated, it must be from about 1937 since it refers to Satyamurti's defeat of the Justice Party candidate in the elections after the Government of India Act of 1935.

73. Kamaladevi Chattopadhyaya, *Indian Women's Battle for Freedom* (New Delhi: Abhinav Publications, 1983), 83-85, and *Inner Recesses, Outer Spaces* (New Delhi: Navrang, 1986), 89-90, 121, 243.

74. Cousins to Sanger, 15 May 1936, Sanger, SSC, B48, F426.

75. A. Moin Zaidi and Shaheda Zaidi, eds., *Encyclopedia of Indian National Congress*, Vol. 11: 1936-1938 (New Delhi: S. Chand, 1980), 409.

76. "Birth Control," *The Sunday Statesman* (24 March 1940), Sanger, LC, C234, Folder I of clippings on India.

BIBLIOGRAPHICAL NOTE

Most of the historical work on Indian women in the colonial period (mainly the nineteenth and twentieth centuries) has been published in journals, but some anthologies have brought together a range of these perspectives. *Separate Worlds: Studies of Purdah in South Asia*, ed. Hanna Papanek and Gail Minault (Columbia, Mo.: South Asia Books, 1982), deals with the location of South Asian women within separate social and political spheres. *Indian Women: From Purdah to Modernity*, ed. B. R. Nanda (New Delhi: Vikas Publishers, 1976), similarly has several useful overviews of attitudes toward women's education and social and political status during and after the colonial period. *The Extended Family: Women and Political Participation in India and Pakistan*, ed. Gail Minault (Columbia, Mo.: South Asia Books, 1981), contains historical discussions on the nature of women's increasing political involvement. Several articles pertaining to the impact of colonial economic and legal policies on the position of women are contained in J. Krishnamurty, ed., *Women in Colonial India* (Delhi: Oxford University Press, 1989). *Recasting Women in History: Essays on Colonial India*, ed. KumKum Sangari and Sudesh Vaid (New Brunswick: Rutgers University Press, 1990), has an insightful introduction and contains important discussions about the construction of Indian womanhood in colonial and nationalist discourse.

A historical approach to contemporary issues facing women in South Asia may be found in Joanna Liddle and Rama Joshi, *Daughters of Independence* (London: Zed Books, 1986). Geraldine Forbes's "The Politics of Respectability: Indian Women and the Indian National Congress," in *The Indian National Congress: Centenary Hindsights,* ed. D. A. Low (Delhi: Oxford University Press, 1988), is a useful introduction to the increasing participation of women in the national movement, especially in the Congress. For a detailed discussion of M. K. Gandhi's articulations on the position of women, see Madhu Kishwar's two-part discussion "Gandhi on Women," *Economic and Political Weekly* 20, no. 40 (Oct. 5, 1985): 1691-1702, and no. 41 (Oct. 12, 1986): 1753-58. A valuable comparative perspective on nationalist mobilization of women in various Third World countries is available in Kumari Jayawardena's *Feminism and Nationalism in the Third World* (London: Zed Books, 1986).

Meredith Borthwick's *The Changing Role of Women in Bengal, 1849-1905* (Princeton: Princeton University Press, 1986) details the effects of the colonial intervention on middle-class women's lives in Bengal. Renu Chakravarty provides an account of women's involvement in the communist movement in India in *Communists in the Indian Women's Movement* (Delhi: People's Publishing House, 1980). The oral testimonies of several women who were involved in the Telengana armed struggle of the 1940s and 1950s have been compiled in Stree Shakti Sanghatana, *"We Were Making History"* (London: Zed Books, 1989).

With increasing attention being paid to representations of women in literature, two recent collections are of importance. Kalpana Bardhan's *Of Women, Outcastes, Peasants and Rebels* (Berkeley: University of California Press, 1990) is a collection of Bengali short stories from the colonial and post-colonial period. Translations of women's writings in Indian languages have been brought together in two recent volumes edited by Susie Tharu and K. Lalita. They are *Women Writing in India,* vols. 1 (600 B.C. to the Early Twentieth Century) and 2 (Twentieth Century) (New York: Feminist Press, 1991).

In addition to these books, the *Economic and Political Weekly* annually features a review of women's studies which brings together the most recent research on Indian women from a variety of perspectives. *Manushi,* an Indian feminist journal published since 1980, focuses primarily on reporting contemporary women's issues; it often carries articles that trace the historical background of Indian patriarchies and the cultural constructions of Indian womanhood. Another journal which occasionally carries articles pertaining to women's history is the *Indian Economic and Social History Review.*

III

Women as Workers

GENDER AND WORKING-CLASS HISTORY
SOUTH AFRICA IN COMPARATIVE PERSPECTIVE

Iris Berger

The continuing struggle against racial domination in South Africa has created an environment in which the actions and attitudes of contemporary popular movements often resonate with historical significance. In this highly politicized atmosphere, interpretations of the past have the power to provoke intense interest and, at times, passionate controversy. Nowhere has this interplay between past and present been more significant than in the trade union movement. As waves of strikes swept the country in 1973-74 and black workers again felt their potential power, labor organizers realized the critical need to understand the successes and failures of earlier working-class organizations. Acutely aware that ruthless government repression had crushed progressive unions during the 1950s and 1960s, new leaders sought to build a movement whose democratic strength would inhibit its destruction.

Yet, because so many union officials had suffered arrest, banning, and exile, important links between generations were weakened or severed; thus, many contemporary activists were unaware of the complex connections over time embodied in their work and their ideas. The silences and distortions of official versions of South African history further reinforced the rift between past and present. When Tembi Nabe shocked some members of the audience at a 1983 labor education workshop by speaking frankly of women's subordination within the household, she never suspected her kinship with Mary Fitzgerald, a flamboyant leader who raised similar issues in the early 1900s. But Nabe's graphic descriptions of women workers providing idle husbands with an endless round of domestic and sexual services closely matched Fitzgerald's critique of domestic inequality.[1] Likewise, in 1983, when the shop stewards at a Dunlop chemical factory successfully laid a trap for a training officer who was requiring sexual favors as a condition of employment, they had no idea of their historical bond with garment strikers who complained in 1931 of "rude and vulgar" treatment and pressure to go out with the foreman or the boss in order to keep their jobs.

In seeking to reknit the continuity among generations of working women and to restore some of the hidden connections between past and present labor struggles, historical studies of working women in other parts of the world and other time periods provide a useful guide to formulating relevant questions and theoretical issues. This material is revealing both for its insights and its shortcomings with respect to South Africa. As the only country on the continent with a relatively long history of industrialization, some aspects of its history conform closely to the experience of Europe and the United States. Yet other features of women's labor and their patterns of proletarianization and family life remain strikingly similar to other African countries where little industrialization has occurred. Nonetheless, historiographical trends in the study of working-class women elsewhere help to frame a context for revealing the complex interplay between gender, class, and race.

The discovery of gold and diamonds in the late 19th century forced South Africa abruptly into the limelight of international capitalism. As extractive industries relying exclusively on male workers took center stage in the economy, most women, black and white, were left outside the networks of wage employment. Only the development of factories producing consumer goods that began during World War I and expanded in the late 1920s drew a significant number of female workers into jobs manufacturing clothing, food, and textiles. In the Cape, most of these women were "colored," a South African designation for people of racially mixed origins; in other areas, they came primarily from impoverished Afrikaans-speaking white families. Following gradual shifts in the industrial labor force in the 1940s and '50s, black women have come, during recent years, to occupy most female industrial positions outside of the .Cape. By state decree, this region remains a "colored" labor preference area.

Despite women's prevalence in certain gender-stereotyped areas of industrial labor, in South Africa, as in many other countries, factories usually have employed men in larger numbers than women. This trend has left women predominant in agricultural labor, domestic work in middle- and upper-class households, and independent "informal" economic pursuits ranging from petty trade to prostitution.[2] In many countries (although less frequently in Africa), home industries have offered jobs to large numbers of women who resisted or were unwelcome in factories.[3] These patterns of women's proletarianization often followed phases of the family cycle, with factories absorbing young, single, and often better-qualified women, while older married women working at home remained part of the "subproletariat."[4] Although their incorporation into factories has varied enormously in different national and local settings, common gender stereotypes have kept women concentrated in low-paid work that is defined as compatible with their "natural" tendencies. Thus, workers in the international electronics industry are valued for their "nimble fingers," as were the legions of late 19th-century female typists in the United States.

Other more concrete similarities in the history of factory employment patterns for women are striking. The three stages of development of the United States garment industry as outlined by Helen Safa are comparable to those in South Africa.[5] The first phase, which relied on a native female labor force, mainly the single daughters of farm families who were working before marriage, parallels a period (albeit a century later) in which newly developing South African factories turned to the daughters of rural Afrikaner families. The successive groups of immigrant women who became clothing workers during the second stage were similar in many respects to the black women who began to fill South African factories after World War II. Like their United States counterparts, they often continued to work after marriage and brought to the urban industrial experience a similar background of ethnic-based (though often disrupted) cultural traditions. Finally, the more recent turn to runaway shops, as the industry branched out into peripheral developing countries, is analogous to the development of rural clothing factories in and adjacent to South African "homelands," where low wages match those of other peripheral centers worldwide.

Although relatively few women have worked in industry by comparison with other occupations, the experience of female factory operatives often has had broad social and political repercussions. Ivy Pinchbeck, for example, in her pioneering study of British women workers, implies that the independence young women developed working in mills and factories influenced the awakening consciousness of middle-class women.[6] In many countries, even if the percentage of women working in factories was relatively low at any given moment, this form of employment was a common phase, a rite of passage through which many young working-class women passed en route to marriage and family. In such instances, the experience might stamp women with a collective awareness that profoundly shaped their consciousness. As David Montgomery has observed in his study of the late 19th-century working class in the United States:

> The young women's work culture . . . confronted supervisors with a paradox. On the one hand, the conviviality and even the fantasy world into which pieceworkers often let their minds slip actually provided a lubrication that helped both workers and their employers accomplish their daily tasks. . . . On the other hand, the bonds that attached young women to one another also fostered a sense of identity and of self-respect that overseers offended at their peril. Clothes, the fashionable attire that invariably shocked upper-class observers as frivolous, became the outward symbol of that identity, on and off the job.[7]

Although expressed partially through fashion, this sense of self was not without a political edge, leading women to express bitterness and anger at "disrespectful" foremen and at many aspects of working conditions, particularly child labor.[8]

The experience of factory work left a particularly strong imprint on many South African women, creating bonds among working women that promoted their involvement in labor resistance. But these ties also might be turned to wider political ends. Thus, when the Federation of South African Women formed in 1954 as a national organization dedicated to fighting racial and gender oppression, trade unionists were disproportionately represented at the initial conference. Equally important, factory work (especially in the 1940s and 1950s) brought together in the same jobs a racially diverse group of women who, under other circumstances, would have had contact with each other only in unequal relationships. (For their male family members, much more closely tracked into racially distinct channels, such proximity would have been unthinkable.)

Thus, working in factories had the potential to extend women's experience in a variety of ways, exposing them to new ideas and to people of other racial and ethnic backgrounds. In some instances, this wider contact reinforced attitudes toward race, class, and the division of authority within the family that women had learned in the more protected world of their households; in others, serious rifts and conflicts might arise between the different, but interrelated realms of work and home. In the Transvaal during the 1940s and early 1950s, white garment workers faced a dilemma. As Afrikaner Dutch Reformed clergy and National Party officials viciously attacked their class-oriented union, many women were torn between family ethnic and political loyalties and attachment to a union responsible for dramatic improvements in wages and working conditions. This example underscores the need to integrate the often-distinct categories of factory, family, and community in order to understand women's lives more fully.

In exploring these connections, recent feminist theory provides useful guidelines for conceptualizing the relationship among these spheres of daily life. Whereas writers in the 1970s often recognized the connections between the opposing categories of public and private, production and reproduction, they sometimes tended to link them in a static, ahistorical fashion. Building on such theoretical dichotomies, writers on South Africa who combined marxist and feminist perspectives repeatedly echoed the functionalist notion that women's reproductive roles subsidized and thereby sustained the capitalist sphere of the economy. But the two were conceptualized as otherwise quite distinct and separate, and gender too often was subsumed within class.[9]

Others have approached the problem of duality with greater historical awareness and have sought to spell out the connections between categories more systematically. Joan Kelly described her view of women's "doubled vision," based jointly on sex oppression and the system of productive relations, asserting that the two needed to be understood simultaneously.[10] Seeking a theory to do so, Belinda Bozzoli turned to the concept of struggle: between women and men within the household and between the domestic sphere and the wider economic system.[11] Though Bozzoli creatively reexamines 20th-century South African history through the use of these concepts, others would caution about viewing racial/ethnic households simply as an arena of conflict, arguing that the family has also acted as a site of resistance to external oppression, and has fostered a great degree of mutual dependence because few men were able to support their families without women's economic contributions.[12]

If these approaches seek connections to bridge dualistic categories, Lourdes Benería and Martha Roldan insist more firmly on the need to understand both the material and the ideological aspects of women's subordination and to see patriarchy and systems of production as interconnected and mutually reinforcing, rather than as dual systems. Since women in real life have no choice but to integrate their lives at work and at home, they suggest that perhaps the only way to confront dualism is not through more elaborate theoretical formulations, but through specific historical analysis.[13] Implied in this approach is the need to overcome yet another division—between history and theory.

Much of the previous writing on South African labor history has been too narrowly conceived to be helpful in bridging any of these gaps between categories of analysis. Perhaps understandably in an era when trade unions were reawakening after a period in which countless activists were imprisoned, banned, and forced into exile, many historians of the late 1970s and early 1980s limited their inquiries to institutional analysis. Though this period produced some important research, only rarely did these writers venture beyond the factories and the union halls to examine workers' family and community lives. And even those who studied predominantly female unions often wrote in a gender-blind fashion, ignoring the issue of whether and how the double or triple burdens of working women influenced consciousness or union participation.[14]

A different problem surfaces in some of the works on South African women in the economy, many formulated as studies of how they were "incorporated" into capitalist or industrial production.[15] Although they are often valuable inquiries into economic structure, these works leave little room either for human agency or for "family strategies" in shaping women's place in the economy.[16] Rather than portraying women as individuals and family members who make their own choices about whether and where they wish to work for wages—however restricted their options—their approach implies a view of people totally manipulated by economic forces that leave them little control over their lives.

This criticism is not intended to suggest that the often-combined weight of race, gender, and class left poor women with a wide range of choice, but rather that even within the confines of their limited economic options, women faced critical decisions about work, marriage, family, and politics. By drawing on husbands, relatives, and children, and on church and community groups, they were able to develop strategies to confront these challenges. To focus exclusively on structures of domination is therefore to ignore individual and collective leverage, creativity, and struggle, however confined the space for its expression, and to neglect the tension between popular pressure and state control.

In reviewing the historical literature on women in industrial production, perhaps no question crops up more frequently than why and how organizing women was different from organizing men. The issue is most often conceptualized as why (in many situations) women were slower to form trade unions than men and, even when organized, took less part in these working-class organizations. Still influenced by this central approach, others have examined successful efforts to involve women in unions or in strikes, or instances where women aggressively took the initiative, asking what made the difference in these particular cases. The problem is particularly pertinent to South Africa where, in varied contexts and periods, observers have often credited women with more fearless and militant behavior than men. Rachael Zeeman, a strike leader in a Cape cannery observed:

> In my opinion, the women in the union achieves more with the bosses than the men. It's like that here as well. The women will insist upon something which would be dropped by a man, women carry on. The women does not give up. She carries on.[17]

In seeking to understand women's relationship to organized labor, historians, until recently, favored two explanations. The first, which attributed women's exclusion to antifemale attitudes among male trade unionists, arose naturally within the context of feminist history in the 1970s. To historians bent on demonstrating the force of patriarchal power across time and culture, sexism embodied in institutional arrangements seemed a logical and historically justifiable reason for women's relative powerlessness in many public settings. Writing on early 20th-century Russia, for example, Rose Glickman argues that male unions mainly ignored women out of an "underlying conviction that women were a lower order of being."[18] The other answer grew from the preoccupation with the dual spheres of women's lives, the split between home and work. Proponents of this view argued that women's heavy involvement in domestic affairs left them neither the time nor the emotional energy to take part in working-class organization.[19] Placing less stress on unions themselves, this explanation implied that circumstances forced women to make choices, and that (under the weight of prevailing cultural norms) they opted for domesticity.

Despite their difference, both formulations tacitly accept the idea that trade unions were the appropriate means of expressing class power and consciousness, and that how women related to these organizations was an index of their class awareness and of unions' gender awareness. Thus, whether through their domestic involvement or through sexism, women often were prevented from developing the attachments that would assure them full membership in "the working class." Yet Temma Kaplan, writing on women in Barcelona, argues that to accept unions alone as the agencies of the working class is to ignore other forms of association connected with the family, the church, cooperatives, and women's groups.[20]

As the focus of women's history has changed, approaches to the question of their involvement in unions have shifted as well. As many women's historians in the later 1970s became more interested in how women have constructed their own autonomous cultures, despite (and in response to) patriarchal constraints, they also began to suggest new ways of integrating gender into working-class history. From the perspective of women's culture, it was easier to dismiss the innuendo that women were remiss in not developing firmer attachments to trade unions, and to argue instead that unions were too narrowly conceived around particular male-defined economic and political issues to reflect women's concerns adequately. If earlier interpretations had found fault in working women for their low level of class consciousness, recent writers have, instead, faulted the unions. Writing from this perspective, for example, Dolores Janiewski turns the old question around and asks, "why are unions irrelevant to so much of women's lives?"[21] Furthermore, analysis based on language and discourse suggested a reason for this masculine emphasis: that, in many instances, the "language of class," the very conception of class and, by extension, of class organizations, was gender-bound, conceiving of male experience as the universal representation of the working class.[22] For much of South African history, it might be added, this portrayal of "the" working class was both male and white.

Answers to the second question concerning women's organization—how to explain examples of successful organization or of strikes with substantial female involvement—draw heavily on the cultural approach to women's history. They show women most inclined to become active union members when they are able to center their participation around work-based and/or community-based culture and networks or where unions have consciously and successfully incorporated women's particular concerns and informal ties.[23] In South Africa, both the Transvaal Garment Workers' Union and the Cape Food and Canning Workers' Union involved members in broad-ranging political and cultural activities. These arguments suggest that the class experience of women includes not simply their conflictual relationship with owners and managers of capital, but their mutual relationships with each other, whether conceptualized as "work cultures" or as "bonds of community." Because these relationships differ from those of working-class men, they are too often dismissed as trivial, while the class content they embody is ignored. Once again, historians generalize from male experience and portray it as the universal norm.

Other discussions of women's involvement in working-class organization and action follow along the lines suggested by Louise Tilly, who hypothesized that different "paths of proletarianization" (including the organization of production and the household division of labor) are linked systematically with particular patterns of collective action.[24] In a similar argument, Carole Turbin proposed that trade union activities or participation in labor unrest may be strengthened when women's families support their involvement. Racial conflict falling along class lines also may prompt such participation by creating a community of interest between women and men.[25] Writing on Latin America, Helen Safa found that female breadwinners, freer from male domination than other working-class women, were more likely to view themselves as "workers." All of these arguments are variations on the idea that particular work and family relationships promote or inhibit women's class action in distinct ways, although Safa's case study emphasizes the absence of an inhibiting factor (male power in the family) rather than the presence of positive reinforcement through family or racial identification. They also underscore the idea that women's propensity to engage in collective action is increased when (for a variety of possible reasons) their behavior is not deemed a threat to male power.

In adopting the more recent approaches to female labor history, historians are implying that congruence between women's lives and culture at work, in the family, and in the community (with different combinations as the salient factors in particular cases) is central to strengthening working women's active class identification, to reshaping "class" in terms that resonate with their own experience. In taking this integrative approach, they follow the lead of social historians like Edward Thompson and Herbert Gutman, who analyze working classes in the combined context of work, family, culture, and community. Yet, there is a crucial difference from some, although not all, of these working-class historians, many of whom write as if "household" and "family" were integrated units, bastions of cultural creativity along class and ethnic lines against the inroads of the dominant classes. The idea of gender conflict at the heart of this haven of communal values is foreign to this perspective as it is often presented.[26]

Following working-class life out of the factory and into the community is clearly critical to any effort at reconceptualizing class to include women's experience. But, in the South African context, and perhaps in others as well, the concept of community advanced by historians such as Herbert Gutman, Virginia Yans-McLaughlin, and Tamara Hareven requires reassessment. Writing on the United States, they speak of "community" in positive terms to refer to groups of geographically proximate people, usually united along class or ethnic lines and embodying critically important pre-industrial, often Old World, cultures and values.[27] The emphasis on culture, whether conceptualized as immigrant, peasant, or preindustrial, is particularly important. In certain respects, such a definition is valuable to African history, reminding us of the worldwide tendency for capitalist encroachment to alter earlier cultural traditions. Yet it also assumes that these working-class families and communities had substantial control over their own working and personal lives, a situation often impossible for black South Africans; harsh economic exploitation and political exclusion have made their lives more comparable to blacks in the United States than to white immigrants.[28]

With South African realities in mind, Belinda Bozzoli has some cautionary insights concerning the complexity of the concept with reference to South Africa. She reminds us, first of all, of the brutal legacy of dispossession, forced removal, and continuing oppression necessarily at the heart of many of South African definitions of "community."[29] In this context, the idea of "struggle" is often critical to any concept of solidarity among working-class people: not simply of contests between laborers and capital or bosses over wages and working conditions, but of struggle against racial legislation, struggle to protect established communities, and struggle to define the meaning of class, ethnicity, and gender. These were often instances, then, in which class (or race) and community reinforced each other, situations that Bozzoli credits with leading to "the most effective and radical forms of class expression."[30]

Bozzoli's discussion also highlights the role, sometimes extremely deliberate and manipulative, of intellectuals in shaping perceptions of community. From them, she argues, come the relatively structured ideologies or systems of ideas that help to form and to restructure individual and collective attitudes.[31] South African labor leaders like E.S. Sachs of the Transvaal Garment Workers' Union and Ray Alexander of the Cape Food and Canning Workers' Union, both from Eastern European communist backgrounds, clearly played such a role within their respective organizations. This insight suggests that any sense of identification with others is not simply a given fact, inherent in people's material lives, but rather needs to be constructed conceptually, emotionally, and historically to have any meaning. Thus, Benedict Anderson's concept of nations as "imagined communities"[32] among people who do not know each other could apply equally well to smaller groupings along lines of gender, race, ethnicity, or class.

Although South Africa has been fragmented in different ways from the United States, its division during most of the 20th century into a black majority of roughly 70 percent of the population, an intermediate mixed-race and Asian group of 10 percent, and a dominant white minority of 20 percent has established a heterogeneous context in which struggles over identity occur. Contests for power among whites have been heightened by persistent tension between the more numerous Afrikaans-speaking segment of the population and those of English-speaking origin. Both African and Afrikaner intellectuals have successfully shaped ideology and political movements around nationalist identification.

Conceptualizing class as one form of "community" (though with social and economic rather than spatial boundaries) immediately raises the question of its connections to other such groupings. On this issue, the work of labor historians writing on the United States is more illuminating for South Africa than that of European historians, who usually write of an undifferentiated working-class experience in the 19th and early 20th centuries. The racial and ethnic diversity of South Africa, like that of the United States, demands a more complex analysis. Thus, Gutman's argument that nonclass elements such as ethnicity and race often generate the appeal of class-based identification[33] is equally cogent for South Africa where, it might be argued, workers have rarely even conceptualized class as transcending racial boundaries.

Since gender so clearly cuts across all other categories, its relationship to them adds another layer of complexity to any analysis. Although women in homogeneous marriages share the inherited ethnic and racial identification of their family and "community," the way they conceptualize and construct this sense of belonging may be very different from that of men. (To my knowledge, this is a largely unexplored topic.) More thoroughly researched is the way in which women's class standing, both objective and constructed, may in certain cases be different from that of their husbands. This is particularly true in many African societies in which the two maintain independent control over their own economic resources.[34] Where gender is more comparable to race and ethnicity in relationship to class are the situations in which gender-based networks and culture among women in a given labor context help to reinforce their solidarity as workers. Countering the argument for separate female and male class positions within individual households, David Montgomery portrays the 19th-century family in the United States as a "nursery of class consciousness," although also a "school for instruction" in women's separate and subordinate sphere.[35]

The idea that a new form of working-class family emerged in Europe and North America during the 19th century is widely accepted among historians. Within this new domestic structure, women, facing strong cultural pressure to retreat to the household if they could afford to do so, became heavily dependent on men's earning power. Black women in South Africa, by contrast, rarely have had the luxury of choosing whether or not to refrain from income-producing labor. The combined pressures of men's low wages, male labor migration, live-in domestic jobs, acute poverty, and state regulation have undermined stable family relationships and intensified women's independence from men.[36] On this issue, black urban women in the United States may be the most apt comparison.

Yet, the contrast between Africa and the west may be less stark than it would appear. Many black South African families tried to replicate the patterns of nuclear family life that European missionaries put forth as a model. Furthermore, like South African women, European and North American women who remained at home sewed, rented rooms to lodgers, and sought other informal means of augmenting scarce family funds. Thus, the differences may be greater in the realm of ideology and expectation than in women's actual lives, although high levels of migrant labor have produced much greater family separation in South Africa than within white households elsewhere.

This discussion of labor history provides a context for understanding working-class women in broad terms that take account of race and ethnicity and insist on the gendered nature of historical experience and perception. This insistence forces historians to examine the connections among aspects of life too often compartmentalized, but clearly critical to our understanding of the past.

Yet the distinct features of South African society make some aspects of comparison more relevant than others. Although the country's racial and ethnic complexity are more comparable to the United States than to Europe (before World War II), the tightly knit ethnic communities of North American immigrants were matched in only a few regions of South Africa. More like African Americans, most blacks who migrated to cities from rural sections of the Transvaal and the Orange Free State came not from integrated peasant societies, but from families of tenant farmers and sharecroppers. And even where peasant communities persisted, most rural areas were profoundly unsettled by the turbulent events of the 19th century. Zulu and Boer expansion uprooted and scattered innumerable communities and brought others under the sway of new conquerors; Christian missionaries created deep cultural and religious rifts between converts and Africans who resisted change; and intensive gold and diamond mining transformed all of southern Africa into a labor reserve for wretchedly paid migrant men. Furthermore, as the commercialization of agriculture and racially based legislation intensified during the early 20th century, land shortages and poverty became increasingly acute. In the wake of these upheavals, the reconstructed cultural traditions and gender relations that developed within urban proletarian communities become as critical to understanding working-class behavior and consciousness as the legacy of precapitalist culture.

South African realities also make state power a critical factor in understanding the lives of working-class women and their families. Often absent from social histories of women, the intrusive, authoritarian presence of the government in all areas of black life has made it impossible to ignore. Since the law governs such basic facts of daily life as who has the right to live in the cities and where urban-dwellers may seek housing, it has left an indelible imprint on the most intimate of family and individual decisions.

In conclusion, the large body of material on working-class women worldwide provides an important context for understanding the lives and experiences of South African women. Certainly, industrial workers there share many attributes of other workers in the Third World periphery, where industries in search of ever cheaper, ostensibly more docile workers have relocated in recent years. The comparison is particularly apt with gar-ment and textile factories in the rural "homelands" and "border areas" (between black and white-designated land) where starvation-level wages are sometimes coupled with restrictions on trade union organizing.

Yet, most studies of women in world-market factories necessarily lack historical depth. Furthermore, South Africa's relatively long industrial past and its high level of wealth makes it comparable in many ways to Europe and the United States. Though with a different demographic bal-ance, the country's multiracial and multiethnic population and its history of white domination also invite comparison more specifically with the United States.[37] Thus, many historical studies of women's organization and of the relationship between family, community, and factory in western countries raise questions and provide insights relevant to both regions.

In two major areas, however, this literature falls short of illuminating the South African experience. Many classic works in labor history (including women's labor history) are concerned primarily with class and, in the case of the United States, with ethnicity. Only a few exceptional works on women are sufficiently concerned with race to be useful in studying South Africa.[38]

Equally serious is the absence of the state. While several critics have noted the propensity of social historians to ignore political power, the South African state, by virtue of its coercive nature, demands inclusion even in the most privately focused historical examinations. Thus, while the study of women in South African industry draws attention to shortcomings in the conceptualization and concerns of labor history, it also underlines the importance of some of the most fundamental concerns of feminist scholarship: the connection between public power and private lives, and the significance of race as well as of gender, class, and ethnicity in shaping women's experience.

Finally, the South African case draws attention to the controversial issue of gender conflict within the family in communities subordinated on racial and class grounds. The strong feminist statements of Tembi Nabe and a few other trade union women notwithstanding, within the larger political environment such women would be unlikely to identify gender as the primary political issue. Within the labor movement, however, they per-ceive women's issues (extending into the household) as extremely urgent. Thus, different political contexts may demand different priorities. Simi-larly, interviews with black working-class women often reveal anger that they alone are expected to cook, clean, and care for children after a full day's work. Yet their comments suggest a deep concern to have men assume greater responsibility for their families, not necessarily a desire for enhanced independence from male domination.

The recent history of labor struggles in South Africa also points to the importance of leaders and intellectuals, both from within and outside the working class, in formulating the discourse that the labor movement adopts. In the 1970s and '80s, for example, the international women's movement has raised the issue of domestic inequality in a way that has influenced women union organizers in South Africa. From this interchange has come a new language for discussing women's position and a view of gender that does not accept the "double day" of working women as inevitable. This shift suggests that, even in a community intensely preoccupied with racial and class exploitation, the meaning and importance of domestic struggle have assumed a different weight in different political contexts. Thus, like class, race, and community, gender has to be understood both in terms of people's objective situation and of how they conceptualize and construct that reality over time.

NOTES

I am grateful to Ron Berger, Peg Strobel, and Gerry Zahavi for their insightful comments on an earlier draft of this article. The essay is based on the introduction to my book, *Threads of Solidarity: Women in South African Industry, 1900-1980* (Bloomington: Indiana University Press, 1992).

1. Tembi Nabe was then an organizer and ex-vice president of the Metal and Allied Workers' Union.

2. The relative lack of transformation in women's work with industrialization is a central argument of the most influential study of European working women, Louise A. Tilly and Joan W. Scott, *Women, Work and Family* (New York: Holt, Rinehart and Winston, 1978).

3. Ester Boserup, *Woman's Role in Economic Development* (New York: St. Martin's Press, 1970), 114-17.

4. Lourdes Benería and Martha Roldan, *The Crossroads of Class and Gender: Industrial Homework, Subcontracting, and Household Dynamics in Mexico City* (Chicago and London: University of Chicago Press, 1987), 102-03.

5. These stages are outlined in Helen I. Safa, "Runaway Shops and Female Employment: The Search for Cheap Labor" *Signs* 7, No. 2 (Winter 1981): 418-33. Her model applies particularly to the northeastern United States. This pattern of development would not apply to the Cape Province of South Africa, where the labor force in the clothing industry did not shift as significantly.

6. Ivy Pinchbeck, *Women Workers and the Industrial Revolution* (1930; London: Virago, 1981), 316. The difference between writers stressing the independent behavior of young, female factory workers and those emphasizing the continued influence of family and household on their actions continues to pervade the literature. See, for example, the references of Tom Dublin and Alice Kessler-Harris to Tilly and Scott, in Dublin, *Women at Work: The Transformation of Work and Community in Lowell, Massachusetts, 1826-1860* (New York: Columbia University Press, 1979), 40, and Kessler-Harris, "Problems of Coalition-Building: Women and Trade Unions in the 1920s," in *Women, Work and Protest: A Century of U.S. Women's*

Labor History, ed. Ruth Milkman (Boston: Routledge and Kegan Paul, 1985), 135, nt. 18.

7. David Montgomery, *The Fall of the House of Labor: The Workplace, the State, and American Labor Activism, 1865-1925* (Cambridge: Cambridge University Press, 1987), 144.

8. Montgomery, *House of Labor,* 145. Leslie Woodcock Tentler, by contrast, suggests in *Wage-Earning Women: Industrial Work and Family Life in the United States, 1900-1930* (Oxford: Oxford University Press, 1982), 4, 9-10, that industrial work, in which women had little power, reinforced circumscribed female roles and women's attachment to the home.

9. This view is expressed in J. Yawitch, "Black Women in South Africa: Capitalism, Employment and Reproduction," B.A. Hons. dissertation, University of the Witwatersrand, 1978.

10. See "The Doubled Vision of Feminist Theory," in *Sex and Class in Women's History,* ed. Judith L. Newton, Mary P. Ryan and Judith R. Walkowitz, (London: Routledge and Kegan Paul, 1983).

11. See Belinda Bozzoli, "Marxism, Feminism and South African Studies," *Journal of Southern African Studies* 9, No. 2 (April 1983): 139-71.

12. Though writing about the United States, this analysis by Evelyn Nakano Glenn, "Racial Ethnic Women's Labor: The Intersection of Race, Gender, and Class Oppression," may also be applicable to South Africa. It appears in Christine Bose, Roslyn Feldberg and Natalie Sokoloff, eds., *Hidden Aspects of Women's Work* (New York: Praeger, 1987), 70-1. Focusing on resistance, Mina Davis Caulfield makes a similar argument in "Imperialism, the Family, and Cultures of Resistance," in *Feminist Frameworks: Alternative Theoretical Accounts of the Relations Between Women and Men,* ed. Alison M. Jaggar and Paula S. Rothenberg (New York: McGraw-Hill, 1984), 374-79.

13. Benería and Roldan, *Crossroads,* 9-10.

14. These accounts include Richard Goode, "For a Better Life: The Food and Canning Workers Union 1941-1975," B.A. Hons. thesis, Cape Town University, 1983; Leslie Witz, "Solly Sachs: Servant of the Workers," M.A. dissertation, Witwatersrand University, 1981, and B.M. Touyz, "White Politics and the Garment Workers Union 1930-1953," M.S. dissertation, Cape Town University, 1979.

15. Among works taking this perspective are: Amelia Marie Mariotti, "The Incorporation of African Women Into Wage Employment in South Africa, 1920-1970," Ph.D. thesis, University of Connecticut, 1979; V.M. Martin and C.M. Rogerson, "Women and Industrial Change: The South African Experience," *The South African Geographical Journal* 66, No. 1 (April 1984): 32-46; Joanne Yawitch, "The Incorporation of African Women into Wage Labor, 1950-1980," *South African Labour Bulletin* 9, No. 3 (December 1983); and Georgina Jaffee and Collette Caine, "The Incorporation of African Women Into the Industrial Work-Force: Its Implications for the Women's Question in South Africa," paper presented to the Southern African Economy After Apartheid Conference, Centre for Southern African Studies, University of York, October 1986. All of these works do not ignore human agency totally, but they rarely see it operating to shape the places women fill in the economy.

16. The use of this concept is explored in Louise A. Tilly, "Women and Family Strategies in French Proletarian Families," *Michigan Occasional Paper* No. IV, Fall 1978.

17. Richard Goode, "Struggle and Strikes in the Cannery: The Great Wolseley Strike," unpublished paper presented to the Conference on the History of the

Western Cape, University of Cape Town, July 1987, 47. Translated from Afrikaans by Goode. Original language of quotations retained.

18. Rose L. Glickman, *Russian Factory Women: Workplace and Society, 1880-1914* (Berkeley and Los Angeles: University of California Press, 1984), 204. She discusses the impact of the legacy of female subordination and submissiveness on women's labor activism on pp. 215-16. Ruth Milkman also discusses the attitudes of male trade unionists in "Organizing the Sexual Division of Labor: Historical Perspectives on 'Women's Work' and the American Labor Movement," *Socialist Review* 49, No. 1 (January-February 1980): 95-150.

19. See, for example, Sheila Rowbotham, *Women, Resistance and Revolution: A History of the Modern World* (New York: Pantheon, 1972), 113.

20. Temma Kaplan, "Female Consciousness and Collective Action: The Case of Barcelona, 1910-1918," *Signs* 7, No. 3 (Spring 1982): 548. Her apparent argument, that women were concerned only with issues of community preservation and survival and not with economic issues, cannot necessarily be generalized to other cases.

21. Dolores E. Janiewski, *Sisterhood Denied: Race, Gender, and Class in a New South Community* (Philadelphia: Temple University Press, 1985), 177. The view of trade unions as inadequate from women's perspective is also strongly expressed in Diane Elson and Ruth Pearson, "Third World Manufacturing," in *Waged Work: A Reader*, ed. Feminist Review [journal's editorial board] (London: Virago, 1986), 89-90; and in Roslyn L. Feldberg, "Women and Trade Unions: Are We Asking the Right Questions?" Bose, *et al.*, *Hidden Aspects*.

22. Joan W. Scott makes this argument in "On Language, Gender, and Working-Class History," *International Labor and Working Class History* 31 (Spring 1987): 1-13.

23. Several of the articles in Milkman, *Women, Work and Protest*, take this approach. See especially Colette A. Hyman, "Labor Organizing and Female Institution-Building: The Chicago Women's Trade Union League, 1904-24"; Ardis Cameron, "Bread and Roses Revisited: Women's Culture and Working-Class Activism in the Lawrence Strike of 1912"; and Alice Kessler-Harris, "Problems of Coalition-Building: Women and Trade Unions in the 1920s." For writing with a focus on work cultures, see the articles in *Feminist Studies* 11, No. 3 (Fall 1985).

24. See Louise A. Tilly, "Paths of Proletarianization: Organization of Production, Sexual Division of Labor, and Women's Collective Action," *Signs* 7, No. 2 (Winter 1981): 400-17.

25. Carole Turbin, "Reconceptualizing Family, Work, and Labor Organizing: Working Women in Troy, 1860-1890," Bose, *et al.*, *Hidden Aspects*, 192; Helen Safa, "Class Consciousness Among Working Class Women in Latin America: A Case Study in Puerto Rico," in *Peasants and Proletarians*, ed. Robin Cohen, Peter Gutkind, and Phyllis Brazier, (New York: Monthly Review, 1979), 447-48; Iris Berger, "Sources of Class Consciousness: South African Women in Recent Labor Struggles," in *Women and Class in Africa*, ed. Claire Robertson and Iris Berger, (New York: Holmes and Meier, 1986), 232.

26. This approach is similar in this respect to those of Evelyn Glenn and Mina Davis Caulfield cited above.

27. Among the works of these authors that establish this perspective are Herbert G. Gutman, "Work, Culture, and Society in Industrializing America, 1815-1919," in *Work, Culture and Society in Industrializing America: Essays in American Working-Class and Social History* (New York: Alfred A. Knopf, 1976); Virginia Yans-McLaughlin, *Family and Community: Italian Immigrants in Buffalo, 1880-1930*

(Ithaca and London: Cornell University Press, 1977); and Tamara Hareven, "Family Time and Industrial Time: Family and Work in a Planned Corporation Town, 1900-1924," in *Family and Kin in Urban Communities, 1700-1930*, ed. Tamara K. Hareven, (New York: New Viewpoints, 1977). In contrast to these approaches, John T. Cumbler emphasizes the formal and informal institutions comprising the new industrial community in *Working-Class Community in Industrial America: Work, Leisure, and Struggle in Two Industrial Cities, 1880-1930* (Westport, Conn.: Greenwood Press, 1979).

28. For two books dealing specifically with work, see Jacqueline Jones, *Labor of Love, Labor of Sorrow: Black Women, Work, and the Family from Slavery to the Present* (New York: Basic Books, 1985) and Joe William Trotter, Jr., *Black Milwaukee: The Making of an Industrial Proletariat, 1915-45* (Urbana and Chicago: University of Illinois Press, 1985).

29. This rich and insightful essay, "Class, Community and Ideology in the Evolution of South African Society," appears in *Class, Community and Conflict: South African Perspectives*, ed. Belinda Bozzoli, (Johannesburg: Ravan Press, 1987), 26.

30. Bozzoli, "Class, Community and Ideology," 6.

31. In this part of her discussion (on pp. 9, 13, and 18), Bozzoli relies on George Rude's distinction between "inherent" traditional attitudes based on direct experience, oral tradition, or folk memory and more structured "derived" ideologies as discussed in *Ideology and Popular Protest* (London: Lawrence and Wishart, 1980), 27-29.

32. Benedict Anderson, *Imagined Communities: Reflections of the Origin and Spread of Nationalism* (London: Verso, 1983). This definition comes from pp. 15-16.

33. Gutman, *Work, Culture and Society*. A.P. Cheater argues for a more complex, situational conception of "worker consciousness" among men as well, one that does not resort to labels like "false consciousness" to explain behavior that fails to conform to narrowly defined marxist norms. See "Contradictions in Modelling 'Consciousness': Zimbabwean Proletarians in the Making?" *Journal of Southern African Studies* 14, No. 2 (January 1988): 293, 303.

34. This is a central theme in many of the essays in Robertson and Berger.

35. David Montgomery, *The Fall of the House of Labor*, 139.

36. Bill Freund suggests this distinction between African and western family patterns in *The African Worker* (Cambridge: Cambridge University Press, 1988), 87. Freund draws his examples from West African cases in which women asserted an extraordinary degree of independence from men.

37. European studies that take into account post-World War II racial diversity tend to rely on sociological rather than historical perspectives and methodologies.

38. The exceptional works on women include Jones, *Labor of Love*, and Janiewski, *Sisterhood Denied*.

BIBLIOGRAPHICAL NOTE

For background on African women, the two most general sources remain Margaret Jean Hay and Sharon Stichter, eds., *African Women: South of the Sahara* (1984; 2nd ed., London: Longman, forthcoming), a topical interdisciplinary survey written for nonspecialists, and the pioneering collection of more specialized articles by Nancy Hafkin and Edna Bay, eds., *Women in Africa: Studies in Social and Economic Change* (Stanford: Stanford University Press, 1976). More recent edited volumes with a thematic focus include Claire Robertson and Iris

Berger, eds., *Women and Class in Africa* (New York: Holmes and Meier, 1986); Sharon Stichter and Jane Parpart, eds., *Patriarchy and Class: African Women in the Home and Workforce* (Boulder, Colo.: Westview, 1988); and Jane Parpart and Kathleen A. Staudt, *Women and the State in Africa* (Boulder and London: Lynne Rienner Publishers, 1990). Monographic studies of African women with a historical emphasis include Margaret Strobel, *Muslim Women in Mombasa, 1890-1975* (New Haven: Yale University Press, 1979); Claire Robertson, *Sharing the Same Bowl: A Socioeconomic History of Women and Class in Accra, Ghana* (Bloomington: Indiana University Press, 1984; repr., Ann Arbor: University of Michigan Press, 1990); Kristin Mann, *Marrying Well: Marriage, Status and Social Change among the Educated Elite in Colonial Lagos* (Cambridge: Cambridge University Press, 1985); and Luise White, *The Comforts of Home: Prostitution in Colonial Nairobi* (Chicago: University of Chicago Press, 1990). For individual life histories from across the continent, see Patricia Romero, ed., *Life Histories of African Women* (London: The Ashfield Press, 1988). *Three Swahili Women: Life Histories from Mombasa, Kenya* (Bloomington: Indiana University Press, 1989), edited by Sarah Mirza and Margaret Strobel, explores the lives of Muslim women on the East Coast.

On South African women, most important for general background are Cheryl Walker, *Women and Resistance in South Africa* (London: Onyx Press, 1982), which traces various resistance movements up to and including the campaign against passes in the 1950s; and Cheryl Walker, ed., *Women and Gender in South Africa* (London: James Currey, 1989), a collection that is important in covering the nineteenth century as well as more recent years. Hilda Bernstein surveys women's lives under apartheid in *For Their Triumphs and for Their Tears: Women in Apartheid South Africa* (London: International Defence and Aid Fund for Southern Africa, 1985). A fuller exploration of the themes of this article is found in Iris Berger, *Threads of Solidarity: Women in South African Industry, 1900-1980* (Bloomington: Indiana University Press, 1992). Two trade union women present their own life stories in Frances Baard, as told to Barbie Schreiner, *My Spirit Is Not Banned* (Harare: Zimbabwe Publishing House, 1986), and Emma Mashinini, *Strikes Have Followed Me All My Life: A South African Autobiography* (London: The Women's Press, 1989). Focusing on another individual life, *Not Either an Experimental Doll: The Separate Worlds of Three South African Women* (Bloomington: Indiana University Press, 1987) by Shula Marks reveals the potentially ambiguous effects of Western education.

Scholarship on feminist theory and women and work is extensive. A good introduction to theoretical issues can be found in Alison M. Jaggar and Paula S. Rothenberg, eds., *Feminist Frameworks: Alternative Accounts of the Relations between Women and Men* (New York: McGraw Hill, 1984). Among the most influential historical accounts of women's labor are Louise A. Tilly and Joan W. Scott, *Women, Work and Family* (New York: Holt, Rinehart and Winston, 1978), which covers Europe, with a particular emphasis on France; Ester Boserup, *Women's Role in Economic Development* (New York: St. Martin's Press, 1970), a book often credited with launching Third World women's studies; and Rose L. Glickman, *Russian Factory Women: Workplace and Society, 1880-1914* (Berkeley and Los Angeles: University of California Press, 1984). On the United States, see Thomas Dublin, *Women at Work: The Transformation of Work and Community in Lowell, Massachusetts, 1826-1860* (New York: Columbia University Press, 1979); Leslie Woodcock Tentler, *Wage-Earning Women: Industrial Work and Family Life in the United States, 1900-1930* (Oxford: Oxford University Press, 1982); Dolores E. Janiewski, *Sisterhood Denied: Race, Gender, and Class in a*

New South Community (Philadelphia: Temple University Press, 1985); Ruth Milkman, ed., *Women, Work and Protest: A Century of U.S. Women's Labor History* (Boston: Routledge and Kegan Paul, 1985); and Jacqueline Jones, *Labor of Love, Labor of Sorrow: Black Women, Work and the Family from Slavery to the Present* (New York: Basic Books, 1985).

INDUSTRIALIZATION AND EMPLOYMENT

POSTWAR CHANGES IN THE PATTERNS OF WOMEN'S WORK IN PUERTO RICO

Luz del Alba Acevedo

Research on the patterns of women's work in Third World countries has been guided until recently primarily by two competing views: the integration and the marginalization hypotheses. These hypotheses are grounded on different theoretical frameworks, namely, modernization and developmentalist theories. They provide contrasting explanations of the differential impact of capitalist development on female employment and social status.[1]

The integration hypothesis developed by modernization theorists argues that there is a positive relationship between economic development and female employment. Proponents of this hypothesis claim that industrialization leads to women's emancipation from traditional subordinate roles and to increased equity between genders by involving women more centrally in economic and political development.[2] Industrialization and its attendant cultural and structural changes tend to involve women significantly in public life. Women are integrated into the modern labor market as new job opportunities are opened up in industry and related services. The integration of women into the labor force increases their financial independence at the same time that it provides them with productive skills and modern values and attitudes.

The marginalization hypothesis was initially derived from Ester Boserup's pathbreaking assessment of the impact of development on the economic roles of women. Later this thesis gained prominence in the radical work of some socialist feminists influenced by the most pessimistic versions of dependency theory.[3] The marginalization hypothesis argues that there is a negative relation between economic development and women's productive work outside the house. Proponents of this hypothesis claim that capitalist industrialization displaces women from production and political power. In precapitalist societies, women were engaged in productive activities of great importance for their households and communities. In these societies, the production and distribution of goods and services were not exchange-oriented. Since wage earning was not the most important activity of the household, women's productive activities were as vital as those of men. The process of industrial development based on foreign investment requires the generalization of market relations throughout the developing society. In this process, men are drawn into the labor force to produce commodities in exchange for wages, while women are relegated to the household. Since women lack the necessary skills to work in the new, growing industries, they are confined to household duties and marginal exchange activities in the tertiary sector of the economy. Here the kinds of jobs available seem to lock them into marginal positions with little opportunity for upward mobility. In other words, industrialization does not incorporate women into the emerging dominant market economy and downgrades the importance that their subsistence-productive activities had in precapitalist production.

More recent sociohistorical studies suggest, however, that neither of these explanations is generalizable, and that changes in the patterns of female employment seem to vary according to the particular conditions of the development process in a given country and the role that a country plays in the international division of labor.[4] The patterns of foreign investment and dependence brought by the new international division of labor since the Second World War are said to have had a dramatic effect on the integration or marginalization of women in the labor market. The internationalization of industrial production on a world scale has brought an increase in women's employment, relative to men, as women constitute the preferred source of labor for transnational corporations (TNC).[5] Thus the key issues emerging from these recent studies are how the patterns of women's work have been affected by postwar industrial development; what types of jobs women are getting; and whether a new gender division of labor is emerging in newly industrializing societies. In other words, what historical transformation is capitalist development effecting in the economic roles of women in newly industrializing countries?

Following the lead of these studies, this essay examines how industrial development affects the distribution of employment by gender over time and how these changes contribute to changes in women's participation in the productive process. The purpose of the study is to assess the changes in the sectoral and occupational distribution of female employment in Puerto Rico since the adoption of an export-led industrial development model in the postwar era. By focusing on the changes in the sectoral and occupational structures of the female labor force, we will be able to examine the changing historical trends in the gender division of labor induced by the new industrial order and to point out the directions and causes of these emerging trends. Moreover, the empirical evaluation of historical patterns will be useful in providing some insights into the complexities involved in the relationship between industrial development policies and the integration and/or marginalization of women in the labor force.

The experience of female employment in Puerto Rico during the course of industrial development is particularly important in the discussion of these issues. The island was one of the first countries in the capitalist periphery to adopt an aggressive, export-led industrialization program during the postwar era. The fact that this industrialization program, popularly known as Operation Bootstrap, has evolved for over three decades, allows for an in-depth analysis of the long-term effects of export-led industrial development on female employment. Puerto Rico's industrialization program has been displayed as a model to be followed by neighboring Caribbean islands and other small countries in the world. Its evaluation becomes relevant as it may help to draw some lessons for those countries that are following a similar path to industrial development.[6]

Industrialization Policy in Puerto Rico

From the American invasion in 1898 until the late 1940s, Puerto Rico's economy was organized around a plantation system based on the production of agricultural commodities for export, mainly sugar cane for the United States market. However, the passage of the Jones Costigan Act of 1934 made it clear that the reign of sugar was coming to an end.[7] This and the problems confronted by Puerto Rican and U.S. policymakers led to profound political changes and to the remapping of the course of the economic development of the island.

With the coming to power of the Popular Democratic Party (PPD) in 1940 and the appointment by President Roosevelt of Rexford Guy Tugwell as governor of Puerto Rico in 1941, a new era began for the economic development of the island. On May 11, 1942, the Puerto Rican legislature, dominated by the PPD, passed the law that initiated the first systematic government-sponsored program to promote the industrialization of the island. Between 1942 and 1947 the industrialization policy implemented by the Puerto Rico Industrial Development Company (PRIDCO) concentrated on establishing manufacturing enterprises utilizing local raw materials in making products destined for the local market. The adoption of an import substitution industrialization strategy was dictated by the constraints imposed on the Puerto Rican economy by World War II. The disruption of normal shipping arrangements between the island and the United States brought about by the presence of German submarines in the Caribbean, and the need to use as much shipping space as possible to supply Great Britain were the key factors that compelled the United States government to allow the establishment of government-owned enterprises to substitute locally produced goods for hard-to-come-by imports.[8]

At the end of the war, the PPD policymakers began to debate the wisdom of continuing the policy of state-based industrialization. In the end the government decided to embark on an industrialization program based on the granting of incentives for private investment. The new development strategy of the PPD was launched under the motto "operación manos a la obra," which became known in English as Operation Bootstrap.

PRIDCO, which later became the Economic Development Administration, popularly known as Fomento, continued as the government agency in charge of implementing the new development strategy. Four industrial incentive laws constituted the backbone of Operation Bootstrap. The main objective of this economic strategy was to attract American capital into Puerto Rico's industrial sector. The centerpiece of the program was full exemption from taxes on income, property, and municipal permits and patents for manufacturing enterprises. The tax-exemption periods ranged from ten to twenty-five years. The major features and changes in the industrial incentive laws passed between 1947 and 1982 are shown in table 1.

Aside from the incentives granted to foreign capital by the industrial incentives laws, there were other economic advantages widely publicized by Fomento: (a) availability of abundant cheap labor with low degree of unionization (or with unions controlled by the government); (b) attractive overhead capital facilities, e.g., low rent for industrial buildings, and low energy cost; and (c) free access to the United States market as a result of the existence of free trade between Puerto Rico and the United States.[9]

Throughout the four decades that Operation Bootstrap has been in effect, the type of industries attracted to the island have changed, and so has the kind of labor force required by them. Law 184 and Law 6 deliberately targeted the attraction of light industries in the areas of textile and electronic products.[10] Although Law 57 was designed mainly to continue to attract U.S. investment in manufacturing in much the same areas as the previous laws, the development of adverse economic conditions for investment in light industries, such as increases in minimum wages and transportation costs between Puerto Rico and the United States, made Law 57 more useful in attracting capital-intensive heavy industries. The longer tax-exemption periods provided by Law 57 and the granting of higher oil import quotas to Puerto Rico by presidential decree in 1964 assured the success of Fomento's campaign to attract oil-refining and petrochemical industries and marked a clear change in Puerto Rico's industrialization policy toward capital-intensive manufacturing.[11]

Law 26 of 1978 expanded the incentive program to include the promotion of service industries. The express goal of the law was to attract foreign investment to the service sector that would generate a substantial number of well-remunerated jobs, in addition to those created in the manufacturing sector. To this effect, Law 26 would grant partial tax exemption to any

TABLE 1
Stages of Economic Development and Industrializaton Policies:
Puerto Rico, 1947-1978

Laws	Tax Exemption	Exemption Period	Type of Industry Attracted
STAGE 1			LABOR-INTENSIVE
Law 184 (1948)	100% income and property tax exemption	July 1, 1947, to June 30, 1959	Apparel, textiles, food, furniture, electrical machinery, and metal products
Law 6 (1953)	100% income tax exemption and property tax exemption according to investment	10 years for industries established between 1954 and 1963	Same as above plus additional branches of the textile and food-processing industries
STAGE 2			CAPITAL-INTENSIVE
Law 57 (1963)	100% income tax exemption and property tax exemption according to investment	10, 12, and 17 years depending on location	Petroleum refining and products, chemicals, pharmaceuticals, and electrical machinery
Law 26 (1978)	90% partial tax exemption for 5 years, 75% for the next 5 years and 55% for up to 15 years depending on location	10, 15, 20, or 25 years depending on location	Pharmaceuticals, electronics, computing equipment, and service industries

Source: Leyes de Puerto Rico Anotadas (1948, 1953, 1963, and 1978).

business or establishment rendering "designated services" on a commercial scale, for markets outside Puerto Rico. The services designated by law can be classified into four categories: data-processing services, communications, consultant firms, and medical and scientific laboratories.

With these laws as landmarks, two stages of development can be identified within Operation Bootstrap: a first stage characterized by the dominance of labor-intensive light industries, and a second stage dominated by capital-intensive industries manufacturing intermediate and finished products for the U.S. market.[12] An ever-present objective of the laws that shaped Operation Bootstrap throughout both stages was to create an industrial structure capable of providing ample employment opportunities to the Puerto Rican population. Thus, before entering into a detailed analysis of the changes in the patterns of women's employment, I shall look briefly at the general impact that this program had on the overall structure of employment by gender.

Industrialization and Employment

An analysis of employment statistics for the period 1950 to 1982 indicates that Operation Bootstrap failed to create enough jobs to satisfy the needs of the working population. During those years, total employment grew from 601,000 to 704,000, an average increase of only 3,219 jobs per year. Table 2 shows low or negative levels of growth in average total employment for every decade between 1950 and 1982. The average male and female rates of employment growth, however, suggest that women were affected less negatively than men. The average employment growth for all four decades combined was 1.7 percent for women and 0.1 percent for men. Thus the employment of women grew at a faster rate than that of men.

TABLE 2
Average Rates of Growth of Employment by Gender in Puerto Rico, 1950-1982

	Women	**Men**	**Total Employment**
1950-59	0.1	-1.0	-0.7
1960-69	3.9	1.7	2.3
1970-79	2.0	0.4	0.9
1980-82	-0.5	-2.6	-1.8

Source: Calculated from Departamento del Trabajo, Serie Historica de Empleo y Desempleo en Puerto Rico (1983).

This inference is reinforced when we examine the average rates of labor-force participation for men and women throughout this period. Table 3 shows that the level of female labor-force participation remained around 27-28 percent, while the average male participation rate decreased from 82 to 59 percent. This led to a reduction in the female/male employment ratio from one woman for every three men employed (.37) to one woman for every two men employed (.51). Thus the reduction in the employment gap between men and women may be attributed to the steady decline in male participation, not to the expansion of female labor-force participation.

The unemployment situation summarized in table 4 shows a similar pattern. While female unemployment grew steadily after the 1970s, male unemployment grew faster during this period. The average rate of female unemployment went up from 12 percent to 14 percent, while the average rate of male unemployment increased from 16 percent to 22 percent. Further, the ratio of unemployed women to men remained around one to three throughout the period.

This brief overview of the employment situation in Puerto Rico suggests that women had a relative advantage over men. Their labor-force participation rate was low but stable, while the rate for men showed a constant

TABLE 3
Average Labor-Force Participation by Gender in Puerto Rico, 1950-1982

	Total Population	Women	Men	Ratio of Women to Men
1950-59	56.1	27.9	82.6	0.37
1960-69	50.3	25.6	75.5	0.39
1970-79	46.3	28.1	66.6	0.47
1980-82	42.4	27.2	59.4	0.51

Source: Calculated from Departamento del Trabajo, Serie Historica de Empleo y Desempleo en Puerto Rico (1983).

TABLE 4
Average Unemployment Rate by Gender in Puerto Rico, 1950-1982

	Total Population	Women	Men	Ratio of Women to Men
1950-59	14.4	14.3	14.4	0.36
1960-69	11.6	8.7	12.6	0.27
1970-79	15.2	12.5	16.5	0.37
1980-82	19.9	14.2	22.8	0.32

Source: Calculated from Departamento del Trabajo, Serie Historica de Empleo y Desempleo en Puerto Rico (1983).

decline. The average rate of employment for women also grew faster than that for men. Such an apparent advantage of women over men could give the impression that the overall employment situation of women improved considerably, probably at the expense of male employment, as women may have displaced men from the labor force. It must be remembered, however, that women's competitive advantage in the labor force lies precisely in their disadvantaged position in society. As women are considered inferior to men, i.e., less productive and skilled, and their incomes are considered supplemental or secondary to the household, they constitute a sizeable source of cheap labor for the newly established industries. In addition, women's lack of participation in labor unions to demand higher wages and other benefits makes female labor even more attractive than male labor to industries eager for profit.

The problem of female employment, however, should be seen in its proper perspective. The policies implemented by the PPD government throughout this period failed to achieve their objective of expanding significantly employment opportunities. The increase in the average unemployment rate, in spite of the emigration of tens of thousands of workers to the U.S. every year, and the decrease in the average growth of total employment since 1970 (tables 2 and 4) clearly indicate that the working population in general was affected negatively.[13] The employment gains in the manufacturing sector did not compensate for the rapid losses in agricultural employment. This stimulated the growth of an industrial reserve army of labor that aggravated the existing problem of surplus labor. In reality, what happened was not that the employment situation of women improved vis-à-vis that of men but that it deteriorated less, in a context in which the employment situation of the population did not improve significantly. This initial evidence disputes the marginalization hypothesis, however.

Industrial Development and Sectoral Changes in Women's Work

If indeed women are not marginalized from the industrialization process, their economic role depends on the kinds of industries (labor-intensive, capital-intensive) and/or the stage (early, advanced) that characterize the process. This premise seems to be historically true in the case of Latin America, where women played a markedly different role at each stage of the process of industrial development. The stages in the path toward industrial development may vary from country to country according to the historical circumstances and the industrialization model followed (e.g., import substitution, export processing).

Studies based on the historical experience of the participation of women in the work force in Brazil have led some scholars to make a distinction between the various stages involved in the process of industrial capitalist development.[14] At each stage of the development process, women played a particular economic role. These stages are (a) the agrarian or pre-industrial stage, in which women participate primarily as members of a peasant family, that is, as both a production and a consumption unit; (b) the early stages of urbanization and industrialization, when women are employed primarily as domestic servants, petty vendors, and unskilled factory workers, particularly in labor-intensive industries such as textiles and food processing; and (c) the expansion of urbanization, capital-intensive industrialization, and state bureaucracy, which leads to an increase in the service sector of the economy and in white-collar jobs for women in clerical work, trade, public administration, social services, etc.

Puerto Rico's industrialization program fits into the last two of the stages described above. The first stage of Operation Bootstrap ran from 1947 to the early 1960s, stimulated by Laws 184 and 6, which resulted in the attraction of labor-intensive industries with relatively low capital requirements. The second stage ran from the mid-1960s to the early 1980s, resulting from the implementation of Law 57, the oil import quota program, and Law 26, which stimulated the attraction of capital-intensive industries and the expansion of the service and public administration sectors during the period 1963 to 1982. (See table 1.)

If we assume that the patterns of female employment are influenced by the stage of industrial development in which a country finds itself, we would expect sectoral variations in the patterns of female participation to occur according to the kind of industries that lead the industrialization process. From this premise we developed five hypotheses about the direction of changes in the patterns of female employment in Puerto Rico during each stage of the industrialization process in five economic sectors: agriculture, manufacturing, trade, service, and public administration.

1. Female agricultural labor in Puerto Rico was always marginal or complementary to male labor. Historically, female participation in the agricultural sector was low, as women played a secondary role in the production of agricultural goods for the market. Therefore, as industrial development progressed and agricultural employment declined, female labor in this sector would become insignificant.

2. Variations in the participation of female labor in the manufacturing sector will depend on the type of industry that leads the industrialization process. Labor-intensive light industries, for example, are characterized by a large absorption of female labor. They generally prefer female labor for two major reasons. On the one hand, these industries depend on the intense use of cheap labor to carry out the different tasks involved in production. The fact that female labor is undervalued in most underdeveloped societies makes it attractive to labor-intensive light industries to recruit large numbers of female workers. The undervaluation of female labor is based on traditional cultural values that assign a subordinate role to women in society. In most Third World countries, where this type of industry is established, women's work is considered to be temporary, and the wages earned are supplemental to the family subsistence. On the other hand, the jobs offered by the light industries are usually in areas associated with the traditional functions of women (e.g., clothing, food processing, etc.), where women have a high level of manual dexterity. This serves as an additional incentive for hiring more female than male labor.[15] During the early stage of economic development in Puerto Rico, the light industries attracted by Law 184 and Law 6 led the industrialization process. The spread of factories engaged in manufacturing activities such as clothing and food processing brought new employment opportunities for women. Therefore, a steady incorporation of women into the manufacturing sector in the early stage of industrialization was expected.

The percentage of women working in industry, however, is expected to decrease during the second stage of the industrialization process, when heavy and capital-intensive industries become the most dynamic component of the manufacturing sector. The explanations for the expected relative decline in women's manufacturing employment in this stage are grounded on a number of interrelated ideological and structural conditions that influence female participation in the labor process.

A key feature of the concentration of economic growth in capital-intensive manufacturing industries is that less employment is generated for a given increase in output or investment. The capacity of those industries to generate new employment opportunities is less than that of labor-intensive industries. Yet the advantage for developing countries in attracting industries of this type is precisely that they are less sensitive to wage-rate increases and thus are less likely to leave the country in response to periodic increases in wage rates. The ideological preconceptions and biases of management and government policymakers, who assume that men are the main breadwinners in a household and consider women's wages complementary, strongly influence the hiring practices of these industries.[16] Since heavy and capital-intensive industries are not as concerned in maintaining rock-bottom wages, the bias for hiring women will not be paramount in these industries. Moreover, the notion that the activities associated with these industries require the kinds of technical expertise and/or physical strength characteristic of the "male nature," prevents women even further from entering these jobs. Thus, the newly created high-paying jobs will be filled mostly by men. Another factor accounting for the decline in female manufacturing employment is the restructuring of the labor process within some industries so that they can remain competitive at the international level. The introduction of labor-saving technologies in industries that traditionally employ large numbers of women, such as textiles, food processing, and electronics, has an adverse effect on the growth rate of women's employment in manufacturing.

3. The economic expansion stimulated by industrial development brings an increase in the commercial activities in a country. With the expansion of the trade sector, new opportunities emerge for the integration of women in the labor force. However, trade has always been viewed in Puerto Rican society as a men's activity. Women are discouraged from pursuing business administration careers, which in time limits their opportunity to take any important trade-related jobs.[17] Thus, the expansion of the trade sector and the new employment opportunities which are created during the first stage of industrial development do not seem to favor the employment of women in that sector. In this sense I did not expect to find a significant growth in the employment of women during the first stage of industrialization.

Interestingly enough, however, I can argue that during the latter stage of industrial development, there are new demands for the expansion and/or creation of employment opportunities in certain areas of the trade sector. During this stage in the industrialization process, retail business and commercial establishments such as big department stores began to flourish in Puerto Rico. The newly created positions could have been taken by women rather than men, since the types of jobs usually available in such stores are traditionally associated with women, i.e., cashiers, salespersons, decorators, etc. Therefore, in the second stage of industrialization, women would be expected to enter the trade sector, probably as "salesgirls."

4. The growth of services associated with industrial development is likely to attract women to jobs in the service sector. As women traditionally have been employed in personal services (e.g., domestic service), one would expect them to take advantage of the expansion of this sector as a means to enter the labor force. However, between the mid-1940s and late 1950s, American private employment agencies recruited significant numbers of Puerto Rican women employed in domestic service to work in private households in the cities of New York, Chicago, and Newark.[18] This stimulated the migration of women who otherwise might have sought employment in the service sector. Therefore, in the first stage of industrialization, we expected to find a very low number of women employed in the service sector, since the largest percentage of women active in the labor force had new options, namely, to seek the jobs offered by the light industries in the manufacturing sectors or to migrate to the United States. Conversely, in the second stage of industrialization, we expected women to enter the service sector at a faster rate. The expansion of social services opens up integration opportunities to a considerable number of women, especially those with relatively high educational levels. The expansion of health services and social administration services, for example, also generates a number of jobs that might be taken by women.

5. The increased demand in public services brought about by the process of industrialization stimulates the growth of the state bureaucracy. This opens up new opportunities for female employment in the public administration sector. However, as politics have traditionally been the domain of men, it is unlikely that in the early stage of industrialization there will be a significant increase in female participation in this sector. Any marked increase in the participation of women in the public administration sector may come in the long run as a result of structural changes and/or changes in the general attitudes of society. The fact that in 1952 the government of Puerto Rico went through a process of reorganization that resulted in the creation of new agencies and governmental departments suggests that the structural conditions for the employment of women at a later stage were prepared. The new job opportunities that were eventually created were for secretaries, stenographers, social workers, etc. These types of jobs were compatible with the roles traditionally played by women; therefore, one would expect to find women entering the public administration sector in the second stage of industrialization.

These hypotheses were modeled into regression equations using time-series data on women's employment in Puerto Rico between 1947 and 1982 to ascertain shifts in the sectoral employment of women. This period was divided into the two stages of development discussed earlier. The empirical analysis measured the effect that each stage had on the distribution of women's employment during the course of industrialization. Four of the five economic sectors under study showed significant results: agriculture, service, manufacturing, and trade.

What follows is a summary of the findings from the time-series analysis.[19]

1. Contrary to what was expected, the percentage of women employed in agriculture during the early stage of industrial development was relatively low, while in the second stage it was relatively high.

2. As expected, women's participation in manufacturing was more intense during the labor-intensive or first stage of industrialization than during the second stage, dominated by capital-intensive industries.

3. Contrary to our expectations, women entered the service sector during the early stage of industrial development, while in the later stage their employment declined.

4. As expected, women's participation in the trade sector grew during the second stage of industrialization.

5. Although the results of the analysis of the public administration sector were not statistically significant, in the early stage of industrialization the employment of women in public administration is insignificant, while in the latter stage there seems to be a slight tendency to incorporate women into the work force in this sector.

Although the changes detected were not always those predicted, and their statistical significance varied, the analysis did establish a clear relation between changes in development policy, as articulated in the different stages, and patterns of sectoral distribution of women's employment. The regression analysis demonstrated that during the first stage of Operation Bootstrap, a large proportion of women were employed in the manufacturing and service sectors, while the proportion of female employment in trade and public administration was relatively low. In the second stage, these trends were reversed. Women's industrial and service-sector participation diminished, as their main job opportunities were opened in the trade and public-administration sectors.

These shifts in the patterns of sectoral distribution of female employment, which are attributable to changes in the industrialization policy, in turn responded to changes in the interests of foreign investors seeking to maintain or increase their competitiveness in the international economy. During the first stage of industrial development, labor-intensive light industries came to the island lured by low wage rates and tax incentives. But the low wage rates that attracted this type of industry had disappeared by the 1960s. While at the onset of Operation Bootstrap the average wage rates in manufacturing in Puerto Rico were 27 percent of the average wage in the United States, by 1970 the average wage on the island was close to that of the southern United States, and three times the wages paid in Mexico.[20] This made it necessary to redefine industrial incentives. Low wages came to play a secondary role to special oil import quotas and enhanced tax advantages for local and U.S. federal taxes. Capital-intensive industries, such as petrochemicals, pharmaceuticals, and to some extent electronics, came to dominate the dynamic sector of the Puerto Rican economy.

These changes in the development strategy, responding to a redefinition of the role of Puerto Rico in the international division on labor, had an uneven effect on women's employment relative to men's. Although women continued throughout the process of development to work on the assembly lines of manufacturing industries, in the long run their participation in this sector diminished, relative to their participation in other sectors of the economy, as men became the preferred labor force for the higher-paying jobs in the capital-intensive industries.

Additionally, the movement of female employment toward the public-administration and trade sectors shows a tendency to the "tertiarization" of women's employment. These changes in the sectoral distribution of women's employment clearly suggest a process of restructuring in the labor market that implies a redefinition in the sexual division of labor.

Occupational Distribution of Women's Employment

In order to look at the more specific aspects of the changes in female employment under Operation Bootstrap, I analyzed U.S. Bureau of Census data on occupational categories for the years 1940, 1950, 1960, 1970, and 1980. Although there are limitations on the comparability of this data, it allows us to make some inferences regarding the changes in the occupational structure of female employment.[21]

Tables 5 and 6 summarize the general tendencies in the changes of women's employment by major occupational category. Table 5 shows that in the census years between 1940 and 1970, female employment grew in the occupational categories of clerical and kindred workers, professionals, service workers, and sales workers, while it significantly declined in the categories of operatives, private households, farm managers, laborers, and farm laborers. Female operatives have substantially declined, yet this category maintains the highest percentage of female employment. In the managers and administrators category, however, female employment fluctuated between 2 and 4 percent. This table suggests that employment shifted from occupations as operatives in manufacturing activities and domestic work to clerical and administrative occupations.

Even though the comparability between tables 5 and 6 is limited because of changes in the classification system used by the census, the latter reveals a similar tendency in the growth and decline of certain occupations. Table 6 shows that female employment in 1980 grew in the categories of administrative support and clerical, professional specialty, service occupations, and sales occupations. The categories where female employment has clearly declined are private households, operatives, farming, forestry and fishing, handlers and equipment cleaners, helpers, and

TABLE 5
Distribution of Women's Employment by Major Occupation, 1940-1970

Occupation	1940	1950	1960	1970
Professionals	6.0	9.8	15.1	17.4
Managers and administrators	1.6	2.6	4.1	3.3
Salesworkers	2.1	2.8	4.6	5.0
Clerical and kindred workers	4.1	9.5	16.4	21.7
Operatives[a]	50.0	39.3	28.0	23.4
Service workers[b]	3.4	8.2	11.8	12.0
Private households	27.5	22.4	13.1	4.5
Craftsmen and kindred workers	0.2	0.4	1.6	2.8
Laborers[c]	2.3	0.6	0.7	1.0
Farm laborers	2.3	2.3	1.3	0.4
Farm managers	2.4	0.6	0.3	0.3

Source: U.S. Department of Commerce, Bureau of the Census (1940-1970).
[a] Except transportation.
[b] Except private households.
[c] Except farm.

laborers.[22] The category of executive administrative and managerial female occupations represents only 6 percent of total female employment. As can be observed, the new occupational categories, such as transportation and material moving, protective services and technicians, and related support occupations, demonstrate that female representation in such categories is still quite low.

A more detailed analysis of female employment by occupation revealed that within the category of professional occupations, female employment grew considerably.[23] Yet when a distinction is made between traditional and nontraditional occupations, the majority of professional women remained in areas of traditional female activity. Despite the fact that the percentage of women employed as teachers declined, more than half of the professional women continued to be teachers. Similarly, the percentage of women employed as registered nurses declined, but this occupation remained second in importance among professional women. The occupation of social and welfare worker grew significantly and became the third most important female occupation during this period. The occupation of librarian was relatively significant; in terms of overall importance, it ranked sixth. The growth of certain professions, such as social and welfare workers and librarians, may be related to the expansion of U.S. federal expenditures on welfare and educational programs in Puerto Rico.[24] The implementation of welfare programs by the government requires the utilization of social and welfare workers to assess the eligibility requirements of potential recipients. Likewise private universities have benefited the most from the federal educational grants for the expansion of their facilities and libraries.

TABLE 6
Distribution of Women's Employment by Major Occupational Category, 1980

Categories	%
Professional specialty	18.7
Executive, administrative, and managerial	6.0
Technicians and related support	2.4
Sales occupation	7.6
Administrative support and clerical occupations	26.9
Private households	1.4
Protective services	0.3
Service occupations[a]	14.4
Farming, forestry, and fishing	0.3
Precision production craft and repair	3.1
Machine operators, assemblers, and inspectors	16.8
Transportation and material moving	0.3
Handlers and equipments cleaners[b]	1.7

Source: U.S. Department of Commerce, Bureau of the Census (1980).
[a] Except protective and household workers.
[b] Includes helpers and laborers.

Among the nontraditional professions, the occupation which has grown the most is that of accountant, ranking fourth in overall importance. In professions such as lawyer, pharmacist, and physician, female participation has also increased, but at a very slow rate. Women in these occupational categories represent only 5 percent of the total female professional work force. Engineering professions continue to be dominated by men. Women in those professions represent less than 1 percent of the total female professionals. Even though the participation of women in nontraditional professions has improved somewhat, the professions which are socially considered highly prestigious—and are usually the most materially rewarding—continue to be overwhelmingly controlled and occupied by men.

Overall, after three decades of industrial development, about three-fourths of the women employed as professionals still held traditional female-associated occupations. In relative terms, however, women made limited progress in the area of nontraditional professions, especially as accountants. Other important areas of growth in female professional occupations were in the categories of college and university professors and writers, artists, and entertainers. In 1980, 2,487 women were employed as college and university professors, representing 4.6 percent of all professional women employed. In the category of writers, artists, and entertainers, there were 1,604 women employed in 1980, which accounted for 3 percent of all professional women employed.

Within the managerial and administrative occupations, there was a significant growth in female occupations related to public administration between 1940 and 1970. However, between 1970 and 1980, women entered this sector at a slower rate. Women entered more rapidly into other occupations such as bank managers and officials, insurance, finance, real estate, and personnel managers. Even though there was a substantial increase in the participation of women in bank management occupations, it is worth noting that of the 1,154 women classified in this category, 680 (59%) were financial officers, and the rest, 474 (41%), were actually managers. Employment of women as managers in the areas of finance, real estate, and insurance has grown at a slower rate than in the area of banking. Nonetheless, a limited improvement in the quality of the occupations of women in these areas can be observed. The breakthrough in female employment as managers in banks, insurance, finance, and real estate firms between 1970 and 1980 may be attributed to the unprecedented expansion of banking and financial services in Puerto Rico during those years.[25] This clearly indicates that women who already had the educational qualifications to work in these areas took advantage of the new employment opportunities which opened up at that particular time. In 1980 there were also a considerable number of women employed as personnel managers. In terms of importance, this occupation ranked second to all other occupations within this category.

While some female occupations grew considerably, others declined dramatically over time. Female employment in retail trade as salaried and self-employed workers, and as managers in the areas of manufacturing, construction, transportation, communications, and utilities, continuously decreased during the period studied. This seems to suggest that in the retail trade, women have increasingly been losing ground to men, indicating that retail trade in Puerto Rico is still fundamentally a male "business."

Another important area of growth in women's employment is that of clerical and kindred workers. Secretaries, typists, and cashiers remained the most important clerical occupations for women. The absolute number of secretaries and typists increased dramatically, and in relative terms these remained about 50 percent of the female clerical workers throughout the period. The expansion of government as well as corporate bureaucracies certainly stimulated the demand for secretarial services. The expansion of trade, particularly the proliferation of commercial establishments such as shopping malls, department stores, etc., may account for the significant growth in the cashiers category. This tendency clearly indicates that the occupations of secretaries and cashiers continued to be considered women's jobs.

Although showing some fluctuations, the occupations of bookkeeper and office machine operator remained relatively important sources of employment for women in the clerical sector. To these sources of employment we can also add receptionists and file clerks. The importance of these categories as sources of employment in this sector serves only to underscore the continued importance of secretarial-associated occupations for women. Finally, it is worth noting that the area of telephone operators has constantly declined in relative terms. This decline may suggest that female employment in this area became less important as new technology was introduced in communications. The installation of electronic switchboards and the use of computers and telecommunications systems may contribute to displace female workers who otherwise would have been employed as telephone operators.[26]

Another relatively important source of women's employment was in sales-related work. The percentage of salespersons and sales clerks in retail trade remained around the 80 percent mark during the period 1940-1970. Between 1970 and 1980, however, it dropped to 72 percent. Despite this late decline, it is reasonable to assert that women employed in these occupations remained basically "salesgirls." Yet the changes reflected between 1970 and 1980 suggest that women began to make inroads into the upper echelons of the sales occupations (e.g., sales representatives).

Among the service occupations, female employment was concentrated mainly in the categories of cooks, janitors, practical nurses, waitresses, and hairdressers and cosmetologists. Of these occupations, the one that saw the most growth throughout this period was that of janitor. However, cooking jobs remained the most important source of employment among service workers. Despite the decline in the number of cooks between 1960 and 1970, this occupation employed the largest number of women, 22 percent of the total service workers. The percentage of practical nurses declined between 1940 and 1970, but it dramatically increased during the years 1970 to 1980. Contrary to this, the percentage of hairdressers and cosmetologists, which had increased constantly between 1940 and 1970, dropped in 1980. The fluctuation in these types of service occupations responded to the changing needs of the commercial activities and health services in Puerto Rico during the decades of the 1960s and 1970s. The flourishing of fast-food services may have contributed to the relative decline in the demand for cooks. Likewise, big chains of beauty-care establishments may have replaced the home-based beauty parlors so popular in the 1960s, while practical nurses found new employment opportunities as nursing aides in hospitals and nursing homes.

Overall, the fact that the percentage of women employed in these occupations combined fluctuated between 60 and 70 percent throughout this period is important. Women's service occupations were very similar to activities they performed at home. In this sense, the economic role played by women in service occupations was still an extension of their traditional roles.

Female employment in manufacturing activities as operatives lost importance throughout this period. Between 1940 and 1960, women were employed in large numbers as dressmakers and seamstresses, tobacco manufacturers, and laundry operatives, and in apparel and textile production. Between 1960 and 1980, however, these occupations (with the exception of apparel and textile production) declined dramatically, while female employment as operatives began to grow in the areas of electrical machinery, chemical products, assemblers, checkers, examiners and inspectors, and packers and wrappers. Female employment as operatives in apparel and textile production fluctuated constantly throughout the period. Apparel and textile production remained the major source of female employment in manufacturing activities. In 1980, female employment in electrical machinery, equipment, and supplies ranked second in terms of relative importance to apparel and textile production. Employment in the chemical industry grew substantially as well. Yet the growth of employment in these industries did not generate large numbers of jobs to compensate for those lost in the apparel and other declining industries.

Overall, the analysis of female employment by occupation suggests the following:

1. There has been a restructuring in the economic role played by women in Puerto Rican society. Where women were once used largely as cheap labor in the apparel industry, they are now employed primarily in clerical occupations.

2. There has been limited improvement in the quality of female occupations, as reflected by the increased share of women in professional occupations and in other office jobs whose conditions and wages are, as a rule, better than those of workers in the apparel industry.

3. Nonetheless, the bulk of female employment remained in traditional occupations such as teachers, nurses, secretaries, and sales. Improvements in nontraditional jobs such as lawyers, physicians, engineers, and, to a lesser degree, bank managers and accountants, have been rather slow, if we take into account that Operation Bootstrap has been in effect for almost four decades.

4. The observed changes in the occupational structure of female employment indicate the emergence of new patterns of job segregation. Gender segregation still appears to underlie the structure of occupational hierarchies in Puerto Rico.

Summary and Conclusions

This study suggests that in the long run there was limited improvement in the employment situation of women, within the larger context of negligible employment growth for the whole population. Between 1950 and 1982, women seemed to have a slight advantage over men in terms of labor-force participation. Their labor-force participation was low but stable, while that of men showed continuous decline. In terms of employment, women also seem to have had a relative advantage over men, as their average rate of employment grew faster than did men's.

The analysis of time-series data supports the assumption that changes in the patterns of female employment were a function of the types of industrial development policies implemented by the government and of the changes in the stages of economic development that Puerto Rico experienced. The evidence demonstrated that during the early stage of industrial development, characterized by the establishment of light industries, a significant percentage of women were employed in the manufacturing and service sectors of the economy. Female employment in agriculture, trade, and public administration was relatively low. Conversely, during the second stage, characterized by the establishment of heavy industries, female employment grew significantly in the trade and public-administration sectors. Female employment in manufacturing and services showed a diminishing trend in comparison with the previous stage. In agriculture, it remained relatively insignificant throughout this period also.

Changes in the industrial development policy also affected the occupational profile of women in Puerto Rican society. In the first stage of industrial development, women were employed in manufacturing activities, especially as operatives in the apparel and textile industries. As industrial development progressed, the operative category lost importance and female employment grew significantly in the clerical and sales occupations, in traditional professions such as nurses, and social workers, and to a much lesser extent in nontraditional areas such as accountants, lawyers, physicians, etc. The increased share of female employment in professional occupations indicates that the occupational situation of women improved slightly. However, a significant part of this improvement occurred in occupations which can be considered an extension of women's household activities.

Overall, the industrial development policy implemented in Puerto Rico since 1947 has slowly contributed to the gradual improvement in the employment situation of women. It has also created, to a limited extent, the conditions for the upgrading of women's work. Yet after four decades of Operation Bootstrap, this has not been fully achieved. Job segregation and high levels of unemployment among women still exist. Only a minority of women have experienced significant positive changes in status and material benefits.

As for whether women have been significantly integrated or marginalized by the development process, the evidence is inconclusive. Although women have increased their labor-force participation in comparison to men, their absolute levels of participation have remained static and their levels of unemployment have increased. It may well be that, as some have argued, Operation Bootstrap has marginalized a substantial proportion of the working population, including women. Moreover, as dependency theory argued, the tendency during the second stage was toward a "tertiarization" of female labor.

In any case, this analysis suggests neither clear-cut marginalization nor full integration and gender equality. What we are just beginning to observe is the emergence of new forms of gender division of labor that deepen women's occupational segregation as large-scale production penetrates all sectors of the economy.

The findings of this study raise some doubts about the adequacy of the integration and marginalization models for the study of gender and work in economic development. The key theoretical issue is not whether women are marginalized from or integrated into the market-oriented productive process, but rather the nature of their incorporation into the labor market in societies where the subsistence sector is disappearing rapidly. The evidence that we presented could be construed as an argument in favor of the integrationist view, as women seem to have entered the labor market in greater numbers than men. However, the key feature of our findings is not this but the persistence of gender segregation in different stages of the export-led industrialization strategy. The new patterns of integration into the international division of labor brought about by the internationalization of production redefined the division of labor by gender, to accommodate the profit-making and labor needs of the transnational corporations that lead the process of industrialization. This generated new patterns of gender segregation across economic sectors and occupations. Gender segregation thus becomes the underlying principle in the organization of production and in the structuring of employment.

The marginalization thesis does not provide an explanation for this contradictory pattern of limited integration and sectoral and occupational segregation. The emphasis placed on technology as the key variable for explaining the marginalization of women from production has tended to overlook the importance of other factors (e.g., politics, ideology, family) that might affect the demand for female labor in capitalist societies. Some women may indeed be marginalized from high-paying manufacturing jobs, while many others are recruited in other sectors of the economy under conditions of social and economic subordination grounded in new patterns of occupational segregation.

The integration thesis gives more attention to occupational shifts in employment as industrialization proceeds, but fails as well to provide a satisfactory account of the continued gender segregation in employment. During the period studied, women were not randomly distributed across the labor market. Gender segregation appeared to be interfering with otherwise competitive market forces. This suggests that the labor market is less receptive to the improvements in "human capital stock" that women were presumed to acquire in the course of modernization than the integration thesis proponents assume. Clearly, the restructuring of the labor force and employment by gender in developing societies need to be studied from a different theoretical framework. Feminist analyses of occupational segregation in relation to the processes of gender construction within the labor process itself constitute a provocative alternative to the study of women's work in newly industrialized societies.

NOTES

This chapter is an abridged version of an article previously published in *World Development* 18, no. 2 (1990).

1. Elliot (1977) and Jaquette (1982). For an in-depth discussion of these hypotheses, see Tiano (1986).

2. See Rosen (1982), Goode (1971), Patai (1967), and Bernard (1971) for examples of studies that have used modernization theory.

3. Boserup (1970). Boserup's theoretical underpinnings fall within the framework of neoclassical economics that in general view modernization as a beneficial process. To Boserup, however, the obstacles to women's integration to development lie in cultural values that prevent them from acquiring the necessary human capital to achieve employment parity with men. This argument is developed by Benería and Sen (1986). For an analysis that uses the marginalization/dependency perspective see Bossen (1975), Saffioti (1978), Chaney and Schmink (1976), Schmink (1977), and Sautu (1980). Other feminists have derived their interpretation of women's marginal role in production from Marxist theories of capital accumulation and world system analysis. See Deere and León de Leal (1982), Deere, Humphries, and León de Leal (1982), and Ward (1982).

4. See, for example, Stolz Chinchilla (1977), Vasques de Miranda (1977), and Wong (1986).

5. Elson and Pearson (1981); Nash and Fernández-Kelly (1983); Safa (1986a).

6. The Puerto Rican model of industrialization was the precursor of the foreign investment-based export-processing manufacturing model of development (later known as *maquiladora*) that has been so widely adopted in the Third World since the 1960s (Pantojas-García [1990], p. 4).

7. This law imposed a quota on sugar imports to the United States. It reduced severely Puerto Rico's export of sugar to the U.S., imposing strict limitations on the growth of the island's sugar industry, which had achieved levels of production far higher than the quota. Cf. Smith and Requa (1939).

8. For a detailed analysis of these processes, see Dietz (1986) and Pantojas-García (1990).

9. These are discussed by, among others, Pantojas-García (1990), p. 72.

10. A good example of the Puerto Rican government's desire and intention to attract these kinds of industries is the study published by the Office of the Government of Puerto Rico in Washington for diffusion among potential investors showing the advantages of Puerto Rico as a location for U.S. textile industries. See O'Connor (1948).

11. For an assessment of the effects that Proclamation 3663 had on the development of the petrochemical industry, see Bohi and Russell (1978), pp. 66-71, 168-74 and Bellah (1970).

12. For a more detailed discussion of these stages, see Dietz (1986), pp. 247-55.

13. Emigration to the U.S. totaled 146,000 in the 1940s, 457,000 in the 1950s, 222,000 in the 1960s, and 29,000 in the 1970s. See Wagenheim (1983) and History Task Force (1979).

14. See Madeiras and Singer (1975), Vasques de Miranda (1977), and Safa (1977).

15. Management preferences for women's labor in a situation of surplus labor are complex; cf. Pearson (1986). The preferences of the garment industry for hiring women in Puerto Rico are discussed in Safa (1986b).

16. This point is made by Robert N. Bellah (1970) in his discussion on the benefits of the oil import program in Puerto Rico.

17 Picó de Hernández (1975).

18. See Rivera (1977), p. 15 for a description of the participation of Puerto Rican women in domestic service during 1940 and 1950.

19. For a full discussion and analysis of the hypotheses and empirical test, see Acevedo (1990).

20. Reynolds and Gregory (1965), p. 27, and Holbik and Swan (1975), p. 45.

21. It should be noted here that the data provided in the 1980 census are not comparable to those of the previous years. For this census all major occupational categories were redefined in order to reflect the "birth of new occupations and the death of others." However, by utilizing the detailed occupational data for 1980, I was able to calculate employment for some specific occupations. For a detailed discussion of the factors that limited the comparability of the 1980 census data from one census to another, see U.S. Department of Commerce, Bureau of the Census (1980), B-15.

22. In 1981, there were 5,000 women engaged in private household occupations working as domestic servants. According to Antonio Soto Rosario, chief of the Employment Statistics Division of Puerto Rico's Department of Labor, the evidence suggests that most of the women employed as domestic servants were not Puerto Rican but immigrants from the Dominican Republic who came to the island in search of better employment opportunities. See Soto-Rosario (1981).

23. The data upon which this analysis is based are presented fully in tables 9-14 in Acevedo (1990).

24. For a discussion of the federal government's expenditures in Puerto Rico in the areas of welfare and education, see U.S. Department of Commerce (1979).

25. On the expansion of banking services in Puerto Rico, see Pantojas-García (1990), chap. 5.

26. For a discussion of the introduction of new technology as a key element in the restructuring of the contemporary office and its effect on women, see West (1982) and Webster (1986).

REFERENCES

Acevedo, Luz del Alba. "Industrialization and Employment: Changes in the Patterns of Women's Work in Puerto Rico." *World Development* 18, no. 2 (1990): 231-55.

Arizpe, Lourdes, and Aranda, Josefina. "Women Workers in the Strawberry Agribusiness in Mexico." In Eleanor Leacock and Helen I. Safa (eds.), *Women's Work* (South Hadley, Mass.: Bergin & Garvey Publishers, 1986), pp. 174-93.

Bellah, Robert N. "The Impact of the Oil Import Program on the Economy of Puerto Rico." M.S.B.A. dissertation, George Washington University, 1970.

Benería, Lourdes, and Sen, Gita. "Accumulation, Reproduction, and Women's Role in Economic Development: Boserup Revisited." In Eleanor Leacock and Helen I. Safa (eds.), *Women's Work* (South Hadley, Mass.: Bergin & Garvey Publishers, 1986), pp. 141-57.

Bernard, Jesse. "The Status of Women in Modern Patterns of Culture." In C. Epstein and W. Goode (eds.), *The Other Half: Roads to Women's Equality.* Englewood Cliffs, N.J.: Prentice-Hall, 1971.

Bohi, Douglas, and Russell, Milton. *Limiting Oil Imports: An Economic History and Analysis.* Baltimore: Johns Hopkins University Press, 1978.

Boserup, Ester. *Woman's Role in Economic Development.* New York: St. Martin's Press, 1970.

Bossen, Laurel. "Women in Modernizing Societies." *American Ethnologist* 2, no. 4 (1975): 587-601.

Chaney, E. M., and Schmink, M. "Women and Modernization: Access to Tools." In June Nash and Helen Safa (eds.), *Sex and Class in Latin America* (New York: Praeger, 1976), pp. 160-82.

Deere, Carmen Diana; Humphries, Jane; and León de Leal, Magdalena. "Class and Historical Analysis for the Study of Women and Economic Change." In Richard Anker, Mayra Buvinic, and Nadia Youssef (eds.), *Women's Roles in Population Trends in the Third World* (London: Croom Helm, 1982), pp. 87-114.

Deere, Carmen Diana, and León de Leal, Magdalena. "Peasant Production, Proletarianization, and the Sexual Division of Labor in the Andes." In Lourdes Benería (ed.), *Women and Development: The Sexual Division of Labor in Rural Societies* (New York: Praeger, 1982), pp. 65-93.

Dietz, James. *Economic History of Puerto Rico.* Princeton, N.J.: Princeton University Press, 1986, chap. 4.

Elliot, Carolyn. "Theories of Development: An Assessment." In Wellesley Editorial Committee (eds.), *Women and National Development: The Complexities of Change* (Chicago: University of Chicago Press, 1977), pp. 1-8.

Elson, Diane, and Pearson, Ruth. "The Subordination of Women and the Internationalization of Factory Production." In Kate Young, Carol Wolkowitz, and Rosalyn McCullagh (eds.), *Of Marriage and the Market* (London: CSE Books, 1981), pp. 144-66.

Escobar, Manuel. *The 936 Market: An Introduction.* San Juan: n.p., 1982.

Goode, William. "Civil and Social Rights of Women." In C. Epstein and W. Goode (eds.), *The Other Half: Roads to Women's Equality* (Englewood Cliffs, N.J.: Prentice-Hall, 1971), pp. 21-29.

History Task Force, Centro de Estudios Puertorriqueños. *Labor Migration under Capitalism: The Puerto Rican Experience.* New York: Monthly Review Press, 1979.

Holbik, Karel, and Swan, Philip L. *Industrialization and Employment in Puerto Rico, 1950-1972.* Austin: Bureau of Business Research, University of Texas at Austin, 1975.

Jaquette, Jane. "Women and Modernization Theory: A Decade of Feminist Criticism." *World Politics* 34 (1982): 265-84.

Madeira, Felicia R., and Singer, Paul. "Structure of Female Employment and Work in Brazil, 1920-1970." *Journal of Interamerican Studies and World Affairs* 17 (1975): 490-95.

Mier, Richard. *Developmental Planning.* New York: McGraw Hill, 1965.

Nash, June, and Fernández-Kelly, María Patricia. *Women, Men and the International Division of Labor.* New York: University of New York Press, 1983.

O'Connor, Donald J. *Puerto Rico's Potential as a Site for Textile, Apparel and Other Industries.* Washington, D.C.: Office of Puerto Rico, 1948.

Pantojas-García, Emilio. *Development Strategies as Ideology: Puerto Rico's Export-led Industrialization Experience.* Boulder/Río Piedras: Lynne Rienner Publishers/University of Puerto Rico, 1990.

Patai, R. E. *Women in the Modern World.* New York: The Free Press, 1967.

Pearson, Ruth. "Female Workers in the First and Third Worlds: the 'Greening' of Women's Labour." In Kate Purcell, Stephen Wood, Alan Waton, and Sheila Allen (eds.), *The Changing Experience of Employment* (London: Macmillan, 1986), pp. 114-31.

Picó de Hernández, Isabel. "Estudio sobre el empleo de la mujer en Puerto Rico." *Revista de Ciencias Sociales* 17, no. 2 (1975): 139-66.

Puerto Rico. *Leyes de Puerto Rico Anotadas.* San Juan: Government of Puerto Rico, 1948, 1954, 1963, and 1978.

Puerto Rico, Departmento de Trabajo. *Serie estadística sobre el empleo.* Puerto Rico: n.p., 1983.

Reynolds, Lloyd G., and Gregory, Peter. *Wages, Productivity, and Industrialization in Puerto Rico.* Homewood, Ill., 1965.

Rivera, Marcia. "Condiciones del empleo doméstico asalariado en Puerto Rico." San Juan: Comisión para el mejoramiento de la mujer, 1977.

_____. "The Development of Capitalism in Puerto Rico and the Incorporation of Women into the Labor Force." In Edna Acosta Belén (ed.), *The Puerto Rican Women* (New York: Praeger, 1979), pp. 8-24.

Rosen, Bernard C. *The Industrial Connection: Achievement and the Family in Developing Societies.* New York: Aldine Publishing, 1982.

Safa, Helen I. "Runaway Shops and Female Employment: The Search for Cheap Labor." In Eleanor Leacock and Helen I. Safa (eds.), *Women's Work* (South Hadley, Mass.: Bergin & Garvey Publishers, 1986a), pp. 58-71.

_____. "Female Employment in the Puerto Rican Working Class." In June Nash and Helen I. Safa (eds.), *Women and Change in Latin America* (South Hadley, Mass.: Bergin & Garvey Publishers, 1986b), pp. 84-105.

_____. "The Changing Class Composition of the Female Labor Force." *Latin American Perspectives* 4 (1977): 126-36.

Saffioti, Heleieth. *Women in Class Society.* New York: Monthly Review Press, 1978.

Sautu, Ruth. "The Female Labor Force in Argentina, Bolivia and Paraguay." *Latin American Research Review* 15, no. 2 (1980): 143-61.

Schmink, Mariane. "Dependent Development and the Division of Labor by Sex: Venezuela." *Latin American Perspectives* 4, nos. 1/2 (1977): 153-79.

Smith, D., and Requa, W. *Puerto Rican Sugar Facts.* Washington: Asociación de Productores de Azúcar de Puerto Rico, 1939.

Soto-Rosario, Antonio. "Los trabajadores en servicio domésticos cuarenta años despues." *Revista del Trabajo* 9, no. 34-35 (1981).

Stolz-Chinchilla, Norma. "Industrialization, Monopoly Capitalism, and Women's Work in Guatemala." *Signs* 3, no. 1 (1977): 38-56.

Tiano, Susan. "Women and Industrial Development in Latin America." *Latin American Research Review* 21, no. 3 (1986): 157-70.

United States Department of Commerce. *Economic Study of Puerto Rico.* Washington, D.C.: Government Prints, 1979, vol. II, chap. X.

United States Department of Commerce, Bureau of the Census. *Census of Population-Puerto Rico.* Washington, D.C.: Bureau of the Census, 1950, 1960, 1970, and 1980.

Vasques de Miranda, Glaura. "Women's Labor Force Participation in a Developing Society: The Case of Brazil." *Signs* 3, no. 1 (1977): 261-74.

Wagenheim, Kal. *Puerto Ricans in the U.S.* New York: Minority Rights Group Inc., 1983.

Ward, Kathryn. "The Economic Status of Women in the World-System: A Hidden Crisis in Development." In Albert Bergesen (ed.), *Crises in the World System* (Beverly Hills: Sage Publications, 1982), pp. 117-39.

Webster, Juliet. "Word Processing and the Secretarial Labour Process." In Kate Purcell, Stephen Wood, Alan Waton, and Sheila Allen (eds.), *The Changing Experience of Employment* (London: Macmillan, 1986), pp. 114-31.

West, Jackie. "New Technology and Women's Office Work." In Jackie West (ed.), *Work, Women and the Labor Market* (London: Routledge & Kegan Paul, 1982), pp. 61-79.

Wong, Aline K. "Planned Development, Social Stratification, and the Sexual Division of Labor in Singapore." In Eleanor Leacock and Helen I. Safa (eds.), *Women's Work* (South Hadley, Mass.: Bergin & Garvey Publishers, 1986), pp. 207-23.

BIBLIOGRAPHICAL NOTE

The number of publications in English on the subject of women, work, and development in Puerto Rico is fairly limited. Most of these publications are found in the form of chapters in collections on Puerto Rico or on women in Latin America, or in specialized journals. Two of the pioneer works on this topic— Marcia Rivera, "The Development of Capitalism in Puerto Rico and the Incorporation of Women into the Labor Force," and Isabel Picó, "The History of Women's

Struggle for Equality in Puerto Rico"—were included in the first edition of Edna Acosta Belén, *The Puerto Rican Women* (New York: Praeger, 1979). This volume included a chapter by Edna Acosta-Belén and Barbara Sjostrom, "The Educational and Professional Status of Puerto Rican Women," which was also a first. The second edition of this book, published in 1986, added chapters by Helen I. Safa, "Female Employment and the Social Reproduction of the Puerto Rican Working Class," and Blanca Silvestrini, "Women as Workers: The Experience of the Puerto Rican Woman in the 1930s." This article appeared first in Ruby Rohrlich-Leavitt (ed.), *Women Cross-Culturally: Change and Challenge* (The Hague and Paris: Mouton Publishers, 1975). The collection edited by June Nash and Helen I. Safa, *Sex and Class in Latin America* (South Hadley, Mass.: Bergin & Garvey, 1980), included Safa's essay "Class Consciousness among Working Class Women in Latin America: Puerto Rico," and reprinted Isabel Picó's "The History of Women's Struggle for Equality in Puerto Rico." Other work by Safa, also a pioneer in the study of women's work in Puerto Rico, includes "Female Employment in the Puerto Rican Working Class," in June Nash and Helen I. Safa (eds.), *Women and Change in Latin America* (South Hadley, Mass.: Bergin & Garvey, 1986), and "Women and Industrialization in the Caribbean," in Sharon Stichter and Jane Parpart (eds.), *Women, Employment and the Family* (London: Macmillan, 1990).

Of particular interest for the topic of women, work, and development are the articles of Palmira N. Ríos, "Export-Oriented Industrialization and the Demand for Female Labor: Puerto Rican Women in the Manufacturing Sector, 1952-1980," *Gender and Society* 4, no. 3 (September 1990), and Luz del Alba Acevedo, "Industrialization and Employment: Changes in the Patterns of Women's Work in Puerto Rico," *World Development* 18, no.2 (February 1990). The first article deals specifically with women in the manufacturing sector, while the latter provides a wider analysis of changes in the patterns of employment in the various economic sectors and occupations. Other articles of related importance are Carlos E. Santiago, "Male-Female Labor Force Participation and Rapid Industrialization," *Journal of Economic Development* 6, no. 2 (December 1981); María del Carmen Baerga, "Wages, Consumption, and Survival: Working Class Households in Puerto Rico in the 1930s," in Joan Smith et al., *Household and the World Economy* (Beverly Hills, Calif.: Sage, 1984); and by the same author, "Women's Labor and the Domestic Unit: Industrial Homework in Puerto Rico During the 1930s," *Centro* 2, no. 7 (Winter 1989-90); Hariet B. Presser and Sunita Kishor, "Economic Development and Occupational Sex Segregation in Puerto Rico, 1950-80," *Population and Development Review* 17, no. 1 (March 1991). A comprehensive annotated bibliography on the general subject of Puerto Rican women listing titles in English and Spanish is Edna Acosta-Belén and Christine E. Bose, *Albany PR-Womenet Database: An Interdisciplinary Annotated Bibliography on Puerto Rican Women* (Center for Latin America and the Caribbean and the Institute for Research on Women, State University of New York at Albany, 1991).

WOMEN, LABOR, AND THE LEFT
ARGENTINA AND CHILE, 1890-1925

Asunción Lavrin

The manner in which women have become "visible" throughout history is one of the most important subjects of concern for the contemporary historian. Visibility leads to a recognition of presence, and once women become "a presence" we can discuss the engagement of both sexes in the activities of gender politics. Gender politics comprise relationships of power and authority between individuals, and as such they are subject to the influence of class, ethnicity, culture, political ideologies and, of course, that of the time period. Gender politics may be studied in many arenas, such as the home, the work place, or national politics. In this paper, I propose to address the interrelation of gender and political ideology by examining the attitudes of the Left (anarchists and socialists) towards women as they began to be an important element in the work force of two South American countries.

In the second half of the 19th century, women became visible by becoming members of the paid labor force as industrial workers, teachers, and a small force of professional and clerical employees. This was a universal phenomenon in many European and North and South American urban centers. Once women appeared in larger numbers in the factories, in the schools, and in the offices, their presence posed questions of a personal, familial, and social character. Would the work of women devalue the wages of men? Would work change women's role at home and family stability be threatened? Was work itself beneficial for women, for the family, and for society? Would women become companions in the struggle that some men envisioned between those who worked and those who owned the means of production? These were, indeed, serious and sometimes deeply troubling questions for men and women at the turn of the 19th century.

The scenario I have chosen for the analysis of these questions is that of two leading nations of the Spanish American southern cone: Argentina

© 1989 JOURNAL OF WOMEN'S HISTORY, VOL. 1 NO. 2 (FALL)

and Chile. The ideology understood here as "the Left" was that of the two main labor groups, socialists and anarchists, and the period, the years between 1895 and 1925. These were years of intense labor agitation in these two countries during which large numbers of women were incorporated into the paid labor market.

In broad terms, Argentina and Chile could be described as export economies. Argentina's exports were largely agricultural (wheat and beef) and expanded nine times between 1880 and 1913. These exports supported the growth of the coastal and river port cities, especially that of Buenos Aires, the federal capital. The labor demanded for this expansion came largely from abroad; immigrants from Spain and Italy flooded the country between 1880 and 1910. Agricultural employment in the pampas, the grain and cattle-producing prairie of central Argentina, was often temporary, and a significant number of the immigrants who stayed in the nation settled in the cities. In 1914, three-quarters of the adult population in Buenos Aires was foreign-born. Forty-six percent of the nation's total population lived in the federal capital and the province of Buenos Aires.

Chile's exports were mineral. Rich nitrate fields in the desertic north had been acquired after a war with neighboring Bolivia and Peru, and they allowed a significant expansion of the economy between 1880 and 1930. Unlike Argentina, Chile did not receive vast numbers of immigrants. Its labor force was largely native-born. Like Argentina, Chile experienced a significant urban expansion between 1880 and 1930, reflected in the fact that by the end of the 1920s almost 50 percent of the population was urban in character.[1]

Despite the differences in the nature of their exports and the composition of their labor force, both countries had some important features in common: neither of them became what we may call "heavily industrialized nations" during this period, despite the growth of their economies; the labor force in the industrial sector was predominantly male; female labor was largely urban and employed in the textile and garment industries, food-processing plants, and in the service sector.

As labor groups began to organize in the mines, ports, and among urban artisans and workers in the late 1880s, European anarchism and socialism found a fertile ground in both countries. Argentina, facing the Atlantic, led the way in the reception of ideas and the organization of workers' groups as its immigrant labor force began to swell in the late 1870s. Ideological followers of Bakunin and Marx launched the first attempts to organize urban workers and published several ephemereal newspapers that broke the ideological ground for the eventual formation of the first anarchist and socialist groups in the 1880s. German immigrants had an important role in the organization of the first workers' associations (Vorwarts) and a marxist socialist newspaper, El Obrero (The Worker), founded by a German immigrant, Herman Avé-Lallemant in 1880, began the task of spreading the tenets of marxist socialism in Buenos Aires.[2]

Anarchism was also introduced in 1880 with the publication of *La Anarquía* and *El Perseguido* (The Persecuted). Political exiles from Germany, France, Italy, and Spain, among them the well-known Enrico Malatesta, began arriving in the mid-1880s, building up the connections between socialism, anarchism, anarcho-syndicalism, and Argentinian workers. Two Argentinian representatives participated in the Second International of 1889. In the mid-1890s, the foundation of a socialist workers' party and a socialist newspaper of marxist bent, *La Vanguardia*, further defined the workers' movement in Argentina. The fact that the majority of the urban labor force was itself foreign-born and literate helps explain the intensity of the activities of the labor movement.[3]

While the introduction of the ideologies of the Left in Chile was not the direct result of a foreign-born proletariat, there were enough European settlers, Uruguayan and Argentinean exiles, and Chilean workers returning from Argentina and the United States to transmit the universal message of justice and equity for the laboring classes proposed by socialism and by anarchism.[4] By the mid-1880s, news of the Knights of Labor and the German Social Democrat Party was reaching the incipient Chilean labor press. The foundation of the Democratic Party in 1887 helped to coalesce artisans, laborers, and a small nucleus of liberals under the banner of socialism. Although the heterogeneous character of its membership precludes its characterization as a socialist venue, socialism became the most important ideological influence in Chilean working circles, as corroborated by the organization of a Social Workers' Center and a Socialist Union in 1896. Anarchism captured the imagination of smaller groups of workers in the ports and mining centers of the nation but it never reached the degree of power and organization of its Argentinian counterpart. A Socialist Party founded in 1897 did not succeed in maintaining its clout, and it was soon challenged by a Socialist Labor Party. For the most part, the Chilean labor movement throughout these formative years lacked a strong nucleation force and remained fragmented in small cells of several shades of the ideological Left. The foundation of the Workers' Socialist Party (*Partido Socialista Obrero*) in 1912 heralded a greater internal organizational and ideological cohesion along the lines of marxist socialism. During these formative years, many working people in both nations grouped around mutualist and resistance societies. The resistance societies were more politically oriented than the mutualist societies, but both fostered labor class consciousness. The mutualist societies provided some services for their members, such as financial aid during times of illness. In sum, it may be stated that the inner struggles and ideological complexities of western socialism and anarchism found a fertile ground in the Argentinian and Chilean labor force. The most important ideological influences were those of Marx, Bakunin, Kropotkin, and August Bebel, but a host of French, Italian, German, and Spanish writers were translated or quoted in the labor press as beacons leading the way to a universal redemption of the working class.

Since I do not intend to trace here the development of the internal struggles of the labor movement itself, I will focus on how socialism and anarchism reacted to the increasing presence of women in the work place, how the male and female leaders of the workers' organizations defined the role of working women at home, in society, and within the labor movement, and how the Left interpreted the dialogue between genders among members of the working class.[5] Using the Left as a broad ideological umbrella, I will, however, make distinctions between anarchists and socialists whenever relevant.

Neither the Argentinean pampas or its docks, nor the Chilean nitrate fields were potential areas for the organization and indoctrination of female workers. Mining and cattle raising were predominantly male activities, and although women worked in certain agricultural crops such as grapes, labor organization and activism outside cities were definitely male domains. On the other hand, the urban work force in both countries had special niches for women. In the last quarter of the century, the textile and garment industries, the shoe industry, and the food processing industries, which in Argentina included females employed in the meat-packing plants, became the foci of female work. Women also began to work in department stores and as telephone operators and government employees in the second decade of the 20th century.[6]

Other forms of female labor remained at the margin of the labor force and labor mobilization: teachers, domestics, and women who worked at home in the putting-out system. These categories formed the bulk of female labor in the period under review. The very nature of their work precluded the inclusion of domestic laborers and teachers in unions or organized groups such as mutualist societies. This was both a question of class and social perception. Teachers were most often urban middle-class women who did not feel class solidarity with industrial workers. Domestics were so poor, isolated, and uneducated that few labor organizations ever considered including them in their agenda. Women associated with the garment industry who worked in the putting-out system resembled servants in their isolation and lack of network contact among themselves. Yet their connection with manufacturing plants built a link between them and labor leaders as well as governmental labor agencies. Although the meagerness of their earnings and their working conditions were bemoaned by labor leaders and social reformists, it was difficult to organize them. Only those needleworkers who labored in factories became objects and subjects of labor mobilization.

The incorporation of women into the labor market—paid labor, whether inside or outside the home—was relatively fast. The demand for services and work never stalled. The 1877 and 1895 Argentinean censuses provided only the most basic information on the categories of female employment. They disclosed a population of women employed mostly as domestics or rendering services as washerwomen and seamstresses. Rural workers were a declining category and were mostly women giving temporary help in the fruit crops. Factory workers were not clearly identified. The number of teachers in the nation was still small as compared with other categories. A 1909 occupational census of the city of Buenos Aires was more precise in its information. It disclosed that although the bulk of employed women were domestics, one-third (32.6 percent) of all people with a known occupation or profession were women. The female labor force had almost as many native Argentineans as foreign women, whereas among male workers foreigners were numerically much greater in number than natives.[7] Industrial female workers—51,629 strong—were 23.7 percent of that occupational category. The 1914 National Census—not a well designed occupational census—showed that although industrial work was predominantly masculine (82 percent of 113,038 industrial workers recorded) women were predominant in certain industries. In the key areas of Buenos Aires and its province, and the leading cities of Santa Fé, Córdoba, and Mendoza, industrial female workers were the backbone of the garment, textiles, and food-processing industries. The salaries paid to women were between one-third and one-half of those paid to men even though in some industries, such as the textile factories, there were twice as many women as men, and they performed most of the work.[8] Women working by the piece at home were 42 percent of the total of 32,855 people so employed. If we were to add the women working at home to the total employed by factories, they would amount to 19 percent of the industrial labor force.

Chilean female employment was similar to Argentinean employment in nature. The 1907 national census categorized seamstresses, washerwomen, embroiderers, and artesanal workers as "industrial," stretching somewhat the meaning of that word. Those thus classified were 92.9 percent of all women employed. Between 1912 and 1925, however, there was a significant change in the occupational profile. In 1916, a national occupational census established that women were 26.2 percent (13,345) of the 50,930 blue-collar workers. Nearly half of these workers (42 percent) were in the garment industry. Food processing, textiles and the shoe and tobacco industries followed in rank, comprising between 11 and 8 percent female workers in their categories.[9] By 1925, women were one-quarter of all workers categorized as "laborers" (blue-collar). The garment, textile, and food industries continued to employ most of the working women. These percentages remained constant throughout 1940.[10] The statistical data, if not perfect, are illuminating. Nearly one-quarter of all industrial workers were women, a fact which has not been given enough attention in labor or social histories of either country.

Female Work: A Blessing or a Curse?

One of the most troubling issues for male workers was how to deal with their female counterparts. The male leadership among the socialists and anarchists, despite intense ideological rivalry, shared mixed feelings about the expanding number of women in the labor force. The increasing momentum of labor organization in the 1890s left both anarchists and socialists little choice in the matter. When these two wings of the Left began to proselytize consistently among the workers of both countries in the mid-1890s, they had to devise some strategies to capture the attention of women workers. Strategically, it did not make sense to ignore their presence and potential contribution to the spread of their respective ideologies. During these few initial years, however, anarchists and socialists had no other tool for this task than the strength of their own theories. The initial discussions of women's work were, therefore, rather theoretical and propagandistic. Anarchists and socialists used newspapers and pamphlets to discuss the advisability of female work, women's place in the labor force and in the ranks of labor organizations, and the social and personal consequences of women's work. The male press, represented by several major newspapers, had the lion's share in this discussion, which was carried out mostly by men, but female writers were occasionally given space in the leading socialist and anarchist newspapers of both countries. Several women's newspapers flowered in the first years of labor organization in both countries, and, although their existence was ephemeral, they opened an invaluable window into the world of women workers.[11]

Argentinean anarcho-communists were the first to address female labor issues in the mid-1890s when several pamphlets directly translated from European materials began to circulate in the country. They discussed the main tenets of anarchism and did not reflect the situation of Argentinean women. Rather, they attempted to raise women's interest in the universal concepts of female emancipation.[12] The message was straightforward: the capitalist exploited the proletariat's work, and this situation had to be redressed through the concerted effort of those who believed in anarchism. Labor, stressed one of these early pamphlets, was not a sacred duty but an economic necessity. These first anarchist propagandists repudiated the notion of the "moral" benefits of labor for the laboring classes and applied it equally to women's work. These propaganda materials did not dwell on the inequalities of women's work or the length of their working days. They focused on women's personal and social emancipation.

The few articles addressed to women and published in one of the most important anarchist newspapers in Buenos Aires, *La Protesta Humana,* as well as the first female anarchist newspaper, *La Voz de la Mujer,* show a similar lack of concrete suggestions for Argentine female workers. This want of focus may have been due to the anarchists' ambiguous feelings in an urban setting in which female labor was still in a state of organizational fluidity. Not until the early 1900s, when socialists and anarchists began a fierce struggle for the control of unions and mutualist societies, did the anarchist message to female workers begin to be more pragmatic and more focused on the conditions of female labor in the country.

Between 1901 and 1902, women began to appear at anarchist meetings, and both in Buenos Aires and Rosario groups of "female libertarians" published broadsheets calling women workers to reflect on their condition and urging them to organize. The exploitation of female workers by capitalists and the economic profit they made on female labor remained important issues, and in 1904-05, years of significant labor unrest in the main Argentinean cities, *La Protesta* expanded its message to address the working conditions, hours of work, and the low wages of women. The nobility of female work was always extolled and contrasted with the capitalists' wicked intentions. A strong and persistent call for joining working women's groups answered the needs of intense recruitment efforts among urban workers of both sexes.[13]

In Argentina, the socialists also began to consider female workers' issues in the early years of the 20th century. The lengthiest and most important discussion of female work by a socialist appeared as a pamphlet in 1903; it was penned by a woman, Gabriela Lapèpierre de Coni, a writer and the wife of an eminent physician. As a member of the Socialist Party in Argentina, she had strong reservations about the advisability of women's work. She was especially concerned about the negative health effects that the adverse working conditions in most factories could have on women and, especially, on their reproductive ability.[14] Coni based her argument on women's physical weakness and their vulnerability to the strain caused by machinery work. Her assumptions were influenced by contemporary medical opinions on the fragility of the female body and the ill-effects of certain forms of stress on their reproductive systems, and she urged women to learn about the potential hazards of overwork. Given the lack of protective legislation in the work place, it was the female workers' duty to guard their own health, which to her, also involved that of future generations.

Coni's ideas were shared by the adult population in general and, more significantly, by working men and women in both Chile and Argentina. Women workers in Chile fully endorsed the need for protecting the female worker in their own independent publications.[15] The universal assumption of the physical frailty of women was a persuasive argument and supported the initial propaganda for the first labor demands on behalf of the "weaker" members of society: women and children. The prohibition of female and child work in certain hazardous jobs and the regulation of their working hours were the first items in labor's agenda for the female sex.

In these first years of the 20th century, labor leaders of all ideological persuasions perceived women's labor as "toil and sweat." Acknowledging that it could also be a form of personal liberation was an ideological stand that demanded time and practical evidence that not only familial but personal economic improvement was involved in women's work. Furthermore, female work had to prove capable of becoming a political issue to be acceptable as a tool for women's liberation from the capitalist system. This transformation began earlier in Argentina than in Chile as the Socialist Party began to campaign for the regulation of women's work and obtained a coup with the approval of a law establishing the blueprint for such restrictions in 1907.[16]

Legislation without effective enforcement was no consolation for some. In 1910, Argentinean socialist Juana María Beguino was still unsure that the new "economic freedom" of women was more important than the physical pressures put on them by unregulated labor and called for a return of married women to the home, "to lull with loving songs the sweet sleep of their children."[17] The theme of women's vulnerability under abusive working circumstances lay behind the organization of mutualist societies in Chile, where such organizations became the most important vehicle for labor organization, and where the organizers urged women to join to protect themselves from the abuses of the factory owners.[18]

Another important component in the discussion of the female labor market was whether or not it was fair for women to compete with men for jobs. Feelings were mixed on this issue, even among the women themselves. In 1907, one of the earliest Chilean female leaders, Esther Valdés de Díaz, a socialist needleworker and the editor of the weekly La Alborada, came to the conclusion that "women who work in factories pushed by the need of earning their daily bread, not only are not in their place, but, without realizing it, are competing with men, and in doing so, becoming victims of capitalism. When women replace men in the work place, they contribute to the devaluation of men's work."[19] This argument was not easy to uproot from labor circles and lingered into the 1920s despite a growing wave of opinion to the contrary. In 1922, the threat of female work was discussed in an Argentinean female anarchist newspaper, and the anonymous writer denounced the current praise of working women by capitalists as a "trap." What capitalists really wanted was to devalue the work of men and displace them with cheap female labor.[20]

In addition to being a threat to women's health and male employment, work outside the home was also regarded as potentially jeopardizing women's moral standards. Moral considerations were important for some of the early female leaders who denounced some occupations as a moral threat to those who were forced to seek employment in certain occupations. Since 1896, the Argentinean Socialist Party's program had included the prohibition of any form of female employment that would endanger women's morality.[21] Chilean La Alborada supported the prohibition of jobs for women in bars in Santiago by the municipality. Although it had deprived 3,000 women from jobs—claimed a 1906 editorial—the economic suffering was preferable to the immorality fostered by such occupation.[22] The exposure of working women to sexual abuse elicited a strong response among men and women on the Left. If working conditions exposed women to "corrupting" influences, the editorialist and activist Esther Díaz was in favor of eliminating the opportunity altogether. Women should not be forced to leave work at night, "exposed to compromise their virtue in the shadows of the night." Díaz painted a dark picture of lusting male "wolves" waiting outside factories for the innocent workers who, having been treated like beasts at work, fell for the sweet enticements of those scoundrels.[23]

One factor that added considerable fuel to the discussion of the nature of female work and to an eventual change of attitudes about it was the emergence of feminism in both countries. First discussed by an Argentinean professional woman in 1901, the shaping of feminism and its intellectual acceptance took place in the first decade of the century and was far from a smooth or straightforward process.[24] Feminism and women's liberation were terms interchangeably used by women and men of several social strata and ideological orientation who, despite important differences, shared a belief in the intellectual equality of men and women and the right of women to a more active and influential participation in the body politic. The professional middle-class women who developed in Argentina before 1910 focused at first on the civil rights and educational aspects of feminism. But their deep sense of social service led them very soon into a long-term commitment to the service of women and children of lesser means. Several of these early feminists were also socialists who helped tighten the connections between feminism and socialism.

The incorporation of feminism in the vocabulary of the Left was best illustrated in several Chilean newspapers. *La Alborada*, a needleworkers' mouthpiece founded in 1905 as a "defender of the proletarian classes," ended its life in 1907 calling itself a "feminist publication" and addressing personal issues of female subordination in addition to those generated by labor conditions. Luis Recabarren, the Chilean socialist editor of *La Reforma* and *El Despertar de los Trabajadores*, discussed feminism and used this term intermittently between 1906 and 1921. This early discussion of feminism in labor circles gives Chilean socialism a unique flavor. Middle-class intellectuals did not join the feminist mainstream in that country until the early 1920s, and when they did they were more inclined to discuss legal and political equality than labor reform legislation.

An increasing political sensitivity and concern for the complex social problems bred by urbanization, lack of labor regulation, housing, and public health problems developed in both countries in the early years of the second decade of the century. This trend, and the changing role forced on women as a result of World War I and suffrage campaigns in both Europe and the United States, gave South American feminists of all ideological inclinations a better sense of direction by the mid-1910s. After 1918, feminism, far from an embarrassing proposition, became the basis for advocating reforms in the Civil Code and social welfare legislation, and for discussing the possible involvement of women in the political process.

The question remained, however, whether feminism would furnish an agenda for individual liberation or buttress the recognition of a special sphere of action for women to which they would bring a distinctive "female" touch. That sphere would be that of family, motherhood, education, and social service. The prevailing attitudes toward gender relations in what were culturally patriarchal societies led Argentinian and Chilean feminists to the acceptance of feminism as a form of asserting women's equality within a feminine—that is separate sphere—context. The input of socialism into the early development of feminism (before 1915) in both countries was significant in that it injected a strong concern for welfare and services that transcended and outlived the ups and downs of the suffrage campaign that began in the late 1910s. In both nations, the Left provided a forceful intellectual foundation to feminism that attempted to combine female equality, social justice, and political clout to their own ranks. The development of these themes was uneven and conditioned by the unique circumstances in which socialism and anarchism evolved in these countries. As I posit below, there were important nuances in gender relations that transcended class consciousness and limited the scope of changes that the Left advocated for the working woman despite its commitment to gender equality.

The mobilization of female workers that began shortly after the turn of the century forced the leadership of the Left in both countries to go beyond mere lip service to women's role as members of the labor force and begin an exploration of the possibilities of matching feminism and socialism in practice. In 1907, *La Vanguardia*, the dean of the socialist newspapers in Argentina, published an article discussing the relationship between women's work, feminism, and female emancipation.[25] Feminism, the author posited, reflected the change in the economic relationship between the genders. Earning a living had put an end to women's subordination. To him, this change was as important for social change as the proposed socialist leveling among the social classes. Thus, he ended: "We consider that [women's] industrial work is a sign of social progress, [and] the first step towards emancipation." A kindred sentiment was expressed by Chilean needleworker Sara Cádiz, who in 1906 stated: "If we want freedom, let us begin by becoming economically independent."[26] By 1911, Argentinean Alicia Moreau, as a young socialist writer, began to argue in defense of female suffrage, especially for working women, precisely because they worked and paid taxes.[27] These were definite departures from the earlier denunciations of female work and heralded a turning point in the perception of women's work as a form of gender and economic empowerment.

Emotional resistance to female work lingered in both countries for many decades, but rising inflation and the several economic crises suffered by both countries between 1915 and 1930 forced many women to seek employment outside the home.[28] Argentinean socialists cashed in on this situation and eventually counted upon an eloquent male and female cadre of supporters of feminism and especially working women's rights in the early 1920s. Because of the weaker nature of organized socialism in Chile, the budding feminism of the needleworkers and the socialists of the Democratic Party waned after the decline of the former from journalistic activism. Feminism maintained its ideological presence within the Chilean Left for as long as Luis Recabarren cared to support it in the pages of *El Despertar de los Trabajadores*. The nature of the message to the women workers remained uplifting and supportive of female work and female organization within the labor movement, but no effort was made to organize support behind any social reform at the legislative level or to transcend the boundaries of class with the broader concept of gender.

During the first two decades of the century, Argentinean socialists and their budding counterparts in Chile were, above all, interested in establishing and retaining their ideological foothold on female labor. Although they continued to use metaphors depicting women's abandonment of the home as rending the family fabric, by the end of the first decade of the century they had accepted the situation as irreversible. Once the inevitability of female labor had been acknowledged, the goals of socialists were to achieve the regulation of that work and, more importantly, a reevaluation of female work through a raise in women's salaries to eliminate their unfair competition. To achieve the latter goal, more working women had to be encouraged to join labor organizations to protect men's earnings. The Tenth Argentinean Socialist Party Congress in 1912 endorsed the concept of a minimum salary, the eight-hour working day, the desirability of regulating female putting-out work, and the support to female labor organizations.[29] The first Chilean Socialist Party's program (1897) did not address the issue of female work, but by 1901 the Democrat-Socialist Party of Valparaíso called for regulation of women's work as part of a program of legislative protection for both sexes.[30] In both countries, the socialist leadership's message after 1906 was one of constant encouragement to women to join their labor organizations to elevate the value of female work and defend the rights of working people in general.[31]

Anarchists, on the other hand, remained torn about regulation of labor by the state and, ultimately, about the expanding frontiers of female labor. Anarchism would have no connection with bourgeois feminism, but because it had always advocated the equality of the sexes, it was difficult for it to accept the fact that an increasing number of people of several political complexions were also promoting the cause of women workers. Argentinean anarchists reiterated their opposition to labor legislation and unleashed their criticism against those who had praised female emancipation and had applauded women who had taken male jobs during the European war years. *La Protesta* argued that performing tasks such as those "ridiculous professions" followed by North American *marimachos* (masculinized women) did not change the fact that most women were still "factory flesh."[32] This uncompromising propaganda ran head on against the tide of the time, and it was partially fueled by the deterioration of the appeal of anarchism among the ranks of labor in the late 1910s. Some anarchists eventually saw fit to return to their praise for female work using the traditional reasons of economic need, but they criticized middle-class women who were joining the professional occupations that had been up to then reserved for men. Some anarchists argued that it was impossible for these women to reconcile their professions to motherhood.[33] What anarchist commentators chose not to discuss was the fact that if professional women had problems in reconciling work and motherhood, this was an even harder task for most female factory workers, since in the early 1920s government regulation of female working hours was not universally enforced, and child care facilities in factories were nonexistent.

Strategies for Organization and Female Leadership

The debate on the advisability of work for women and their competition with men in the labor market did not deter the process of women's incorporation into the labor force and their participation in the activities of labor associations of the several ideological orientations of the Left.[34] The manner whereby women joined these associations and the role they played within them in the first quarter of the century is an important indicator of how male and female interacted within the ranks of labor. By the end of the 19th century, women in both countries had organized mutualist societies of their own, had joined labor associations and their activities, and had joined and organized strikes, but the fragmented nature of such efforts rendered them ineffectual. One cannot talk about an effective female organizational network in either country until the early 1900s.[35]

The strategies in both nations for organizing women's activities as a potential element of political support for the fledgling labor movement had some points in common and some differences. Chilean mutualist societies gained a vigor and a centrality that was not found in Argentina where the energies were channelled through organizations of the political Left. Women organized their first mutualist society in Valparaíso in 1887 (Sociedad de Obreras No. 1), and by 1905, with the encouragement of several male socialist leaders, dozens of women's workers groups were formed in textile, cigar, and garment factories.[36] Humble washerwomen, shoefactory-, and needleworkers heard the call to form resistance societies in Santiago, Antofagasta, and Valparaíso and formed cells whose later fate remains shrouded by a lack of information.[37] The enterprising character of some of these women is best illustrated again by Esther Valdés de Díaz who, having organized a mutualist society, proceeded to found and sustain one of the few female workers' newspapers (*La Alborada*) in addition to holding a job in a garment factory. Other Chilean working women such as Eloisa Zurita, Mercedes and Carmela Jeria, and Sara Cádiz gained recognition for their leadership abilities and their uplifting writings in labor newspapers. Unfortunately, these women were able to carry out their activities for only a few years in the first decade of the century and disappeared from the labor profile after 1910.

Both in Argentina and Chile, gender separation in labor organizations was the rule. Between 1902 and 1903, the Argentinean socialists founded two organizations to serve the needs of women, the Socialist Feminine Center and the Feminine Guild Union. The latter, which aimed at proselytizing among women workers, seems to have faded by 1907, while the former, more social in character, survived through the 1930s.[38] Baldomero Loyola, a Chilean writing for *La Alborada*, extolled women of the northern mining areas for their untiring organizational efforts. Women fought alongside their male companions, he said, "separating only to organize in associations, as it was imperative due to their sex."[39] Women attended workers conventions representing their own organizations. Thus, Carmela Jeria, a female printer, attended the Fourth Worker's Convention in Chillán in 1905.[40] In 1907, the celebration of the May 1st day in Santiago brought together male and female workers. Four of 11 speakers were women.[41] The fact that the Chilean labor movement did not gain coherence within a central organization until 1916 constrained the emerging female groups, which remained relatively small and centered on their own activities.

The tone of the mutualist societies' propaganda was uplifting and sometimes utopian, but while advocating a new society in the future, they adopted pragmatic plans that would give their members financial help in case of sickness, loss of job, or death. The oldest women's mutualist society in the country, located in the port of Valparaíso, offered the use of a *carro fúnebre* (hearse) and money for burial. In 1906, under the increasing influence of organized labor, the newly founded needleworker association hoped to be able to provide medicine and medical attention and a job directory to its members. They also hoped to form a consumers' cooperative, a savings bank, and a retirement fund.[42] Quite likely, these plans never materialized, but they point to these women's interest in welfare and services, as well as their confidence in their own abilities to administer this complex project.

When Emilio Recabarren founded the Socialist Workers' Party in 1912, he sought to strengthen the concept of female workers' organizations he had been personally encouraging for several years. The first visit to the northern mining towns of a notable female Spanish anarchist, Belén de Zárraga, gave Recabarren the opportunity to support the foundation of numerous women's clubs bearing the name of Belén de Zárraga. The Belén de Zárraga centers were defined as anticlerical and freethinking, but among their objectives was to teach the basis of socialism to working women, who were expected to lend their support to the men's efforts in the struggle for the organization of labor. The weekly lines allocated in Recabarren's newspaper *El Despertar de los Trabajadores* to the activities of these clubs suggest that within them women began to acquire the bases of a political education, but we do not know how or whether they extended these activities beyond the meetings. The net result was that few women achieved any position of leadership in the Chilean labor movement or its mouthpiece, the Socialist Labor Federation of Chile (FOCH), founded in 1916.[43]

Labor organization in Argentina offered a similarly interesting, but different, picture. The greater influx of foreign socialists and anarchists into Argentina kindled a strong rivalry among the several anarchist groups and the socialists. As part of their effort to capture the workers' allegiance, they encouraged women's participation as speakers and activists. A center of anarchist women was founded in Buenos Aires in 1907, and although its development remains obscure, we know that women anarchists founded others in at least half a dozen provincial cities that were still meeting in the early 1920s.[44] For their part, socialists organized the womens'centers mentioned above to recruit members among women in the Buenos Aires' factories. Argentinean anarchists and socialists seated women in their respective congresses between 1903 and 1904, but in the long run the socialists were more successful in maintaining a visible presence of women within their own ranks. They gathered a brilliant group of women in the Buenos Aires Socialist Feminine Center that soon became the main core of female activities through the whole period under review. In the late 1920s, the Center was still serving as a forum for female and male speakers and provided some of the services that working mothers needed most: child care and a place to gather and socialize in a family atmosphere. They also gave instruction in needlework, typing, and secretarial services. At a more political level, the Center supported women's issues and eventually declared in favor of suffrage and feminist principles.[45]

The adoption of universal male suffrage in 1912 and the first popular elections in 1918 strengthened the socialist party, which by the mid-1920s had elected several deputies and senators. This newly-gained political strength was, in part, used to promote legislation favoring what they understood as the needs of working women and the proletarian family. Women socialists leaders supported the party from within their special niche in it. They were strong and effective backers and, in some instances, superb propagandists. However, at no point did they rise to the leadership of the party.[46] Instead, they reaffirmed their separation by founding a magazine of their own (*Nuestra Causa*) in 1918. A survey of the contents of this publication show that despite being nominally a mouthpiece of the working woman, between 1918-20 it was largely dedicated to the promotion of such middle-class feminist objectives as suffrage, the active participation of women in national politics, and the promotion of legal equality through the reform of the nation's civil and penal code.[47]

What we know today of the bold, determined, and articulate women who participated in the activities of labor associations of the Left in both countries is not enough to support a general group profile. Were they all working-class women, or were they middle-class professional women with a strong commitment and a sense of mission? The picture is mixed. Several well-educated middle-class women in the Socialist Party such as the Russian emigré sisters Fenia, Mariana, and Adela Chertcoff, Alicia Moreau, Petrona Eyle, and Gabriela Lapèpierre rendered invaluable services to the Party. The socialists also included women of working-class origin such as Carolina Muzilli. We are not sure of the social origins of the early Argentinean anarchist women, but all indications are that they emerged from the ranks of the workers, as did the members of Chilean mutualist societies. Thus, it is fair to say that genuine working women in both countries joined the ranks of the Left and actively participated in its activities at least during the first two decades of the century. Most of them were self-educated women such as Carolina Muzilli and Juana Rouco Buela in Argentina, and Carmela Jeria and Esther Díaz in Chile. Their writings and organizational activities demonstrated that able female leadership was possible within the body of female workers.

Leadership was open to those who could fulfill the objectives of mutualist societies and working women groups: raising individual morale in the work place, inspiring confidence in the ability to obtain redresses for the workers, and generating allegiance to the ideology of the guiding organizations. To achieve the latter, education in either socialism or anarchism was a *sine qua non.* Ephemeral working women's magazines were the means of communication and diffusion, the backbone of female networking in those days. Men worked with these female organizations, either as mentors, advisors, or collaborators. In the process, women were trained to speak and to lead. Some of the women surprised the men as their untapped leadership abilities developed and were put into practice. They dealt capably with the same intellectual issues men discussed, and, in addition, they were able to carry a special gender message to their female coworkers.

Chilean women workers wrote of the "perfume of confraternity" that male and female workers shared in the newly discovered equality that was theoretically accepted and extolled during the initial years of the century when the struggle to organize labor was more intense and members of both sexes fraternized in meetings for the first time.[48] This initial fraternization, however, was enjoyed mostly by the limited number of gifted women who became leaders in several of the labor groups. A disquieting note was already heard in 1905 when an anonymous writer for the Chilean *La Alborada* accused the selfishness of those who had denied women's access to a workers' association.[49] Both societies were still sex-segregated in education as well as in other social activities, and it would have been against the grain of such cultural constraints to expect full gender coparticipation in the labor organizations.

As time passed, women's functions within the associations were redirected towards their own peer group, a situation that seemed to have jelled by the middle of the second decade of the century. Sex segregation was not, however, a totally undesirable situation. For many working women in the capital and provincial cities of both countries, the resistance groups, the mutualist societies, the Argentinean anarchist clubs "Luisa Michel," and the Chilean "Belén de Zárraga" associations were gathering places where networking and reciprocal support could be found. Poor women had no alternative means of fraternizing. These gathering places offered them the only schooling in ideas and the only stages for peer socialization and recognition that they would ever know.[50]

The Dialogue of Power Between the Sexes

The channeling of women's activities into female organizations meant that they were effectively removed from the most important political activities of either the party or the original nuclear association. The evolution from integrated participation to formation of women's group responded to a deeply-seated tradition of gender relations in the late 19th century. Before World War I and in some instances up to the end of the second decade of the century, male and female anarchists and socialists in Argentina and Chile showed significant ambiguities on the role of women— especially working women—in society and within the family.

Neither anarchists nor socialists of either gender could completely tear themselves away from the patriarchal model of the family or the illusion of the home as an oasis of happiness. Such model was built upon the unquestioned acceptance of the physical weakness of the female sex, an ideology which had first served as the basis for questioning the female presence in the work place and for urging the restriction of certain occupations to the male. Women needed male protection at the personal level as much as they needed labor associations to defend them against oppressive social institutions and the economic interests of capitalism. Uplifting words encouraging women to rescue their rights and seek their happiness notwithstanding, women were more often than not depicted as men's companions—if not followers—and providers of solace and tenderness to the head of the house. Woman's role was to sweeten the "bitter hours of he who sustains, guides and pilots the ship of his home."[51] In exchange, men's duty was to love and protect women, and be truly responsible for the welfare of their families.[52]

The role of women as followers is often subtly reiterated by the use of the verb *secundar*—best translated as to second. Women's support of men at home was naturally extended to the public arena as their helpers in the organization of protests and strikes. The Argentinean female anarchist newspaper *Nuestra Tribuna* printed an article in 1923 in which a proud woman writer proclaimed that women had achieved the same degree of cultural and mental elevation as men and were ready to become social assets as educators and complements (*complementos*) of men in all literary and scientific activities.[53]

The enthusiastic participation of women in the anarchist and socialist groups in Argentina and Chile had not taken place without opposition. Ironically, anarchists had the greatest problems in agreeing how independent the "new women" they wished to help shape could be. The first female Argentinean anarchist newspaper *La Voz de la Mujer* recorded male hostility, and even opposition, to their activities and their newspaper.[54] Anarchist women were again criticized in 1904 for joining male resistance unions instead of developing truly "feminist propaganda," that is, a separate set of female organizations.[55] The first Chilean socialist female organizers seemed also to have received criticism from some men for having failed to succeed in their organizational efforts.[56] The worst example of ideological intransigence, however, was the radical anarchists' critique of Juana Rouco Buela's foundation of the newspaper *Nuestra Tribuna* in 1923. Rouco Buela had hoped that the newspaper would become a vehicle for the expression of the concerns of female anarchists. She was sharply criticized by the orthodox leadership for running against the seam of true anarchism, in which men and women were totally equal and had no need for gender differentiations.[57] Since in the early 1920s the anarchists were losing their grip on the Argentinean labor movement, this stringent criticism of women seeking their own identity seemed to have been an effort to retain internal unity. In addition, the ideological split between socialists and anarchists in Argentina created a tense atmosphere of gratuitous criticism against the activities of the women in each other's group that took place every time they took positions on important issues, such as labor legislation or suffrage.

The resistance and/or criticism of women among the Argentinean and Chilean Left are indications of deeper problems in gender relations. The official ideological position of gender equality of both socialists and anarchists did not necessarily imply its observance in the reality of daily life. Originally, anarchists such as Kropotkin did not support the highlighting of women's special interests within the movement. Others, such as German socialist August Bebel, defended vigorously the concept of female liberation based on the specifically feminine needs and forms of expression and oppression.[58] The most difficult aspect of equality was how to enforce it in the intimate realm of the home. In Chile, a few socialists of both sexes undertook the bitter task of writing about this touchy subject. Recognizing that not all their male coworkers practiced what they preached or had heard preached, they verbally lashed proletarian men who beat and abused their wives.[59] But even this effort to convey the concept of the equality of husband and wife within the family was fraught with problems. The self-analysis of these critical writings was burdened by images of women being abused and exploited or, contrarily, they described them as meek followers and supporters of men and family. Women assumed to be either victims or subservient followers could not receive the full impact of the message of gender equality. Thus, the emphasis of these writings was put on the future redemption of the female sex rather than on its immediate liberation.

Did socialists and anarchists change the tone of the dialogue of power between the genders? The answer must take into consideration the patriarchal culture of these two countries and must be, of necessity, opaque rather than clear. The Left made an honest attempt to face the social subordination of women in society. Their ideological stand gave them handles to challenge the character of the relations among the sexes, but some of the issues were enormously difficult to tackle, and their impact on the nature of gender relations in Argentina and Chile was minimal.

Most anarchists and a few radical socialists endorsed sexual liberation, but the majority of socialists extolled the bonds of responsible manhood and the protection of the family. The Argentinean anarchists' search for the *personal* liberation of women expressed itself best through the rejection of marriage as a hypocritical institution that encouraged women to "sell" themselves to men through marriage to gain economic security. Support for "free love" in anarchist newspapers in Buenos Aires was intense, and reflected a belief in the unfettered expression of human sexuality.[60] The discussion of sexuality in Argentina, however, was handled mostly by men. Their writings reflected a masculine perception of sexual relations in which men were seen as fertilizing women and giving them the ultimate happiness of motherhood and family within the framework of freedom provided by anarchism. Despite their rejection of social institutions, many men writing for the anarchist *La Protesta* clung to the concept of the family. As they advocated free love, they wished to redefine the basis of gender relations on a personal and not a familial basis. As one writer put it, what mattered was to put an end to the "brutal pretensions of the male to become the owner of the female."[61]

Just as important was the anarchists' advocacy of birth control. Their objective in supporting birth control was social and political, as a tool for depriving the capitalists of future labor. This subject, however, also posed important nuances of female self-control over their bodies. Although in Argentina few women wrote on this theme, the anarchist message on reproductive control was rapidly picked up by some alert female leaders in Chile. In August 1908, the short-lived needleworkers' newspaper *La Palanca*, carried a powerful article on the right of women to control their own motherhood. This unsigned article attacked men and women who engaged in the "selfish, brutal and mechanical satisfaction" of their own sexual needs without further thoughts to their social consequences. It also assailed male "scientists," whose criminal insensitivity to women's needs deprived the latter of the knowledge of their own bodies and their reproductive functions so that they could plan their motherhood.[62]

Another Chilean working woman, signing as Clara de la Luz, injected ideology and the issue of class into the discussion of birth control. Capitalism and clericalism, she argued, encouraged blind procreation as a means to maintain the working class in slavery. She urged Chilean mothers to consider restricting the number of their offspring. These writings show that at least some working women had a clear grip on the relationship between class, gender, poverty, and procreation. Yet the message of female control over their reproductive functions was subsumed under the political and class agenda; it did not stress the individual choice of the woman herself.

Discussion of birth control was limited to a few voices. Other Chilean working women were even more ambiguous and less forceful about challenging the system of power established through sexual relations, birth control, and gender relations within the home. When they did, they mixed satire and criticism and did not abandon the belief that men owed women certain traditional gestures of gallantry and gentle treatment.[63] The Chilean male socialist press, as represented by its most powerful newspapers, Recabarren's *La Reforma* and *El Despertar de los Trabajadores*, did not discuss birth control or sexual relations, leaving the comments of a few radical women workers as the only records of the Chilean Left on the subject. Neither liberated sexuality nor the control of reproduction had a great impact on the working class in Chile or Argentina. Not only were the medical means for birth control imperfect and unavailable to them, but the cultural reverence for motherhood was as deeply rooted among the workers as it was among the middle class.

Unlike anarchists, socialists in both countries opted for the family and motherhood. After allying themselves with the emergent feminist movement in the second decade of the century, Argentinean socialists spilled much ink reassuring all those concerned that they endorsed neither the masculinization of women nor the antagonism of the sexes. By devoting their energies to seeking protection for mothers and children through regulatory legislation, they implicitly accepted the sexual division of work and the traditional social roles of the genders.

Ultimately, the perception of the possibility of a change in the power relationship between the sexes was not based on the subversion of their sexual roles. It was based on the understanding that women should not be "more like men," but should climb the intellectual ladder to be their equals. Socialists and anarchists had faith in the potential of the feminine sex, but they departed from the assumption that women were not, as yet, up to meeting male intellectual and political standards. In many subtle ways, women were portrayed as still lacking maturity but slowly evolving towards it through the adoption of their respective ideologies. One of the metaphors most often used by both socialists and anarchists to describe the process of change among women was that of awakening from sleep— or less charitably, from stupor. The light of either socialism or anarchism was finally dispelling the darkness of the long night in which the female brain had been kept by ignorance and prejudice. *Luz al cerebro* (Light to the brain) proclaims an illustration in the Chilean *El Despertar de los Trabajadores,* showing a woman receiving the beneficial rays of the sun above.[64] To be sure, women were not responsible for their own ignorance. The church and the capitalists were to blame for having either maintained women at the margin of progress or having fed them with lies and sophisms. Nonetheless, the assumption was that women were ignorant and in need to be enlightened.

Socialists and anarchists did not believe in the intellectual inferiority of women. They firmly upheld their equality in intelligence and ability, but they knew that among female workers education left much to be desired, and they saw their role as one of "enlightening" women. This was a task to be carried out by both men and women. The development of female leadership after 1900 had precisely that purpose, and, indeed, both ideologies were successful in attracting a number of bright women. The presence of these female leaders, however, did not obliterate the image of the woman in need of help. The ironic fact is that even women's newspapers carried articles that portrayed women lagging behind men and in need of help to free themselves from the bondage of ignorance, oppression, and exploitation. "We wish the miserable slave of yesterday, today's exploited woman, to receive light in her brain through the beneficial rays of instruction. We want the proletarian woman educated, that she may suffer no longer the ignominious yoke of despotism. We ask education for the inseparable companion of man, for the mother of future generations."[65]

That role of mother was one that not even the anarchists could or would challenge, despite their theoretical support for sexual freedom. Motherhood retained its powerful message as the crowning experience in women's lives, the supreme form of personal fulfillment. Note, however, that the anarchist and the socialist mother was an educated one, not the ignorant mother of generations past. If the proletariat would have had educated mothers, lamented Chilean Luis Recabarren in 1914, the working class would have been spared a great deal of exploitation.[66] What type of education should a woman receive for motherhood? Education in freedom through the dogma of socialism, stated Recabarren in 1916. "Socialism wants to see woman free and capable of educating her children . . . *totally* dedicated to the education of her children. When the education of woman is undertaken according *to her maternal mission,* when instead of prayer she is taught anatomy, obstetrics, psychology, biology, etc then she becomes free and she brings forth free children who live in the respect of everybody's freedom."[67] The last metaphor, in Recabarren's own language, was that of women as fecund wombs. "Let women be the precious wombs where tomorrow will germinate, where new life will be given to the new and modern men and women."[68]

In this dialogue between poor working women and the Argentinean-Chilean Left, all the terms were known to each party and accepted by both. There were feminine reproaches as well as strong criticism, but as a whole the relations among the sexes did not change drastically despite the increasing number of women joining the labor force. The changes proposed by anarchists and socialists were of an economic nature and addressed to an insensitive capitalist society. Within the male-female partnership in the Left, the juxtaposition of class and gender created no turmoil. During the formative and activist years, leadership among women emerged from either the working class itself or from socially-conscious middle-class women. The Left, represented by its male and female leadership, consistently addressed the needs of working women throughout the first two decades of the century. This situation changed somewhat in Argentina as socialists threw their support behind women's suffrage and began speaking a more "gentrified" language. However, this departure was born out of necessity, as the contours of the Argentinean politics changed after 1918 and the party hoped to broaden its political base.

The Left's pragmatic formula to mobilize women achieved a modest degree of success among the industrial workers of the main urban centers. The objectives of having working women awake slowly, develop their own leadership, and speak with their own voices was fulfilled during the first quarter of the century as they organized their own associations, participated in strikes when the situation demanded it, and learned the ropes of mobilization. Women, however, remained segregated in special feminine niches within the labor organization. Neither men nor women of the Left challenged the pattern of gender relationships within or outside the home or the work place. Within the labor movement, women remained evolutionaries rather than revolutionaries with the acquiescence of men. They wished to be liberated, but they also wished to remain "the tender companion of man." Gender relations were dominated by the image of women as females—that is, a physically fragile being with specific functions predetermined by their sex. The Left endorsed a gender politics of adjustment and compromise. Its challenge was social, but at the personal level men and women leaned towards the preservation of traditional sexual and social roles.

NOTES

1. For general historical information on these two nations, see James R. Scobie, *Argentina: A City and a Nation*, 2nd ed. (Oxford: Oxford University Press, 1971); David Rock, *Argentina, 1516-1982: From Spanish Colonization to the Falklands War* (Berkeley: University of California Press, 1985); Brian Loveman, *Chile: The Legacy of Hispanic Capitalism* (New York: Oxford University Press, 1979). For an overall view of the history of labor, see Charles Bergquist, *Labor in Latin America: Comparative Essays on Chile, Argentina, Venezuela, and Colombia* (Stanford: Stanford University Press, 1986).

2. For a brief study of Germán Avé-Lallemant, the founder of *El Obrero*, see Leonardo Paso, *La clase obrera y el nacimiento del marxismo en la Argentina* (Buenos Aires: Editorial Anteo, 1974).

3. Among the important sources for the study of the labor movement in Argentina in the first quarter of the twentieth century are Samuel Baily, *Labor, Nationalism and Politics in Argentina* (New Brunswick, N.J.: Rutgers University Press, 1967); Hobart A. Spalding, Jr., *La clase trabajadora argentina: Documentos para su historia, 1890-1912* (Buenos Aires: Editorial Galerna, 1970) and *Organized Labor in Latin America: Historical Case Studies of Workers in Dependent Societies* (New York: New York University Press, 1977); Richard J. Walters, *The Socialist Party of Argentina* (Austin: University of Texas Press, 1977); Iacod Oveed, *El anarquismo y el movimiento obrero en Argentina* (Buenos Aires: Siglo XXI, 1978); José Ratzer, *Los marxistas argentinos del 90* (Córdoba: Ediciones Pasado y Presente, 1969); Diego Abad de Santillán, *El movimiento anarquista en la Argentina desde sus comienzos hasta el año 1910* (Buenos Aires: Editorial Argonauta, 1930) and *La F.O.R.A. Ideología y trayectoria* (Buenos Aires: Editorial Proyección, 1971). Abad de Santillán was a notable Spanish anarchist deeply involved in the Argentinean movement.

4. For the history of the Chilean labor movement, see Hernán Ramírez Necochea, *Historia del movimiento obrero: Siglo XIX* (Santiago: n.p., 1956); Peter De Shazo, *Urban Workers and Labor Unions in Chile, 1902-1927* (Madison: University of Wisconsin Press, 1983); Jorge Barría Serón, *Los movimientos sociales de Chile desde 1910 hasta 1926* (Santiago: Editorial Universitaria, 1960); Moisés Poblete Troncoso, *La organización sindical en Chile y otros estudios sociales* (Santiago de Chile: Imprenta R. Brias, 1926); Virginia Kresminski, "Alessandri y la cuestión social," in Claudio Orrego, comp., *Siete Ensayos sobre Arturo Alessandri* (Santiago: Instituto Chileno de Estudios Humanísticos, 1979), 165-258. Julio Heise G. presents information on the labor press, labor struggles, and anarchism in Chile. See *Historia de Chile: El período parlamentario, 1861-1925* (Santiago de Chile: Editorial Andrés Bello, 1974), 341-46, 383-88, 402-16. With few exceptions, most of these sources focus on male labor only.

5. A recent analysis of the role of women in the French socialist Parti Ouvrier Français may be used in conjunction with this essay to compare French and South American attitudes of the ideological Left toward women. See Patricia Hilden, "Rewriting the History of Socialism: Working Women and the Parti Ouvrier Français," *European History Quarterly* 17, no. 3 (July 1987): 285-306. See also Jane Slaughter and Robert Kern, *European Women on the Left: Socialism, Feminism, and the Problems Faced by Political Women, 1880 to the Present* (Westport, Conn.: Greenwood Press, 1981).

6. Julio Mafud, *La vida obrera en la Argentina* (Buenos Aires: Editorial Proyección, 1976), passim.

7. The male-oriented categorization of occupations in the national censuses of the late nineteenth century is itself a significant statement on the perception of female workers. Elena Gil, *La mujer en el mundo del trabajo* (Buenos Aires:

Ediciones Libera, 1970), 43; James R. Scobie, *Buenos Aires: Plaza to Suburb, 1870-1910* (New York: Oxford University Press, 1974), 216; *Censo general de la ciudad de Buenos Aires* (1909) 3 vols. (Buenos Aires: Compañía Sud-Americana de Billetes de Banco, 1910); "Población obrera de la República Argentina," *Boletín del Departamento Nacional del Trabajo* 16 (March 1911): 24-31. According to this source, in the city of Buenos Aires, women were 27 percent of the industrial labor force, 10 percent of those in commerce, 26 percent of those in the "health profession" (midwives), and 33 percent of those in education.

8. *Boletín del Departamento del Trabajo* 12 (March 1910): 8-22. One of the shoe factories surveyed in 1910 employed only 22 percent male labor. In one of those factories, "La Argentina," women performed all the manufacturing operations. See Carolina Muzilli, "El trabajo femenino," *Boletín Mensual del Museo Social Argentino* 11, no. 15 (April-May 1913): 65-90.

9. *Anuario Estadístico de la República de Chile*, IX (Santiago de Chile: Soc. Imp. y Lit. Universo, 1917). Fifty-eight percent of all female workers were employed in Santiago. Valparaíso ranked second with 17.8 percent, and the three provinces of Concepción, Talca, and Aconcagua employed 11 percent of the female working population.

10. *Anuario Estadístico* (Santiago de Chile: Oficina Central de Estadística, 1914), VIII, passim; Robert McCaa, comp., *Censo de la Población, 1940* (Santiago: Centro de Demografía Celade, 1976), 119-20.

11. For Argentina I have used the anarchist newspaper *La Protesta Humana*, which turned into *La Protesta*, and its socialist counterpart *La Vanguardia*, both published in Buenos Aires in the years under review. For Chile, *La Reforma* and *El Despertar de los Trabajadores* expressed the leading socialist ideas in the first years of the century and after 1912 respectively, and are the best sources for materials on women. *La Palanca* and *La Alborada* are two female newspapers published by needleworkers in Santiago between 1904 and 1907. Another important source is the anarchist *Nuestra Tribuna* (1922-24) published in Argentina by Juana Rouco Buela, a self-educated working woman.

12. Italian anarchist Enrico Malatesta founded syndicalist anarchism in Argentina. He promoted the publication of a series of pamphlets called *La Question Sociale* beginning in 1885. The titles aimed at women were *A las muchachas que estudian* (To Girls Who Study, 1895), *A las hijas del pueblo* (To the Daughters of the People, 1895), and *A las proletarias* (To Proletariat Women, 1895). They were translated by a female Spanish anarchist, Soledad Gustavo. See also Maxine Molyneux, "No God, No Boss, No Husband: Anarchist Feminism in Nineteenth Century Argentina," *Latin American Perspectives* 13, no. 1 (Winter 1986): 119-45; Iacod Oveed, *El anarquismo*, 35-35.

13. Scanning *La Protesta Humana* and its sequel *La Protesta* between 1900 and 1923 yielded considerable information on the activities of anarchists of both sexes throughout these years. See, as examples of early female involvement in anarchist organizations and activities, issues of *La Protesta Humana*, 13 July 1901, 12 September 1902; *La Protesta*, 16 November 1904, 8 December 1904.

14. Gabriela Coni, *A las obrera. Consideraciones sobre nuestra labor*, "Biblioteca de Propaganda," IX (Buenos Aires: C. Gallarini, 1903).

15. See the Chilean counterpart to Coni's ideas in the writings of the female labor leaders writing for *La Alborada*, a weekly published in Santiago de Chile between 1905 and 1907. In vol. 2, no. 20, 18 November 1906, Esther Valdés wrote: "La mujer por su constitución física, es más débil que el hombre, señalándole de esta manera la Naturaleza un trabajo mas moderado" (Woman is physically weaker than man, and Nature has assigned to her more moderate tasks). Since women

worked longer hours than men for a lower salary, she argued for the regulation of their labor.

16. Walter, *The Socialist Party*, 90.

17. *Primer Congreso Femenino Internacional de la República Argentina* (Buenos Aires: Imprenta A. Ceppi, 1910), 233. In 1890 French socialist Paul Lafargue called for a return of women to the home. The possibility of Lafarguian influence on some members of Argentine socialism remains an interesting speculation. See Hilden, "Women and the Parti Ouvrier Français," 294-99.

18. Sara Cádiz B., "Sobre organización femenina," *La Reforma*, 28 June 1906.

19. *La Alborada* 2, no. 42, 19 May 1907. In 1907 labor demand and exports were at a peak in Chile.

20. *Nuestra Tribuna* 1, no. 3, 15 September 1922.

21. Hobart Spalding, *La clase trabajadora*, 266, 267, 270, 273, 279.

22. *La Alborada* 2, no. 24, 16 December 1906. Editorial "Las mujeres en las cantinas" (Women as waitresses in bars).

23. *La Alborada* 2, no. 40, 21 April 1907; 2, no. 49, 19 May 1907. In Argentina and Chile, only women of ill repute walked alone after dark. See Blas Alberti, *Conversaciones con Alicia Moreau de Justo y Jorge Luis Borges* (Buenos Aires: Ediciones del Mar Dulce, 1985), 41-45, 50, 65, 108-10. "In those days [ca. 1900-1905] a young woman who went out alone, especially at night, was labeled [as a bad woman]." The first women to attend the socialist centers for women met between 5 and 7 P.M. in order to return home before night, "because a woman returning to her home alone at late hours was judged to be something else." On prostitution in Argentina during that period, see Donna Guy, *Sex and Danger in Buenos Aires: Prostitution, Family, and Nation in Argentina* (Lincoln: University of Nebraska Press, 1991).

24. Elvira López, *El movimiento feminista*, doctoral thesis in Philosophy and Letters (Buenos Aires: Imprenta Mariano Moreno, 1901). In 1903 the Argentinean scientific journal *Archivos de Psiquiatría, Criminología y Ciencias Afines* published an anonymous review of the feminist debate in Europe. See 2 (1903): 181-85. I thank Prof. Donna Guy for calling my attention to this source.

25. *La Vanguardia*, 8 September 1907.

26. Sara Cádiz B., "Sobre organización femenina obrera," *La Reforma*, 28 June 1906.

27. Alicia Moreau, "Feminismo y evolución social," *Humanidad Nueva* 3, no. 4 (1911): 356-75.

28. For a discussion of middle-class and working-class feminism in the nations of the Southern Cone, see Asunción Lavrin, "The Ideology of Feminism in the Southern Cone, 1900-1940," The Wilson Center Working Papers: Latin American Program Paper no. 169 (Washington, D.C.: The Wilson Center, 1985). For a review of the literature on feminism in general, see Sandra McGee Deutsch, "Feminist Studies," in *Latinas of the Americas: A Source Book*, ed. K. Lynn Stoner (New York: Garland Publishing, 1989), 129-52. For comparative purposes, see Sally M. Miller, ed., *Flawed Liberation: Socialism and Feminism* (Westport, Conn.: Greenwood Press, 1981); Mari Jo Buhle, *Women and American Socialism, 1879-1920* (Urbana: University of Illinois Press, 1981); Charles Sowerwine, *Sisters or Citizens? Women and Socialism in France since 1876* (Cambridge: Cambridge University Press, 1982).

29. Muzilli, "El trabajo femenino," 65-90.

30. Ramírez Necochea, *Historia del movimiento obrero*, 235-36, 247.

31. See writings of Luis Eduardo Díaz, Esther Valdés de Díaz, and Sara Cádiz in *La Reforma* and, more important, the general tone of articles printed in *La*

Alborada. La Vanguardia of Buenos Aires was consistent in its support of socialist women's activities and of the organization of women workers.

32. *La Protesta,* 17 September 1918. See also 1 August 1913; 16, 24 October 1914.

33. *La Protesta,* 17 September 1918; 16 September 1923.

34. In this essay I do not deal with Catholic confessional unions, which were also important in organizing a significant sector of the artisanal female labor in both countries. On this topic, see Sandra F. McGee, "Female Right-Wing Activists in Buenos Aires, 1900-1932," in Barbara J. Harris and Jo Ann K. McNamara, eds., *Women and the Structure of Society* (Durham, N.C.: Duke University Press, 1984), 85-97; "The Visible and Invisible Liga Patriótica Argentina, 1919-29: Gender Roles and the Right Wing," *Hispanic American Historical Review* 64, no. 2 (May 1984): 233-58.

35. Donna Guy, "Women, Peonage and Industrialization: Argentina, 1810-1914," *Latin American Research Review* 16, no. 3 (1981): 65-89; De Shazo, *Urban Workers,* 100-101.

36. *La Alborada* 2, no. 19, 11 November 1906. *La Aurora,* in its edition of 1 April 1903, printed the photograph of Francisca Quezada, president of "La Protección de la Mujer," another mutualist society. "Protection, Saving, and Defense" was the motto of a needleworkers' association founded by Esther Valdés de Díaz in Valparaíso, Chile.

37. Between 1905 and 1907, *La Alborada* reported female mutualist societies in Chillán, Linares, Antofagasta, Valparaíso, and Santiago. In 1926 Moisés Poblete Troncoso reported 47 female and 312 mutual societies. See *La organización sindical en Chile y otros estudios sociales,* 74.

38. Nicolás Coello, *Ejemplo noble de una mujer* (Buenos Aires: n.p., 1936); Fenia Chertcoff de Repetto, "El movimiento socialista femenino en la República Argentina," *Almanaque de Trabajo* 1 (1918): 141-45.

39. *La Alborada* 2, no. 24, 16 December 1906.

40. *La Alborada* 1, no. 1, 10 September 1905.

41. *La Alborada* 2, no. 42, 19 May 1907. The presence of columns of marching women was hailed by this newspaper.

42. *La Alborada* 2, no. 30, 3 February 1907.

43. De Chazo, *Urban Workers,* 86, 100.

44. *Nuestra Tribuna* 1, no. 1, August 1922; 1, no. 2, September 1922; 2, no. 24, September 1923; 3, no. 39, July 1924.

45. Asunción Lavrin, "Socialists, Anarchists, and Working Women in Argentina, 1890-1940," paper presented at the XIII International Congress, Latin American Studies Association, Boston, October 1986. Information on the activities of the Socialist Feminine Center can be followed in the pages of *La Vanguardia.*

46. Richard Walters, *The Socialist Party,* makes this point obvious throughout his narrative.

47. One of the few articles addressed to working women appeared in 1, no. 4, August 1919. It was signed by Virgilia Sánchez, secretary of a Feminine Labor Federation in the city of Corrientes. It praised female work as a vehicle of female equality and endorsed feminism.

48. *La Alborada* 1, no. 2, October 1905. Throughout this newspapers's initial numbers, its dating was loosely printed as first or second fortnight of the month. In subsequent numbers the date was more accurately printed.

49. *La Alborada* 1, no. 5, November 1905.

50. "La sociedad de resistencia es lo único que puede suplir la escuela" (Resistance societies are the only venues to supplement the school), statement by a woman in *El Despertar de los Trabajadores,* 12 December 1912.

51. *La Alborada* 1, no. 12, 12 April 1906.

52. Labor writer Ricardo Guerrero, otherwise a strong supporter of women's emancipation in Chile, expressed this view in *La Alborada* 1, no. 11, April 1906. Similar views were expressed by another writer in 1, no. 12, second fortnight of April 1906. Some men lacked *hombría* (masculinity) and failed to fulfill their responsibility to sustain their families, allowing their women to be exposed to shameful occupations, such as bar maids. *La Alborada* 2, no. 24, December 1906.

53. *Nuestra Tribuna* 2, no. 27, 15 October 1923.

54. Molineux, *No God,* 127-28. *La Voz de la Mujer* was founded in 1895 and folded in 1896.

55. *La Protesta,* 3 December 1904. The lack of feminine organizations was a tactical mistake that, in the opinion of the writer, should be superseded. He encouraged women to form their own associations. He used the word *feminist* to mean women-only associations.

56. *La Alborada* 2, no. 27, 13 January 1907. Esther Valdés de Díaz stoutly defended the women who participated in strikes even if they were unsuccessful, arguing that men had also been defeated in their efforts before. She reminded her readers that, in addition to lacking experience and time away from home, women had to cope with either the indifference or the lack of support of their male companions and coworkers.

57. *Nuestra Tribuna* 1, no. 2, 15 September 1922. A few years earlier, an anarchist woman had rejected the concept of female-only anarchist groups. See *La Protesta,* 6 February 1918. Since many small clubs of women anarchists were reported in the provinces of Argentina in the early 1920s, the inference is that the radical stand against women's associations was unheeded, at least beyond the confines of Buenos Aires.

58. Molineux, *No God,* 129. Kropotkin and Bebel were translated and published in both male and female workers' newspapers in Argentina and Chile.

59. *La Alborada* 1, no. 14, May 1906. See also 12 April, 18 November, 6 December 1906. Carmela Jeria G. voiced one of the most bitter criticisms of the hypocrisy of the men who outside the home proclaimed to support female liberation, while treating their wives like slaves. See 2, no. 29, 27 January 1907. Chilean socialists were willing to expose problems within the working-class family during these years, but they preferred to blame bourgeois laws as hypocritical for allowing such abuses. One article in *El Despertar* faulted marriage legislation for its contribution to the slavery of women within marriage, citing the examples of working women who had to bear their husbands' mistreatment knowing that, at most, the men would be fined twenty pesos for physical abuse. See 29 March 1923.

60. See, for example, *La Protesta Humana,* 30 August 1902, 26 January 1919; "La unión libre," in *A las muchachas que estudian.*

61. For a sampling of the nuances of interpretation in sexual relationships, see *La Protesta Humana,* 13 June 1897; *La Protesta,* 29 December 1904, 5 August 1905, 19 February 1910, 26 January 1919. The use of the term *macho y hembra* by anarchist writers underlined the directness of their discourse, since that term was used to refer more to animals than to people.

62. *La Palanca* 1, no. 4, August 1908. Writing about male doctors, the article stated, "Que nada hacen para hacer comprender a la mujer, que ella debe disponer de su cuerpo, que ella solo tiene derecho de disponer, para ser madre prudentemente, en la medida de sus fuerzas i de sus medios económicos,

escojiendo el momento oportuno" (They do not teach women how to control their bodies. Women alone have the right to determine their motherhood, prudently and according to their strength and economic means, choosing the opportune time to do so).

63. *La Alborada* 2, no. 26, 26 December 1906.

64. *El Despertar*, 6 February 1915. Among the numerous quotes in many newspapers, some are emblematic. See, for example, Juan Vargas M., "Feminismo. La mujer obrera," in *La Reforma*, 4 October 1906. "Que exija . . . la disminución de las horas de trabajo, para que pueda tambien saciar i nutrir su cerebro con las suaves luces de la ilustración" (Let her demand a reduction in working hours so that she may feed and nourish her brain with the soft light of enlightenment); Sara Cádiz, in "Sobre organizacion femenina obrera" (On organizing female workers), *La Reforma*, 28 June 1906, stated: "Es verdad que no somos culpables de nuestro atraso intelectual; son muchos los factores que influyen en contra de nuestro desarrollo mental" (We are not responsible for our intellectual backwardness; the factors conspiring against our mental development are manifold). See also Luis Eduardo Díaz, "Instrucción para la mujer," *La Reforma*, 29 June 1906; Abel Cruz Cañas, "La educación de la mujer," *El Despertar de los Trabajadores*, 12 March 1912; and "Mujeres, despertad," 28 October 1913.

65. *La Alborada* 2, no. 19, 11 November 1906; 2, no. 20, 18 November 1906; 1, no. 17, July 1906. "Las proletarias de Chile, las víctimas del taller, están despertando del sopor en que han permanecido la mayor parte de su vida. El pesado velo de ignorancia que ante su vista se estendía esta próximo a caer hecho girones, dando paso en su mente a la Verdad y a la Ciencia" (Chilean proletariat women are awakening from the stupor in which they have spent most of their lives. The heavy veil of ignorance covering their eyes will soon be torn, and Science and Truth will reach their minds).

66. *El Despertar de los Trabajadores*, 21 April 1914. "Si madres instruídas hubieramos tenido, la suerte del proletariado no estuviera hoy en las garras de la explotacion" (If we had had educated mothers, the proletariat's fate would not be today in the claws of exploiters).

67. Luis Emilio Recabarren, *La mujer y su educación* (Punta Arenas: Imp. "El Socialista," 1916). No pagination. Emphases are mine.

68. Recabarren's words in a speech recorded in *El Despertar de los Trabajadores*. 21 April 1914.

BIBLIOGRAPHICAL NOTE

The history of women in twentieth-century Latin America is in the process of being recovered and recounted. No general history of women in this century is yet available, and the interested reader has to rely on a few monographic studies on several key historical topics. Sociologists, political scientists, anthropologists, and economists are currently enriching gender literature with studies from the 1960s to the present. Given this situation, it is not surprising that there are no major studies, in either English or Spanish, of women in the labor force and in the labor movement in Argentina and Chile in the early twentieth century. Several labor histories have bits and pieces of information scattered throughout the text, but the topic is still awaiting monographic treatment.

This bibliography contains titles that will introduce the reader to the study of women's history in twentieth-century Spanish and Portuguese America, and will encourage further inquiry into more specialized works. Bibliographical guides to the field are especially recommended for surveying the state of the art in several disciplines. Stoner's *Latinas of the Americas* is particularly useful for its fifteen bibliographical sections preceded by excellent essays. In this suggested reading list, I have included a selected number of works on feminism because of its historical concern with the issues of working women, and some key works on contemporary issues.

Bibliographical Sources and Historiography

Deutsch, Sandra McGee. "Feminist Studies." In K. Lynn Stoner, ed., *Latinas of the Americas: A Source Book.* New York: Garland Publishing, 1989, pp. 129-52.

Greenberg, Janet. "Toward a History of Women's Periodicals: A Working Bibliography." In Seminar on Women and Culture in Latin America, *Women, Culture and Politics*, 182-231.

Hahner, June. "Recent Research on Women in Brazil." *Latin American Research Review* 20, no. 3 (1985): 163-79.

Lavrin, Asunción. "Women, the Family, and Social Change in Latin America." *World Affairs* 150, no. 2 (Fall 1987): 109-28.

Stoner, K. Lynn. *Latinas of the Americas: A Source Book.* New York: Garland Publishing, 1989.

Zabaleta, Marta. "Research on Latin American Women: In Search of Our Political Independence." *Bulletin of Latin American Studies* 5, no. 2 (1986): 97-103.

Women's History and Studies: General Works

Acosta-Belén, Edna, and Christine E. Bose, eds. *Integrating Latin American and Caribbean Women into the Curriculum and Research.* Albany: CELAC-IROW, 1991.

Alvarez, Sonia E. *Engendering Democracy in Brazil: Women's Movements in Transition Politics.* Princeton: Princeton University Press, 1990.

Carlson, Marifran. *Feminismo!: The Woman's Movement in Argentina from Its Beginnings to Eva Perón.* Chicago: Academy Chicago Publishers, 1988.

Chaney, Elsa. *Supermadre: Women in Politics in Latin America.* Austin: University of Texas Press, 1979.

French, John, and Mary Lynn Pedersen. "Women and Working-Class Mobilization in Postwar Sao Paulo, 1945-1948." *Latin American Research Review* (1989): 99-125.

Guy, Donna. "White Slavery, Public Health, and the Socialist Position on Legalized Prostitution in Argentina, 1913-1936." *Latin American Research Review* 23, no. 3 (1988): 60-80.

_____. "Prostitution and Penal Criminality in Buenos Aires, 1875-1937." In Lyman Johnson, ed., *The Problem of Order in Changing Societies: Essays on Crime and Policing in Argentina and Uruguay, 1750-1940*. Albuquerque: University of New Mexico Press, 1990.

_____. *Sex and Danger in Buenos Aires: Prostitution, Family, and Nation in Argentina*. Lincoln: University of Nebraska Press, 1991.

Hahner, June. *Emancipating the Female Sex: The Struggle for Women's Rights in Brazil, 1850-1940*. Durham, N.C.: Duke University Press, 1990.

Jaquette, Jane S. *The Women's Movement in Latin America: Feminism and the Transition to Democracy*. Winchester, Mass.: Unwin Hyman, 1989.

Jelin, Elizabeth, ed. *Women and Social Change in Latin America*. London: Zed Books, and United Nations Research Institute for Social Development, 1990.

Lavrin, Asunción. "The Ideology of Feminism in the Southern Cone, 1900-1940." The Wilson Center Working Papers: Latin American Program Paper no. 169. Washington, D.C.: The Wilson Center, 1985.

Little, Cynthia Jeffress. "Education, Philanthropy, and Feminism: Components of Argentine Womanhood, 1860-1926." In Asunción Lavrin, ed., *Latin American Women: Historical Perspectives*. Westport, Conn.: Greenwood Press, 1978, pp. 235-53.

Macias, Anna. *Against all Odds: The Feminist Movement in Mexico to 1940*. Westport, Conn.: Greenwood Press, 1982.

Mallon, Florencia E. "Patriarchy in the Transition to Capitalism: Central Peru, 1830-1950." *Feminist Studies* 13, no. 2 (Summer 1987): 379-407.

Masiello, Francine. "Women, State, and Family in Latin American Literature in the 1920s." In Seminar on Feminism and Culture, *Women, Culture and Politics*, pp. 27-47.

Miller, Francesca. "Latin American Feminists in the Transnational Arena." In Seminar on Feminism and Culture in Latin America, *Women, Culture and Politics*, pp. 10-26.

Nash, June, and Helen Safa, eds. *Women and Change in Latin America*. South Hadley, Mass,: Bergin & Garvey, 1985.

Patai, Daphne. *Brazilian Women Speak: Contemporary Life Stories*. New Brunswick, N.J.: Rutgers University Press, 1988.

Seminar on Feminism and Culture in Latin America. *Women, Culture, and Politics in Latin America*. Berkeley: University of California Press, 1990.

_____. "Toward a History of Women's Periodicals: An Introduction." In *Women, Culture and Politics*, pp. 173-82.

Stoner, K. Lynn Smith. *From the House to the Streets: The Cuban Feminist Movement For Legal Reform*. Durham, N.C.: Duke University Press, 1991.

WOMEN SCHOOL TEACHERS IN THE MEXICAN REVOLUTION
THE STORY OF REYNA'S BRAIDS

Mary Kay Vaughan

The Mexican Revolution of 1910 was reputedly not a revolution for women: women did not vote in national elections until 1958, they were marginalized from industrial work, discriminated against in divorce cases, and told that domesticity and motherhood constituted their citizenship.[1] Yet this revolution opened a field for creativity and self-realization for hundreds of Mexican women of humble, provincial backgrounds who became rural school teachers. They filled the ranks of the only profession opened to women since the nineteenth century and took up a crusade for "civilization." The school of the Mexican Revolution was not a simple school for teaching people to read and write. It aimed at a social and political literacy that would change the way people ate, raised children, relaxed, worked, and viewed the world, themselves, and their Patria.

In this essay, I probe the lives of three women school teachers, Reyna Manzano Carmona, Socorro Rivera Rodríguez, and Isaura Martínez Guzmán, to understand their empowerment as women, professionals, and revolutionary teachers.[2] I ask what difficulties accompanied women's entry into the teaching profession in a fundamentally agrarian society in which only 25 percent of women over 12 years of age were literate in 1910. Because rural school teachers were part of a revolutionary process of change and state formation, I probe the experiences of these women to gain insight into a central issue in Mexican revolutionary historiography: the interaction between the individual, socio-political movements, and the revolutionary state in the period 1920 to 1940.

Revisionist historians treat the state as the organizer and victor of the Mexican Revolution. They marginalize the role of popular forces to focus attention on state formation and on ambitious politicians who manipulated mass organizations and issues to gain power.[3] A number of works, including my own, have interpreted public education as a channel for state domination and the imposition of a western, capitalist paradigm on the peasantry and working class.[4] As historians question the revisionist approach and explore ways of understanding the role of individuals and social movements in the revolutionary process, teachers and schooling offer an intriguing field for study. Teachers were individuals who became employees of a revolutionary state. Many worked among peasants, or campesinos, major historical actors in the revolutionary process who were beneficiaries of land reform, and subjects to be co-opted by the emerging state. Education was a mechanism of incorporation. The process of empowerment of the school teacher was bound up with what may be viewed as a process of subordinating the campesino. However, I hypothesize here, on the basis of data limited to the Mexican state of Puebla, that teachers and campesinos had negotiating power in the formation of the state and that their revolutionary participation resulted in their simultaneous empowerment and domination.

Oral history is an approach to understanding the interaction between social subject, popular movements, and the state.[5] These teachers' testimonies capture the bravery, imagination, terror, and commitment with which they confronted opportunities and obstacles created by the revolution. Oral history uncovers the ideological notions they learned in childhood from families, teachers, and others and carried into the teaching profession. It conveys their sense of autonomy in relation to the state and the communities in which they worked. It reveals their willingness to subordinate themselves to the state and the peasantry and their ability to negotiate with both.

Oral history also has limitations as a source for historical analysis. The experiences of Reyna Manzano Carmona, Socorro Rivera Rodríguez, and Isaura Martínez Guzmán are unique and may not be generalized. Like many rural teachers of the 1920-40 period, they came from modest, small-town backgrounds and semiliterate to literate families, separated in some way from precapitalist social formations or what François-Javier Guerra calls traditional organic collectivities (villages of subsistence farmers, indigenous communities, haciendas).[6]

However, the specificities of these teachers' experiences require definition. One specificity is temporal. Born between 1914 and 1922, they began their careers between 1935 and 1940 during the presidency of Lázaro Cárdenas. In this period, the Mexican Revolution reached its zenith of reform in the distribution of thousands of hectares of land to peasants, the winning of trade union rights and collective bargaining contracts by industrial and urban workers, the nationalization of foreign-owned oil wells and other properties, and the implementation of a policy of "socialist" education, which instructed teachers to act as leaders of reform. Simultaneously, worker and peasant organizations were consolidated into the single state political party, the Partido Nacional Revolucionario, renamed the Partido Revolucionario Mexicano, known as the PRI after 1946. In retrospect, the Cárdenas reforms served to eliminate obstacles to industrialization (inefficient large landed estates and foreign control over natural resources) and to consolidate political power in the central state and PNR (PRM/PRI) after decades of dispute and centrifugality. That is, these teachers participated in a moment of profound contradiction in the revolution: an unprecedented level of organized mobilization for social justice simultaneous with a centralization of political power, which contributed to 30 years of capitalist growth and relative political quiescence after 1940.[7]

A further specificity in the experience of Reyna Manzano, Socorro Rivera, and Isaura Martínez is ideological. They shared the zeal for social justice and nationalism that animated Cárdenas' many supporters. Not all female primary school teachers were so enthusiastic. At the beginning of the Cárdenas presidency, antireligious aspects of socialist educational policy alienated many women teachers and led to their resignation or dismissal in several parts of the country.[8] Reyna Manzano, Socorro Rivera, and Isaura Martínez came from liberal political backgrounds. Although they may have held religious beliefs, they supported the secularizing policies of the state.

A third specificity is geographical. These teachers lived and taught in the state of Puebla (see map). Like every Mexican region, Puebla had its own socio-economic, cultural, and political particularities. On the eve of the Mexican Revolution of 1910, Puebla was typical of central Mexico in its abundant indigenous and mestizo communities living in varying degrees of subordination to large haciendas or commercial *cacicazgos* (personal-familial networks of power). Although the women teachers examined here shared a liberal, secular political culture nurtured in parts of Puebla, Catholic sentiments wary of secularization were also deeply embedded in Puebla's social fabric. The society was strongly hierarchical with sharp racial and class distinctions. Partly because it was poorer and more agrarian than northern Mexico and partly because its social relations were less dominated by commerce and the market place, in 1910, Puebla had a smaller literate population than the north: 17 percent of women over 12 and 26 percent of the men versus 43 percent of the women and 48 percent of the men in the north.[9]

In the revolution, different sectors of the rural population (subsistence village farmers, peons on haciendas, medium-size landowners, merchants, artisans) challenged the structure of wealth and power and initiated a struggle for a redistribution of resources that was not resolved or brought under state control until the late 1930s. Not all regions of Mexico were as contentious and mobilized as Puebla between 1910 and 1940. Puebla was not a hospitable environment for the state's modernizing school project in the 1920s and 1930s.[10] Although the rural population mobilized for

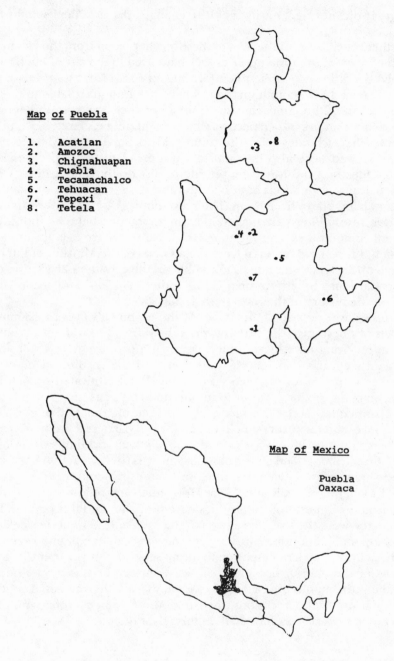

Map of Puebla

1. Acatlan
2. Amozoc
3. Chignahuapan
4. Puebla
5. Tecamachalco
6. Tehuacan
7. Tepexi
8. Tetela

Map of Mexico

Puebla
Oaxaca

change, it did not necessarily seek the changes that teachers sought to introduce.

Further specificities in the lives of these teachers stem from the fact that for a long span of their mature lives they have lived in the city of Puebla in material conditions of modest comfort and freedom from want, disease, and drudgery. These conditions would have been unimaginable to them in their youth. Although each came from a provincial background, today they articulate an urban perspective, which might not be shared by women school teachers who never left the countryside or small towns. The teachers interviewed here also internalize a notion of history's progressive nature. Questions motivated by postmodernist doubts about history as progress or marxist notions of public education as a form of state domination draw blank stares from them. Their testimonies cannot wholly explain their own revolutionary participation as an interaction between individuals, rural communities, and the state. To arrive at a more balanced interpretation, I have used material from the archives of the Ministry of Public Education (Secretaría de Educación Pública), the presidential archives of Lázaro Cárdenas in the Archivo General de la Nación, and secondary works on the history of the revolution in that state.

In this essay, I describe four phases of these women's lives to examine four sets of questions. The first concerns the difficulties women encountered in receiving an education and entering a profession in a still predominantly agrarian society in transition. Did the revolution make a difference in promoting women's schooling? What motivated women to pursue teaching careers? The second question concerns the professional lives of women teachers in a society still suspicious of women in public life. Did the revolutionary process help to break down barriers to women's participation in public life? What were the possibilities and limits of professional advancement? The third question concerns the interaction between these women school teachers and the campesino communities they worked in between 1935 and 1945. How much negotiating power did teachers and campesino communities have over the school program? To what degree were the teachers agents of the state and to what degree did they enjoy some autonomy? In their interaction with campesina women, did the school teachers empower them or seek to control them in the interests of the state or dominant classes? Fourthly, I wish to raise questions about the mature phase of these women's lives: their material conditions, their political perceptions, their notions of women's roles, and the impact their experiences have had on their daughters.

Being Taught and Becoming Teachers

Although Reyna Manzano, Socorro Rivera, and Isaura Martínez attended primary school during the 1920s when the federal government launched its school crusade, their education was influenced by nineteenth century traditions. They were from provincial towns and villages where schools had opened in the course of the nineteenth century. Their families belonged to the small literate sector, 29 percent of Mexico's adult population in 1910.[11] They were poor but not impoverished. They were products of mestizaje, or racial mixture: each family was mestizo with at least one indigenous grandparent. The women came from secular, pro-schooling environments fed by a liberal ideology that celebrated principles of citizenship, equality, and patriotism and regarded education as a necessary step in self-improvement. This political culture had been fed by historical experience so that collective memory in their home regions recalled participation in the patriotic struggles against the Spanish in 1810 and the French in the 1860s.[12] These teachers' families had separated themselves from traditional collectivities (agrarian villages, indigenous communities) and looked to mobility and education for self-improvement and self-realization. However, even after the Revolution reaffirmed liberal principles and an ideology of change, the environment was fraught with obstacles to literacy acquisition: poverty, class hierarchies and distinctions, and a general skepticism as to literacy's utility.

Reyna Manzano's experience illustrates the obstacles to education persistent in a proeducation, revolutionary environment. She was born in 1921 in a poor barrio of Tetela de Ocampo, a district in Puebla's Sierra Norte, the mountainous escarpment separating the central plateau and hacienda district from the coastal lowlands. A region of small-scale mestizo property owners, merchants, and artisans dominating indigenous farming communities, Tetela was Puebla's heartland of liberal pedagogy and an exporter of teachers.[13] A member of the Bonilla family, Tetela's leading family, always directed or taught in the state normal school in the capital of Puebla since its foundation by family patriarch Juan Crisóstomo Bonilla when he was state governor in 1879. An appreciation of schooling developed among Tetela's mestizo sector, to which Reyna Manzano belonged. Although she came from a poor carpenter's family, she had an aunt who was a teacher. As a young child, she dressed up in her mother's high heeled shoes and played at being a teacher.

In the poverty of Reyna's family lay both the difficulty and the drive behind her dream. Although both her parents had some primary education and sent their children to school, they of necessity valued work first. Because her father drank his weekly earnings on Saturday nights, the burden of subsistence fell on his wife and children. Reyna had to help her mother grind corn, sell tamales and bread in Tetela and nearby villages, and bring in the bean and corn harvests on the family plot. She is constantly reminded today of how her bare feet froze on the icy stones as she walked to markets.

For Reyna, as perhaps for many Mexican children, school was a release from the painful drudgery of everyday life. The playtime aspect of school

had to have enormous attraction given the opprobrium she was forced to
endure to stay in school. Class distinctions were embedded in the schooling process in Tetela despite the district's liberalism. She came to school
barefoot and poorly dressed. Children moved away from her. She was
always punished for coming late, a condition she could not avoid given the
distance she lived from school and the work tasks she had to complete for
her mother. She was short on school supplies and books because her
mother could not afford them. She never played outside during recess for
fear of being beaten up. She stayed in the classroom and studied. Despite
the hardships of homelife and her mother's need for her help, Reyna's
mother convinced her to remain in school at critical moments when she
was close to dropping out.

Another sustaining factor in Reyna's education was the network of
female school teachers who encouraged her and to whom she looked for
support, protection, and dreaming. In the late 1920s and early 1930s when
Reyna attended school, Mexico was looking for women teachers. The
women teachers of Tetela had a deep sense of mission predating the revolution. They searched among their students for new converts. Asuncion
Bonilla, Trinidad García Islas, Dolores Posadas Olayo, Carmen Caballero
de Córtes, Alicia Braun—all formed part of Reyna Manzano's nurturing
network. By the time she completed the fifth grade, she was in top place in
her class and living in the home of one of her teachers.

Nonetheless, the feminine network was not enough to catapult Reyna
out of Tetela into a teaching career. This required "divine" male intervention. Upon a visit to Tetela, Alicia Braun's sister, a spiritist who talked with
the dead, engaged Reyna and the other women teachers in a seance. An
old Indian voice spoke to Reyna half in Nahuatl and half in bad Spanish.
It was Juan Francisco Lucas, patriarch of the Sierra Norte, leader of Indian
armies against the French in the battle of Puebla in 1862, a staunch
believer in schools, dead now for 15 years.[14] "You want to be a teacher," the
old cacique told the young girl, "I will help you to be a teacher. You will be
a teacher."

In fact, her female mentors launched Reyna's career. Spiritually, their
support helped her to overcome the guilt she felt in leaving the family she
had helped to sustain. In November 1936 at the age of 15, Reyna Manzano
left Tetela for the first time in her life. Her braids, an Indian custom bor-
rowed by some mestizo women in Tetela, symbolized her sense of social
and gender subordination as well as her provincialism. She rode on horse-
back in the company of one of her teachers to the train station in
Chignahuapan. The roar of the train whistle and the clouds of steam from
the locomotor petrified her, but she boarded with the excitement and conviction that a new day was about to dawn. That day took long in coming.
Once in Puebla in the home of her teacher's mother, the mother turned
the girl from the countryside into a maid. "I had to do all the housework.
She made me sleep on newspapers on the cold floor. I had to suffer insults

and humiliations as if poor people had no rights to anything." No matter how great her grief, she was determined not to return to Tetela where more poverty and discrimination awaited her. Several months later, her teacher secured her a teaching post in the town of Huatlatlauca in the district of Tepexi.

The path which led Isaura Martínez into a teaching career was less tortuous than Reyna Manzano's. Although Acatlán in southern Puebla had a proeducation liberal heritage, it was weaker and more disputed than Tetela's. In the largely Mixtec-speaking municipality of San Gerónimo, where Isaura was born, only seven percent of the population was literate in 1900.[15] Isaura's parents were among the literate. Her father and his brothers were a notch above ordinary campesinos because they were musicians, a talent in demand for religious and patriotic village functions. With the exception of Isaura's father, the Martínez brothers were not convinced believers in the improving power of schooling: basic literacy was sufficient for men and of little use to women. Isaura's maternal grandfather was, however, a believer in education. This Mixtec-speaking farmer chided her for playing outdoors as a child and insisted that she read. Her father was an active man. He distinguished himself from his brothers by leaving San Gerónimo for the district capital and by promoting his daughter's education.

Unlike Reyna Manzano, Isaura Martínez was an only child and the focus of her father's attention. "You have two choices in life," he told her, "You can be a servant or you can be a teacher." He proposed that she become a teacher. To ensure her education he moved from Acatlán to Veracruz to Puebla. Although her father did not participate in the Mexican Revolution as a combatant, he took advantage of the atmosphere of rapid change it generated. By the mid-1920s, this *tocador* (player) of sacred music from rustic San Gerónimo was playing in a jazz quartet in the cosmopolitan port of Veracruz. Here, Isaura attended primary school which she completed in Puebla when her family moved there to promote her career. Protected, encouraged, and exposed to new environments, Isaura Martínez entered the normal school in Puebla in 1934 and performed as a model student.

Socorro Rivera's educational experience falls between that of Reyna and Isaura. She was born in Chatzumba, Oaxaca, in 1914 into a family that was more educated, more dedicated to reading, and more self-consciously liberal than Reyna's or Isaura's. Her uncle Hilario Salas was a member of the Partido Liberal Mexicano, the political organization which mobilized opposition to the dicatatorship of Porfirio Díaz between 1906 and 1910. A one-time textile worker in Orizaba, Veracruz, where he had come into contact with opposition journalists in Mexico City, he became PLM organizer in southern Mexico and in 1906 led an uprising of peasants in Acayucán, Veracruz. Socorro's father was a school teacher and one of two men who had left his village to study in Oaxaca. He educated his children in the local primary school, then sent them off to perfect their studies in Oaxaca,

Puebla, and Mexico City. He valued professional advancement through
education. For women, the path was normal school, which Socorro
attended briefly in Oaxaca but left when she developed malaria. She
returned to Chatzumba to become the primary school teacher with little
more than a primary school education. In 1935, she came to Puebla with a
brother to seek a teaching position in the federal schools.

The youthful experiences of Reyna, Isaura, and Socorro raise certain
questions about women's access to education and motivation for seeking a
teaching career in the early years of the Mexican Revolution. The prerevolutionary entry of women into education set the stage for post-
revolutionary expansion. As opportunities for education opened after the
revolution, what factors encouraged more women to go to school and
what factors discouraged them? Were literate parents, role models, and
support networks important motivators, as they were in the cases of Reyna,
Isaura, and Socorro? The life histories of these women show how revolutionary ideology reaffirming liberal principles of equality, democracy, and
self-improvement motivated individuals who had no direct participation in
political struggle. On the other hand, were regional cultures of popular
liberalism, nurtured in the nineteenth century, decisive breeding grounds
for future women teachers? The case of western Mexico, where an acti-
vated popular Catholicism flourished at the end of the nineteenth century
and similarly produced women teachers, would suggest a more complicated picture.

Why was the motivation to pursue schooling so much weaker among the
campesina women and girls whom Reyna, Socorro, and Isaura encountered when they entered teaching? Although the campesina women faced
the same obstacles that poverty and low social status created for Reyna,
many guarded a more profound moral skepticism about revolutionary
schooling than did these women teachers who shared a faith in modernity
and change. What were the ingredients of their resistance?

The revolution increased and legitimized a process of social mobility
well underway with economic growth in the late nineteenth century.
Women's leaving home became more acceptable. Teaching was an outlet
for women's creativity that opened wide as revolutionary governments
made primary education a priority. When Socorro, Reyna, and Isaura took
up teaching, they seem not to have been motivated by any desire to escape
marriage nor did they work because they had not found husbands. Each
pursued it with a will to realize herself in nontraditional ways. Reyna, the
little mestizo girl with Indian braids, fought hard to overcome discrimination and poverty in order to be a person. In pursuing a teaching career,
she may have sought to escape the fate of her mother, burdened with an
unproductive husband and condemned to support the family with meager
resources. Socorro, encouraged by a brood of brothers and sisters and a
supportive father, came from a teaching family and moved with ease into
this career. Isaura's father doted on his only daughter and realized part of

his own aspirations for upward mobility in sponsoring her entry into teaching. How generalizable are their cases?

Professional Conditions

Although the opportunity to become rural school teachers opened to women on an unprecedented scale, they faced precarious working conditions in Puebla in the 1930s. The anarchy that prevailed in the countryside masked an intense contest for power and resources among different sectors of the rural population. The ambience of violent dispute made it difficult to carry out schooling on a regular basis.

When Reyna Manzano set out to take her first job in Huatlatlauca, Tepexi, she took a bus and a train, then rode on a burro accompanied by the mailman to the town of Tepejic where the local doctor was to give her directions for the rest of her journey. The doctor could not receive her because he was overburdened with autopsies of the victims of robberies and feuds. On his table were the bodies of a campesina woman and her baby, knifed in their home. The doctor sent Reyna to a neighbor's house. Here she met a woman and her daughter who were recuperating from an ordeal in which the young woman's boyfriend and his companions had taken her off to the mountains and repeatedly raped her. The next day, two people were brought into town near death after having been assaulted on the road by Ajamilpa, a favorite point of attack for El Tallarín, Puebla's most intrepid bandit.[16]

Fifteen years old and scared to death, Reyna too had to travel the road to Ajamilpa. Little wonder that when she arrived in Huatlatlauca, she almost immediately married the director of the village school, Celerino García. He seemed to her a source of protection. When Socorro Rivera took her first job in the remote Indian village of Xitlama in southern Tehuacán, her father and sister accompanied her. She married a man who worked in Obras Públicas and was not always with her, but a brother, sister, or cousin almost always lived with her in the villages where she taught. Army troops escorted her to Centros de Cooperación, biweekly pedagogical seminars held by the Secretaria de Educacion Publica(SEP) to train teachers.

Under the best of circumstances, in a society unaccustomed to women in public life, the single woman was suspect and the object of taunting and rumor. She was thought to be loose because in her work she associated with male teachers in Centros de Cooperación, union meetings, and other events. In a normal situation, she was the target of male pursuit; in a revolutionary situation in the countryside, she was fair game for rape. In April 1935, a woman teacher was abducted by rebels protesting socialist education in the district of Teziutlán and taken to the hill of Cihuitl where rebels gang-raped her for a week.[17]

In such an environment, women teachers often sought marriage as a source of protection. Their professional environment did not provide them with the rights and space they needed as single women. Too often male school inspectors took advantage of female teachers. If a young woman accepted the inspector's conditions, she was favored in salary and placement. If she refused, she might be sent to an inhospitable village or shamed as a "bad element" in teachers' assemblies. State teachers may have been more vulnerable to inspectors than federal teachers. The latter formed a solid trade union in the 1930s while the state teachers' efforts to unionize did not pay off until the late 1950s. The union itself did not bring full protection and rights to women. Socorro Rivera was one of the few women to participate in the formation of the Puebla section of the national federal teachers' union in the 1930s. Her participation was short-lived. As a rule, the male-dominated union has tended to discriminate against the promotion and advancement of women. In part, this discrimination stems from the self-perception of women of Socorro's generation. They viewed their role as teachers as one of service, not formal politics. Their duties to their husbands and families often prevented them from taking a role in union affairs. However, once a particular style of male-dominated politics became imbedded, it was difficult for women to penetrate without compromising themselves.[18]

The exception to these observations is Isaura Martínez, professionally the most successful of the three teachers. She is the only one to have received a normal school degree, which became her armor in a male world. The normal school gave her role models of remarkable women leaders who held their own in a public world of men. Adela Márquez de Martínez was a towering figure in the Puebla normal school, a superb and meticulous pedagogue, the leader of a prolonged, bitter teachers' strike in 1923-24. Isaura was close to Adela Márquez de Martínez and her son, Enrique Martínez Márquez, who became a power in Puebla education. With a normal school degree, Isaura Martínez was placed in less danger-ous, more hospitable jobs than Reyna Manzano and Socorro Rivera. She entered teaching in 1939 when the violence had subsided and a consensus around schooling was rapidly taking shape. Unlike Reyna Manzano, who believes that marriage and family prevented her from upgrading her qual-ifications, Isaura Martínez never married and was able to obtain a degree from the Escuela Normal Superior that entitled her to teach in high school. For 32 years, she has been a key administrator in the Centro Esco-lar de Niños Heroes de Chapultepec, the jewel in the Puebla state school system founded by Adela Márquez de Martínez and her son, Enrique Martínez Márquez. Protected by her degrees, her status, and her connec-tions, Isaura Martínez took a leadership role in the formation of the state teachers' union in the late 1950s. Well placed from the beginning of her career, she successfully played the rules of clientelist politics to secure a maximum professional self-realization.

Historians ought to explore the effect of revolutionary violence on the status of women. Did it generally force them to seek the protection of men? Although male-monopolized violence may have acted as a deterrent to women's rights and public self-expression, can it not also be hypothesized that the revolution gave women school teachers an opportunity to cast themselves as makers of history, a role they otherwise would not have had? Can we generalize about the service mentality and limited role in union affairs for women who came of age in the mid-1930s? The contrast between Isaura, on the one hand, and Reyna and Socorro, on the other, would suggest not.

Schooling as Negotiated Change

If the families of Reyna, Socorro, and Isaura belonged to the small literate sector of Puebla in 1910, it was the other 75 percent of Puebla's people whom revolutionary governments hoped to educate in reading and writing, citizenship, hygiene, and market economics.[19] Toward them, the energies of Reyna, Socorro, and Isaura were directed. The resistance that Puebla's rural communities showed toward schooling was widespread through the mid-1930s. Culture, poverty, and revolution contributed to resistance.

As James Scott has written, the moral economy of the subsistence farmer is bound up with a spiritual ethos suspicious of the new, the uncertain, and the extra-local.[20] As schools opened in Puebla in the nineteenth century, indigenous communities often ignored them in an effort to protect their cultural autonomy. Mestizo communities frequently suspected secular education for its lack of religious content and its portent of change.[21] As market penetration and state formation undermined the organic unity of agrarian communities, they could stimulate an interest in schooling as a tool for survival or empowerment. Scholars note the positive impact of modern market penetration on creating a demand for schooling by increasing commerce and literate occupations, introducing new printed information, and encouraging mobility. However, modern market penetration can also create misery and reduce people's capacity to invest in schooling. On the eve of the revolution, economic growth had impoverished hundreds of *poblano* villagers on their small plots of land. They sold their labor at low rates to haciendas. They sold their crops at low prices to haciendas and merchants and bought necessities at rapidly rising prices. Literacy rates were stagnant or declining in the hacienda districts of central Puebla in 1910. Even in communities that maintained schools, only a small percentage of children attended them, and resentment toward supporting them with the mandatory headtax lay just beneath the surface. In 1910, when the onset of the Mexican Revolution produced widespread revolt in rural Puebla, one of the first acts of the rebels was to refuse to pay taxes, a large share of which went to pay the school teachers.[22]

The revolution temporarily strengthened resistance to schooling in Puebla. Many agrarian villages mobilized to reclaim lost rights, resources, and space. The inability of any political faction to consolidate power at the state level between 1910 and 1930 led to a reassertion of local autonomy. Village elites and local powerholders often viewed the school and the teacher as suspect representatives of national ideology and authority—with good reason. Unlike the prerevolutionary school which taught the three "r's" and Mexican patriotic history, revolutionary education challenged the fabric of rural life. It sought to penetrate the community and to invade the home with pretensions of modernization and improvement. Most of Puebla's peasant communities lived at a precarious subsistence margin. Frequent drought and frosts made hunger a persistent reality. Disease and death permeated daily life and were spiritually integrated into mentalities. The encounter between these communities and an aggressive minority certain that it held the tools for eliminating disease, death, and hunger had to have been dramatic and charged. The trauma of the encounter is best illustrated by vaccination against small pox and other contagious diseases, a process which began in the late nineteenth century and became a major task of the revolutionary school. With protection from army troops, teachers often injected unwilling communities. Mistakes abounded. Sometimes they did not inoculate properly and caused deaths. In other instances, the sick asked for shots when it was too late. Families and friends believed they died from the vaccine.[23]

The encounter between teacher and community could have been eased if teachers had had organic links with community leadership or had been members of the communities. In Puebla through the mid-1930s, teachers tended to be outsiders. Their links with community leadership were weak. Because the men of the communities were engrossed in an intense struggle with each other and with outside powerholders over a redistribution of resources (land, water, commerce, and political office), they paid scant attention to the school. Campesina women were a primary target for the school program, which envisioned transforming their homes into models of urban orderliness, hygiene, and nutrition so that they would raise healthier, more productive children. But campesina women were even more distant from the school than men. The notion of women's education was alien to most of them. The violent ambience around them discouraged them from letting their daughters out of their sight. Families firmly resisted sending adult women and young girls to night classes because of dangers at dusk and because classes were coeducational. They were equally afraid to leave young girls with male teachers.[24]

To complicate further the encounter between community and teacher, neither side had the resources to bring about the kind of transformation for which the Secretaría de Educación Pública (SEP) called. SEP discourse enunciated a broad array of tools and methods to sanitize communities: vaccination, water purification, crop and diet diversification, modern medicines and antiseptic first aid, eradication of flies, garbage removal, sewage disposal, building latrines, getting the animals out of the house, bathing, changing clothes. But, even after receiving land, communities had few resources for such experimentation. Who could grow lettuce or bathe without water? Teachers lacked resources, know-how, and training. Deep-water wells were expensive undertakings beyond their engineering or fiscal capacities. Building outhouses and septic tanks were major tasks for the novice teachers.

Between 1934 and 1936, resistance reached a pitch of intensity when the national policy of socialist education challenged religious values.[25] In Puebla, the few children in rural schools left them. So intense was the reaction in many parts of Mexico that President Cárdenas abandoned anticlericalism to emphasize social reform through the school. Between 1936 and 1945, resistance began to subside. Between 1936 and 1938 in Puebla as in the rest of the nation, the political machine of the official state party (PNR-PRM) was consolidated. Competing peasant and worker associations were organized into state-level federations, brought into national confederations, and integrated into the party. State political machines incorporated local powerholders. Puebla's governor rid the countryside of bandits and disarmed the peasants.[26] Once integrated into the state, their local disputes temporarily resolved, community leaders could turn their attention to schooling. In this gesture, they were encouraged by the PNR-PRM and the national peasant confederation.[27]

A political explanation for the transition is inadequate. In the process of encounter between school and community from 1921, each side negotiated with the other the parameters and content of the school program. The negotiation was painful, hesitant, and indirect. In the process, a rapidly changing environment helped to demonstrate the utility of literacy and certain other elements in the formal school program. Women like Reyna Manzano, Socorro Rivera, and Isaura Martínez played a vital role in this negotiation. The female teacher was the critical interlocutor between the school's program and campesina women. The empowerment of these three teachers as women and as citizens derives from this negotiating experience. However, it is difficult to obtain from them a balanced picture of the encounter because they measured their success by the changes they made in communities and because they have little critical perspective on their "civilizing" mission. They could never understand how delousing children's hair and encouraging bathing were acts of cultural aggression. If told they acted as agents of state domination, they would wonder because what they taught often came out of their own backgrounds and was not an official instruction.

Reyna Manzano and Socorro Rivera were improvised teachers who taught what they knew from their own lives. Much of their modernizing message was not a state imposition but a spontaneous articulation of their values and aspirations in a revolutionary setting. When Socorro Rivera started teaching in Nahuatl-speaking Xitlama in the sierra east of Tehuacán, she attracted young men to night classes with an old hand-driven Victrola. The machine was her entrée in introducing the townfolk to urbanity, Mexico, capitalism, and notions of social justice in a masterful complexity of ideas, values, and programs that synthesized the ideology of the Mexican Revolution:

> I told them there were big cities, like Coxcatlán, because they sold fruit there, but even bigger than Coxcatlán, with many children and many trucks. The children knew how to read and write and the big *señores* earned a lot of money. I told them they should change their lives—put on a pair of pants, a decent shirt, and get on the ball! I played music on my Victrola—the Flor de Maíz and the Zacatecas March, music of the day. I taught them to sing the Agrarista Hymn. I told them that we had just fought a revolution, a fight for land on the part of those who had lost it, and that everyone deserved justice.

She was 17 years old and without training from the Secretaría de Educación Pública. She had learned the Agrarista Hymn from her primary school teacher. Many recipes she taught to campesina women were her mother's. Using the *huizache* plant to make ink was an old trick of her schoolmaster father. Similarly, Reyna Manzano brought her burning sense of equality into her classroom with no official encouragement. Petlalcingo, Acatlán, was divided between comfortable, urban, Spanish-speakers with some education and non-Spanish-speaking agricultural laborers. They did not mix, but in her classroom "all were equal." Although coeducation was prohibited by community fiat, she encouraged competition in academic contests between boys and girls to "bring girls up to the level of the boys."

This is not to suggest that the SEP had no influence. Teachers learned through biweekly Centros de Cooperación and through the SEP publication, *El Maestro Rural.* They used SEP texts when they received them. Further, these women entered teaching when an accelerated process of bureaucraticization was reducing teacher autonomy. It might be argued that their brief autonomy was merely apparent because what they taught through improvisation was compatible with what the state wanted: a little reading and writing, a lot of patriotism, and some middle class notions about productivity, mobility, cleanliness, and change. But the teachers themselves shared many of the programmatic principles of the SEP. Their success in implementing these depended upon their imaginations and the responses of peasant communities.

While Ministry of Education officials had a notion of the homogeneity of rural life, these women teachers were sensitive to its specificities. One town would be spotlessly clean, another squalid. In one village, a group of women could be organized to support the school; in another, they scurried off with their baskets to market. The specificities of rural life also demanded that the teachers honor SEP instructions more in principle than in practice. They learned that direct approaches got them nowhere. They were often rebuffed when they visited campesino homes. If the teachers wanted to change the way campesina women cooked, it was most effectively done through preparing a collective meal at a patriotic fiesta under the teacher's direction. If they wanted to change the campesina household, the best way was to make the teacher's home a model with her notion of a kitchen, furniture, mattresses, latrines. When Reyna Manzano wanted to improve domestic hygiene in the town of Amozoc near Puebla, she had to begin with the children in her classroom in a five-year project that slowly built up trust through its demonstration effect. Despite the official anticlerical ideology of socialist education between 1934 and 1936, the teachers did not challenge religious values. Socorro Rivera attended mass in order to hear what the priest said about her and the other teachers. In Hueyotlipán, she made a friend of the priest who helped her mount patriotic theater productions.

There were two basic changes that the school helped to affect in campesino family life: inoculation and the raising of the hearth from ground to waist level. Over time, families came to recognize that the inoculated survived more epidemics than those who were unprotected. They came to accept shots. Prior to the introduction of antibiotics after World War II, inoculation was the best shield yet found against child mortality. Like inoculation, the transfer of cooking from the ground to waist level was occurring independently of the school. Teachers hastened the change but did not complete it. Traditionally, campesina women cooked on the ground on a *tecuile*, which consisted of three stones placed in a triangle around a fire. On them rested the *comal* for heating tortillas and beside it the *metate* for grinding corn. Families sat on the ground around the tecuile and used tortillas as eating utensils. The project of the school was to raise the hearth to waist level in a hygienic and labor-saving innovation which would at the same time remove the smoke from the home through a chimney. Families would be obliged to eat at a table with spoons and forks in a "civilized" manner. Of these proposals, raising the hearth to waist level caught on among many campesina women because it saved their backs.

Otherwise, the rural communities of Puebla tended to drive the school back to the classroom and to limit its direct role in community life to teaching children, fomenting sports, and celebrating patriotic ritual. The school's elaboration of patriotic ritual, replete with civic fiestas full of oratory, drama, music, fireworks, and food, was a nineteenth century phenomenon familiar to communities. The revolution added new elements: athletic competitions, notions of social justice, agrarian reform, workers' rights, and equality enshrined in the Constitution of 1917, the collective quest for modernity and national dignity independent of foreign powers and identified with the Partido Nacional Revolucionario.[28]

Although Mexican women did not vote in national elections until 1958, women teachers played an enormous role in cementing Mexican citizenship. The Mexican government's expropriation of foreign-owned oil wells in March 1938 became the act through which Mexicans became conscious of their citizenship. Teachers guided a spontaneous popular reaction and orchestrated a vast campaign to raise funds to compensate the foreign owners. They turned this event into a thoroughly didactic experience. Socorro Rivera was working in Ajalpam, a district of textile workers and campesinos near Tehuacán. Although the people of Ajalpam had never responded to the school's social projects, they mobilized when they learned of the oil expropriation. Socorro recalls:

> It was a marvelous moment for all the people, the workers, the campesinos, the children, the merchants, everyone. The emotion was precious— precious to remember, I cry thinking about it. Every Monday morning, the children came to school with their centavitos to pay for the oil. Everyone helped. We organized fiestas, kermesses, and dances. We made wreaths of flowers, confetti, and streamers. The *señoras* prepared *chalupas* and *tamales*. We sold them to pay for the oil. And the workers! You cannot imagine with what *cariño* they came to give their money! It was so moving because you saw people so poor, who had no money, not even for their daily needs, but with what *cariño* they brought the little they had to pay the national debt!

A massive, collective school lesson opened for the teachers around the oil expropriation. They taught children and adults where the oil came from, what it did for production and could do, who owned it, for whose benefit, how poorly the foreigners paid the Mexican workers, how miserably they lived without schools, hospitals, and decent housing.

In 1939 Isaura Martínez, the youngest of the three teachers, entered teaching service. She began in Cañada Morelos, Tecamachalco, a community of ejidatarios, land reform recipients of much struggle and fame. She began to teach at the moment when resistance was subsiding. Her explanation is somewhat official; of course, everyone loved the school. The campesinos knew that their children's future depended upon it. Literacy had proved itself indispensable to their own keeping of accounts in the management of their lands. How different things were from the Porfiriato when the campesinos were cheated by the company store because they could not count. But six years before, the local teacher would have been frustrated by children who did not attend, by women who fled in the other direction, by men who paid scant attention. Seven years later in 1946 in another community of Tecamachalco, the ejidatarios presented Reyna Manzano and her husband with a plaque for their service—a photograph of palm trees and the seashore. They handed them an envelope of money to show their gratitude. They gave the children candy for excellence in performance on their examinations. One father was delighted when his son could answer questions he himself could not. Reyna Manzano chuckled, convinced that they wanted to be literate in order to be equal to the "cultos" (the educated) of the community. Important as well was the school inspector's observation. As trucks and buses came through on the new highway, many a youngster wanted to drive one, and that required a primary school certificate.[29]

Was the empowerment of these women school teachers at the expense of campesina women and their communities? My study of revolutionary primary education in the state of Puebla has persuaded me that it was less a process of explicit state domination than one of negotiation. In a period of intense popular mobilization, incipient bureaucracy, and a relatively weak state, both peasant communities and teachers had some degree of power and autonomy in defining the school program and its outcome. By the time teachers were effectively subjected to bureaucratic controls and peasants integrated into the new state, peasant communities had successfully driven education out of private life and back to the classroom and basketball court. Teachers like Reyna Manzano, Isaura Martínez, and Socorro Rivera did not abandon their attempts to diversify the campesino diet or get the flies and animals out of the homes, but they worked "with" people rather than "on" them.

To what degree did the school teachers empower campesina women? To what degree did their teaching contribute to controlling and dominating them as subjects of a capitalist state? Like the revolutionary state's educational policy, the women teachers examined here never had an ideology of feminism that challenged domesticity or women's fundamental roles as mothers. I have no evidence that they ever directly challenged male dominance in the campesino household. In fact, Reyna Manzano kept her hair in braids and was a faithful servant of her husband. Indirectly, however, it can be argued that the teachers challenged gender inequalities. For one, they sought to communicate directly with campesina women without the intermediation of men about issues relevant not only to the organization of their lives and those of their families but about citizenship and the wider world. Two, the very existence of the school implicitly empowered campesina women in the public world. As the traditional guardians of their children's socialization, mothers' participation was required by the school—even if that participation at first took the form of refusing to send children to school. Three, the women teachers were vigorously committed to the education of young girls as a mechanism for equalizing their opportunities. Probably more than Reyna Manzano and Socorro Rivera, Isaura Martínez promoted the physical education of girls, that is, their participation in sports and games, because her normal school training legitimized this. Within the sphere of domesticity, the women teachers attempted to reduce the burdens of women through such gestures as raising the hearth to waist level. In matters of sexuality, neither the women teachers nor the campesina women allowed the state to interfere. Repeated attempts on the part of educational policy makers to introduce sexual education and sex hygiene met with limited success.

On the other hand, it can be argued that the women teachers participated in wresting control over children's socialization from campesino mothers and placing a large portion of socialization in the hands of the state. It can be argued that in their awe for modernity, they disparaged aspects of peasant life that had given women power and respect, such as traditional healing. It can be hypothesized that by using textbooks that pictured campesino families as equal members of the Mexican nation, the teachers beguiled them and contributed to false consciousness. There is little doubt that the Mexican Revolution facilitated a rapid transition from an agrarian to an industrial society. This involved the disintegration of pre-capitalist social formations within the context of capitalist growth. Hence, the revolutionary school fostered integration into a new world. The school was—and is—an ideological apparatus of domination. On the other hand, because of the very high level of social mobilization and the relative weakness of the state in the years of revolutionary consolidation, the school did not articulate a set of purely bourgeois values but was—and is—a negotiation in which campesino values and interests influenced what was taught and what was learned. In this sense and in the sense that education provides indispensable survival skills in the modern industrial world, the argument for the school as a reified apparatus of domination requires more careful scrutiny.

Although these issues cannot be resolved in an essay of this scope, a number of questions can be posed for research. When rural girls started to attend school in large numbers, was the decision to send them the decision of mothers or fathers? What reasoning lay behind the decision? What role did the female teacher play in arriving at this decision? As rapid market penetration and village impoverishment turned more and more campesina women into single heads of household responsible for their children's futures, what role did education play in their strategies for survival? Did the female teacher help to devise these strategies?

Conclusion: Mature Lives, Rich Legacies

Reyna Manzano and Socorro Rivera bore and raised many children while they taught school. They kept them in cradles in the classrooms and hid them when the inspectors came around. Their children grew up to become professionals. In 1972 when she was 50 years old, Reyna Manzano's husband left her. At that moment, she undid her braids and assumed full personhood. She guided her children into adulthood and initiated many community projects, building chickencoops in Tetela and a children's playground in the neighborhood in which she lives in Puebla. She traveled to the Soviet Union, Canada, Cuba, western Europe, and the United States. Socorro Rivera lives with her daughter, who is a teacher, in the teachers' colony of Puebla where she is organizing the building of a new church. Isaura Martínez continues to administer the Centro Escolar and, in 1989, was awarded the Gabino Barreda prize for 50 years of outstanding educational service by the governor of Puebla.

Still women of service, they serve no master. Although as a professional, Isaura Martínez is the most successful of the three, Socorro Rivera and Reyna Manzano have left as important a legacy to their daughters. Both women are freer than Isaura Martínez to criticize the authoritarian nature of the Mexican political system and the failures of the revolution to realize social justice, material abundance, and democratic rights. Reyna and Socorro, like Isaura, know that they made history, that they were part of what they believe to be the most constructive element of the Mexican Revolution. This sense of having participated in nation-building combines with a profound sensitivity and identification with the lives of the rural poor. These sentiments they have passed on to their daughters, who are school teachers. The consciousness of their daughters is different from their mothers. Like them, they are engaged in service, but they feel less guilty about balancing family and work. They are more professionally assertive and less subservient to men. They are more politically engaged in unions, educational bureaucracies, and opposition movements. In assessing the impact of the Mexican Revolution on women, we should not underestimate events and processes in post-1940 Mexico that have allowed for a growth in consciousness in this sector of professional women. Nor should we forget that in many ways the growth in consciousness stems from the historical legacy of their mothers who taught school.

NOTES

1. For analysis of women in the Mexican Revolution, see, among other works, Dawn Keremitsis, "Latin American Women Workers in Transition: Sexual Division of the Labor Force in Mexico and Colombia in the Textile Industry," *The Americas* 40 (1984): 491-504; "La industria de empaques y sus trabajadoras: 1910-1940," *Encuentro: Estudios sobre la mujer (Ciencias Sociales y Humanidades)* 2 (1984): 57-74; Anna Macías, *Against All Odds. The Feminist Movement in Mexico to 1940* (Westport, Conn.: Greenwood Press, 1982); "Women and the Mexican Revolution: 1910-1920," *The Americas* 37 (1980): 53-81; Barbara Ann Miller, "Women and Revolution: The Brigadas Femeninas and the Mexican Cristero Rebellion, 1926-1929," *Journal of Third World Societies* 15 (1981): 57-66; Barbara Ann Miller, "The Roles of Women in the Mexican Cristero Rebellion: Las Señoras y las Religiosas," *The Americas* 40 (1984): 303-324; Maria Antonieta Rascón, "La mujer y la lucha social," in Elena Urrutia, *Imagen y realidad de la mujer* (Mexico: SepSetentas, 1975), 139-74; Shirlene Ann Soto, *The Mexican Woman: A Study of Her Participation in the Revolution,*

1910-1940 (Palo Alto, Calif.: R & E Associates, 1979); Mary Kay Vaughan, "Women, Class, and Education in Mexico, 1880-1928," *Latin American Perspectives* 4 (1977): 63-80.

2. I am deeply indebted to these women who have shared their life experiences with me in interviews I conducted on repeated occasions between 1984 and July 1989 in the city of Puebla. Any direct references to these women's experiences are derived from these interviews and are not further cited in the text. I am equally indebted to their children and their friends—Ida García Manzano, Victor Hernández Alva, Irma Martínez Rivera, Conrado Quintero, and Gloria Chantres— for opening the world of Mexican teachers to me. I would also like to express my gratitude to Federico Lazarín Miranda and Claudia Tapia for the extraordinary support they have given me in the archives of the Secretaría de Educación Pública in Mexico City.

3. Exemplary of works focusing on the state as organizer of the revolution is Arnaldo Córdova, *La política de masas del cardenismo* (Mexico: Ediciones Era, 1974); *La ideología de la Revolución mexicana: la formación del nuevo régimen* (Mexico: Ediciones Era, 1973). For works focusing on political leadership, see Romana Falcón, *Revolución y caciquismo. San Luis Potosí, 1910-1938* (Mexico: El Colegio de México, 1984); various essays in David Brading, ed., *Caudillo and Peasant in the Mexican Revolution,* (Cambridge: Cambridge University Press, 1982); Alicia Hernández Chávez, *La mecánica cardenista. Historia de la Revolución mexicana,* 23 vols. (Mexico: El Colegio de México, 1979), 16. For a critique of revisionist scholarship on the Revolution, see Alan Knight, "The Mexican Revolution: Bourgeois? Nationalist? Or Just a 'Great Rebellion'?," *Bulletin of Latin American Research* 4 (1985): 1-37; Alan Knight, "Recent Interpretations of the Mexican Revolution," Paper presented to the Symposium on Twenty Years of Mexican Historiography, Oaxtepec, October 12-15, 1988. For a more neutral analysis of revolutionary historiography, see Thomas Benjamin, "The Leviathan on the Zócalo: Historiography of Postrevolutionary Mexican State," *Latin American Research Review* 20 (1985): 195-217.

4. Mary Kay Vaughan, *The State, Education, and Social Class in Mexico. 1880-1928* (Dekalb: Northern Illinois University Press, 1982); see also Marjorie Becker, "Black and White and Color: Cardenismo and the Search for a Campesino Ideology," *Comparative Studies in Society and History* 29 (1987): 453-65. For an attempt to relate this thesis to women and women's education, see Vaughan, "Women, Class, and Education in Mexico," 63-80.

5. Mine is not the first use of teacher oral testimony. Dawn Raby relied on oral interviews and correspondence with teachers in her pioneer study of teacher activism in the Cárdenas period, *Educación y revolución social* (Mexico: Sepsetentas, 1974). Recently, the Secretaría de Educación Pública called upon teachers to articulate their teaching experiences in essay form. A selection of these essays has been published in Secretaría de Educación Pública, *Los maestros y la cultura nacional, 1920-1952,* 5 vols. (Mexico: Museo Nacional de Culturas Populares, Dirección General de Culturas Populares, 1987). These testimonies have been examined by Salvador Camacho Sandoval, "Los maestros rurales en la educación socialista," *Historias* 17 (1987): 85-93.

6. François Javier Guerra, *Le Mexique de l'ancien régime à la révolution,* 2 vols. (Paris: Editions L'Harmattan, 1985) 1: 120-30.

7. On the Cárdenas period, see Nora Hamilton, *The Limits of State Autonomy: Post-Revolutionary Mexico* (Princeton, New Jersey: Princeton University Press, 1982); Hernández, *La mecánica cardenista;* Benjamin, "Leviathan on the Zocalo," 195-217. On socialist education, see, among others, John A. Britton, *Educación y radicalismo*

en México, 2 vols. (Mexico: Sepsetentas, 1976); Arnaldo Córdova, "Los maestros rurales en el cardenismo," *Cuadernos Políticos* 2 (1974): 77-92; Victoria Lerner, *La educación socialista: Historia de la Revolución Mexicana*, 23 vols. (Mexico: El Colegio de México, 1979), 17; Victoria Lerner, "Historia de la reforma educativa (1933-1945)," *Historia Mexicana* 113 (1979): 91-132; Raby, *Educación y revolución social*; Mary Kay Vaughan, "La política comparada del magisterio en Puebla y Sonora en la época cardenista," *Crítica, Revista de la Universidad Autónoma de Puebla* (1987): 90-100; Mary Kay Vaughan, "The Implementation of National Policy in the Countryside: Socialist Education in Puebla in the Cárdenas Period," in *Ciudad y campo en la historia de México*, Ricardo Sánchez, Eric Van Young, and Gisela von Wobeser, eds., 2 vols. (México City: Instituto de Investigaciones Históricas, Universidad Nacional Autónoma de Mexico, 1991); Josefina Zôraida Vazquez, "La educación socialista en los años treinta," *Historia Mexicana* 18 (1969): 408-23.

8. See, for example, Salvador Camacho Sandoval, "La educación socialista en Aguascalientes," Tesis de Maestría, Departamento de Investigaciones Educativas, Centro de Estudios Avanzados, Instituto Politécnico Nacional, Mexico, 1989, pp. 59-103; see also Lerner, "Historia de la reforma educativa," 110-11; Jorge Mora Forero, "Los maestros y la práctica de la educación socialista," *Historia Mexicana* 113 (1979): 135-51.

9. I have examined literacy trends in Puebla between 1895 and 1910 in Mary Kay Vaughan, "Economic Growth and Literacy in Late Nineteenth Century Mexico: The Case of Puebla," Paper prepared for Session A-5, Education and Economic Development since the Industrial Revolution, International Economic History Congress, Leuven, Belgium, August 1990. Statistics are taken from the *Tercer censo de la población. Mexico. 1910* (México: Ministerio de Fomento, Dirección General de Estadística, 1918).

10. No comprehensive study of the Mexican Revolution in Puebla has as yet appeared. For important contributions to an analysis, see Jesús Márquez Carrillo, "Los origenes del Avilacamachismo. Una arqueología de fuerza en la constitución de un poder regional. El estado de Puebla, 1929-1941," Tesis de Licenciatura, Colegio de Historia, Universidad Autónoma de Puebla, 1983; Julio Glockner Rossainz, *La presencia del estado en el medio rural. Puebla, 1929-1941* (Centro de Investigaciones Filosóficas, Instituto de Ciencias, Universidad Autónoma de Puebla, 1982) and David La France, *The Mexican Revolution in Puebla, 1908-1913: The Maderista Movement and the Failure of Liberal Reform* (Wilmington, Del.: Scholarly Resources, 1989).

11. The figure is derived from the *Tercer censo de la población. Mexico. 1910* (Mexico: Ministerio de Fomento, Dirección General de Estadística, 1918). I have discussed issues of literacy in late nineteenth century Mexico in Mary Kay Vaughan, "Primary Education and Literacy in Nineteenth-Century Mexico: Research Trends, 1968-1988," *Latin American Research Review* 25 (1990): 31-66; and "Economic Growth and Literacy in Late Nineteenth Century Mexico: The Case of Puebla," 1-5.

12. The historical development of a liberal political culture in the subregions from which these women came is an important point for discussion in current Mexican historiography. While most historians of nineteenth-century Mexico have suggested that liberalism was snuffed out by positivist ideology and the political authoritarianism of the Porfirio Díaz regime (1876-1910) and the French historian François Guerra has recently argued that liberalism was only superficially grafted on to more traditional sets of social relations and values, Alan Knight has argued that a popular liberalism took root in certain regions of Mexico through grass-roots protests and patriotic struggle in the course of the nineteenth century (Knight,

"El liberalismo mexicano desde la Reforma hasta la Revolución: una interpretación," *Historia Mexicana* 35 [1985]: 59-85). For a sensitive and penetrating case study supportive of Knight's thesis, see Guy P.C. Thomson, "Bulwarks of Patriotic Liberalism: The National Guard, Philharmonic Corps and Patriotic Juntas in Mexico, 1847-1888," Paper presented at the 46th International Congress of Americanists, Amsterdam, July 1988, 1-44. Thomson's essay discusses the district of Tetela, home of Reyna Manzano Carmona.

13. For background on the genesis and practice of liberalism in Tetela, see Guy P.C. Thomson, "Conservative Mobilization, Liberal Insurrection, and Indian Rebellions in the Sierra Norte of Puebla, 1854-1876," Paper presented to the Society of Latin American Studies, Warwick University, March 29-31, 1985; "Regional Power Groups in Mexico in the Inter-War Years. Montana and Llanura in the Politics of Southeastern Mexico: The Case of Puebla, 1820-1920," CEDLA Workshop, Amsterdam, June 1987; and "Bulwarks of Patriotic Liberalism," 1-44. For specific focus on education and literacy in the Sierra and its relationship to educational trends in the state of Puebla, see Vaughan, "Economic Growth and Literacy in Late Nineteenth Century Mexico," 7, 13-15.

14. On Juan Francisco Lucas, see David LaFrance and Guy P.C. Thomson, "Juan Francisco Lucas: Patriarch of the Sierra Norte of Puebla," in William Beezley and Judith Ewell, eds., *The Human Tradition in Latin America* (Wilmington, Del.: Scholarly Resources, 1987), 1-12.

15. Secretaría de Fomento, Colonización e Industria, Dirección General de Estadística, *Censo verificado el 28 de octubre de 1900. Estado de Puebla* (Mexico: Oficina Tipográfica de la Secretaría de Fomento, 1902), 380.

16. For a discussion of banditry in Puebla in this period based upon materials in the Cárdenas archives (AGN), the Puebla press, Secretaría de Educación Pública documents, and U.S. Military Post Reports (U.S. National Archives), see Vaughan, "The Implementation of National Policy in the Countryside"; see also Glockner, *La presencia del estado*, 91-92; and Jesús Márquez Carrillo, "Los orígenes del Avilacamachismo," 145-47.

17. Interviews with Joel Delgadillo, July 19, 1989, Puebla, and Victor Hernández Alva, July 22, 1989, Puebla. Delgadillo, who entered teaching in the Cárdenas period, provided interesting insights on perceptions of women teachers in the 1930s. Victor Hernández Alva's mother was a teacher and single head of household in the same period; his wife is a teacher today. On violence specifically directed against school teachers in Puebla in the Cárdenas period, see Vaughan, "The Implementation of National Policy in the Countryside," in which much of my understanding of violence against teachers is based upon a reading of correspondence in Archivo General de la Nación, Ramo Presidentes, Fondo Lázaro Cárdenas, Expediente 545.2/2.

18. For a discussion of women teachers in relation to their trade unions, see Regina Cortina, "Power, Gender, and Education: Unionized Teachers in Mexico City" (Ph.D. Dissertation, School of Education, Stanford University, 1985).

19. Many works describe the formal revolutionary educational program and changes within it between 1921 and 1940. See, for example, John A. Britton, "Moisés Sáenz, nacionalista mexicano," *Historia Mexicana* 22 (1972): 79-98; *Educación y nacionalismo*, 1, 48-72, 122-53; Engracia Loyo, "Lecturas para el pueblo, 1921-1940," *Historia Mexicana* 33 (1984): 298-345; Guadalupe Monroy Huitron, *Política educativa de la revolución, 1910-1940* (Mexico: Sepsetenas, 1975); Augusto Santiago Sierra, *Las misiones culturales, 1923-1973* (México: Sepsetentas, 1973); Dawn Raby, "Ideology and State-Building: The Political Function of Rural Education in Mexico 1921-1935," *Ibero-Amerikanisches Archiv* (Berlin: Neue Folge Colloq-

ium Verlag Berlin, 1978), 21-38; Ramon Eduardo Ruiz, *Mexico: The Challenge of Poverty and Illiteracy* (San Marino, Calif.: Huntington Library, 1963); Vaughan, *The State, Education, and Social Class*, 127-189; Vaughan, "Ideological Change in Mexican Educational Policy Programs and Texts, 1920-1940," *Proceedings of the VI Conference of Mexican and United States Historians* (California: UCLA, Forthcoming); Josefina Zoraida Vázquez, *Nacionalismo y educación en México* (Mexico: El Colegio de Mexico, 1970), 151-82.

20. James Scott, *The Moral Economy of the Peasant. Rebellion and Subsistence in Southeast Asia* (New Haven, Conn.: Yale University Press, 1976), 13-34.

21. Puebla, *Memoria instructiva y documentada que el Jefe del Departamento Ejecutivo del Estado presenta al XV Congreso Constitucional*, 2 Vols. (Puebla: Imprenta de la Escuela de Artes y del Estado, 1899), 1, 126. For sympathetic, insightful discussions of peasant resistance to modern state schooling, see for example François Furet and Jacques Ozouf, *Reading and Writing: Literacy in France from Calvin to Jules Ferry* (Cambridge: Cambridge University Press, 1982), 154-55; Eugen Weber, *Peasants into Frenchmen: The Modernization of Rural France, 1870-1914* (Palo Alto, Calif.: Stanford University Press, 1976), 320-26.

22. Puebla, *Periódico Oficial*, Vol. 89, 42, November 24, 1911. I have examined literacy trends in Puebla in this period in Vaughan, "Economic Growth and Literacy in Late Nineteenth Century Mexico."

23. On inoculation, see, for example, Archivo Histórico de la Secretaría de Educación Pública (hereafter cited as SEP), Departamento de Escuelas Rurales (hereafter cited as DER), Caja 905, Jesús H. González, Informes Bimestrales, Tecamachalco, May, June, October, November 1932.

24. See, for example, *ibid.*, Jesús H. González, Informe Bimestral, Tecamachalco, April 1932; DER, Caja 969, Jesús H. González, Informe Bimestral, Tecamachalco, March 1933; Dirección General de Enseñanza Primaria (hereafter cited as DGEP) Expediente 206.7, Jesús H. González, Informe Bimestral, Tecamachalco, July-August 1935.

25. For religious reaction in Puebla, see Vaughan, "The Implementation of National Policy in the Countryside," 1-25; Márquez Carrillo, "Los orígenes del Avilacamachismo," 152-54. See also references in Dawn Raby, "Los maestros rurales y los conflictos sociales en México (1931-1940)," *Historia Mexicana* 18(1968): 190-226. General treatments of the religious reaction on a national scale can be found in Josefina Zoraida Vázquez, "La educación socialista," 408-23, and Victoria Lerner, *La educación socialista*, 32-58; "Historia de la reforma educativa," 111-17.

26. On the consolidation process in Puebla, see Márquez Carrillo, "Los orígenes del Avilacamachismo," 9-11, 154-55, 211-43; Julio Glockner Rossainz, "La presencia del estado," 27-45; Mary Kay Vaughan, "La política comparada del magisterio en Puebla y Sonora," 90-100.

27. Letters expressing support for schooling and settlement of disputes with schools and teachers are particularly abundant in the as yet unclassified individual school archives in the Archivo Histórico de la SEP. See, for example, Sacramento Joffre, Comunidades Agrarias y Sindicatos Campesinos del Estado de Puebla, to SEP, Chalchicomula, June 30, 1938; Francisco Galicia, Presidente del Comisariado Ejidal, et al. to SEP, Quecholac, February 8, 1944; Aniseto López, Presidente del Comisariado Ejidal et al., to SEP, Perisotepec, Tlacotepec, December 6, 1946; Enrique Mellado, Presidente del Comisariado Ejidal to SEP, Puerto Cañada, Cañada Morelos, November 23, 1938; Francisco Orduña, Presidente del Comisariado Ejidal, et al., to SEP, April 23, 1942, Puerto Cañada, Cañada Morelos, April 23, 1942. Although uncatalogued to date, this material is available to researchers.

28. On amplified patriotic ritual and celebration, see, for example, SEP, DGEP, Expediente 316.1, Jesús H. González, Informe, Tecamachalco, May 30, 1936; Informe Bimestral, May 1936; Informe, August-September 1936; Expediente 315.8, Rogelio Coria, Informes Bimestrales, April, May, August 1936; Expediente 315.10, Lino García, Tecali-Tepeaca, Informe General 1935, December 31, 1935; Plan de Trabajo 1936, n.d.; Informes Bimestrales, March, May, July, September 1936; Programa cultural que se desarrollara en la reunion social del Instituto de Mejoramiento Profesional, Tecali, March 14, 1936. For the nineteenth century roots of the patriotic fiesta, see Alan Knight, "Intellectuals in the Mexican Revolution," Paper presented at the Conference of Mexican and United States Historians, Chicago, September 1981, 26-34.

29. SEP, DGER, Caja 905, Jesús H. González, Tecamachalco, Informe Bimestral, August 1932.

IV

*Issues in Methodology
and Analysis*

WHAT'S SO FEMINIST ABOUT DOING WOMEN'S ORAL HISTORY?

Susan Geiger

There's a long running review in Minneapolis called "What's so funny about being female?" While the cast of comedians changes, the show usually features six or seven women whose routines are as diverse as their ages, sizes, delivery styles, and material. On the occasions I've seen this review, I've found some of the sketches to be very funny while others don't tickle me at all. Among the women I consider very funny, some do what I and they call "feminist humor." But others who don't identify themselves as feminist make me laugh anyway, and not all of the self-identified feminist comics seem funny to me. Nevertheless, all of them think they have something funny to say about being female, and Dudley Riggs, who hires them, thinks so too. But when I'm in the audience, I make up my own mind as to whether the words, the process, and the presentation are funny, feminist, both, or neither. I have certain guidelines and standards for doing this, of course; and I can usually tell by their responses whether others in the audience agree with me.

Just as there is nothing inherently feminist about women comics talking about women, neither is there anything inherently feminist about women's oral histories or women doing women's oral histories. What, then, makes their gathering, production, and publication a feminist act? To answer this, we need to consider a set of prior issues including the objectives of the researcher, the questions addressed in the research, the evidence against which oral data are verified or evaluated, the character of the research relationship, the intended audience for the "product(s)" of the research, and the potential beneficiaries of the transformation of oral into written history. In addition, of course, we need a working definition of the term "feminist," which I offer under "objectives" below.

© 1990 JOURNAL OF WOMEN'S HISTORY, VOL. 2 NO. 1 (SPRING)

Objectives

It is important to begin with the issue of objectives precisely because oral history is not a new activity or concept; nor is it a new research method. As an activity, it predates writing and transcends research institutions. Women's oral histories are not inherently feminist nor is the telling necessarily a feminist act. Moreover, the gathering of oral histories began long before the current wave of feminist movement and cannot be considered, automatically, a feminist research method. Nor is the activity of the listener/recorder feminist simply because she is a woman researcher.

Oral history only becomes a *method* in the hands of persons whose interests in it go beyond the immediate pleasure of hearing/learning the history being told. As scholars, we *use* information derived from oral history, and, in that way, it becomes a method, and methodological questions arise about it. But it can only become a feminist *methodology* if its use is systematized in particular feminist ways and if the objectives for collecting the oral data are feminist.

Feminist objectives include at least one of the following characteristics: they presuppose gender as a (though not the only) central analytical concept; they generate their problematic from the study of women as embodying and creating historically and situationally specific economic, social, cultural, national, and racial/ethnic realities; they serve as a corrective for androcentric notions and assumptions about what is "normal" by establishing or contributing to a new knowledge base for understanding women's lives and the gendered elements of the broader social world; they accept women's own interpretations of their identities, their experiences, and social worlds as containing and reflecting important truths, and do not categorize and, therefore, dismiss them, for the purposes of generalization, as *simply* subjective.

According to Gelya Frank and Elizabeth Hampsten, feminist objectives emphasize *understanding* rather than *controlling* the material or information generated and conceptualize the interpretive task as one of *opening* rather than *closure.*[1] There are also objectives that may not be feminist but neither are they antifeminist nor inherently "bad." Many of us who call ourselves feminists have certain perfectly reasonable objectives in our scholarly work and research that do not meet or relate to the above criteria. But I believe we deny the term "feminist" all meaning if we insist that it includes everything we happen to do; that it means anything we want it to mean; or that it refers to everything positive and good as opposed to negative and bad.

Questions

As scholars, we seek and develop methodologies to answer questions that interest us. But what makes our questions feminist? Our objectives will obviously influence the kinds of questions we will address in collecting oral histories. In my view, questions that in their content or formulation presume the accuracy of existing partial, androcentric, or ethnocentric constructions of the lives or situations of women are not feminist. For example, if, as Sally Green suggests, we assume, in our construction of questions to be posed with respect to the lives of Middle Eastern women, that "a 'harem' was a storehouse of lovers . . . and that . . . polygamy and seclusion [are] intrinsically evil"—both elements in the western image of the Middle East as "other"—we are unlikely to get beyond "the woman as a black sack of potatoes, shuffling after her husband, as a fleshy, gyrating belly dancer, as a longing face peering through the lattice."[2]

But my own reading of many women's life histories,[3] with a particular focus on the scholarly terms of analysis, has led me to conclude that the problematic for feminists resides most importantly in the fundamental concepts underlying the *framing* of questions; and that until certain intractable propositions and concepts are shaken up, perfunctory or automatic "answers" to the "wrong" questions are likely to continue to cloud imagination as well as understanding.

Let us consider, for example, two of the most common concepts employed in anthropological and historical analysis of "the person" and available to those of us trained in the western intellectual tradition: *marginality* and *representativeness.* These concepts have been presented *as if* they are appropriate to objective analysis and somehow identifiable from some stance of "ungendered point of viewlessness."[4] Yet both concepts require that the observer recognize the reality of what Alcoff calls "positionality," a concept she offers to identify not only the **relational** and "constantly moving" context that constitutes our reality, but as the "place from which values are interpreted and constructed rather than as [the] locus of an already determined set of values."[5]

All too frequently, questions that presume or identify the marginality of an oral historian[6] or the place from which she speaks do not situate the narrator and her world; rather, such questions expose the researcher's preconceived notion of the narrator's world and of her own centrality, or, at least, the *centrality/power* of her own place in the world. For example, if a set of questions put to a woman trader in the Makola #1 market in Accra, Ghana, assumes and adopts the marginalizing economic terminology currently operating in much of the mainstream African literature on trade and commerce (that is, the terms "petty," "informal," "casual," "small-scale"), an understanding of the trader's actual relations to the state, to her suppliers and buyers, to her fellow traders, and to her own business might well be lost or at best obscured.[7]

Of course, a sense of marginality can, in fact, be expressed in the articulated experience of oral historians. Thus, the Jewish women rabbis interviewed by anthropologist Gelya Frank felt that their own sense of religious experience left them marginalized in the context of mainstream Judaism.[8] On the other hand, neither the lesbian women who created their own bar culture as a space for socializing, nor the African-American women writers studied by Elizabeth Kennedy and Nellie McKay, respectively, considered themselves marginal, thus rendering the concept inappropriate to an interpretation these authors wished to give to their lives.[9]

The point is, then, that marginality cannot be assumed, nor will questions that predict the marginality of the person to whom they are put yield particularly interesting insights into the self-perceptions or life of the oral historian. Marginality is best understood as a relational concept, the "truth" of which depends on the acceptance or affirmation of both parties to that characterization of the relationship,[10] and to the context in which the relationship occurs.

Even when something called marginality can be carefully defined, identified, and contextualized historically and geographically, as Africanist historian Marcia Wright has pointed out,[11] we still do not automatically or necessarily know what it is we have identified or how it operates. Moreover, there are historical circumstances in which even externally imposed economic, social, or political marginalization has been beneficial. In other words, "marginal" is not always a bad way or place to be in the world or in a given society; on the contrary, it can be a protection against certain destructive or negative forces. For example, African women in the Cape, Natal, and Transvaal provinces of South Africa were considered marginal to the wage labor needs of the economy and were therefore exempt, until the 1950s, from the pass requirements and laws through which the white minority regime controlled, intimidated, and oppressed African men.[12]

Questions that **derive from** the concept of *representativeness* and the assumptions underlying this concept constitute the other side of the same coin. Such questions necessarily presume norms against which the words, position, or experience of the oral historian are measured and in which the validity and, more tellingly, the significance and usefulness of her information is judged. But what determines, in this prior way, what or who is "representative" and, therefore, the norm against which all in a given society are to be judged? Not surprisingly, it is frequently the same scholarly tradition that established marginality as a useful category and concept. This is not to say that these concepts should be completely discarded. My point is simply that questions that presume their relevance ultimately shape and can certainly distort what is learned in the course of oral history work. On the other hand, if an attempt to address the issue of an individual's representativeness within carefully determined parameters

follows rather than preceeds the formulation of questions, useful contextulization occurs and assists understanding. Thus, Marjorie Shostak, in presenting the life story of Nisa, eventually situates Nisa's life history within a framework that includes the life stories of seven other !Kung women and statistical materials including the age curve of first marriage for !Kung girls, the usual numbers of marriages and children, and so forth. Had Shostak worried about Nisa's "representativeness" to begin with, she would have abandoned their interviews on the grounds that Nisa, who was first married at the age of nine, eventually experienced five marriages, had no living children, and was "unusually uninhibited, if not an outright extrovert,"[13] was not sufficiently typical of other !Kung women to bother with.

A particular pitfall for western feminist scholars is encountered when the concept of "representativeness" gets collapsed into a tendency to "represent" particular "Third World" women, including oral historians, as a kind of universalized "other." As Chandra Mohanty has observed, a homogenization necessarily occurs in this process that creates an "object status" for Third World women. In this scenario, western feminists remain "true subjects" while Third World women "never rise above their generality. . . ."[14] Aihwa Ong further notes that "by portraying women in non-Western societies as identical and interchangeable, and more exploited than women in the dominant capitalist societies, liberal and socialist feminists alike encode a belief in their own cultural superiority."[15]

In some instances, as Julia Swindells has observed, what can be usefully characterized as representative is not, in any case, the individual member of a group but rather the conditions or circumstances within which that person operates. Thus, Hannah Culwick, the Victorian maidservant whose 17 diaries were written essentially for the pleasure of her master and patron, Arthur Munby, was not herself "representative" of Victorian maid servants; but the general conditions she experienced, far from being unique to herself, were characteristic of her age, time, and class.[16]

An oral history methodology that features as major conceptual organizers the positional markers of marginality and representativeness automatically privileges certain voices and obstructs others through the very framework imposed. As feminists, we should be acutely aware of whose voices are obstructed. In contrast to questions flowing from assumptions of marginality and representativeness, questions that seek larger meaning and relevant concepts from oral historians themselves are likely to yield new and significant insights.

In listening to Italian wage earning women of Turin talk about their lives between the world wars, historian Luisa Passerini found that models of rebelliousness were frequently exchanged and shared through "habit[s] of reciprocal narration, based, in turn, on family oral traditions."[17] These narratives, juxtaposed against parallel narratives, told by the same individuals of their lives as exemplary wives, workers, and mothers were important symbolically in the context of a tradition of literary representation of women rebels. In discovering both where the models for their lives came from and how these women developed their own counter-narratives and models for truth and for a "good life," Passerini moved beyond those questions calling for answers that can be tested for simple factual accuracy. Instead, she concerned herself with the ways of deriving *meaning* from the oral histories and narratives collected. And meaning, as Passerini has so carefully established, lies in the silences and contradictions contained in a life story just as certainly as it lies in what is said.[18] Memory in turn *is* a construction of meaning—significant for feminists only if we are attentive to its shape and importance.

Authority

I have raised the issue of the validation or dismissal of oral accounts on the basis of a factual standard that privileges certain kinds of historical information, that is, dates, names, and numbers. Qualitative responses, textural evidence, reflections on social consequences of events, the popular memory of "what happened," and so forth are frequently dismissed as insubstantial within the scholarly domain or hedged around with multiple qualifiers designed to demonstrate scholarly skepticism. A related issue concerns the authority against which oral evidence is verified.

The "authority" or "authorities" on whom researchers draw helps determine whether or not a methodology is feminist. Most of us have learned to regard information generated by "experts" and found in archives, libraries, classrooms, and universities as "reliable." These are the repositories of knowledge against which we have been taught to measure any "new" information we might collect or discover. If we insist that the validity of women's oral accounts must be—can only be—evaluated against existing knowledge or affirmed through the prism of the "latest" in fashionable social analysis, we are *not* following a feminist methodology in our oral history work with women. The question is this: Why isn't the written word, the received understanding, or the "latest" in analytical virtuosity tested against women's oral testimonies instead of the other way around? This is the method Carolyn Steedman uses in remembering, reconstructing, and presenting the working-class childhoods of her mother and herself. Finding that neither the accepted authorities on or iconography of "the working-class" and on working-class motherhood nor those on childhood or femaleness capture the realities or "truths" of her mother's life and how those truths shaped her own, Steedman scrutinizes these authorities for their political and emotional agendas and lacks. She then uses her mother's story "to subvert" idealized accounts of the working class in order that her own, her mother's, and the lives of working-class women should not be found "wanting."[19]

The degree of academic panic or ridicule registered when feminist scholars insist upon the reconsideration and reconceptualization of everything we "know" is often a measure of the general malaise in the fields and disciplines from which these responses emanate. A "crisis of representation" is only a crisis for those who worry that their fundamental beliefs are about to crumble and with them, the power that the centrality of their point of view has brought. This is why many feminists don't consider the "crisis" a crisis at all but, rather, an opportunity. A "feminist" methodology is, in Adrienne Rich's words, prepared to be "disloyal to civilization."[20]

Oral Historian/Researcher Relationship

The issue of authority—one's own as a scholar, as well as the existing knowledge upon which one depends—is linked to that of the relationship between the researcher and her living "source." It is easier to characterize the possible polarities in this relationship than it is to clearly articulate what might constitute a feminist alternative. At one end of the spectrum of such relationships lies erasure of the *person* of the oral historian through anonymous generalization from her story or through a third person rendering of her words that objectifies her as just another "text." At the other end lies total identification or attempted merger with the "source" in an attempt to erase not the person herself but the reality of differences and disparities. The latter extreme is often a heartfelt response to the recognition and simultaneous rejection of inequalities separating researcher and oral historian. But it is not a particularly useful response and is, in a sense, as misleading and dishonest as the other extreme. Neither is likely to produce interpretations that have the possibility of transforming our understanding of the world.

In a feminist relationship between oral historians and researcher, existing differences will be recognized and conditions of mutual respect will be sought. Ways of sharing the "authority" expressed in written renditions of the oral account or exchange will be explicitly discussed, as will the nature of the working relationship itself and what is to be produced from it.[21] A feminist research relationship will also be characterized by honesty about its limitations; that is, that the relationship is a particular kind of association, at least with respect to the work being done in its context. Whether a different kind of relationship is built into or results from that between scholar and oral historian is another issue. Doing oral history within a feminist methodological framework is about intellectual work and its processes, not about the potential for or realization of a relationship beyond or outside that framework.

This distinction is not always easy to bear in mind because the relationship is obviously being shaped from two directions, and the oral historian's will and intent can be just as strong as the researcher's. Frequently, for example, a young researcher will find herself in the position of being considered a daughter—and certainly a child if the age difference is quite great. Other familial ties may be claimed or asserted, for example, sister, auntie, or mother, if the age difference is closer or reversed. There is something very comforting about having the relationship characterized in familial terms, especially for researchers who have (understandable) doubts about the validity of what they are doing. Moreover, certain kinds of information may only be shared among particular categories of people. Anthropologists have long depended upon, and even capitalized on, this aspect of their chosen form of scholarly work. In almost any circumstance, it is useful to be considered "not-a-stranger." But as feminist researchers, I believe we must think long and hard about these fictive relational assertions and the extent to which we are willing not only to enjoy their benefits but to meet the obligations that necessarily accompany their creation and whatever privileges flow from them.[22]

There is a correlation between what I am trying to suggest with respect to a feminist research relationship and what Bettina Aptheker terms "pivoting the center." As Elsa Barkley Brown notes, this concept calls for the ability to center the experience of another person (or society) without denying the validity of one's own: neither "norm" nor "center"—in the sense of a place from which everything else is "marginal" are relevant in these conceptualizations.[23]

Audience

Authority and audience are also linked. Not surprisingly, but all too frequently, they are comprised of the same people. This is the case, for example, if the audience for one's oral history research and production are the gatekeepers and acclaimed superstars of the discipline, the admired mentors/critics whose assessments determine promotion and entrance into an exclusive club of "first rate" scholars. A doubting thesis adviser also constitutes authority and audience in one, as, with increasing frequency, does a self-constituted feminist jury. In any of these cases, it is unlikely that the product(s) resulting from the oral history research can be feminist, and it is, therefore, unlikely that something called a feminist methodology will have been employed.

These audience issues reflect the peopling of our heads with critics whose judgment of our work matters because of the positions they occupy. These critics often have power, both real and imagined, over our scholarly actions and intellectual decisions. It is easier for most of us to identify this audience for ourselves than it is to identify or characterize its opposite: an audience that liberates us from self-censure based on fear and allows us to explore a range of ways of thinking about oral histories that are not easily categorized or contained within pre-established contexts.

In part, it seems to me that a researcher who undertakes oral history work in the context of a feminist methodology needs to imagine and position as an audience for the "results" several groups of people and perhaps several different "products." Certainly, women of the oral historian's community should be regarded as a significant "audience" for the work and interpretations produced by the researcher. These persons, as individuals and as a collective of sorts, have undoubtedly occupied a prominent place in the researcher's life and mind for the length of the period of collection. To assume that their role and place and function end once their words are recorded on tape or paper is to objectify them as "data."

But identifying this group as part of an audience does not mean that one's interpretation must be *the same as* their interpretation of themselves or their lives; nor does it mean that *everything* a researcher writes must be written in terms or in a context to which oral historians necessarily have direct access.[24] Nevertheless, the oral historians should "be there" in the sense that a feminist methodology cannot be one that wittingly or unwittingly violates the words of the individuals that have become the "subject matter."

Other members of a liberating audience might include fellow feminist scholars working in or with oral histories, feminist students and scholars more generally, and sympathetic "others." I have chosen to emphasize here the audience one constructs in the process and production stages of research. Ultimately, of course, a researcher's audience is not restricted to people visualized or chosen. It includes anyone who happens to have access to what we write and say.

Who Benefits?

The final issue, initially raised as a precurser to, if not determinant of whether oral history might constitute a feminist methodology, concerns the beneficiaries of the relational process and its product(s) or publication(s). The idea that someone besides the researcher should benefit from one's research or its conclusions or findings is hardly unique to feminist scholarship. Much of social science research is presumed to be useful to one group or other: a community, a local government, a society. "Action," participatory or policy oriented research in anthropology and sociology, history workshop productions and virtually all of psychology, are designed to be more than intellectual exercises undertaken by scholars for the edification of other scholars. And several of these groups are equally insistent that their studies not harm those who have been studied or those who have participated. "Human Subjects" regulations exist in most universities in order to prevent harm, intended or unintended, to people who constitute

the focus of academic research. In any case, to have or claim to have an
ethics of caring and concern may well be an aspect of feminist methodology but it is not unique to feminism.[25]

Nevertheless, the conduct of oral history research *does* require an attentiveness to the concerns, interests, and circumstances of oral historians
themselves. The specifics of this attentiveness—the way it can be expressed
or realized—will vary according to the conditions of collection, the community or social group involved, and the amount of time spent with oral
historians, among other factors. The benefits accruing to researcher and
to oral historian(s) need not be, nor are they likely to be, the same. What
constitutes the feminist part of attentiveness to the question of benefits is
a willingness on the part of the researcher to be both flexible and creative—responsive to the fact that oral historians themselves often know
how they can and would like to benefit from the work.

In my own research, for example, many of the women whose life histories constitute the base of my understanding of nationalist politics in Tanzania[26] have wanted and received the Swahili transcripts or versions of their
life stories. They have wanted these for themselves, their children and
grandchildren and for other reasons—their reasons. In earlier oral history
work,[27] I was asked to find out what had happened to claims regarding a
dispute in the 1930s that had been put forward by people I was interview-
ing in the late 1960s. It is not uncommon to be asked to act as a conduit
for the testimonies or explanations of oral historians. And some oral historians may wish further discussion of certain issues because the act of relating has provoked additional thoughts or clarified previously murky ideas.
A feminist researcher's methodology must be receptive to these strains in
the overall process, even where "strain" has a double meaning as simultaneously "tension" and "strand." This means, of course, that there must be
time to spare in the research—time that is not seen or experienced by the
researcher as "time wasted."[28] And just as feminist objectives validate and
concern women centrally and fundamentally, so too it is unimaginable
that a feminist methodology should not produce ideas that benefit women
through the revelation of historical experience. Finally, as Jacquelyn Dowd
Hall points out, men who are open to "multiple voices rather than competing orthodoxies" are likely beneficiaries as well.[29]

Truths and Transformations:
Interpretation as the Radical Act in Feminist Scholarship

Many of us share the view that in order to be feminist, our methodology
must be about transforming the world. Indeed, feminist disillusionment
frequently sets in at the point where we presume more power over change
than we actually have. This is a major reason ironically, that women less
privileged than ourselves perceive us as *more* rather than *less* like the male

imperialists from whom we seek to distance ourselves. If we remember that within our chosen arena of operation, scholarly work, our main contribution will necessarily be an intellectual one, we can relieve ourselves of the immobilizing and counter-productive burdens of frustration and guilt—feelings that too often emerge to inhibit women's ventures into the lives of women different from themselves through a medium like oral history research.

To be more specific: even as we know that "disloyalty to civilization" must inform a feminist methodology, we need to remain realistic and reasonably modest in our understanding of the part of the transformative project on which we **as** academics, feminist or otherwise, have some influence. Thus, for example, we cannot usually or in any immediate and substantive way change the lives of women living in tragic or difficult circumstances. What we might be able to do, however, is change the ways their lives are interpreted, appreciated, and understood.

This, in fact, is not such a modest project. It involves engaging in the process and practice of interpretive shifts, large and small, the sum total of which may transform and must certainly complicate thinking on how and why the world **is** and is *gendered* in the various ways it is and why this matters profoundly in ways with which we are only begining to come to terms. It is a project that demands placing all accepted texts in question, not with the deconstructionist purpose of upsetting projects of explanation but with the feminist purpose of exposing the interests served by prevailing doctrine. This, in turn, requires understanding the ideological conditions under which norms and binary modes of thought are created and explaining why particular points of view—standpoints—were and are granted the status of (sole) "correct" interpretation and by whom. Most importantly, it involves releasing **multiple truths** into the scholarly environment.

It is hardly surprising that an acceptance of—indeed, insistence upon—"multiple" or "plural" truths should be expressed in the work and thought of many feminist scholars today. In the recently published volume of essays *Interpreting Women's Lives*, the Personal Narrative Group editing and contributing to the organizational and theoretical framework for the collection settled on "Truths" as the title for the book's concluding essay.[30] Aptheker's insistence on "numerous centers" and the need to "pivot the center";[31] Hall's conclusion that we need to accept the idea of all representations of reality as "partial truths"; Passerini's insight that it is the task of interpreters to discover "in which sense, where,[and] for what purpose" autobiographic memory is true[32]—these assertions all point to our grappling with the meaning of women's experiences over time and in an environment of vital criticism and self-criticism.

There is an interesting parallel, I think, between Jacquelyn Hall's call "for a historical *practice* [my emphasis] that turns on partiality, that is self-conscious about perspective"[33] and the stories and life stories oral historians relate, which are themselves partial, perspectival, and self-conscious.

Feminist oral history methodology reflects and values these parallel activities—the practice of the researcher, the practice of the oral historian. Neither practice stands for the other, but if she is careful, the feminist historian's own interpretive product will encompass radical, respectful, newly accessible truths, and realities about women's lives.

NOTES

I want to thank Margaret Strobel, whose critical comments and suggestions on an earlier version of this essay informed my final revision. The gaps and inadequacies remaining are obviously my responsibility.

1. Transcript, "Autobiographies, Biographies and Life Histories of Women: Interdisciplinary Perspectives" Conference. University of Minnesota, May 23-24, 1986, 9 (Frank); 20, 23-24 (Hampsten).

2. Sally Green, "Reading Middle Eastern Women Writers," *American Book Review* 11 (1989).

3. Susan Geiger, "Women's Life Histories: Method and Content," *Signs* 11 (1986): 334-51.

4. Catharine A. MacKinnon, "Feminism, Marxism, Method and the State: Toward a Feminist Jurisprudence," *Signs* 8 (1983): 638-39.

5. Linda Alcoff, "Cultural Feminism versus Post-Structuralism: The Identity Crisis in Feminist Theory," *Signs* 13 (1988): 433.

6. I am using the term "oral historian" as Marjorie Mbilinyi uses "life historian" to designate the individual relating history/her history to the researcher. The more commonly employed terms "informant" and even "subject" suggest to me a less important place in the research process and relationship than the term "oral historian," which, despite the fact of who is narrating and who receiving the oral history content, is usually reserved, in academic circles, for the researcher. For Mbilinyi's usage, see Marjorie Mbilinyi, "I'd Have Been a Man," in *Interpreting Women's Lives: Feminist Theory and Personal Narratives,* ed. Personal Narratives Group (Bloomington: Indiana University Press,1989), 204-27.

7. See Gracia Clark, "Introduction," in *Traders versus the State: Anthropological Approaches to Unofficial Economies,* ed. Gracia Clark (Boulder, Col.: Westview Press,1988), 1-16.

8. Gelya Frank, Transcript, 5.

9. Elizabeth Kennedy, Transcript,11-12; Nellie McKay, Transcript, 70-71.

10. This is a view derived from Carolyn Steedman, *Landscape for a Good Woman* (London: Virago, 1986).

11. Marcia Wright, Transcript, 31.

12. See Julia C. Wells, "The War of Degradation: Black Women's Struggle Against Orange Free State Pass Laws, 1913," in *Banditry, Rebellion and Social Protest in Africa,* ed. Donald Crummey (Portsmouth,N.H.: Heinemann, 1986), 253-70.

13. Marjorie Shostak, "What the Wind Won't Take Away," in *Interpreting Women's Lives,* 231.

14. Chandra Talpade Mohanty, "Under Western Eyes: Feminist Scholarship and Colonial Discourses," *Boundary* 2, 12:3/13, 1 (1984 [published 1986]): 351.

15. Aihwa Ong, "Colonialism and Modernity: Feminist Re-presentations of Women in Non-Western Societies," *Inscriptions* 3/4 (1988): 85.

16. Julia Swindells, Transcript, 238-39.

17. Luisa Passerini, "Women's Personal Narratives: Myths, Experiences, and Emotions," in *Interpreting Women's Lives*, 190.

18. Luisa Passerini, Transcript, 202.

19. Carolyn Steedman, *Landscape*, 7-24, esp. 8-10.

20. Adrienne Rich's phrase "disloyal to civilization" is in turn derived from the insight of Lillian Smith, who notes in "Autobiography as a Dialogue between King and Corpse" (1962) "what [Freud] mistook for her lack of civilization is woman's lack of loyalty to civilization." Adrienne Rich, *On Lies, Secrets, and Silences* (New York: Norton, 1979), 277-78.

21. For contrasting but, I believe, equally respectful approaches that take into account the different conditions and contexts of the oral history research, see Margaret Strobel and Sarah Mirza, "Introduction," in *Three Swahili Women: Life Histories from Mombasa, Kenya*, ed. and trans. Sarah Mirza and Margaret Strobel (Bloomington: Indiana University Press,1989), 4-6; and Marjorie Mbilinyi, "I'd Have Been a Man," *Interpreting Women's Lives*, 204-27.

22. Carol A.B. Warren, *Gender Issues in Field Research* (Beverly Hills, Calif.: Sage,1988) provides a useful overview of the gendered complexities of researcher-informant relations. See esp. sections 2 and 3.

23. Elsa Barkley Brown, "African-American Women's Quilting: A Framework for Conceptualizing and Teaching African-American Women's History," *Signs* 14 (1989): fn. 1, 921-22, citing Bettina Aptheker, *Tapestries of Life: Women's Work, Women's Consciousness and the Meaning of Daily Life* (Amherst: University of Massachusetts,1989).

24. Compare this view with Jacquelyn Dowd Hall, "Partial Truths," *Signs* 14 (1989): 911.

25. There are clearly other assertions I make about feminist methodology in this essay that concern ideas and positions that are not the exclusive property of feminists. Here I agree with Deborah Gordon who, in her criticism of *Writing Culture*, points out that to expect "feminist claims to be exclusively feminist (an impossibility by definition as long as the world isn't feminist—at which point the word 'feminism' would cease to exist) . . . creates a double bind. Feminism must produce innovation that is completely distinct from any other; if it doesn't live up to this impossibility then it ceases to be either feminist or innovative." (See Deborah Gordon, "Writing Culture, Writing Feminism: The Poetics and Politics of Experimental Ethnography," *Inscriptions* 3/4 [1988]: 15; also, Frances E. Macia-Lees, Patricia Sharpe, and Colleen Ballerino Cohen, "The Postmodernist Turn in Anthropology: Cautions from a Feminist Perspective," *Signs* 15 [1989]: 7-33.)

26. Susan Geiger, "Women in Nationalist Struggle: TANU Activists in Dar es Salaam," *International Journal of African Historical Studies* 20 (1987): 1-26. But as Margaret Strobel notes, "it is easier to give something back when people themselves are organized and/or have some consciousness [of the significance of documentation]." Of the three women whose life histories she recorded in Mombasa, Kenya, only the youngest, whose political consciousness and sense of history were considerable, wanted a copy of the taped interview and history of the Muslim Women's Institute she had narrated to Strobel. Moreover, Strobel's desire to insure that Swahili women in Mombasa in general had access to a Swahili version of the three life histories she and Mirza painstakingly transcribed and organized was thwarted by Kenyan publishers who maintained that there was no market for "serious" Swahili literature and were, therefore, not interested in local publication (Margaret Strobel, personal communication, September 29,1989).

27. Susan [Geiger] Rogers, *The Search for Political Focus on Kilimanjaro: A History of Chagga Politics, 1916-1952, with Special Reference to the Cooperative Movement and Indirect Rule* (PhD dissertation, University of Dar es Salaam, 1973).

28 Compare with Mbilinyi, "I'd Have Been a Man," *Interpreting Women's Lives.*

29. Jacquelyn Dowd Hall, "Partial Truths," 911.

30. See *Interpreting Women's Lives*, 261-64.

31. Elsa Barkley Brown, "African-American Women's Quilting."

32. Luisa Passerini, "Women's Personal Narratives," *Interpreting Women's Lives.*

33. Jacquelyn Dowd Hall, "Partial Truths," 908.

BIBLIOGRAPHICAL NOTE

On life histories as potential examples of oral histories of women undertaken from a feminist perspective, see my "Women's Life Histories: Method and Content," *Signs* 11 (1986): 334-51. For an excellent example of recent feminist life-history work, see Margaret Strobel and Sarah Mirza, *Three Swahili Women: Life Histories from Mombasa, Kenya* (Bloomington: Indiana University Press, 1989). Other life histories that convey the richness and depth possible in this kind of account include Ida Pruitt, *A Daugher of Han: The Autobiography of a Chinese Working Woman* (Stanford: Stanford University Press, 1967); Fran Leeper Bliss, *La Partera: Story of a Midwife* (Ann Arbor: University of Michigan Press, 1980); and Elisabeth Burgos-Debray, *I, Rigoberta Menchu: An Indian Woman in Guatemala*, trans. Ann Wright (London: Verso Editions, 1984).

The following essays in the Personal Narratives Group (eds.), *Interpreting Women's Lives: Feminist Theory and Personal Narratives* (Bloomington: Indiana University Press, 1989), offer useful ideas on the doing of women's oral history: Karen Brodkin Sacks, "What's a Life Story Got to Do with It?" 85-95; Luisa Passerini, "Women's Personal Narratives: Myths, Experiences, and Emotions," 189-97; Marjorie Mbilinyi, " 'I'd Have Been a Man': Politics and the Labor Process in Producing Personal Narratives," 204-27; and Marjorie Shostak, " 'What the Wind Won't Take Away': The Genesis of *Nisa—The Life and Words of a !Kung Woman,"* 228-40.

SIX (OR MORE) FEMINISTS IN SEARCH OF A HISTORIAN

Sharon Sievers

Feminist #001 (Jane): "**WHY** *are we* still *arguing about the definition of feminism!*"

Feminist #002 (Gayatri): "*This is not about definition. It is about meaning.*"

Feminist #003 (Fumiko): "*Well, we're still arguing, that much is clear.*"

Feminist #004 (Céline): "*Ah yes, Fumi-chan, but only that is clear.*"

Feminist #005 (Kate): "*Our only experience is what we see and hear at this moment?*"

Feminist #002 (Gayatri): "*Can you be sure that women truly experience anything?*"

Feminist #006 (Pilár): "*This is precisely the reason feminism is so useless! At least give us analysis grounded in history—something we can use!*"

We know that feminism—even at a safe historical distance—is seen by many women outside of the United States and Europe as another form of "cultural imperialism" whose white, capitalist, and imperialist associations make it virtually useless in the analysis of their own history. Unlike marxism, which is, on one level, a western critique of the west, feminism has rarely been thought of, except by a few feminists, as a revolutionary ideology in its own right. We all recognize that there are many complex reasons for this, none of which have to do with the failure of feminism to produce its own Marx. I raise these issues as a reminder that, large as they are, questions of ethnocentric bias and a lack of revolutionary content in feminism represent only a glimpse of the difficult issues we face as we begin to develop the history of feminism.

Currently, there is little appreciation of the significant differences that might exist between women's history and the history of feminism. Reading through various responses to a book I wrote some time ago—a book that was taken by most to be a history of women, though in fact it was a history of feminism in Japan—taught me something about the importance of the distinction. It is time to explore those differences and to begin thinking of

© 1989 JOURNAL OF WOMEN'S HISTORY, VOL. 1 NO. 2 (FALL)

the history of feminism as an enterprise different from, though clearly related to, the history of women in spite of strong tendencies to deny the validity of feminism as a historical experience. The arguments that deny a history to feminism may be similar to earlier objections to women's history, but in their cross-cultural expression, denials are clearly linked to the notion that feminism has always been a western experience, defined narrowly in terms of (earlier) women's rights and (later) radical separatism. My argument is that only by developing the history of feminism will we be able to confront problems of definition, links to theory, the politics of feminism, and its processes.

It is impossible not to notice the ambiguities in recent historical descriptions of feminism, many of which are included within the framework of competing world views. Feminism is often characterized as a movement that makes all men the enemy in a sexual/political struggle, forcing women (always) to choose between, for example, nationalism or socialism. That remains the favored description in spite of the fact that feminist history has most often been one of coalition. On the other hand, recent feminists have claimed "sisterhood" as an ideal, though it is clear that all women—even within the same family—have not been sisters in that idyllic sense we once imagined possible.

What little we know of feminist history suggests that coalition has been possible; that cooperation across barriers of class and race have been rare, but possible; that white feminists raised in capitalist society have taken their feminism to black struggles in Third World countries; that Japanese women, the "professional mothers" of a postindustrial society, have protested "sex tours" to Korea because the practice is symbolic of the sexism of the two societies, as well as of a continuing imperialist relationship to which women are often held hostage.

Writing the history of feminism means exploring these examples of our history in more detail; it means making clearer choices about what is and is not universal about feminism; it means establishing more clearly the motivation and scope of coalition. The connection between feminism and white imperialism should be explored, not erased or papered over, because only by asking questions about that experience will we begin to get a sense of the historical complexity and contradictions of feminism.

Writing the history of feminism will broaden the debate over its meanings and its breadth, though the work of Karen Offen[1] and Nancy Cott[2] already testify to the movement away from earlier constructs that limited feminism to a few European and U.S. suffragists. Gerda Lerner was among the first to call attention to the important distinction between "women's rights" and "women's emancipation," a division that in significant ways echoes the differences between the history of women and the history of feminism. Similarly, Nancy Cott's introduction to *The Grounding of Modern Feminism* argues for a history of feminism that does not "render [feminism] meaningless" by "equating [it] with 'what women did.' "[3] Karen

Offen, who has done more than anyone else to pin down the history of the term feminism,[4] argues for redefinitions that implicitly require more feminist history. Without it, there is no way to reverse the ethnocentrism of many North American formulations, no way adequately to sort through the tangled politics from which feminism emerged in Europe, and certainly no way to comprehend the complexities of global feminism. As Offen puts it,

> the evidence from comparative history also suggests that in order to fully comprehend the historical range and possibilities of feminism, we must locate the origins and growth of these ideas within a variety of cultural traditions, rather than postulating a hegemonic model for their development on the experience of any single national or sociolinguistic tradition. . . . Put differently, feminism must itself be "revisioned" by expanding our investigative horizons.[5]

It is not surprising that the most interesting attempts to define feminism have come from scholars whose work has been the history of feminism; that they do not agree whether feminism is revolutionary, evolutionary, a movement, a process, or a state of mind should not discourage us. It simply reinforces the notion that we are unlikely to appreciate fully how unruly and complex a dragon feminism is without historians of feminism—many more than we have now.

Some of the common characteristics of recent definitions of feminism are inclusiveness, flexibility, and a willingness to accept historically grounded contradiction. If, however, we have still done too little to define feminism in historical contexts that translate across cultures, is it because ethnocentrism is still alive and well in spite of our new-found inclusiveness? My answer to that is yes, but it is a qualified yes.

Ethnocentrism is, of course, a problem even (or as someone might say, especially) for feminists; we have proved many times over that we, the latest in a long line of putative "universalists," carry our cultures with us—sometimes as a kind of intellectual baggage that crushes every effort at communication across cultures. Yet even ethnocentrism among self-proclaimed feminists deserves more analysis and careful consideration by those of us interested in the history of feminism than we have so far given it.

How, for example, do we distinguish between ethnocentrism, ignorance, and what some critics have described as the "false universalism" of feminism? Several years ago, two of the first readers of an article I wrote on a 19th-century Japanese feminist (Kishida Toshiko) asked if Kishida had not read Mary Wollstonecraft. It was a logical and not unexpected question; logical because there are apparent similarities in the arguments about education made by both women; expected, too, because of the natural curiosity one feels at the discovery of kindred consciousnesses in unexpected places. But whether or not such questions bubble from ethnocentric springs is often a difficult determination for anyone to make. Certainly, my questioners did not subscribe, as some feminists do, to the assumption that all "women's rights" (and, therefore, all feminist) arguments have originated in the west.

There may be some feminists who continue to exhibit a classic kind of bias engendered by the inability to see anything valuable in another culture that is not rooted in one's own cultural/historical experience, as in Arthur Koestler's 1960 description of Japan as a reflection "in a distorting mirror," a caricature "of our western civilization held uncomfortably close to one's face."[6] But even though a majority of western feminists may not subscribe to such views, we are indelibly linked to them by our history and culture; views like Koestler's reverberate with a hollow sense of western superiority rooted in the experience and processes of imperialism. To the extent that we in the west symbolize such hegemonic views to women elsewhere, we should not be surprised to find a reverse devaluation of western culture and "feminism" with it.

One area of our work that generates concern about these issues is theory. It is clear that, while the historical development of feminist theory should be the province of historians of feminism, feminist theorists tend to claim both women's history and feminist history as their domains. It is the burden of feminist theory to account for the asymmetry, dissonance, and, yes, oppression women have faced. Precisely for this reason, theory can become a historical enterprise, carried on by people who are not historians and who are not trained to interpret multicultural worlds of development and change. Gerda Lerner's *Creation of Patriarchy*[7] is an exception, since Lerner, though she is here writing theory, is a skilled historian. Still, she is a U.S. historian, working far from home, and that fact, for all of the reasons outlined here, has already made her work controversial.

Recently, in a sometimes ironic and paradoxical effort to widen the application of theory to demonstrate the universality of women's experience, feminist theorists have written and rewritten the history of the world. The results of this effort have been mixed but largely predictable: feminists with good intentions have found themselves attacked by critics who often charge them with a misrepresentation of the past that is tinged with ethnocentric bias. Mary Daly, who demonstrated the faults of her virtues with the publication of *Gyn/Ecology*,[8] is a case in point. Spinning out theory in a historical setting that has been the target of angry criticism by Audre Lorde, Hannah Papanek, and others, Daly, a respected theorist, seemed to symbolize for many women the worst habits of "orientalism" and the hegemonic assumptions of the west. Why? In her search for common ground, Daly resurrected some of the offensive metaphors of imperialism, occasionally blundered into the use of previously discredited sources, and unintentionally set up a hierarchy of "civilized" customs. For example, as a theorist taking up the central question of feminist theory and locating the roots of women's oppression, she found herself in unfamiliar territory—in the middle of South Asia and a history of women there that is still very much in process. It is an interesting fact that the history contained in de Beauvoir's *The Second Sex*[9] or Adrienne Rich's *Of Woman Born*[10] has seemed less objectionable than *Gyn/Ecology* to the world's feminists. Certainly, the general recognition that both women were writing history out of necessity since so little had been written is one way of explaining the difference; another is that neither work ventures far beyond the confines of Euro-U.S. history.

Even so, as Karen Offen reminds us, there can be contextual problems in Euro-U.S. settings as well. Offen, obviously chagrined at the lack of historicity in the development of feminist theory among U.S. feminists, argues for a new feminist politics that can accommodate itself to the historical diversity of feminist expression—particularly relational forms that "[seek] to destroy masculinist hierarchy but not sexual dualism." Offen is implicitly calling for theory informed by history, with (in this case) a greater appreciation of historic links with Europe and the European theoretical heritage among U.S. feminists.[11]

Beyond ethnocentrism and the difficulty we have had wedding history with theory, there may be other sources of the widely-held perception that feminism and feminist theory are pristinely western creations. We have not often tried to define feminism in historical contexts that translate across cultures; when we have made the effort, our tendency has been to attach disproportionate weight to western political and philosophical theory, in all their binary brilliance. We have, to an embarrassing degree, used political theory as a guide to feminist theory, and, partly as a consequence, read the discourse of feminism too literally and too narrowly.

In spite of the fact that feminist theory is now a subcategory of political theory in many graduate programs, I would argue that the history of feminism is, like feminist theory, too important to be left to political scientists. My objection stems partly from the numbers of books and articles in recent years that fail to distinguish theory from history, much less put theory in any historical context. More important is the fact that, in the hands of many political scientists, feminist history and theory become ever more culture-bound. There is a general recognition that political science, law, and philosophy, particularly in their theoretical expressions, are fiercely attached to The Western Tradition. History on the other hand, while not perfect, seems at least pretentious enough to want to claim the rest of the world as an object of study.

It is typically the political scientist, or the lawyer, or the philosopher who tells us that all democratic traditions spring from western culture, in spite of the fact that there are major debates over this issue in many parts of the world—debates that center on historical perceptions of "rights" and reciprocity in culture and politics. By extension, feminism, in the hands of the political scientist, becomes a western creation whose theories ultimately are derived from western political philosophy. Similarly, if we limit our

exploration to the familiar dichotomies of the west—for example, public/
private, reason/emotion, culture/nature—we will by definition be looking
chiefly at the west and/or its influence outside of Europe and the United
States. We are also likely to produce feminist criticism, theory, and history
that are both limiting and irrelevant in the present age. It seems likely that,
if there is something universal in feminist experience—something that
transcends the rather narrow boundaries of political "rights," "democracy," and "law" as they have been transmitted from western traditions—
historians, anthropologists, sociologists, and other comparativists will have
to find it.

Among many recent examples of culture-bound accounts of feminism
and feminist theory, Jean Elshtain's *Public Man, Private Woman* is among
the most ambitious and offers a history of feminism and feminist theory, a
theoretical critique of both, and a view of the future.

> In bringing feminist imperatives to a critical examination of the tradition
> of Western political thought and going on to locate the insights and
> concerns of political theory in the heart of the feminist enterprise, I
> implicitly, and, at times, explicitly indicated that I had an alternative to
> offer which would forge links between the Western tradition and feminist
> thinking in a way that served to illumine the past, instruct the present,
> and presage a reconstructive future.[12]

But it is jarring to one's historical consciousness to read the theories of
de Beauvoir, Firestone, and Cixous as if they were cogs in a feminist mono-
lith, operating in some sphere beyond time, and distressing to see the
ideas of Shulamith Firestone presented as if they were a reading of the
contemporary theoretical scene. *The Dialectic of Sex*[13] was written in 1970;
some would call that recent, but a good historian judges the quality and
pace of change, and given the speed with which feminist theory has developed, Firestone's ideas are light years away from the feminism Elshtain
purports to describe in 1981. Still, this is not just a bad history of feminist
theory that gives us little or no sense of change, let alone the motivation
for it. *Public Man, Private Woman* is also a text derived exclusively from western traditions of political philosophy—something that helps to account
for its complete lack of any discussion of sexual politics, a point astutely
made by Judith Stacey.[14] It is one of the reasons that the institution central
to the book's argument—the family—is so narrowly construed: first, to
mean the western family, and ultimately, the U.S. family. It is one of the
reasons Elshtain mistakes Rosaldo's description of "primitive" behavior
for a model of social existence Elshtain knows cannot fit postindustrial
America.[15] If one considers carefully the implications of Elshtain's views, it
will be clear that, even though she admits our ideas stem from "a set of
pan-cultural, bedrock imperatives,"[16] she is not very familiar with any models outside of the west, and not really eager to entertain the possibility that
wider worlds—the sort that Rosaldo explored—have important implica-

tions for our own time and place. These biases are, I think, precisely what we should avoid as we write the history of feminism.

We need to expand our sense of what feminism is, and has been, in order to write effectively its history. Certainly, we need a sharper sense of how the politics of feminism has functioned historically, and that means moving beyond the limits of "traditional" political theory, as well as of 20th-century feminism as we have come to know and love it. And if we are sensitive to our own history, we will develop definitions and discourse that are inclusive and inherently cross-cultural. Writing the history of feminism will also force us to confront in a different way the built-in competition between feminism, nationalism, and socialism that has marked our history in the modern period. So far, all that theory and history have managed to do is to tell us what feminism has *not* been relative to other ideologies; women's history has taught us something about feminist coalition and the motivation for it, but because we have not fully defined feminism in its own terms, or because we have defined it too narrowly as a western construct, we have not said much about the intellectual accommodation involved in such coalition; we have also not said what feminism has offered that may have been different—though I suspect that one of those things might be characterized as a kind of "sexual politics" that, like the term *feminism* can transcend chronology.

Let's begin at the beginning, with the question of broadening and making more inclusive our historical definitions of feminism. We have, for the most part, gone at this in a strange way; we have often asked, "was _____ a feminist?" Occasionally, we have been quick to character-ize someone in history cautiously on this point, as in, "she certainly did not consider herself a feminist, but. . . ." or "she would not have been con-sidered a feminist by 20th-century standards, but. . . ." or (one of my favor-ites) "Charlotte Gilman could not really be characterized as a feminist because she was opposed to women's suffrage." It is, perhaps, not unusual to want to define historical moments through individuals and groups, but the central problem remains that we do not yet have a clear enough sense of feminism as a set of ideas marked by time and place, as well as continu-ities. And until we do, it will be difficult to place feminists in history and to read some collective sense of the "feminism of the age" in their individual lives.

What we have tended to do (though there are notable exceptions) has been to judge historical feminism and its advocates by contemporary expressions of both feminism and feminist theory. Our problem is to define in the broadest sense (consistent with time and place) the entire complex of issues specific to women and their concerns—issues that fit our historical sense of what might constitute feminism.

All of us realize the term *feminism* itself can pose problems, particularly when it is used literally and exclusively. One characteristic of transforming social movements is moral passion, derived from what may be an innate or learned sense of social justice, that is, the "shoulds" of human existence. Feminism may be the name that has been given to a particular set of organizing principles and ideas about women, but universally such sentiments—the moral passion that precedes organizing principles—are present long before we have names for them. Or, as Margot Badran comments in a recent article on feminism and nationalism in Egypt,

> Egyptian women first used the term *feminism* in public in 1923. The term *women's liberation* or *the liberation of the woman* . . . made a controversial public appearance in Egypt in 1899 when Qasim Amin used it as the title of a book. . . . In this paper, I use *feminism* as an analytical concept including within its range a nascent awareness that women have been oppressed because of their sex, and extending to a more complex analysis of oppression and liberation of women and an agenda of activism. Historically, some women in different parts of the world have had a concept of feminism before they had a precise term for it. . . . When I speak of feminist consciousness raising in the nineteenth-century Egyptian harem, I refer to that phenomenon in terminology not used at that historical moment. In fact, for nearly the entire period dealt with in this paper, the word *feminism* was not used in Egypt.[17]

In Japan, the term *feminism* has a very checkered history, though *women's liberation* (*onna kaiho*) was not an unfamiliar rallying cry in the 19th-century. In the narrowest sense, the Japanese equivalent of western feminism in the 19th-century was probably *danjo dōken*, equal rights for men and women. The term *feminīsto*, on the other hand, referred initially to a man who made too much of women: who opened doors for them, gave up his train seat to them, and generally did not fit Japanese definitions of manhood. *Ūman rību*, or "woman's lib," used in the late '60s and '70s, generally refers to militant women whose behavior in pursuit of their goals is thought to have undercut any possibility of wide-spread support among Japanese women; *feminīzmu*, the most recent arrival, seems to refer to Euro-American feminism, and for many women, fits the Third World perception of feminism as a kind of cultural imperialism.

I am not at all in agreement with those who think we should give up the term *feminism* on grounds that it is not translatable across cultures and the barriers of 20th-century politics; I believe that there is a kind of historicity and continuity about the term that is valuable—even though we certainly need to broaden its content. Whether or not you agree that Japanese feminism, like Egyptian feminism and European feminism, developed long before the term was developed *does* ultimately depend on how broad your historical definition of feminism is; that question, in turn, goes to the issue of cross-cultural connection.

Johanna Handlin, in a description of 16th-century China, tells us that feminist questions were asked in places other than Europe long before the 18th-century. Writing in 1975, Handlin asked us to look at the impact of increased literacy among women, as well as other kinds of social change in which they were directly involved, as background to the concerns of writers like Lu K'un in 16th-century China.

> Accordingly, the presence of a female audience influenced Lu's consciousness. The idealized view of the position of women had gone unaltered for centuries, but in the sixteenth century widespread female literacy provoked men for the first time to perceive not the equality of women but their comparability, and to ask just how, given their obvious talents, they differed from men. These questions, once articulated during the late Ming, continued to worry writers during the Ch'ing. Thus a study of sixteenth-century attitudes toward women will suggest that long before the intrusion of the West, the serious literature of the scholar-official class had laid the foundation for the presumably revolutionary twentieth-century belief in the equality of the sexes.[18]

All of us know that, given the nature of the beast we are trying to describe, the further back in history we push our search for something we can call *feminism* the more male thinkers we will include in our history. That makes some of us very uneasy, particularly when we are still trying—with little success—to find women who expressed feminist sentiments in that earlier period. It has also been irritating for many of us to find the men of the 19th century given the lion's share of the credit for the expression of feminist ideas—whether John Stuart Mill, Fukuzawa Yukichi, or K'ang Yu-wei. But the truth is that we need to make the effort, not only to find documentation in "traditional" sources before the 18th-century. We need to look carefully at the kinds of contexts Handlin describes and to weigh carefully the motives men and women might have had for expressing a nascent feminism. We need to look at differences in perceptions of existing problems involving women: were there gender-based differences, were they significant?

A great deal of work has already been done on the 19th-century, work that seems to have produced an uneasy consensus: advocates of education and power for women, even if that advocacy limited women's power to the private sphere, should be included in the history of feminism. This seems to be the case, irrespective of divergent motivation for such advocacy (religious beliefs, a sense of nationalism, or ordinary pragmatism) and irrespective of gender. That is not to say that we might not *prefer* Susan B. Anthony to Catherine Beecher, or Ueki Emori (who wanted equality for women written into Japan's 1889 constitution) to Mori Arinori (who wanted to increase the power of Japanese women in the family), but we seem willing to include them all at this stage, even though we may insist on making distinctions, for example, between support for private and support for public roles for women in a 19th-century context. And in the end, I have a feeling we will find it simpler to untangle the relationship between Harriet Taylor and John Stuart Mill than to determine what motivated

16th-century Chinese philosophers or a 17th-century Japanese novelist like Saikaku to write as they did, because the 19th-century is more familiar, the sources more accessible and plentiful, and so many of the issues already defined. Trying to determine why Lu K'un or Saikaku saw women as comparable, if not equal, to men requires more stretching and more creativity; just as looking for new sources on missing women, or using old sources in new ways, or revising traditional historical treatments has required a great deal of intellectual stamina.

We also need to look again at a fundamental question, one that—to oversimplify the argument—I will put this way: should Catherine Beecher's ideas be included in the history of feminism? Or, is it possible to include an Indian woman who performs sati, not in acquiescence to the demands of Indian tradition but in protest of them? What about Chinese mothers who created a kind of "uterine politics" that tied their sons to them and gave them protection—often, if not always, at the expense of daughters-in-law? Or women who engage willingly in a veiling ceremony because they feel it is not only a rite of passage but protection? Are they less representative of feminism than Chinese women who refused to marry, lived separately from men, and convinced an entire region of the rightness of their action by tying it to religious beliefs? Or is it only those who protest footbinding in a public arena who belong to the history of feminism?

The questions embedded in this list are: how is the history of feminism different from the history of women? how is it different from the history of feminist theory? if there is significant overlap between them (and there is), why should we fragment a history that is still in its infancy? My tentative answer is that, in my experience, they are different and require different questions, even though women's history may contain the history of feminism, just as the history of feminism contains the history of theory. Beyond that, recognizing that feminism has a history that is sometimes separate from women's history will help us clarify the content and continuity of feminism. We will be able to show, for example, that there are times when women going out on strike belong not only to women's history or economic history but to the history of feminism. That, in turn, may help us find answers to difficult questions: why, for example have women so often been the first workers in industrializing societies to go on strike?

Is the history of feminism by definition the history of reform, or subversion, or simply social change? Were feminists chiefly motivated by intellectual curiosity, a desire for social justice, a belief in a rational world, or religion? What are the major differences in feminism before and after the 18th century? Can we translate those differences across cultures? Again, there are no answers here; the important issue is whether we can agree on the questions.

Finally, what is the connection between theory and the history of feminism? It is clearly a more intimate connection than the ties between women's history and the history of feminism. Feminist theorizing is an eclectic, cross-pollinating enterprise that reflects back and forward in time and is not confined by the geographic limits of Europe and North America. Occasionally in concert with other well-established ideologies focused on social justice, and sometimes on its own, feminist theory has assumed the responsibility of finding the roots of women's oppression and devising ways out of that oppression.

We know that ideas do not develop in a vacuum, and we need to fill out the contexts and contours of feminist theory. In the 20th century, for example, it seems likely that theory has been developed in part as a result of coalitions made in the day-to-day decision making that is feminist politics. Some forms of theory, it is held, can even be explained on the basis of sexual identification. But is it historically accurate to link lesbianism with radical feminist theory? In all times and places? And who, over time, is going to sort out the complicated connections between deconstruction, postmodernism, and feminist theory? Why are feminist theorists in the forefront of intellectuals both who have used deconstruction as a tool and who are among its severest critics? As Mary Poovey tells us, the value of deconstructive techniques is compromised for feminists by a lack of historicity, and, by implication, political commitment.

> My original problem, then, returns with a vengeance born of my political commitment to the future as well as to the present. Because of its ability to dismantle binary logic and deconstruct identity, I do think deconstruction has provided and continues to offer an essential tool for feminist analysis. But in order for this double-edged blade not to reproduce the system it purports to cut apart, deconstruction itself must be historicized and subjected to the same kind of scrutiny with which it has dismantled Western metaphysics. . . . Ultimately, my prediction is that feminists practicing deconstructive and other post-structuralist techniques from an explicitly political position will so completely rewrite deconstruction as to leave it behind, for all intents and purposes, as part of the historicization of structuralism already under way in several disciplines.[19]

Feminists have made good use of deconstructive and postmodernist techniques not simply to analyze work in their own disciplines; they have encouraged the dismantling of western imperialism by calling into question the superiority of western culture. But what have feminist theorists added to the analytical tools we have to undertake the history of feminism? It seems to me that, in addition to legal rights and equality, terms that are often limited to very specific historical time and place, we have the open-ended, multicultural language of theory—sex/gender systems or sexual politics, for example—with which we can begin to analyze the history of feminism. We might find that sexual politics—as both a marker and a tool of analysis—has been as critical to feminism as class struggle has been to marxism. The use of theory by historians will certainly help us discover how gender differs from sexuality and should reemphasize the importance of the history of sexuality to the history of women and of feminism.

Feminism is no longer, as Ti Grace Atkinson remarked in the early '70s, "a movement without an idea." The question for us is, is feminism a movement without a history?

NOTES

1. Karen Offen, "Defining Feminism: A Comparitive Historical Approach," *Signs* 14, No. 1 (Autumn 1988): 119-57.

2. Nancy Cott, *The Grounding of Modern Feminism* (New Haven: Yale University Press, 1988).

3. Cott, *Grounding of Modern Feminism.*

4. Karen Offen, "On the French Origins of the Word Feminism and Feminist," *Feminist Issues* 8, No. 2 (Summer 1988): 45-51.

5. Offen, "Defining Feminism," 150-51.

6. Arthur Koestler, *The Lotus and the Robot* (London: Hutchinson & Co., 1960), 181-82.

7. Gerda Lerner, *The Creation of Patriarchy* (New York: Oxford, 1986).

8. Mary Daly, *Gyn/Ecology* (Boston: Beacon, 1979).

9. Simone de Beauvoir, *The Second Sex* (New York: Knopf, 1953).

10. Adrienne Rich, *Of Woman Born* (New York: Norton, 1976).

11. Offen, "Defining Feminism," 151.

12. Jean Bethke Elshtain, *Public Man, Private Woman* (Princeton: Princeton University Press, 1981): 298.

13. Shulamith Firestone, *The Dialectic of Sex* (New York: Morrow, 1970).

14. Judith Stacey, "The New Conservative Feminism," *Feminist Studies* 9, No. 3 (Fall 1983): 559-83.

15. Elshtain, 338-40.

16. Elshtain, 339.

17. Margot Badran, "Dual Liberation: Feminism and Nationalism in Egypt, 1870's-1925," *Feminist Issues* 8, No. 1 (Spring 1988): 16.

18. Johanna Handlin, "Lu K'un's New Audience: The Influence of Women's Literacy on Sixteenth Century Thought," in *Women in Chinese Society,* ed. Roxanne Witke and Margery Wolf (Stanford: Stanford University Press, 1975), 26.

19. Mary Poovey, "Feminism and Deconstruction," *Feminist Studies* 14, No. 1 (Spring 1988): 61-62.

CONTRIBUTORS

Luz del Alba Acevedo is a lecturer in the Departments of Latin American and Caribbean Studies and Women's Studies at the State University of New York at Albany, and a Ph.D. candidate in Political Science at the University of Illinois at Chicago. She specializes in women and development, and gender and politics in the Third World. Her articles have appeared in *World Development* and *Homines.*

Janet Afary is Assistant Professor of History and Women's Studies at Purdue University. She received her Ph.D. from the Department of History and Near Eastern Studies at the University of Michigan. Her dissertation is about the Iranian Constitutional Revolution of 1906-11.

Iris Berger is Associate Professor of History, Africana Studies, and Women's Studies and Director of the Institute for Research on Women at the State University of New York at Albany. She is the author of *Threads of Solidarity: Women in South African Industry, 1900-1980* and *Religion and Resistance: East African Kingdoms in the Precolonial Period* and is the co-editor (with Claire Robertson) of *Women and Class in Africa.*

Susan Geiger is an Associate Professor and Chair of the Women's Studies Department at the University of Minnesota. A co-editor, with other members of the Personal Narratives Group, of *Interpreting Women's Lives: Feminist Theory and Personal Narratives*, she has written on life history research, on feminist pedagogy, and on African women's history. She is currently writing a history of Tanzania's nationalist movement based on the life histories of women activists.

Karen Tranberg Hansen is Associate Professor of Anthropology at Northwestern University. In addition to her interest in gender and imperialism, she is exploring broad questions of political economy in terms of class, race, and gender. Her several rounds of fieldwork in Zambia have resulted in the publication of articles on gender, the informal sector, housing, and urbanization. She is the author of *Distant Companions: Servants and Employers in Zambia, 1900-1985* and is editor of an anthology of interdisciplinary essays, *African Encounters with Domesticity.*

Emily Honig is the author of *Sisters and Strangers: Women in the Shanghai Cotton Mills, 1919-1949* and (with Gail Hershatter) of *Personal Voices: Chinese Women in the 1980's.* She is currently an Associate Professor in the Department of History and the Women's Studies Program at Yale University.

Cheryl Johnson-Odim is Assistant Professor of History at Loyola University of Chicago. She has chapters in the books *Women and Class in Africa, Nigerian Women in Historical Perspective*, and *Third World Women and Feminism*, as well as several articles in journals such as the *African Studies Review* and

Tarikh. With Margaret Strobel, she co-edited *Restoring Women to History.* She is currently completing a biography of Funmilayo Ransome-Kuti (with Nina Mba) and is working on a study of African-American women in Chicago, 1880-1930.

Asunción Lavrin is Professor of History at Howard University. She is the editor and co-author of *Latin American Women: Historical Perspectives* and *Sexuality and Marriage in Colonial Latin America.* She is currently finishing a study of feminism, women, and social change in the southern cone nations of South America.

Janaki Nair has recently completed her dissertation entitled "The Emergence of Labor Politics in South India: Bangalore, 1900-1947" in the Department of History at Syracuse University. She will be Visiting Assistant Professor in the Department of History at Colgate University from Fall 1991.

Cynthia Nelson, Professor of Anthropology at the American University in Cairo, has lived and taught in Cairo since the 1960s. She has published articles on the women's movement in contemporary Egypt, income-generating strategies and other women's development issues, and Middle Eastern women.

Barbara N. Ramusack is Professor of History at the University of Cincinnati. Her research specializations are the princes of India, the interaction among Western and South Asian women, and women's rights issues. She has published *The Princes of India in the Twilight Empire: The Decline of a Patron-Client Relationship, 1914-1930* and is currently working on a volume on the Indian princes and their states for the New Cambridge History of India. She has also published several articles on British feminists and Indian women's organizations.

Sharon Sievers, Professor of History and formerly Director of the Women's Studies Program at California State University, Long Beach, is author of a prizewinning history of feminism in Japan, *Flowers in Salt.* She has been the recipient of various research awards and currently teaches courses on feminist theory and the history of women in Asia.

Margaret Strobel is Professor of Women's Studies and History at the University of Illinois at Chicago. Her book *Muslim Women in Mombasa, 1890-1975* was co-winner in 1980 of the Herskovits Prize awarded by the African Studies Association. She has also published *Three Swahili Women: Life Histories from Mombasa, Kenya* (co-edited, in English and Swahili, with Sarah Mirza), *European Women and the Second British Empire,* and *Complicity and Resistance: Western Women and Imperialism* (co-edited with Nupur Chaudhuri). With Cheryl Johnson-Odim, she co-edited *Restoring Women to History* (vol. 3), a 500-page summary of the history of women in Africa, Asia, Latin America and the Caribbean, and the Middle East, which is intended to help teachers integrate women's history into history survey courses. Her current project is a study of socialist feminist women's unions in the U.S., which focuses on the Chicago Women's Liberation Union.

Mary Kay Vaughan is Associate Professor of Latin American Studies and History at the University of Illinois at Chicago. Author of *The State, Education, and Social Class in Mexico* and numerous articles on Mexican education, she is completing a book on the practice of "socialist" education in the states of Sonora and Puebla in Mexico under the presidency of Lázaro Cárdenas (1934-1940).

E. Frances White is an Associate Professor of History and Black Studies at Hampshire College. She has written on African women in history and is now at work on a book about black feminist theory, *Transformations: Race, Gender, and Sexuality.*

Anand A. Yang, Chair, Department of History, University of Utah, is the editor of the journal *Peasant Studies*. He has edited the book *Crime and Criminality in British India*, has authored the study *The Limited Raj: Agrarian Relations in Colonial India, 1793-1920*, and is currently completing the book *The Colonial Bazaar: Peasants and Markets in Gangetic India, 1765-1947.*